Over 300 scrumptious recipes to help you enjoy life and stay well

eat to beat
diabetes

edited by
ROBYN WEBB, M.S.

Author of the *Flavorful Seasons Cookbook* and
Diabetic Meals in 30 Minutes or Less

METRO BOOKS
New York

PROJECT STAFF

Editor Neil Wertheimer
Writer and Recipe Editor Robyn Webb, M.S.
Copy Editor Jeanette Gingold
Nutritionist Madelyn Wheeler, Ph. D.
Designer Amy Trombat
Prepress Manager Douglas A. Croll
Manufacturing Manager John L. Cassidy
Production Coordinator Leslie Ann Caraballo

READER'S DIGEST HEALTH PUBLISHING

Editor in Chief and Neil Wertheimer
Publishing Director
Managing Editor Suzanne G. Beason
Design Director Michele Laseau
Marketing Director Dawn Nelson
Vice President and Keira Krausz
General Manager

READER'S DIGEST ASSOCIATION, INC.

President, Eric W. Schrier
North America
Global Editor-in-Chief

Photographers
Sue Atkinson, Martin Brigdale, Gus Filgate,
Amanda Heywood, Graham Kirk, William Lingwood,
Sean Myers, Simon Smith

The recipes in the *Eat to Beat Diabetes Cookbook*
were drawn from the Reader's Digest *Eat Well, Live
Well* series.

Note to Readers
The information in this book should not be substituted for, or used to alter, any medical treatment or
therapy without your doctor's advice.

METRO BOOKS
New York

An Imprint of Sterling Publishing
387 Park Avenue South
New York, NY 10016

METRO BOOKS and the distinctive Metro Books logo are trademarks of
Sterling Publishing Co., Inc.

© 2003 by The Reader's Digest Association, Inc.

This 2010 edition published by Metro Books
by arrangement with The Reader's Digest Association, Inc.

ISBN: 978-1-4351-2563-6

For information about custom editions, special sales, and premium
and corporate purchases, please contact Sterling Special Sales
at 800-805-5489 or specialsales@sterlingpublishing.com.

Manufactured in China

4 6 8 10 9 7 5 3

www.sterlingpublishing.com

introduction

Welcome to some of the most delicious and creative recipes ever offered for people with diabetes. Inside these pages you will find wonderful combinations of ingredients, great flavors, and a diverse range of cooking styles and techniques. A quick look at the photographs says it all, doesn't it? When it comes to eating to beat diabetes, fresh, enticing food is the order of the day. Better still, none of these dishes are hard to make. A little chopping, a quick sauté, a fast sauce, and—voilà!—a luscious meal is served.

Of course, plenty of cookbooks deliver great-tasting recipes. But what makes this book different is obvious: Here are delicious, interesting recipes that help you beat diabetes! Five years ago, such a sentence would be an oxymoron. How could you possibly create exciting, tasty meals when diabetes mandated that you avoid so many ingredients? The answer, of course, is that the rules have changed. In recent years, science has learned that most people with diabetes don't need to be so restricted. Rather, the goal is to eat a diversity of nutrients in proper portion sizes, spread evenly through the day. Sugar is fine, for example, if eaten in small portions and balanced well with proteins, fats, and more beneficial carbohydrates.

The more than 300 recipes inside all represent this new thinking; they are nutritious, diverse, and created to help keep blood sugar levels stable. In addition to the recipes, we've provided a thorough reading section on the art and science of eating for diabetes. You'll discover the newest nutritional information, sample meal plans, ideas for shopping, hints and tips for combining ingredients, and much more. Read it now, read it later—but be sure to read it!

You'll also discover in this book a crucial fact: Eating well for diabetes is becoming increasingly similar to eating well for almost any health goal or concern. The recipes inside are great for heart health, cancer prevention, hypertension control, and everyday well-being. They are rich in nutrients—particularly phytochemicals, the ingredients in fresh produce that have many specific health benefits—but also well flavored with the healthy fats that doctors and nutritionists are talking so much about.

So while we have worked hard to deliver the best cookbook possible for people with diabetes, we have also made sure we delivered a cookbook that the entire family can embrace. To reinforce that, we make a point of detailing many of the health benefits of the recipes that go beyond diabetes management.

Diabetes is a serious disease, and its spread is becoming an epidemic. Eating healthy, delicious food in proper portions is perhaps the very best way to combat it. We can't imagine a much better treatment than the recipes inside. Give them a try!

Robyn Webb

contents

breakfast

drop scones

Drop scones, also called Scotch pancakes, are easy and fun to make, and perfect for breakfast on the weekend or even as a simple dessert. Served with creamy low-fat vanilla yogurt and sweet, succulent berries, they are quite irresistible.

Preparation time **10 minutes**   Cooking time **15–20 minutes**   *Serves 6 (makes about 24 drop scones)*

Scones

1 cup self-rising flour

2 teaspoons sugar

1 egg, beaten

1 tablespoon reduced-fat margarine spread, melted

1/2 cup 1% milk

Cooking spray

Garnish

1 cup blueberries

1 cup raspberries

1 container (8 ounces) fat-free vanilla yogurt

1 Combine the flour and sugar in a medium bowl. Make a well in the center of the dry ingredients, and add the egg, melted margarine, and a little of the milk. Gradually stir the flour into the liquids and add the remaining milk a little at a time, to make a fairly thick, smooth batter.

2 Coat a large nonstick skillet with cooking spray and heat over medium-high heat. For each scone, drop a heaping tablespoon of batter onto the hot surface. When bubbles form on the surface of the scones, use a spatula to turn them and then cook until the underside is golden brown, about 1 minute.

3 Remove the scones from the skillet and keep warm under a clean cloth. Cook the rest of the batter in the same way.

4 Place the blueberries and raspberries in a bowl and lightly crush the fruit, leaving some berries whole. Serve the scones warm with the berries and vanilla yogurt.

(Some More Ideas) Instead of serving the drop scones with the crushed fruit, top each one with a dab of yogurt and a little jam.

Apple drop scones: Stir 1 cored and finely diced sweet apple into the batter with a pinch of ground cloves. Serve the scones dusted with a little sifted confectioners' sugar.

Parmesan and herb drop scones: Instead of sugar add 1 tablespoon snipped fresh chives, 1 tablespoon chopped fresh oregano, and 2 tablespoons freshly grated Parmesan cheese to the flour. Serve the drop scones topped with low-fat plain yogurt or cottage cheese and halved cherry tomatoes.

Plus Points

• Homemade drop scones contain less fat and sugar than store-bought scones, and serving them with low-fat yogurt instead of butter keeps the total fat content low.

• The scones are served with a crushed berry sauce, eliminating the need for pancake syrup, which is high in sugar and calories.

Exchanges	
carbohydrate 2	

Each serving provides calories 152, calories from fat 21, fat 2g, saturated fat 1g, cholesterol 37mg, sodium 319mg, carbohydrate 27g, fiber 3g, sugars 8g, protein 5g. Excellent source of phosphorus. Good source of calcium, riboflavin, thiamine, vitamin C.

blueberry popovers

Similar to Yorkshire puddings, popovers are a much-loved American classic, and the slightly sweet version here is perfect for breakfast or brunch. Plenty of juicy blueberries are folded into the batter, and then it is baked in deep muffin tins. The popovers are served with a fresh berry salad to add extra vitamin C.

Preparation time **20 minutes**   Cooking time **25–30 minutes**   *Serves 8 (makes 8 popovers)*

Popovers

Cooking spray
1 cup plain flour
Pinch of salt
1 teaspoon sugar
2 eggs
1 cup 1% milk
1/2 cup blueberries
1 tablespoon
Confectioners' sugar

Salad

1 cup raspberries
2 teaspoons sugar
1 cup thickly sliced strawberries
1 cup blueberries

1 Preheat the oven to 425°F. Coat an 8-cup muffin pan or popover pan with cooking spray.

2 To make the popovers, sift the flour, salt, and sugar into a mixing bowl and make a well in the center. Break the eggs into the well, add the milk, and beat together with a fork. Using a wire whisk, gradually work the flour into the liquid to make a smooth batter.

3 Divide the batter evenly among the prepared muffin cups. They should be about 2/3 full. With a spoon, drop a few blueberries into the batter in each cup, dividing them equally.

4 Bake in the middle of the oven until the popovers are golden brown, well risen, and crisp around the edges, about 25 to 30 minutes.

5 Meanwhile, make the berry salad. Puree 1/2 cup of the raspberries in a blender. Strain the raspberries in a sieve to remove the seeds. Add 2 teaspoons sugar. Add the rest of the raspberries to the bowl, together with the strawberries and blueberries. Drizzle the raspberry sauce over the fruit.

6 Using a knife, unmold the popovers and dust with confectioners' sugar. Serve hot, with the berry salad.

(Some More Ideas) Use frozen blueberries, thawed and well drained, if fresh are not available. You can use thawed frozen raspberries and blueberries for the berry salad as well.

Plus Points
• Blueberries, like cranberries, contain anti-bacterial compounds called anthocyanins. These are effective against the *E. coli* bacteria that cause gastrointestinal disorders and urinary tract infections.
• Ounce for ounce, strawberries contain more vitamin C than oranges.

Exchanges

starch 1 fruit 1/2 fat 1/2

Each serving provides calories 131, calories from fat 22, fat 2g, saturated fat 1g, cholesterol 56mg, sodium 38mg, carbohydrate 23g, fiber 3g, sugars 8g, protein 5g. Excellent source of vitamin C. Good source of folate, riboflavin, thiamine.

blueberry popovers, *p10*

apricot-pecan muffins, *p15*

apple and hazelnut drop scones, *p12*

breakfast muffins, *p13*

apple and hazelnut drop scones

Drop scones are an almost instant sweet snack or breakfast treat. The thick batter is made by simply stirring together a few basic pantry ingredients, and the scones cook in minutes. Here they are flavored with diced apple and toasted hazelnuts. Top with a little light maple syrup and enjoy warm from the pan.

Preparation time **15 minutes**   Cooking time **20 minutes**   *Makes 15 scones*

3 tablespoons hazelnuts, chopped
1 cup flour
1/2 teaspoon baking soda
Pinch salt
2 tablespoons sugar
1 large egg
1 1/4 cups fat-free buttermilk
1 apple, cored and finely chopped
Cooking spray
4 tablespoons light maple syrup

1 Heat a large nonstick skillet over medium-high heat. Toast the hazelnuts in the pan until golden brown and fragrant, stirring and tossing constantly. Place the toasted nuts in a small bowl and set aside.

2 Sift the flour, baking soda, salt, and sugar into a large mixing bowl. Make a well in the center of the dry ingredients. Lightly beat the egg with the buttermilk and pour into the well. Gently stir the flour mixture into the buttermilk mixture to make a smooth, thick batter. Fold in the apple and toasted hazelnuts.

3 Coat the same large skillet with cooking spray and heat over medium-high heat. For each scone, drop a heaping tablespoon of batter onto the hot surface. When bubbles form on the surface of the scones, use a spatula to turn them and then cook until the underside is golden brown, about 1 minute.

4 Remove the scones from the skillet and keep warm under a clean cloth. Cook the rest of the batter in the same way.

5 When all the drop scones are cooked, quickly heat the maple syrup in a small saucepan just to warm it. Drizzle the syrup over the warm drop scones and serve immediately.

(Some More Ideas) *Apricot and walnut or pecan drop scones*: Use 1/2 cup finely chopped dried apricots instead of the apple, and 2 tablespoons walnuts or pecans instead of the hazelnuts.

Fresh berry drop scones: Add 3/4 cup blackberries or raspberries to the batter in place of the apple, and season with a good pinch of ground cinnamon. Omit the hazelnuts, if you prefer.

Plus Points

• Buttermilk is the liquid left over after cream has been turned into butter by churning. Contrary to its name, buttermilk does not contain butterfat, but it does provide protein and minerals. Buttermilk can easily be made at home by mixing 1 cup fat-free milk with 1 tablespoon lemon juice and allowing it to stand for 5 minutes.

• Apples are a good source of soluble fiber in the form of pectin. Eating apples with their skins offers the maximum amount of fiber. Research has shown that eating apples can also benefit the teeth, as it appears to help to prevent gum disease.

photo, page 10

Exchanges

carbohydrate 1

Each serving (one scone) provides calories 70, calories from fat 14, fat 2g, saturated fat 0g, cholesterol 15mg, sodium 84mg, carbohydrate 12g, fiber 1g, sugars 5g, protein 2g.

breakfast muffins

Muffins are the perfect portable breakfast. They are easy to grab "on the run" and provide the energy boost the body needs to start the day. This particular recipe is packed full of hearty ingredients such as whole-wheat flour, wheat germ, and raisins, which contribute fiber, vitamins, and minerals to the diet.

Preparation time **15 minutes**   Cooking time **15–20 minutes**   *Makes 12 muffins*

1/2 cup whole-wheat flour
3/4 cup all-purpose flour
2 teaspoons baking soda
Pinch salt
1/4 teaspoon ground cinnamon
1/4 cup brown sugar
2 tablespoons wheat germ
3/4 cup raisins
1 container (8 ounces) plain low-fat yogurt
3 tablespoons canola oil
1 egg
Zest of 1/2 orange
3 tablespoons orange juice

1 Preheat the oven to 400°F. Line 12 muffin cups with paper liners or coat with nonstick cooking spray. Set aside.

2 Sift the flours, baking soda, salt, and cinnamon into a large bowl. Stir in the sugar, wheat germ, and raisins, and make a well in the center of the dry ingredients.

3 Lightly whisk together the yogurt, oil, egg, orange zest, and juice. Pour the liquid ingredients into the well of dry ingredients and stir together, mixing only enough to moisten. Do not beat or overmix.

4 Spoon the mixture into the muffin tray, dividing it equally among the cups. Bake until the muffins are golden brown and the centers are firm when gently touched, about 15 to 20 minutes. Leave muffins to cool in the tray for 2 to 3 minutes, then turn out onto a wire rack. The muffins are best eaten freshly baked, preferably still slightly warm from the oven, but can be cooled completely and then kept in an airtight container for up to 2 days.

(Some More Ideas) Substitute chopped prunes or dried dates for the raisins.

Carrot and spice muffins: Add a dash of nutmeg, stir 2 small grated carrots into the flour mixture with the wheat germ, and reduce the amount of raisins to 1/4 cup.

Blueberry and walnut muffins: Instead of raisins use 1 cup blueberries, and add 1/3 cup chopped walnuts.

Plus Points
• Breakfast is a good opportunity to increase fiber intake for the day, which is why eating a high-fiber cereal is usually recommended. These muffins are another good choice, as they offer plenty of dietary fiber from the whole-wheat flour, wheat germ, and raisins.
• Wheat germ is the embryo of the wheat grain and as a result contains a high concentration of nutrients, intended to nourish the growing plant. Just 1 tablespoon of wheat germ provides around 25% of the average daily requirement for vitamin B6. Wheat germ is also a good source of folate, vitamin E, zinc, and magnesium.

photo, page 10

Exchanges	
carbohydrate 1 1/2	fat 1

Each serving (one muffin) provides calories 45, calories from fat 40, fat 4g, saturated fat 1g, cholesterol 19mg, sodium 232mg, carbohydrate 24g, fiber 1g, sugars 12g, protein 4g

summer berry muffins

Fresh summer berries not only add delicious flavor and color to these tempting muffins, they also make them more nutritious. The muffins are at their best when served warm, fresh from the oven, but will be enjoyed just as much once cooled—an ideal addition to a family breakfast, or for breakfast on the go.

Preparation time **10 minutes**   Cooking time **about 20 minutes**   *Makes 9 muffins*

1/2 cup whole-wheat flour
1/3 cup white flour
1 tablespoon baking powder
Pinch salt
3/4 cup mixed fresh berries, such as blueberries and raspberries
2 tablespoons reduced-fat margarine spread
1/4 cup light brown sugar
1 egg, beaten
1 cup fat-free milk

1 Preheat the oven to 375°F. Use paper muffin liners to line a 9-cup muffin tray or coat with cooking spray.

2 Sift the flours, baking powder, and salt into a bowl. Gently fold in the mixed berries.

3 Melt the margarine gently in a small saucepan, then add the sugar, egg, and milk and mix until smooth. Make a well in the center of the dry ingredients and pour the liquid ingredients into the well. Gently fold the ingredients together, mixing just until combined. The batter will be lumpy.

4 Spoon the batter into the muffin cups, filling each about two-thirds full. Bake until the muffins are golden brown, about 18 to 20 minutes.

5 Transfer to a wire rack to cool slightly, then serve warm. The muffins can be kept in an airtight container for 1 to 2 days.

(Some More Ideas) Instead of a mixture of white and whole-wheat flour, use all white or all whole-wheat flour.

For a hint of spice, add 1 1/2 teaspoons ground mixed spice, ginger, or cinnamon with the flour.

Replace the berries with other fresh fruit, such as chopped apples, apricots, peaches or strawberries, or dried fruit, such as raisins, chopped apricots, dates or figs.

Pear and cinnamon oatmeal muffins: Mix 3/4 cup self-rising whole-wheat flour, 1/4 cup oat bran, 1 teaspoon baking powder, 1 1/2 teaspoons ground cinnamon, and a pinch of salt in a bowl. Fold in 1 peeled and chopped pear. In a separate bowl, mix together 2 tablespoons melted reduced-fat margarine spread, 1/4 cup granulated sugar, 2 eggs, and 1/2 cup plus 2 tablespoons orange juice. Pour this over the flour mixture and fold the ingredients together. Spoon into 9 muffin tins and bake as in the main recipe.

For mini muffins, divide the batter among 30 mini paper muffin cups and bake for 10 minutes.

Plus Points

• Combining whole-wheat flour with white flour increases the fiber content of these muffins and adds valuable nutrients such as B-group vitamins.
• Fresh berries are naturally low in fat. They offer dietary fiber and make a good contribution to vitamin C intake. Raspberries also supply vitamin E, and blueberries, like cranberries, contain a compound that helps to prevent urinary-tract infections.

Exchanges
carbohydrate 2 fat 1/2

Each serving (one muffin) provides calories 98, calories from fat 18, fat 2g, saturated fat 0g, cholesterol 24mg, sodium 162mg, carbohydrate 18g, fiber 1g, sugars 8g, protein 3g. Excellent source of phosphorus. Good source of calcium.

apricot-pecan muffins

Any time can be muffin time, especially when you bake up these fresh apricot-pecan muffins. They come out of the oven light, moist, and smelling of cinnamon. Wheat bran is added to the recipe for flavor and extra nutrition. If fresh apricots are not in season, any type of fresh fruit, such as blueberries, strawberries, or bananas, can be used instead.

Preparation time **25 minutes**   Baking time **20 minutes**   *Makes 12 large muffins*

2 1/4 cups all-purpose flour

1 cup packed light brown sugar

3 tablespoons wheat bran

1 tablespoon baking powder

1 teaspoon ground cinnamon

1/2 teaspoon grated lemon zest

1/4 teaspoon salt

2 large eggs

6 tablespoons low-fat unsalted butter, melted and cooled

1 cup fat-free milk

5 apricots, peeled, pitted, and coarsely chopped, about 1 cup

1/4 cup chopped pecans

1 Preheat the oven to 375°F. Lightly coat a 12-cup muffin pan with cooking spray or line with paper baking cups.

2 In a large bowl, mix the flour, sugar, wheat bran, baking powder, cinnamon, lemon zest, and salt. Make a well in the center of the dry ingredients and set aside.

3 In a large measuring cup, whisk the eggs until frothy and light yellow. Beat in the butter, then the milk, until well blended. Pour this mixture into the well in the center of the flour mixture. Stir just until the dry ingredients are moistened. The batter will be slightly lumpy. Do not overmix the batter or the muffins will be tough. With a rubber spatula, gently fold in the apricots and pecans.

4 Spoon the batter into the prepared muffin pan, filling the cups 3/4 full. Bake the muffins until the muffins are peaked and golden brown, about 20 minutes. The muffins are done when a wooden toothpick inserted in the center comes out almost clean, with a few moist crumbs clinging to it. Let the muffins cool in the pan for 3 minutes before removing them. These muffins are best when served piping hot or within a few hours of baking.

(Some More Ideas) *Banana-nut muffins*: Use 1 cup mashed ripe banana instead of the apricots.

Blueberry-nut muffins: Substitute 1 teaspoon grated orange zest for the lemon zest. Substitute 2 cups fresh blueberries for the apricots and 1/4 cup chopped walnuts for the pecans.

Strawberry muffins: Substitute 2 cups coarsely chopped, ripe strawberries for the apricots.

Peach muffins: Use 2 cups coarsely chopped, peeled, ripe peaches (1 pound) instead of the apricots.

High-fiber muffins: For the flour, use 2 cups all-purpose flour and 1/4 cup whole-wheat flour.

Plus Points

• Health experts regularly recommend increasing the amount of fiber in our diet. These muffins help to do just that, especially when made with 1 cup chopped dried apricots instead of fresh ones. The muffins contribute both soluble and insoluble fiber, which is good for digestion, and also helpful in controlling the fat and sugar in the blood.

• Wheat bran is the indigestible outer fibrous part of the wheat grain. It is one of the richest sources of dietary fiber that helps keep the digestive system healthy.

photo, page 10

Exchanges

carbohydrate 2 1/2 fat 1

Each serving (one muffin) provides calories 236, calories from fat 62, fat 7g, saturated fat 3g, cholesterol 43mg, sodium 170mg, carbohydrate 40g, fiber 2g, sugars 21g, protein 5g. Excellent source of phosphorus. Good source of calcium, folate, iron, riboflavin, thiamine, vitamin A.

cinnamon-raisin bread

This whole-wheat bread loaf studded with raisins tastes good plain or can be served spread with a little honey or jam. It's also wonderful toasted for breakfast, when the gentle aroma of warm cinnamon makes a soothing start to the day.

Preparation time **20 minutes, plus 1 hour rising**   Cooking time **30 minutes**   *Makes 1 large loaf (cuts into 16 slices)*

5 cups whole-wheat flour

1 1/2 teaspoons salt

2 teaspoons ground cinnamon

1 package instant dry yeast

2/3 cup raisins

3 tablespoons sugar

3 tablespoons unsalted butter

1 cup fat-free milk, plus 1 tablespoon to glaze

1 egg, lightly beaten

1 Lightly coat a 2-pound loaf pan with cooking spray and flour. Sift the flour, salt, and cinnamon into a large mixing bowl. Stir in the yeast, raisins, and sugar, and make a well in the center.

2 Gently heat the butter and milk in a small saucepan until the butter has melted and the mixture is just warm. Pour into the well in the dry ingredients and add the beaten egg. Mix together to make a soft dough.

3 Turn the dough out onto a lightly floured surface and knead until smooth and elastic, about 10 minutes. Shape the dough into a loaf and place in the prepared pan. Cover with a clean towel or plastic wrap that has been coated with cooking spray and leave to rise in a warm place until doubled in size, about 1 hour.

4 Toward the end of the rising time, preheat the oven to 425°F. Uncover the loaf and brush with the milk to glaze. Bake until it sounds hollow when removed from the pan and tapped on the bottom, about 30 minutes. Cover the loaf with foil toward the end of the cooking time if the top is browning too much.

5 Turn out onto a wire rack and leave to cool. The bread can be kept, wrapped in foil, for 2 to 3 days.

(Some More Ideas) *Cinnamon-raisin-walnut bread*: Add 1/3 cup chopped walnuts to the flour mixture before adding the liquid ingredients.

Any type of dried fruit can be substituted for the raisins. Try adding 2/3 cup dried cherries, cranberries, blueberries, or chopped dried apricots in place of the raisins.

Cinnamon-raisin rolls: instead of forming the dough into a loaf after the first rising, divide it into 2-ounce pieces. Shape each piece into a round ball and place on a sheet pan coated with cooking spray. Cover the dough with plastic wrap or a towel and allow to rise according to the recipe. Bake the rolls on the same sheet pan until they sound hollow.

Plus Points

• Instant dry yeast can be combined with the dry ingredients and added directly into a bread recipe. This eliminates the need to dissolve the yeast in warm milk or water and to let it stand for 5 minutes prior to use.

• When cooking for a diabetic, whole grains and complex carbohydrates should be used whenever possible. Whole-wheat flour can be substituted for at least half the amount of white flour in almost all recipes to increase the fiber, vitamin, and mineral content of a baked good.

Exchanges

starch 2 1/2

Each serving (one slice) provides calories 198, calories from fat 30, fat 3g, saturated fat 1g, cholesterol 19mg, sodium 234mg, carbohydrate 38g, fiber 6g, sugars 8g, protein 7g. Good source of iron, magnesium, niacin, phosphorus, riboflavin, thiamine.

smoked haddock soufflé

Light, fluffy soufflés rarely fail to impress, yet they are surprisingly easy to make. This recipe uses the fish-poaching milk to make the soufflé base, and fresh herbs and chopped tomatoes are added for a lovely flavor. Serve straight from the oven, with a piece of crusty whole-wheat bread on the side.

Preparation time **35 minutes**   Cooking time **35 minutes**   *Serves 6*

2/3 pound smoked haddock fillet

1 1/4 cups 1% milk

1 teaspoon butter

1 tablespoon Parmesan cheese

1 tablespoon fine dry bread crumbs

3 tablespoons flour

3 eggs, separated

2 tomatoes, peeled, seeded, and diced

1 teaspoon coarse mustard

2 tablespoons finely chopped parsley

2 tablespoons finely snipped fresh chives

1 egg white

Salt and pepper

1 Place the haddock and milk in a saucepan and heat until simmering. Simmer gently until the fish will just flake when tested with a fork, about 8 minutes. Remove the pan from the heat and leave the fish to cool in the milk. When the fish is cool enough to handle, remove it, and flake the flesh, discarding the skin and any bones. Set the poaching milk aside to cool.

2 Preheat the oven, with a metal baking sheet inside, to 375°F. Lightly grease a 6-cup soufflé dish with the butter. Mix together the Parmesan and bread crumbs, and sprinkle over the bottom and side of the dish, turning the dish to coat evenly. Shake out any excess crumb mixture and reserve.

3 Mix the flour with a little of the reserved, cold poaching milk to make a smooth paste. Heat the remaining milk in a small saucepan until almost boiling, then pour into the flour mixture, stirring constantly. Return to the pan and bring to a boil, stirring to make a thick sauce.

4 Pour the sauce into a large mixing bowl. Add the egg yolks, one by one, beating them thoroughly into the sauce. Stir in the flaked haddock, tomatoes, mustard, parsley, chives, and salt and pepper to taste.

5 In a clean, dry mixing bowl, whisk the 4 egg whites until stiff enough to hold soft peaks. Fold 1/4 of the whites into the sauce mixture to lighten it, then gently fold in the remaining whites.

6 Spoon the mixture into the prepared soufflé dish and sprinkle the top with the reserved Parmesan and bread crumb mixture. Set the dish on the hot baking sheet and bake until well puffed and golden brown, about 35 minutes. Serve immediately.

(**Some More Ideas**) *Mediterranean-style goat cheese soufflé*: Place 1/2 cup sun-dried tomatoes in a small bowl and pour over boiling water to cover. Leave to soak for 30 minutes, then drain, and finely chop. In Step 3, make the thick sauce base with 3 table-spoons flour and 1 1/4 cups 1% milk. After beating in the egg yolks, add 1/3 cup low-fat goat cheese and beat until smooth. Stir in the sun-dried tomatoes and the herbs, and sea-son with salt and pepper to taste. Fold in the stiffly whisked egg whites, then spoon the mixture into the soufflé dish. Finish and bake as in the main recipe.

photo, page 21

Exchanges

carbohydrate 1/2 meat (lean) 2

Each serving provides calories 160, calories from fat 43, fat 5g, saturated fat 2g, cholesterol 150mg, sodium 500mg, carbohydrate 9g, fiber 1g, sugars 4g, protein 20g. Excellent source of phosphorus, riboflavin, vitamin B12. Good source of calcium, magnesium, niacin, potassium, vitamin A, vitamin B6, vitamin C. Flag: High in sodium.

huevos rancheros

In order to refuel and stabilize blood sugars in the morning, it is important to have a balanced breakfast consisting of a small amount of protein along with carbohydrates, dairy, and fruit, or vegetables. For a fun weekend brunch, serve this perfectly balanced Mexican-style dish of poached eggs, warm flour tortillas, a fresh tomato and chile salsa, and toppings of low-fat grated cheese and sour cream, scallions, and fresh cilantro.

Preparation and cooking time **35 minutes, plus 30 minutes marinating**   *Serves 4*

Salsa

5 medium tomatoes, finely chopped

1 mild fresh red chile, seeded and finely chopped

1 small red onion, finely chopped

1 small garlic clove, finely chopped

2 tablespoons finely chopped fresh cilantro

1 tablespoon olive oil

2 to 3 teaspoons lime juice

Salt and pepper

Eggs

4 (10 inch) flour tortillas

1 teaspoon vinegar

4 eggs

2 ounces coarsely grated reduced-fat cheddar cheese

6 tablespoons low-fat sour cream

4 scallions, chopped

Garnish

Chopped fresh cilantro

Lime wedges

1 First make the salsa. Place the chopped tomatoes in a bowl and stir in the chile, red onion, garlic, and cilantro. Add the oil and lime juice to taste. Set aside to marinate for about 30 minutes, then season lightly with salt and pepper to taste.

2 Preheat the oven 350°F. Wrap the stacked-up tortillas in foil and put them in the oven to warm for 10 minutes.

3 Meanwhile, half-fill a large skillet with water. Heat until just starting to simmer, then reduce the heat so the water does not boil. Add the vinegar. Break the eggs into the water, one at a time, and poach for 3 minutes. Toward the end of cooking, spoon the water over the yolks. When cooked, remove the eggs with a slotted spoon and drain on a paper-towel-lined plate.

4 Place the warmed tortillas on plates. Spoon over a little salsa, then put the eggs on top and season with salt and pepper to taste. Let everyone help themselves to the rest of the salsa, the grated cheese, sour cream, and scallions, plus chopped cilantro for sprinkling over the top and lime wedges for squeezing.

(**Some More Ideas**) Add these quick homemade refried beans for a very hearty brunch dish. Heat 2 teaspoons canola oil in a saucepan. Add 1 finely chopped garlic clove and 1/2 teaspoon ground cumin, and cook for a few seconds. Stir in 1 can (14 ounces) pinto beans, drained, and 1/2 cup water. Cover and simmer until the beans are soft enough to mash, about 5 minutes. Roughly mash them with a fork, then cook, uncovered, for 3 minutes. If the mixture is too runny, cook for a few more minutes. Season lightly with salt.

Plus Points

• Chile peppers are a good source of vitamins A, C, and E, as well as folic acid and potassium. Capsaicin is the compound in chiles that gives them their fiery nature. In order to make chiles milder, the seeds and membranes must be removed.

• Low-fat dairy products are an excellent source of calcium. It is recommended that Americans consume at least 3 servings of low-fat milk, cheese, or yogurt each day.

photo, page 21

Exchanges

starch 2 1/2   vegetable 3
meat (medium fat) 1   fat 2 1/2

Each serving provides calories 459, calories from fat 171, fat 19g, saturated fat 7g, cholesterol 231mg, sodium 554mg, carbohydrate 55g, fiber 5g, sugars 11g, protein 20g. Excellent source of calcium, folate, iron, phosphorus, potassium, riboflavin, thiamine, vitamin A, vitamin C. Good source of magnesium, niacin, vitamin B6, vitamin B12.

stuffed eggs

The hollows in hard-boiled egg halves make perfect containers for a tasty filling. In this recipe, the creamy filling is made with grated carrots and chives. Low-fat mayonnaise and yogurt are used to lower the fat and cholesterol content. The stuffed eggs are served on a bed of ribbon vegetables and crunchy lettuce leaves drizzled with a tarragon vinaigrette dressing. All you need is some interesting bread, such as whole-wheat with sunflower seeds, to make a satisfying lunch.

Preparation and cooking time **25 minutes**   *Serves 8*

Eggs

8 eggs, at room temperature

2 tablespoons low-fat mayonnaise

2 tablespoons plain low-fat yogurt

1 teaspoon mustard powder

1 medium carrot, finely grated

2 tablespoons snipped fresh chives

Dressing

1 1/2 tablespoons olive oil

2 teaspoons tarragon vinegar

1 teaspoon Dijon mustard

Salt and pepper

Salad

1 medium carrot

1 small bulb of fennel

2 small zucchini

4 cups Boston or Bibb lettuce

1 First, hard-boil the eggs. Place in a large saucepan, cover with tepid water, and bring to a boil. Reduce the heat and simmer for 7 minutes. Remove the eggs with a slotted spoon and place in a bowl of cold water to cool.

2 Meanwhile, make the dressing. Put the olive oil, vinegar, and mustard in a screw-top jar with salt and pepper to taste. Shake well, then set aside.

3 Peel the eggs and cut each in half lengthways. Scoop out the yolks into a bowl, using a teaspoon. Set the whites aside.

4 Add the mayonnaise, yogurt, mustard powder, grated carrot, and half of the chives to the egg yolks, and mash together. Season lightly with salt and pepper. Using a teaspoon, spoon the egg-yolk filling into the hollows in the egg-white halves, mounding it up attractively.

5 Using a vegetable peeler or a mandoline, shave thin ribbons lengthways from the carrot, fennel, and zucchini. Put the vegetable ribbons in a mixing bowl with the lettuce. Shake the dressing again, then pour over the salad, and toss together.

6 Divide the salad among 8 plates and top each with 2 stuffed egg halves. Sprinkle the top of the eggs with the remaining chives, and serve.

(Some More Ideas) For a lightly curried filling, mix the egg yolks with 4 tablespoons reduced-fat cream cheese instead of mayonnaise, 1 teaspoon curry paste, 2 finely chopped scallions, and the grated carrot.

Try adding 3 to 4 finely chopped radishes to the stuffing mixture.

Plus Points
• Eggs have often been given bad press because of their cholesterol content. When eaten in moderation (2 to 3 per week), eggs should have little effect on blood cholesterol levels.
• Preparing vegetables just before use helps to minimize vitamin loss.
• By using a combination of low-fat mayonnaise and plain yogurt rather than using mayonnaise alone, the fat and calorie content of this dish is reduced.

Exchanges

vegetable 1 meat (medium fat) 1 fat 1/2

Each serving provides calories 129, calories from fat 73, fat 8g, saturated fat 2g, cholesterol 213mg, sodium 134mg, carbohydrate 7g, fiber 2g, sugars 4g, protein 8g. Excellent source of riboflavin, vitamin A. Good source of folate, phosphorus, vitamin B12, vitamin C.

stuffed eggs, *p20*

tomato and pecorino cheese pudding, *p22*

smoked haddock soufflé, *p18*

huevos rancheros, *p19*

tomato and pecorino cheese pudding

For this attractive pudding, sweet cherry tomatoes are baked in a light, fluffy batter flavored with grated pecorino cheese. Many egg dishes are made with whole eggs and cream. Here the batter is made with a combination of whole eggs, egg whites, and low-fat sour cream to make a delightfully lower-fat version. Make individual servings in small ramekins or one large one, and serve for a simple lunch or supper. Boiled new potatoes and fresh green beans are excellent accompaniments.

Preparation time **20 minutes**   Cooking time **30–35 minutes**   *Serves 4*

Cooking spray
1 pound cherry tomatoes
4 tablespoons snipped fresh chives
1/3 cup coarsely grated pecorino romano cheese
3 large eggs
3 egg whites
2 tablespoons flour
3 tablespoons low-fat sour cream
1 1/4 cups 1% milk

1 Preheat the oven to 375°F. Lightly spray 4 shallow ovenproof dishes, each about 5 to 6 inches in diameter. Divide the cherry tomatoes among the dishes, spreading them out, and sprinkle over the chives and 4 tablespoons of the cheese.

2 Break the eggs and egg whites into a bowl and whisk them together, then gradually whisk in the flour until smooth. Add the sour cream, then gradually whisk in the milk to make a thin, smooth batter. Season lightly with salt and pepper.

3 Pour the batter over the tomatoes, dividing it evenly among the dishes. Sprinkle over the remaining cheese and an extra grinding of pepper. Bake until set, puffed, and lightly golden, about 30 to 35 minutes.

4 Remove the puddings from the oven and leave to cool for a few minutes before serving, as the tomatoes are very hot inside.

(Some More Ideas) Bake one large pudding, using a lightly sprayed 9-inch round ovenproof dish that is about 2 inches deep. Increase the baking time to 35 to 40 minutes.

Substitute torn fresh basil leaves or chopped fresh oregano for the chives.

Plus Points
• Pecorino is a hard Italian cheese made from sheep's milk. Like Parmesan, it is quite high in fat, but can be used in small quantities, as it has a rich, strong flavor.
• Two egg whites can be used in place of one whole egg in almost all recipes. This eliminates the yolk of the egg, which contains 218mg cholesterol. The substitution is particularly useful in recipes for baked goods such as cakes and quick breads.

photo, page 21

Exchanges
carbohydrate 1/2 vegetable 1
meat (lean) 1 fat 1/2

Each serving provides calories 193, calories from fat 80, fat 9g, saturated fat 5g, cholesterol 178mg, sodium 272mg, carbohydrate 14g, fiber 1g, sugars 7g, protein 15g. Excellent source of calcium, phosphorus, riboflavin, vitamin A, vitamin C. Good source of folate, potassium, thiamine, vitamin B12.

strawberry-yogurt smoothie

When summer arrives and strawberries are in season, it is the perfect time for this flavorful drink. Whirl up the berries with yogurt and fresh orange juice to create this creamy, refreshing smoothie that's high in vitamin C. It makes a fast and healthy breakfast shake or a delicious low-calorie snack-in-a-glass, any time of the day.

Preparation time **10 minutes**   *Serves 4*

Smoothie

1 quart (4 cups) ripe strawberries
1 cup plain low-fat yogurt
1/2 cup fresh orange juice
1 tablespoon sugar, or to taste

Garnish (optional)

4 small strawberries with leaves
4 thin round slices of unpeeled orange

1 Rinse and drain the strawberries and place them in a food processor or blender. Add the yogurt, orange juice, and 1 tablespoon sugar. Process on the highest speed until a well-blended puree forms, about 15 seconds, stopping to scrape down the sides of the container once or twice. Taste the mixture and sweeten with a little more sugar, if you wish.

2 For a very smooth beverage, strain the mixture, using a wooden spoon to push the drink through. Discard the strawberry seeds.

3 Pour into 4 tall glasses and serve immediately. If you wish to decorate the drinks, slit the strawberries and the orange slices halfway through the centers. Attach one berry and one orange slice to the rim of each glass.

(Some More Ideas) *Banana-berry smoothie*: Add 1 small banana, cut into quarters (Step 1). Because bananas tend to thicken drinks, increase the orange juice to 3/4 cup. Taste the smoothie before adding the tablespoon of sugar (you may not need it).

Apricot-berry smoothie: For the fruits, use 2 cups peeled apricot slices and only 2 cups of ripe strawberries.

Plus Points

• Strawberries are not only naturally sweet and delicious but also an excellent source of vitamin C. Ounce for ounce, strawberries provide more vitamin C than fresh oranges. Vitamin C is an antioxidant that helps protect against cancer, may slow the aging process, and helps maintain the immune system.

• Yogurt contains active bacterial cultures that "eat" the milk sugar (lactose), making yogurt a great dairy product for those people who have a milk intolerance.

• Low-fat plain yogurt is lower in calories than yogurt that is sweetened with fruit purees.

photo, page 25

Exchanges
carbohydrate 1 1/2

Each serving provides calories 108, calories from fat 14, fat 2g, saturated fat 1g, cholesterol 5mg, sodium 45mg, carbohydrate 21g, fiber 4g, sugars 17g, protein 4g. Excellent source of vitamin C. Good source of calcium, folate, phosphorus, potassium, riboflavin.

mint and orange scented melon cup

This is a perfect light summertime treat, a combination of colorful ripe fruits and pieces of crisp cucumber, drizzled with orange-flavored liqueur and garnished with fresh mint. The salad is served in hollowed-out melon shells for an elegant presentation, and slices of star fruit add another intriguing touch. Serve the salad at an afternoon picnic or for Sunday brunch.

Preparation time **25 minutes**   Marinating time **20 minutes**   *Serves 6*

Melon Cup

1 small cantaloupe (about 1 pound)

1 small honeydew melon (about 1 pound)

1 pint ripe strawberries, hulled and sliced (1 1/2 cups)

1 large pear, cut into 1/2-inch pieces

1/2 small cucumber, diced (1/2 cup)

2 star fruits, sliced 1/4 inch thick

6 tablespoons Grand Marnier or brandy

2 tablespoons shredded fresh mint

Garnish

Fresh mint sprigs

1 Cut both melons in half crosswise and scoop out the seeds from the center. Using a melon baller or a small spoon, scoop out balls of melon into a large bowl. With a tablespoon, scoop out any remaining melon into the bowl, leaving smooth shells.

2 Add the strawberries, pear chunks, and diced cucumber to the melon in the bowl. Set aside 4 star-fruit slices for decoration. Dice the remaining slices and add to the bowl.

3 Drizzle the Grand Marnier over the fruit, sprinkle with the mint, and toss gently to mix well. Cover with plastic wrap and let macerate in the refrigerator for 20 minutes.

4 Pile the fruit mixture into the shells and decorate with the reserved slices of star fruit.

(**Some More Ideas**) *Nonalcoholic fruit basket*: For the Grand Marnier, substitute a mixture of 3 tablespoons fresh orange juice and 3 tablespoons honey.

Luncheon salad: For the fruits and vegetables, use 1 small honeydew melon, 1 1/2 cups sliced, hulled strawberries, 1 large crisp red apple such as Delicious or Cortland, 1 cup seedless green grapes, 2 peeled sliced kiwis, and 1/2 cup diced cucumber. Omit the cantaloupe, pear, star fruits, and Grand Marnier. In a large bowl, toss 6 cups mesclun salad leaves, 2 cups watercress, and 1/2 cup chopped scallions. Arrange on 6 salad plates and spoon the fruit on top. Add a scoop of low-fat cottage cheese and sprinkle with the shredded fresh mint.

Plus Points

• This delicious combination of fresh fruits provides a healthy serving of fiber and vitamins, especially vitamin C. The orange-fleshed melon contributes beta-carotene, which the body converts into vitamin A, an important antioxidant.

• Fruit-based desserts are sweet enough to cap off a delicious meal, but are generally lower in fat and calories than desserts that are laden with chocolate, sugar, and butter.

Exchanges

fruit 1 1/2

Each serving provides calories 107, calories from fat 5, fat 1g, saturated fat 0g, cholesterol 0mg, sodium 8mg, carbohydrate 20g, fiber 3g, sugars 17g, protein 1g. Excellent source of vitamin C. Good source of potassium, vitamin A.

mint and orange scented melon cup, *p24*

orchard spread, *p27*

strawberry-yogurt smoothie, *p23*

berry salad with passion fruit, *p26*

berry salad with passion fruit

Tart, sweet, and juicy, berries come in many varieties—from bright and delicate raspberries to sweet strawberries, from plump little blueberries to rich, fragrant blackberries. Thanks to importers, you can buy almost all berries in any season. If one kind is not available, you can substitute another. Fresh-squeezed passion-fruit juice adds a tart edge to the berries in this salad.

Preparation time **10 minutes**   *Serves 6*

1 quart (4 cups) ripe strawberries, hulled and cut in half

1/2 pint (1 cup) fresh red raspberries

1/2 pint (1 cup) fresh blackberries

1/2 cup fresh blueberries

1/2 cup mixed fresh red currants and black currants, removed from their stalks (optional)

2 passion fruits

3 tablespoons sugar, or to taste

1 tablespoon fresh lime or lemon juice

1 In a large serving bowl, combine the strawberries, raspberries, blackberries, blueberries, red currants, and black currants in a bowl.

2 Cut each passion fruit in half. Holding a strainer over the bowl of berries, spoon the passion fruit and seeds into the strainer. Press the flesh and seeds with the back of a spoon to squeeze all of the juice through the strainer onto the berries. Reserve a few of the seeds left in the strainer and discard the rest.

3 Add the sugar and lime juice to the berries. Gently toss. Sprinkle with the reserved passion-fruit seeds. Serve the salad immediately or cover and chill briefly.

(Some More Ideas) Instead of passion-fruit juice, add 3 tablespoons crème de cassis. Chill the salad until ready to serve.

Berry salad with fresh peach sauce: Omit the passion fruit. Peel, pit, and puree 2 large, ripe peaches. Sweeten with 3 tablespoons sugar, 1 tablespoon fresh lemon juice, and 1/2 teaspoon pure vanilla extract. Drizzle with 1 tablespoon peach brandy, if you wish.

Fresh berry sundae: Scoop 1/2 cup low-fat vanilla frozen yogurt onto 6 dessert plates and spoon the berries over the top. Sprinkle with a few toasted almonds, if desired.

Plus Points
• Comparing the same weight of each fruit, fresh black currants weigh out on top in vitamin C. One 1/4 cup serving of black currants contributes 90mg of vitamin C, as compared to fresh strawberries with 28mg, fresh raspberries with 13mg, and fresh blackberries with 11mg.
• This feast of summer fruits is particularly healthful. It's rich in dietary fiber and vitamin C. Passion fruit adds vitamin A, which is essential for healthy skin and good vision; it also contains beta-carotene, which is an important antioxidant.

photo, page 25

Exchanges

fruit 1 1/2

Each serving provides calories 89, calories from fat 6, fat 1g, saturated fat 0g, cholesterol 0mg, sodium 4mg, carbohydrate 22g, fiber 6g, sugars 15g, protein 1g. Excellent source of vitamin C.

orchard spread

Save the fat calories by using this rich, lightly spiced puree of fresh and dried fruit instead of butter on warm toast or muffins. The recipe makes 4 cups, far more than is needed for one breakfast, but the spread keeps well in a covered jar in the refrigerator. Another day, try it for lunch in a sandwich with peanut butter or cheddar cheese.

Preparation time **30 minutes**   Cooking time **35 minutes**   Cooling time **at least 1 hour**   *Makes 1 quart (4 cups)*

1 pound tart cooking apples (such as Jonathan, McIntosh, Rome Beauty), peeled, cored, and coarsely chopped (3 cups)

1 1/2 cups dried pears

1 1/2 cups dried peaches

1 1/2 cups apple juice

1 1/2 cups water

1 teaspoon ground allspice

1 1/2 teaspoons fresh lemon juice, or to taste

1 In a large, heavy saucepan, place the apples, pears, peaches, apple juice, water, and allspice. Bring the fruit mixture to a boil over high heat, stirring occasionally.

2 Reduce the heat to low and simmer, uncovered, until the mixture is reduced to a pulp and no liquid is visible on the surface, about 30 minutes. Stir frequently to prevent the mixture from sticking to the bottom of the pan.

3 Remove the pan from the heat and let the mixture cool slightly. Stir in the lemon juice, then taste and add a little more lemon juice if the mixture is too sweet.

4 Transfer the fruit mixture to a food processor or blender and process until a thick puree forms. Let the spread cool at room temperature for about 1 hour before serving. The spread can be kept in a covered jar, refrigerated, for up to a week.

(**Some More Ideas**) Just before serving, stir in some finely chopped blanched almonds. Tip: Add nuts just to the portion of the spread you are serving, as the nuts will soften if stored for more than a few hours.

Mixed-fruit spread: Substitute 3 cups dried mixed fruits, such as blueberries, cranberries, pineapple, and golden raisins, for the dried pears and peaches. Substitute 1 1/2 cups fresh orange juice for the apple juice and 1/2 teaspoon ground ginger for the allspice.

Vanilla peach spread: Increase the dried peaches to 3 cups and omit the dried pears. Substitute 1 1/2 cups fresh orange juice for the apple juice. Replace the allspice with a vanilla bean, discarding it after cooking (Step 3) and before adding the lemon juice.

Orange cranberry spread: Replace the dried peaches and pears with 3 cups dried cranberries and substitute 1 1/2 cups cranberry juice for the apple juice. Add 2 teaspoons finely grated orange zest with the allspice.

Plus Points
• Apples are a good source of soluble fiber called pectin, which helps to absorb large amounts of water from the intestinal tract, helping to prevent constipation.
• Dried peaches are a good source of vitamin A, iron, and potassium. Plus, they contain carotenes, which protect against some cancers.
• The sweetness of fresh fruit is concentrated in its dried form, so a spread such as this one does not need additional sugar.

photo, page 25

Exchanges

fruit 1   **Each serving (one ounce) provides** calories 59, calories from fat 2, fat 0g, saturated fat 0g, cholesterol 0mg, sodium 2mg, carbohydrate 15g, fiber 3g, sugars 9g, protein 1g.

27

lunch

tarragon chicken salad

Tahini, a paste made from ground sesame seeds, is a favorite ingredient in Middle Eastern cooking. Available from most large supermarkets, it adds a nutty taste and creaminess to the dressing for this colorful and nutritious chicken salad. The chicken is served on a bed of crisp spinach leaves and topped with crunchy toasted almonds for a delightful presentation.

Preparation time **25 minutes**   Cooking time **15 minutes**   *Serves 4*

1 pound boneless, skinless chicken breasts

1 1/2 cups low-fat, reduced-sodium chicken or vegetable broth

1 small bunch fresh tarragon

1 small lemon

3 black peppercorns

2 tablespoons sesame tahini

1 head chicory or other head lettuce

2 cups baby spinach leaves

2 oranges

1/4 cup toasted sliced almonds

Salt and pepper

Plus Points

• Tahini contains 18 grams of fat per 2 tablespoons. Only a little of the potent ingredient is needed along with the broth to make a very flavorful and unique dressing for this salad.

• Chicory was used by the ancient Egyptians, Greeks, and Romans, both for its medicinal properties and for cooking. It was believed to stimulate the digestive juices and strengthen the liver.

1 Place the chicken breasts in a shallow pan, in one layer, and pour over the broth. Remove the tarragon leaves from the stalks and set them aside. Lightly crush the tarragon stalks with a rolling pin to release all their oils, then add to the pan. Using a vegetable peeler, remove a small strip of zest from the lemon and add this to the pan together with the peppercorns.

2 Set the pan over medium heat and bring the broth to a boil. Turn down the heat so the broth just simmers gently and cover the pan. Cook until the chicken is cooked all the way through, about 15 minutes.

3 Remove the chicken breasts, using a slotted spoon, and leave to cool on a plate. Strain the broth into a bowl and discard the tarragon stalks, lemon zest, and peppercorns. Set the broth aside. When the chicken has cooled, cut it into thick strips.

4 Add the tahini to a mixing bowl and gradually whisk in 4 tablespoons of the reserved broth to make a smooth, creamy dressing. If the dressing is a bit thick, whisk in another 1 to 2 tablespoons of the broth. Squeeze the juice from the lemon and stir it into the dressing. Chop enough of the tarragon leaves to make 1 tablespoon, and add to the dressing with salt and pepper to taste.

5 Cut the chicory or other head lettuce across diagonally into slices about 1 inch thick. Arrange the chicory and spinach in a large salad bowl.

6 Peel the oranges, then cut between the membrane into segments. Scatter the segments over the salad leaves, followed by the toasted almonds. Place the chicken strips on top, and spoon over the tahini tarragon dressing. Serve immediately.

(Some More Ideas) *Asian chicken salad*: Poach the chicken in broth flavored with 3 thin slices fresh ginger and 3 black peppercorns. Combine 2 cups shredded bok choy, 2 cups torn romaine lettuce, and 1 cup watercress in a large salad bowl, and arrange the sliced chicken on top. Scatter over 3 peeled and diced kiwifruit. For the dressing, whisk together 2 tablespoons tahini, 1 crushed garlic clove, 1 teaspoon finely chopped fresh ginger, the grated zest and juice of 1 lemon, 1 tablespoon light soy sauce, a good pinch of five-spice powder (optional) and 3 to 4 tablespoons of the reserved poaching broth until smooth. Spoon the dressing over the salad, sprinkle with 1 tablespoon sesame seeds, and serve with warm pita breads.

Exchanges

fruit 1 meat (very lean) 4 fat 1 1/2

Each serving provides calories 273, calories from fat 101, fat 11g, saturated fat 1g, cholesterol 67mg, sodium 127mg, carbohydrate 14g, fiber 5g, sugars 8g, protein 30g. Excellent source of niacin, phosphorus, riboflavin, vitamin C. Good source of calcium, folate, iron, magnesium, potassium, thiamine, vitamin A, vitamin B6.

watermelon and feta salad

In this salad, the salty tang of creamy feta cheese contrasts with pieces of sweet watermelon and juicy golden nectarines. A mix of arugula, endive, and leaf lettuce adds a slightly peppery taste, while the toasted pumpkin seeds give a crunch. The dressing is light and zesty, complementing the flavors of the salad perfectly. Serve with whole-wheat bread for a light lunch or dinner meal.

Preparation time **20 minutes**   *Makes 4 main-dish servings*

Salad

1 small watermelon
(about 1 pound)

2 large nectarines or peaches

6 cups mixed salad greens,
including arugula, endive,
and leaf lettuce

1 cup crumbled feta cheese

2 tablespoons toasted
pumpkin seeds or
sunflower seeds

Lemon Dressing

3 tablespoons olive oil

2 tablespoons fresh
lemon juice

1/4 teaspoon salt

1/4 teaspoon freshly ground
black pepper

1 First, make the dressing. Place the oil, lemon juice, salt, and pepper into a 2-cup jar or container with a tightfitting lid. Cover and shake until well blended.

2 Using a serrated knife, cut the watermelon into bite-size chunks, discarding the rind and all of the seeds. Toss into a large salad bowl.

3 Cut the nectarines in half (do not peel) and pit them. Place the nectarines on a cutting board, cut side down, and cut lengthwise into thin slices; toss with the watermelon chunks. Tear the salad greens into bite-size pieces and add to the fruit. Toss to mix.

4 Crumble the feta cheese over the salad. Sprinkle the seeds over the top and drizzle with the lemon dressing; serve.

Tip: *To serve the salad later, prepare the salad through Step 2, cover with plastic wrap, and refrigerate. Proceed with Steps 3 and 4 right before serving.*

(Some More Ideas) *Pear and Gorgonzola salad*: Instead of the watermelon and nectarines, use 1 pound ripe, cored, thinly sliced red Bartlett or Comice pears, and 3 cups sliced ripe strawberries. Use 1 cup creamy Gorgonzola cheese instead of the feta cheese. Include radicchio in the mix of salad leaves.

Try using toasted walnuts in place of the toasted pumpkin or sunflower seeds.

Plus Points

• The golden nectarines and peaches contain the antioxidant beta-carotene, which the body converts into vitamin A. Watermelon contains a fair amount of vitamin C.

• Feta cheese is relatively high in sodium, and actually contains more than twice as much sodium as found in the same quantity of cheddar cheese. To reduce the salt, soak the feta in milk for 30 minutes. Then rinse the cheese in a strainer under running water and pat dry on paper towels.

• Sunflower seeds are one of the best sources of vitamin E, which helps to maintain red blood cells and muscle tissue.

photo, page 35

Exchanges

fruit 1/2 vegetable 1
meat (high fat) 1 fat 1

Each serving provides calories 198, calories from fat 131, fat 15g, saturated fat 5g, cholesterol 22mg, sodium 386mg, carbohydrate 13g, fiber 2g, sugars 9g, protein 6g. Excellent source of vitamin A, vitamin C. Good source of calcium, folate, magnesium, phosphorus, riboflavin, vitamin B6.

eastern salad

Based on fattoush, the colorful, crunchy salad served throughout the Middle East, this version adds tuna fish for extra flavor and protein. Make sure you grill the pita bread until really crisp to prevent it from going soggy when mixed with the other ingredients, and serve the salad as soon as possible after making.

Preparation time **about 15 minutes**   Cooking time **about 5 minutes**   *Serves 4*

4 small whole-wheat pita breads

1 1/2 tablespoons olive oil

Juice of 1 lemon

6 scallions, sliced

3/4 pound ripe tomatoes, chopped

1 small cucumber, diced

1 can (7 ounces) tuna in spring water, drained and flaked

2 tablespoons coarsely chopped fresh flat-leaf parsley

1 tablespoon coarsely chopped fresh cilantro

1 tablespoon coarsely chopped fresh mint

Salt and pepper

1 Preheat the oven broiler. Place the pita breads on a baking sheet and warm under the broiler, 6 inches from the heat source, for a few seconds or until puffy, then carefully split them open through the middle and open out each one like a book. Return to the broiler and toast on each side or until lightly browned and crisp, about 2 to 3 minutes. Roughly tear the pita into bite-size pieces and set aside.

2 Whisk together the olive oil and lemon juice in a large serving bowl, and season lightly with salt and pepper. Add the scallions, tomatoes, cucumber, and tuna, and toss gently to coat with the oil and lemon juice.

3 Add the parsley, cilantro, mint, and torn pita pieces to the serving bowl and toss quickly to mix. Serve immediately.

(Some More Ideas) Make a more substantial salad by adding 1 can (15 ounces) black-eyed peas.

Mediterranean-style vegetable salad: Whisk together 1 teaspoon Dijon mustard, 1 teaspoon finely grated lemon zest, 1 crushed garlic clove, 2 teaspoons red wine vinegar, 1 1/2 tablespoons olive oil, 1 tablespoon chopped fresh oregano, and salt and pepper to taste in a large serving bowl. Quarter 1/2 pound baby plum tomatoes and add to the bowl. Add 2 medium zucchini, 1 small bulb of fennel, and 1 red onion, all coarsely chopped. Toss to coat the vegetables with the dressing.

Plus Points

• When cooking with scallions, use both the white bulb and leaves of the onions to increase the beta-carotene provided. The antioxidant is found in the green part of the vegetable.

• This salad can be served as a main dish and a complete meal because it contains a source of carbohydrate (pita), protein (tuna), and vegetables.

photo, page 35

Exchanges

starch 2   vegetable 1   meat (very lean) 1   fat 1

Each serving provides calories 270, calories from fat 64, fat 7g, saturated fat 1g, cholesterol 13mg, sodium 296mg, carbohydrate 38g, fiber 4g, sugars 6g, protein 18g. Excellent source of niacin, phosphorus, thiamine, vitamin B12, vitamin C. Good source of folate, iron, magnesium, potassium, vitamin A, vitamin B6.

LUNCH

citrus and spinach salad

Fresh leaf spinach pairs well with citrus fruits, melon, and prosciutto. Here the spinach is tossed with the fruits and their juices and then drizzled with a creamy and sweet balsamic dressing. The prosciutto is used in a small amount to top the salad, so you get the flavor without adding much fat!

Preparation time **30 minutes**   *Serves 6*

Salad

2 large navel oranges

1 large ruby-red grapefruit

6 cups baby spinach leaves, washed

1 small cantaloupe, peeled and cut into bite-size chunks

4 scallions, white parts only, very thinly sliced

4 ounces thinly sliced prosciutto, cut into shreds

Dressing

3 tablespoons balsamic vinegar

3 tablespoons olive oil

2 tablespoons light cream

2 teaspoons honey

1/4 teaspoon salt

1/4 teaspoon freshly ground black pepper

1 First, make the dressing. Place the vinegar, oil, cream, honey, salt, and pepper into a pint-size jar or container with a tightfitting lid. Cover and shake until well blended.

2 To make the salad, use a citrus zester or peeler to remove fine shreds of zest from one orange. Set aside. Working over a medium bowl to catch the juices, peel the oranges and grapefruit using a serrated fruit knife; be sure to remove all of the white pith.

3 Cut between the membranes of the fruits, lift out the fruit sections, and place in the bowl with the juices.

4 Add 2 tablespoons of the combined grapefruit and orange juices to the dressing and shake again to blend. Taste and add more citrus juice, salt, and pepper, if desired.

5 Place the spinach in a large serving bowl. Add the orange and grapefruit sections and any juices in the bowl, the cantaloupe, and scallions. Toss to evenly distribute the ingredients among the spinach leaves. Shake the dressing once more, then pour it over the salad and toss again. Scatter the shredded prosciutto over the top of the salad and sprinkle on the orange zest. Serve the salad immediately.

(Some More Ideas) *Zesty spinach salad:* To add a peppery flavor to this salad, use only 4 cups of spinach leaves and add 2 cups of watercress leaves. Remove the watercress leaves from their stems; use only the leaves, discarding the stems.

Citrus, spinach, and Gorgonzola salad: Make a vegetarian salad by omitting the prosciutto. Substitute 3 ounces of bite-size chunks of creamy Gorgonzola cheese for the prosciutto.

Variations for the dressing: In place of the balsamic vinegar, use 3 tablespoons raspberry, apple cider, or white wine vinegar in the dressing.

Plus Points

• This salad is an excellent source of vitamin C, thanks to all of the fruits as well as the spinach. Because cooking and cutting foods destroys vitamin C, it is best to leave the spinach leaves whole and to serve the salad as soon after tossing as possible.

• Cantaloupe contains the antioxidant beta-carotene, which is converted into vitamin A by the body.

Exchanges

fruit 1 meat (lean) 1 fat 1 1/2

Each serving provides calories 193, calories from fat 97, fat 11g, saturated fat 3g, cholesterol 21mg, sodium 471mg, carbohydrate 19g, fiber 3g, sugars 14g, protein 7g. Excellent source of folate, vitamin A, vitamin C. Good source of magnesium, potassium, riboflavin, thiamine, vitamin B6.

34

watermelon and feta salad *p32*

grilled salmon in ciabatta *p37*

citrus and spinach salad *p34*

eastern salad *p33*

summer salmon and asparagus

Fresh young vegetables and succulent salmon make this an excellent speedy dish to prepare for special occasions, especially when home-grown asparagus is in season. Slivered leeks, tender asparagus, and sugar snap peas all cook quickly and look superb. Serve with boiled new potatoes for a memorable meal.

Preparation time **10 minutes**   Cooking time **about 20 minutes**   *Serves 4*

Salmon and Asparagus

4 skinless salmon fillets
(about 4 ounces each)

2 leeks, thinly sliced

8 ounces asparagus spears

1 cup sugar snap peas

4 tablespoons dry white wine

1 cup reduced-sodium
vegetable broth

Salt and pepper

Garnish

1 tablespoon snipped
fresh chives

Exchanges

vegetable 2 meat (lean) 3

1 Run your fingertips over each salmon fillet to check for any stray bones, pulling out any that remain. Arrange the leeks in a single layer in the bottom of a large Dutch oven coated with cooking spray. Lay the pieces of salmon on top. Surround the fish with the asparagus and peas. Add the wine and broth and season lightly with salt and pepper.

2 Place the Dutch oven over medium-high heat and bring broth to a boil, then cover the pan with a tightfitting lid and reduce the heat to low. Cook the fish and vegetables until the salmon is pale pink all the way through and the vegetables are tender, about 12 to 14 minutes. Sprinkle the chives over the salmon and serve.

(Some More Ideas) Mackerel fillets can be prepared in the same way. Season the mackerel fillets and fold them loosely in half, with the skin outside. Use baby carrots, or large carrots cut into short, thick sticks, instead of the asparagus. Add 2 sprigs of fresh rosemary to the vegetables before arranging the mackerel on top and pouring in the wine and broth.

For a quick Asian-flavored dish, use cod or halibut fillet instead of salmon, 4 scallions instead of the leeks, and 8 ounces whole button mushrooms instead of the asparagus. Arrange the vegetables and fish as in the main recipe, adding 4 tablespoons Chinese rice wine or dry sherry with the broth instead of the white wine. Sprinkle with 1 tablespoon light soy sauce, 1 tablespoon grated fresh ginger, and 1 teaspoon toasted sesame oil over the fish. Garnish with chopped fresh cilantro instead of chives.

Plus Points
• Asparagus contains asparagine, a phyto-chemical that acts as a diuretic.
• This dish is easy to prepare and delightfully low in fat. The fish and vegetables are lightly poached in the wine and broth, infusing all of the flavors together.

Each serving provides calories 234, calories from fat 90, fat 10g, saturated fat 2g, cholesterol 70mg, sodium 99mg, carbohydrate 8g, fiber 2g, sugars 6g, protein 26g. Excellent source of folate, niacin, phosphorus, thiamine, vitamin B12, vitamin C. Good source of iron, magnesium, riboflavin, potassium, vitamin B6, vitamin A.

grilled salmon in ciabatta

Here fresh salmon fillets are marinated, then lightly grilled and served in warm ciabatta rolls with mixed salad leaves and a basil mayonnaise, to create a very tempting and special lunch dish. Using low-fat mayonnaise and yogurt reduces the fat without losing any of the creaminess.

Preparation time **15 minutes**   Marinating time **30 minutes**   Cooking time **10 minutes**   *Serves 4*

Juice of 1 lime

3 tablespoons chopped fresh basil

4 (4 ounce) skinless salmon fillets

2 1/2 tablespoons plain low-fat yogurt

2 1/2 tablespoons low-fat mayonnaise

1/2 teaspoon finely grated lime zest

4 ciabatta or whole-wheat rolls, about 2 ounces each

Salt and pepper

Mixed salad leaves, such as arugula, baby spinach, and red chard

1 Mix together the lime juice, 2 tablespoons of the basil, and salt and pepper to taste in a shallow, nonmetallic dish. Add the salmon fillets and turn them in the mixture to coat well all over. Cover and leave to marinate in the refrigerator for 30 minutes.

2 Meanwhile, mix together the yogurt, mayonnaise, lime zest, and remaining 1 tablespoon basil in a small bowl. Season lightly with salt and pepper. Cover and refrigerate until needed.

3 Preheat the oven to 425°F. Remove the salmon fillets from the marinade and place on a ridged grill pan. Or alternatively, preheat the oven broiler and place the salmon on a foil-lined broiler rack. Brush the salmon with a little of the marinade, then grill until the fish is just cooked and the flesh is beginning to flake, about 4 to 5 minutes on each side, brushing again with the marinade after you have turned the fillets. While the fish is cooking, place the ciabatta rolls, wrapped in foil, in the oven to bake for about 5 minutes.

4 Split the ciabatta rolls in half and spread the cut sides with the basil mayonnaise. Put a cooked salmon fillet on the bottom half of each roll and top with a few mixed salad leaves. Put the top half of each roll in place and serve immediately.

(**Some More Ideas**) Use other types of bread, such as whole-wheat English muffins or small, seeded whole-wheat rolls.

Grilled tuna sandwiches with tomato and ginger relish: Use 4 (3 ounce) fresh tuna steaks, and marinate them in a mixture of 2 teaspoons finely chopped fresh rosemary, the juice of 1 orange, and salt and pepper to taste. Meanwhile, to make the relish, sauté 1 finely chopped small red onion, 1 crushed garlic clove, and 1 tablespoon finely chopped fresh root ginger in 2 teaspoons olive oil until softened, about 8 to 10 minutes. Remove from the heat and add 4 chopped plum tomatoes, 1 or 2 tablespoons chopped fresh basil, and salt and pepper to taste. Mix well. Grill the tuna for 3 minutes on each side or until cooked to your taste, then serve on whole-wheat rolls with salad leaves and the relish.

Plus Points
• Adding low-fat yogurt to the mayonnaise not only reduces total fat, it also increases the nutritional value of the dish, in particular adding calcium, phosphorus, and vitamins B2 and B12.
• Salad leaves such as arugula are useful sources of the B vitamin folate and of beta-carotene.

photo, page 35

Exchanges
starch 2 meat (lean) 3 fat 1/2

Each serving provides calories 356, calories from fat 114, fat 13g, saturated fat 2g, cholesterol 78mg, sodium 429mg, carbohydrate 30g, fiber 2g, sugars 6g, protein 28g. Excellent source of niacin, phosphorus, riboflavin, thiamine, vitamin B6, vitamin B12. Good source of copper, folate, iron, magnesium, potassium.

smoked haddock and potato pie

Fish pie is usually popular even with people who may not otherwise be keen on fish. In this version, leek and watercress are added to boost the vitamin content, and sliced potato and cheese make an appealing, crispy topping. Serve the pie with roasted vine tomatoes, cooked for about 15 minutes alongside the pie, and steamed broccoli.

Preparation time **40 minutes**   Cooking time **25–30 minutes**   *Serves 6*

Pie

2 1/4 cups plus 3 tablespoons fat-free milk

1 pound smoked haddock fillets

1 bay leaf

1 large leek, halved lengthways and sliced

1 pound russet potatoes, peeled and cut into 1/4 inch thick slices

3 tablespoons cornmeal

2 cups watercress, thick stalks removed

1/2 cup coarsely grated reduced-fat cheddar cheese

Salt and pepper

Garnish

Chopped parsley

1 Pour the 2 1/4 cups milk into a wide skillet. Add the haddock and bay leaf. Bring to a gentle simmer, then cover and cook until the haddock is just cooked, about 5 minutes.

2 Lift out the fish with a slotted spoon and allow to cool slightly, then peel off the skin and break the flesh into large flakes. Set aside. Strain the milk, reserving 2 cups, as well as the bay leaf.

3 Place the leek in the skillet and add the reserved milk and bay leaf. Cover and simmer until the leek is tender, about 10 minutes.

4 Meanwhile, cook the potatoes in a saucepan of boiling water until they are just tender, about 8 minutes. Drain gently. Preheat the oven to 375°F.

5 Remove the bay leaf from the leeks and discard. Mix the cornmeal with the remaining 3 tablespoons cold milk to make a smooth paste. Add to the leek mixture and cook gently, stirring, until slightly thickened.

6 Remove the skillet from the heat and stir in the watercress, allowing it to wilt. Season lightly with salt and pepper. Add the flaked haddock, folding it in gently. Transfer the mixture to a 9-inch pie plate.

7 Arrange the potato slices on top of the fish mixture, overlapping them slightly.

Sprinkle with the cheese, and season with salt and pepper to taste. Bake until the fish filling is bubbling and the potatoes are turning golden, 25 to 30 minutes.

8 Sprinkle the top of the pie with parsley and allow to stand for about 5 minutes before serving.

(Some More Ideas) *Spinach fish pie*: Use 2 sliced leeks. Omit the watercress and instead, in Step 4, add 2 cups of baby spinach leaves to the potato slices for the last 1 to 2 minutes of the cooking time. Drain well. Make a layer of the potatoes and spinach on the bottom of the pie dish. Spoon the hot fish and leek filling over the top, sprinkle with the cheese, and broil for 5 to 10 minutes or until bubbly and golden.

Smoked haddock, pepper, and fennel pie: Cook 1 seeded and chopped red bell pepper, 1 small chopped onion, and 2 chopped garlic cloves in 2 teaspoons olive oil in a large skillet until the onion is soft. Add 1 cup thinly sliced fennel bulb and cook for 5 minutes, stirring occasionally. Stir in 1 can (15 ounces) chopped tomatoes, with their juice, and season lightly with salt and pepper. Cover and simmer until the fennel is tender, about 25 minutes. Meanwhile, cut the potatoes into chunks instead of slices and cook until tender, about

Exchanges

**starch 1 vegetable 1
meat (lean) 1**

Each serving provides calories 224, calories from fat 28, fat 3g, saturated fat 1g, cholesterol 67mg, sodium 714mg, carbohydrate 23g, fiber 2g, sugars 5g, protein 26g. Excellent source of calcium, niacin, phosphorus, potassium, vitamin B6, vitamin B12. Good source of folate, iron, magnesium, riboflavin, thiamine, vitamin A, vitamin C.

10 minutes. Pour the pepper and fennel sauce into the pie dish. Lay the skinned smoked haddock fillets on the top (cut to fit if necessary) and sprinkle with the drained potatoes. Sprinkle with 1/2 teaspoon crushed dried chiles and 2 tablespoons freshly grated Parmesan cheese. Bake until golden and bubbly, about 20 minutes.

Plus Points

• Haddock is a very mild-flavored white fish. When introducing fish into the diet, haddock is a good type to start with because it does not have a strong fishy taste. It is excellent when baked with a simple bread-crumb topping and served with lemon wedges.

• Watercress, like other dark green leafy vegetables, is an excellent source of many of the antioxidant nutrients, including beta-carotene, vitamin C, and vitamin E. Many recipes for fish pie contain butter and cream, which are used to make the creamy filling. In this recipe, fat-free milk is thickened and used as a low-fat substitute with very similar results.

monkfish and mussel kebabs

To create these succulent mini kebabs, marinated cubes of monkfish fillet and fresh mussels are threaded onto skewers with a selection of colorful vegetables, then lightly grilled. They make an extra-special hot appetizer for a buffet or celebration party.

Preparation time **20 minutes, plus 1 hour marinating**   Cooking time **8–10 minutes**   *Makes 16 kebabs*

Kebabs

Finely grated zest and juice of 1 lemon

Juice of 1 lime

1 tablespoon olive oil

2 teaspoons honey

1 garlic clove, crushed

1 tablespoon chopped fresh oregano or marjoram

1 tablespoon chopped parsley

7 ounces monkfish fillet, cut into 16 small cubes

16 shelled fresh mussels

1 small yellow bell pepper, seeded and cut into 16 small chunks

1 zucchini, cut into 16 thin slices

16 cherry tomatoes

Salt and pepper

Garnish

Lime or lemon wedges

1 Place the lemon zest and juice, lime juice, oil, honey, garlic, chopped oregano or marjoram, parsley, and salt and pepper to taste in a shallow nonmetallic dish. Whisk together, then add the monkfish cubes and mussels. Turn the seafood to coat all over with the marinade. Cover and marinate in the refrigerator for 1 hour.

2 Meanwhile, put 16 wooden skewers in warm water and leave to soak for 10 minutes. Drain. Preheat the grill or oven broiler to medium-high.

3 Onto each skewer, thread 1 cube of monkfish, 1 mussel, 1 piece of yellow bell pepper, 1 slice of zucchini, and a cherry tomato. (Reserve the marinade.) Leave the ends of the skewers empty so they will be easy to hold.

4 Place the kebabs on the grill rack or broiler pan and grill or broil until the monkfish is cooked and the vegetables are just tender, turning occasionally and brushing frequently with the marinade, about 8 to 10 minutes. Serve hot, garnished with lime or lemon wedges.

(Some More Ideas) *Scallop and shrimp kebabs:* Use 16 large sea scallops and 16 raw large peeled shrimp in place of the monkfish and mussels.

Tuna or swordfish kebabs: Cut 12 ounces fresh tuna or swordfish fillet into 16 small cubes and marinate in a mixture of the finely grated zest and juice of 1 lime, 1 small crushed garlic clove, 2 teaspoons olive oil, 1 teaspoon Cajun seasoning, and salt and pepper to taste. Seed 1 red bell pepper and cut into 16 small chunks, and quarter 4 shallots or baby onions. Thread the marinated fish onto skewers with the prepared vegetables and 16 very small button mushrooms. Grill as in the main recipe.

Plus Points

• Monkfish has a huge, ugly head, and only the tail is eaten. The firm flesh tastes a lot like lobster. Monkfish is an excellent source of phosphorus and a useful source of potassium, which is vital to help regulate blood pressure.

• Mussels provide several minerals, in particular iron, zinc, copper, and iodine. Mussels are also an extremely good source of vitamin B12, needed for the maintenance of a healthy nervous system.

photo, page 43

Exchanges	
vegetable 1	meat (very lean) 1
	fat 1/2

Each serving (two kebabs) provides calories 90, calories from fat 28, fat 3g, saturated fat 0g, cholesterol 17mg, sodium 84mg, carbohydrate 7g, fiber 1g, sugars 5g, protein 9g. Excellent source of vitamin B12, vitamin C. Good source of iron, phosphorus.

chicken and cashew pancakes

Chicken stir-fried with carrots, celery, cabbage, and cashew nuts, then lightly flavored with orange and sesame, makes a delicious filling for thin, savory pancakes. This dish is sure to meet with the entire family's approval.

Preparation time **20 minutes**   Cooking time **about 30 minutes**   *Serves 4*

Pancakes

1/2 cup flour
1 egg, beaten
1 1/4 cups fat-free milk
1 teaspoon canola oil
Salt and pepper

Filling

1/4 cup halved cashews
2 teaspoons canola oil
12 ounces skinless, boneless chicken breasts, cut into strips
1 garlic clove, crushed
1 teaspoon finely chopped fresh ginger
1 fresh red chile pepper, seeded, deveined, and finely chopped (optional)
2 carrots, cut into thin sticks
2 celery stalks, cut into thin sticks
Grated zest of 1 orange
1 cup Savoy cabbage, shredded
1 tablespoon light soy sauce, plus extra for serving
1/2 teaspoon toasted sesame oil

1 To make the pancakes, sift the flour into a bowl and add a little salt and pepper to taste. Make a well in the center. Mix the egg with the milk, then pour into the well. Gradually whisk the flour into the egg and milk to form a smooth batter.

2 Use a little of the oil to lightly grease an 8-inch nonstick pancake pan, and heat it over medium heat. Pour in a little of the batter and swirl it evenly across the surface, then cook for 2 minutes to form a pancake. Toss the pancake or flip it over with a spatula and cook on the other side for about 30 seconds. Slide out onto a warm, heatproof plate and cover.

3 Cook the remaining batter in the same way, making 8 pancakes in all and stacking them up, placing wax paper between each pancake. When all the pancakes have been made, cover the pancake stack with foil, sealing it well. Place the plate over a pan of gently simmering water to keep the pancakes warm while you prepare the filling.

4 Heat a wok or large skillet. Add the cashews and stir-fry them over a medium heat for a few minutes or until golden. Remove to a plate and set aside.

5 Add the oil to the wok or skillet and swirl it around, then add the chicken, garlic, ginger, and chile pepper, if using. (Wear gloves when handling chiles; they burn.) Stir-fry for 3 minutes.

6 Add the carrot and celery, and stir-fry for 2 minutes. Add the orange zest and cabbage, and stir-fry for 1 minute. Sprinkle over the soy sauce and sesame oil, and stir-fry for another minute. Return the cashews to the pan and toss to mix with the other ingredients.

7 Divide the stir-fry filling among the warm pancakes and fold them over or roll up. Serve immediately, with a little extra soy sauce on the side.

(**Some More Ideas**) Add 2 teaspoons finely chopped fresh ginger and the grated zest of 1 orange to the pancake batter.

When in a time crunch, you can use pre-made Chinese pancakes. Find the pancakes in specialty grocery stores and Asian markets. The stir-fry can also be served over steamed brown rice instead of pancakes.

Plus Points

• Cashew nuts are a rich source of protein, fiber, and minerals such as iron, magnesium, and selenium.
• Stir-frying is a healthy way to cook, because only a little oil is needed, any meat or poultry used is very lean, and cooking is done quickly over a high heat so that the maximum amount of nutrients in the vegetables is retained.

photo, page 43

Exchanges

**starch 1   vegetable 2
meat (very lean) 3   fat 2**

Each serving provides calories 320, calories from fat 107, fat 12g, saturated fat 2g, cholesterol 106mg, sodium 296mg, carbohydrate 26g, fiber 3g, sugars 8g, protein 27g. Excellent source of niacin, phosphorus, riboflavin, vitamin A, vitamin B6, vitamin C. Good source of calcium, folate, iron, magnesium, potassium, thiamine, vitamin B12.

chicken jamboree

This healthy chicken and vegetable casserole is cooked in one pan and makes an easy mid-week meal. To make it even quicker, you can use prewashed baby carrots and cut broccoli. Serve the dish with a mixture of steamed wild and brown rice.

Preparation time **15 minutes**   Cooking time **about 25 minutes**   *Serves 4*

Cooking spray
12 ounces skinless, boneless chicken breasts, diced
1 small onion, chopped
8 ounces button mushrooms
1 bay leaf
2 large sprigs fresh thyme or 1/2 teaspoon dried thyme
3 large sprigs fresh tarragon or 1/2 teaspoon dried tarragon (optional)
Zest of 1 small lemon
1/2 cup dry sherry
1 1/4 cups boiling water
1 cup baby carrots
Salt and pepper
1 cup broccoli florets
1 tablespoon flour
3 tablespoons fresh parsley, chopped

1 Heat a large nonstick skillet, coated with cooking spray, over medium-high heat. Add the chicken and cook for 3 minutes, stirring constantly. Reduce the heat to medium. Stir in the onion, mushrooms, bay leaf, thyme, tarragon (if using), and lemon zest. Cook until the onion and mushrooms are beginning to soften, about 4 minutes.

2 Add the sherry, water, carrots, salt, and pepper and stir well. Bring to a boil, then reduce the heat to low and cover the pan. Simmer for 5 minutes.

3 Add the broccoli florets. Increase the heat to bring the liquid back to a steady simmer. Cover the pan and cook until the pieces of chicken are tender and the vegetables are cooked, about 5 minutes. Remove and discard the bay leaf, sprigs of thyme, and tarragon (if using fresh herbs).

4 Blend the flour and 2 tablespoons cold water to form a smooth paste. Stir the flour mixture into the skillet and simmer, stirring constantly, until thickened and smooth, about 2 minutes. Sprinkle with parsley and serve.

(Some More Ideas) Tiny pattypan squash look nice in this dish. Trim off and discard the stalk ends from 8 ounces squash and slice them horizontally in half. Add them to the pan with the broccoli. When cooked, the pattypan should be tender but still slightly crunchy.

Creamy chicken and mushroom casserole: Increase the quantity of button mushrooms to 12 ounces and omit the broccoli. Simmer for 5 minutes longer in Step 2. Stir in 4 tablespoons fat-free half-and-half after thickening with the flour, and heat for a few more seconds. Prepared stir-fry strips of turkey, lean pork, or chicken are ideal for this casserole. They reduce preparation time and cook quickly.

Plus Points

• Wild rice is actually not a type of rice at all. Instead, it is a long-grain marsh grass that is native to the northern Great Lakes area. It has a rich, nutty flavor and slightly chewy texture that works well when combined with long-grain brown rice. It is considered a whole grain and can contribute to your daily fiber needs.

Exchanges

vegetable 3	meat (very lean) 1

Each serving provides calories 170, calories from fat 23, fat 3g, saturated fat 1g, cholesterol 51mg, sodium 66mg, carbohydrate 12g, fiber 3g, sugars 6g, protein 22g. Excellent source of niacin, phosphorus, riboflavin, vitamin A, vitamin B6, vitamin C. Good source of folate, iron, potassium, thiamine.

chicken jamboree p42

monkfish and mussel kebabs p40

chicken and cashew pancakes p41

chicken yakitori p44

chicken yakitori

These delicious Japanese-style bites of chicken speared with green bell pepper and scallions can be assembled in advance and then grilled just before serving. For the best flavor, leave the chicken to marinate for several hours or overnight, and remember to soak the skewers first so they do not burn under the grill.

Preparation time **20 minutes, plus at least 1 hour marinating**   Cooking time **10–15 minutes**   *Makes 30 kebabs*

3 tablespoons light soy sauce

3 tablespoons sake or dry sherry

1 tablespoon toasted sesame oil

1 garlic clove, crushed

1 tablespoon finely chopped fresh ginger

2 teaspoons honey

1 pound skinless, boneless chicken breasts, cut into 1-inch cubes

1 large green bell pepper, seeded and cut into 30 small cubes

4 large scallions, cut across into 30 pieces

1 Place the soy sauce, sake, sesame oil, garlic, ginger, and honey in a shallow dish and stir together to mix. Add the chicken pieces and spoon the marinade over them. Cover and marinate in the refrigerator for at least 1 hour or overnight.

2 Just before cooking, put 30 short wooden skewers in warm water and leave to soak for 10 minutes. Preheat a grill or oven broiler to medium.

3 Thread about 2 pieces of chicken onto each skewer, alternating with a piece of pepper and one of scallion, threaded widthwise. Place the kebabs on the grill or broiler rack and cook until tender, turning from time to time and brushing with the marinade, about 10 to 15 minutes. Serve hot.

(**Some More Ideas**) Sprinkle the kebabs with a few sesame seeds toward the end of the grilling time.

An alternative marinade is 3 tablespoons hoisin sauce mixed with 2 tablespoons Chinese rice wine or dry sherry and 1 teaspoon sesame oil. If desired, add 1 teaspoon five-spice powder or 1 finely chopped, seeded, and deveined fresh red chile pepper (use gloves; they burn).

Instead of green bell pepper, use pieces of red or orange bell peppers, zucchini, or tiny mushroom caps.

Grilled salmon: Use 1 pound skinless salmon fillet and marinate in a mixture of 3 tablespoons soy sauce, 2 tablespoons dry sherry, 1 teaspoon sesame oil, 1 crushed garlic clove, 1 teaspoon honey, and the grated zest of 1 small orange for about 30 minutes. Thread onto soaked wooden skewers, alternating the cubes of salmon with whole firm cherry tomatoes and pieces of scallion. Grill for 10 to 15 minutes, turning and basting frequently with the marinade.

Plus Points

• Party nibbles made with puff pastry are high in fat and calories. These little kebabs, made with lean chicken and vegetables, offer a lower-fat choice and look really appealing.

• Honey, used since ancient times as a sweetener and preservative, has a higher fructose content than sugar, which makes it sweeter. Its higher water content also makes it lower in calories on an ounce for ounce basis. Just be sure to count honey as part of your carbohydrate intake for the day.

photo, page 43

Exchanges
meat (very lean) 1 fat 1/2

Each serving (one skewer) provides calories 56, calories from fat 15, fat 2g, saturated fat 0g, cholesterol 18mg, sodium 139mg, carbohydrate 3g, fiber 0g, sugars 2g, protein 7g. Excellent source of vitamin C. Good source of niacin.

chinese-style lemon chicken

A savory light lemon sauce seasoned with a hint of sesame tastes fabulous with tender chicken and a tantalizing array of crunchy vegetables. Serve over a bed of plain rice to add some satisfying carbohydrate.

Preparation time **25 minutes**   Cooking time **about 25 minutes**   *Serves 4*

Cooking spray

12 ounces skinless, boneless chicken breasts, thinly sliced

1 onion, thinly sliced

1 green bell pepper, seeded and cut into thin strips

1 garlic clove, chopped

1 tablespoons finely chopped ginger

2 carrots, thinly sliced

1 can (8 ounces) water chestnuts, drained and sliced

1 1/2 cups low-fat, reduced-sodium chicken broth

3 tablespoons dry sherry

2 tablespoons flour

1 teaspoon sugar

3 tablespoons light soy sauce

1 teaspoon toasted sesame oil

Zest of 2 lemons

Juice of 1 lemon

1 1/2 cups green beans, cut into 2-inch pieces

1 cup bean sprouts

1 Heat a large Dutch oven coated with cooking spray over medium-high heat. Add the chicken and cook until the meat is just turning white, about 1 minute. Add the onion, pepper, garlic, and ginger, and cook over medium heat, stirring often, until the onion is softened but not browned, about 5 to 6 minutes.

2 Add the carrots and water chestnuts. Pour in the broth and sherry, and heat until simmering. Cover and simmer for 10 minutes, stirring occasionally.

3 Meanwhile, mix the flour and sugar with the soy sauce in a small bowl to make a smooth paste. Add the sesame oil and lemon zest and juice, stirring well with a whisk. Add the flour mixture to the broth in the Dutch oven and bring to a boil, stirring constantly. Add the green beans, cover the pan, and simmer for 2 minutes. Add the bean sprouts and simmer for 2 minutes. Serve immediately, before the bean sprouts soften.

(Some More Ideas) Fresh shiitake mushrooms are also good in this dish—add 1 cup sliced shiitake mushrooms with the green beans so that they will be just lightly cooked.

Try adding 8 ounces baby corn instead of the water chestnuts and 1 1/2 cups shredded baby bok choy instead of the bean sprouts. For a slightly hotter dish, add 1 seeded and chopped fresh green chile pepper with the vegetables in Step 1.

This is a good recipe for firm, meaty fish, such as swordfish (used in place of the chicken). Cut the fish into chunks and add to the dish in Step 2 with the carrots and water chestnuts.

Plus Points

• Bean sprouts and other sprouted beans and seeds are rich in vitamins B and C.
• Canned water chestnuts are light and crunchy. Mixed with other vegetables, they can help to extend a modest amount of chicken or meat to make a satisfying meal. They also contribute small amounts of phosphorous and potassium.
• Meals like this, with a base of fresh vegetables and a moderate amount of protein and rice, are perfectly balanced and help maintain blood sugar at an even level.

photo, page 47

Exchanges	
starch 1	vegetable 3
meat (very lean) 2	fat 1/2

Each serving provides calories 247, calories from fat 34, fat 4g, saturated fat 1g, cholesterol 51mg, sodium 713mg, carbohydrate 30g, fiber 6g, sugars 13g, protein 24g. Excellent source of niacin, phosphorus, potassium, vitamin A, vitamin B6, vitamin C. Good source of folate, iron, magnesium, riboflavin, thiamine.

sausage, grilled pepper, and tomato bruschetta

This open sandwich of toasted ciabatta bread with a mixed bell-pepper topping is typical of the style of food enjoyed in Mediterranean countries, where bread, along with plenty of fruit and vegetables, is a mainstay of the diet. A little chorizo sausage adds a spicy note to the mix of bell peppers.

Preparation time **about 20 minutes**   Cooking time **about 30 minutes**   *Serves 10*

1 medium ciabatta loaf or medium French bread

1 red bell pepper, halved and seeded

1 yellow bell pepper, halved and seeded

2 ounces chorizo sausage, thinly sliced

1 cup quartered cherry tomatoes

2 tablespoons tomato relish or chutney

1/2 cup torn fresh basil leaves

1 tablespoon olive oil

1 garlic clove, crushed

Black pepper

1 Preheat the oven to 400°F. Wrap the ciabatta bread in foil and bake for 8 to 10 minutes. Remove from the oven and place on a wire rack to cool. Preheat the oven broiler to high.

2 When the broiler is hot, place the peppers skin side up on a baking tray and broil until the flesh softens and the skin begins to blister and char, about 8 to 10 minutes. Transfer the peppers to a plastic zipper bag, seal, and set aside until cool enough to handle.

3 While the peppers are cooling, sauté the chorizo sausage slices in a small skillet until the oil runs out and the sausage slices start to crisp, about 3 to 4 minutes. Drain on a paper towel.

4 Place the chorizo in a bowl and add the tomatoes, relish or chutney, and basil. Remove the cooled peppers from the bag and peel away their skins. Roughly chop the flesh and add to the bowl. Season lightly with pepper and mix well. Set aside while you prepare the toasts.

5 Cut the baked ciabatta across into 5 pieces, then cut each piece in half horizontally. Mix the olive oil with the garlic and brush this mixture onto the cut sides of the ciabatta pieces. Place them cut side up under the broiler and toast until golden and crisp, about 2 to 3 minutes.

6 Top the toasted ciabatta with the pepper and chorizo mixture and serve immediately.

(Some More Ideas) For a vegetarian topping, omit the chorizo and sprinkle the pepper and tomato mixture with 1/4 cup toasted pine nuts. Or, replace the chorizo with 2 ounces crumbled feta or goat cheese.

Plus Points

• Chorizo is a popular Spanish sausage made with pork and pimiento, a Spanish pepper. Though chorizo has a high fat content, this can be substantially reduced by using a small amount and by sautéing the sausage in a dry pan and draining it well.

Exchanges

starch 1 1/2 vegetable 1

Each serving provides calories 150, calories from fat 23, fat 3g, saturated fat 1g, cholesterol 3mg, sodium 387mg, carbohydrate 27g, fiber 2g, sugars 2g, protein 5g. Excellent source of thiamine, vitamin C. Good source of folate, niacin, riboflavin, vitamin A.

sausage, grilled pepper, and tomato bruschetta *p46*

chinese-style lemon chicken *p45*

bolognese beef pot *p48*

mushroom and thyme toasts *p49*

bolognese beef pot

Lemon and fennel bring wonderfully fresh flavors to familiar braised ground beef in this Italian-inspired dish, making it as good for al fresco summer dining as it is for a light winter supper. Adding diced potatoes to the deliciously tangy tomato sauce rounds out the meal. Serve with a tossed green salad drizzled with a light vinaigrette.

Preparation time **10 minutes**   Cooking time **25 minutes**   *Serves 4*

Beef Pot

12 ounces extra lean ground beef

1 onion, chopped

2 garlic cloves, crushed

1 pound potatoes, scrubbed and finely diced

2 cans (14 1/2 ounces) chopped tomatoes

3/4 cup low-fat, low-sodium chicken broth

Zest and juice of 1 lemon

1/2 teaspoon light brown sugar

Salt and pepper

1 fennel bulb, thinly sliced (reserve the leaves)

1 cup frozen green beans

Garnish

Chopped fennel leaves

Chopped fresh flat-leaf parsley

1 Place the ground beef, onion, and garlic in a large saucepan and cook over medium heat, stirring frequently, until the meat is evenly browned, about 5 minutes.

2 Stir in the potatoes, tomatoes with their juice, broth, half the lemon zest, the sugar, salt, and pepper. Bring to a boil, then reduce the heat to low and simmer the mixture for 10 minutes, stirring once or twice to ensure that the potatoes cook evenly.

3 Stir in the fennel, frozen beans, and lemon juice. Cover the pan again and simmer until the potatoes are tender and the fennel and beans are lightly cooked but still crisp, about 5 minutes.

4 Spoon the mixture into serving bowls. Garnish with the remaining lemon zest, the chopped fennel leaves, and flat-leaf parsley.

(**Some More Ideas**) Ground turkey, chicken, pork, or lamb can be substituted for the ground beef.

Carrots and canned beans can be substituted for the potatoes. Add 1 can (15 ounces) cannellini beans, drained and rinsed, and 1 cup finely diced carrots to the dish.

A green salad tossed with thinly sliced red onion, a handful of fresh basil, a few black olives, and a lemon–olive oil dressing tastes excellent with this dish, providing contrasting texture as well as flavor.

Plus Points

• Extra lean ground beef contains 9.6 grams fat per 3 1/2-ounce serving. Provided you use a heavy-based or good-quality nonstick pan, there is no need to add any fat when browning ground meat.

• Tomatoes are a rich source of vitamin C—fresh raw tomatoes contain 17 milligrams per 3 1/2 ounces and canned tomatoes about 12 milligrams.

• Scrubbing potatoes rather than peeling them retains vitamins and minerals found just beneath the skin. The skin also provides valuable fiber.

photo, page 47

Exchanges

starch 1 1/2 vegetable 4
meat (lean) 2

Each serving provides calories 334, calories from fat 76, fat 8g, saturated fat 3g, cholesterol 57mg, sodium 599mg, carbohydrate 43g, fiber 8g, sugars 14g, protein 25gExcellent source of: Iron, magnesium, niacin, phosphorus, potassium, thiamine, vitamin B6, vitamin B12, vitamin C, zinc. Good source ofcalcium, copper, folate, riboflavin, vitamin A.

mushroom and thyme toasts

Prepare these toasts for a satisfying snack or a quick lunch paired with fresh fruit. The smooth flavor of the mushrooms is enhanced by cooking them with garlic, herbs, and a dollop of tangy low-fat sour cream. The mushrooms taste wonderful piled on top of whole-grain toast spread with ricotta cheese.

Preparation time **10–15 minutes**   Cooking time **10 minutes**   *Serves 8*

1/2 cup part-skim ricotta cheese

2 celery stalks, finely chopped

3 tablespoons finely chopped parsley

Good pinch of cayenne pepper

1 pound button mushrooms

1 garlic clove, crushed

2 tablespoons chopped fresh thyme

2 tablespoons low-fat sour cream

1 teaspoon lemon juice

8 thick slices cut from a small loaf of whole-grain bread

1 Place the ricotta, celery, parsley, and cayenne pepper in a bowl and mix well. Refrigerate until needed. Preheat the oven broiler to high.

2 Leave any small mushrooms whole and halve larger ones. Place them in a large, heavy, nonstick skillet and add the garlic, thyme, sour cream, and 1 teaspoon water. Cover and cook gently until the mushrooms are just tender and have given up their juices, about 3 to 4 minutes. Add the lemon juice and season lightly with salt and pepper.

3 While the mushrooms are cooking, toast the bread slices on both sides under the broiler. While still warm, spread one side of each piece of toast with some of the ricotta mixture, then cut it in half.

4 Arrange the toasts on individual serving plates. Spoon the hot mushroom mixture over the toasts and serve immediately.

(Some More Ideas) *Deviled mushroom toasts*: Heat 1 tablespoon olive oil in a nonstick skillet, add 1 thinly sliced onion and cook over medium heat until softened. Stir in 1 crushed garlic clove, 1 pound halved mushrooms, and 1 seeded and diced red bell pepper. Cook, stirring frequently, for 2 minutes, then stir in 2 teaspoons Worcestershire sauce, 1 teaspoon Dijon mustard, and 1 teaspoon dark brown sugar. Lower the heat and cook gently for 5 minutes, stirring occasionally. Add 2 tablespoons chopped parsley and season lightly with salt and pepper. Toast the bread and spread with 1/2 cup low-fat soft goat cheese. Spoon the hot deviled mushroom mixture over the toasts and serve immediately.

Plus Points
• Though there are over 2,500 varieties of mushrooms grown throughout the world, not all are edible and some are poisonous. All edible mushrooms are a useful source of several B vitamins.
• Like other cheeses, ricotta is a good source of protein and calcium. Because of its high moisture content, it is lower in fat than many other varieties of soft cheese.

photo, page 47

Exchanges	
starch 1 1/2 fat 1/2	

Each serving provides calories 148, calories from fat 32, fat 4g, saturated fat 1g, cholesterol 6mg, sodium 261mg, carbohydrate 24g, fiber 4g, sugars 3g, protein 8g. Excellent source of riboflavin. Good source of folate, iron, magnesium, niacin, phosphorus, potassium, thiamine, vitamin C.

pea curry with indian paneer

Paneer is an Indian cheese, similar to ricotta but drier. It is often combined with peas in a curry. This delicious version uses homemade paneer, which is simple to make. The cheese is also high in protein, making it a useful meat substitute in vegetarian meals. Serve the curry with basmati rice and steamed fresh carrots for color.

Preparation time 15 minutes, plus about 45 minutes draining, 3 hours pressing   Cooking time **about 20 minutes**   *Serves 8*

Paneer

8 cups 2% milk
6 tablespoons lemon juice

Pea and Tomato Curry

2 teaspoons canola oil
1 large onion, chopped
2 garlic cloves, finely chopped
1 (2 inch) piece fresh ginger, finely chopped
1 fresh green chile, seeded and thinly sliced
1 tablespoon coriander seeds, crushed
1 tablespoon cumin seeds, crushed
1 teaspoon turmeric
1 tablespoon garam masala
1 pound firm tomatoes, quartered
1 1/2 cups frozen peas
3 cups spinach leaves
2 tablespoons fresh cilantro, chopped
Salt to taste

1 First, make the paneer. Pour the milk into a large saucepan and bring to a boil. Immediately reduce the heat to low and add the lemon juice. Stir until the milk separates into curds and whey, about 1 to 2 minutes. Remove the pan from the heat.

2 Line a large sieve or colander with cheesecloth, or a clean, tight-knit dishcloth, and set over a large bowl. Pour in the milk mixture. Leave to drain until cool, about 15 minutes. Bring together the corners of the cloth to make a bundle containing the drained curds. Squeeze them, then leave to drain until all the whey has dripped through the sieve into the bowl, about 30 minutes. Reserve 1 cup of the whey.

3 Keeping the curds wrapped in the cloth, place on a board. Set another board on top and press down to flatten the ball shape into an oblong block. Place cans or weights on top and leave in a cool place until firm, about 3 hours.

4 Carefully peel off the cloth and cut the cheese into 1-inch squares. Heat 1 teaspoon of the oil in a large nonstick skillet and cook the paneer until golden, about 1 to 2 minutes on each side. As the pieces are browned, remove from the pan with a slotted spoon and set aside.

5 For the curry, heat the remaining 1 teaspoon oil in the pan. Add the onion and cook gently until softened, about 5 minutes. Stir in the garlic and ginger, and cook gently for 1 minute, then stir in the chile, coriander and cumin seeds, turmeric, and garam masala. Cook for 1 minute, stirring constantly. Add the tomatoes, the reserved whey, and a pinch of salt, and stir well to mix. Cover and cook gently for 5 minutes.

6 Add the peas and bring back to a boil, then reduce the heat, cover, and simmer for 5 minutes. Add the spinach, stirring it in gently so as not to break up the tomatoes too much. Simmer until the spinach has just wilted and the peas are hot and tender, about 3 to 4 minutes. Stir in most of the chopped cilantro, then transfer the curry to a serving dish and scatter the paneer on top. Spoon the curry gently over the paneer to warm it, then sprinkle with the rest of the cilantro and serve.

(Some More Ideas) For a cottage cheese and vegetable curry, which is similar but much quicker to make, cook 1 1/4 pounds peeled potatoes, cut into large chunks, in a large pan of boiling water for 5 minutes. Add 1 1/2 cups cauliflower florets to the pan and

Exchanges

carbohydrate 1 1/2 meat (lean) 2

Each serving provides calories 200, calories from fat 54, fat 6g, saturated fat 4g, cholesterol 51mg, sodium 261mg, carbohydrate 20g, fiber 4g, sugars 10g, protein 21g. Excellent source of calcium, phosphorus, riboflavin, vitamin A, vitamin C. Good source of folate, iron, magnesium, potassium, thiamine, vitamin B6.

cook for 5 more minutes. Add 1 cup halved green beans and cook until all the vegetables are tender, about 3 to 4 minutes. While the vegetables are cooking, place 1 1/2 cups cottage cheese in a sieve and leave to drain off any excess liquid. Cook the onion and spices as in Step 5 of the main recipe, then add 10 ounces vegetable stock and cook gently for a further 5 minutes. Add the drained potatoes, cauliflower, and beans to the spiced sauce and stir to coat. Season lightly with salt. Fold in the cottage cheese and heat through gently. Serve hot, with whole-wheat naan or flat bread.

Plus Points

• When planning a diabetic meal, half of the plate should be filled with vegetables. The remaining half should be composed of half starch and half protein. Spinach is an incredibly nutritious vegetable that is packed with iron and vitamins A and C. It can be used raw in salads or cooked for a healthy side dish.

pears broiled with pecorino

From the countryside of Tuscany comes this traditional pairing of sweet, juicy pears with savory pecorino cheese. Depending upon the pecorino you choose, the flavor can be creamy and mild or hard and pungent. Some of the cheese is melted over the pears, and the rest is tossed with sweet grapes, arugula, and watercress. The salad is drizzled with a simple balsamic vinaigrette and served while the cheese is still warm.

Preparation time **20 minutes**   Broiling time **about 2 minutes**   *Serves 4*

Salad

4 ounces (about 6 cups) arugula, leaves removed from stems

1 bunch (2 cups) watercress, leaves removed from stems

1 cup halved seedless green grapes

3 ounces pecorino cheese

2 large, ripe pears, such as Comice or Bartlett

Vinaigrette

1/4 cup olive oil

3 tablespoons balsamic vinegar

1 teaspoon Dijon mustard

1/2 teaspoon sugar

1/4 teaspoon salt

1/4 teaspoon freshly ground black pepper

1 First, make the dressing. Place the oil, vinegar, mustard, sugar, salt, and pepper into a 2-cup jar or container with a tight-fitting lid. Cover and shake until well blended. Chill the dressing until you're ready to use it.

2 In a large salad bowl, toss the arugula, watercress, and green grapes. Using a vegetable peeler or cheese slicer, cut the pecorino cheese into very thin slices. Roughly chop half of the slices and toss into the salad bowl. Set aside the rest of the slices for melting on the pears.

3 Preheat the broiler to high and line a baking sheet with foil. Peel the pears, cut in half, and core.

4 Arrange the pear halves, cut sides down, on the baking sheet. Top the pears with the reserved cheese slices, overlapping them. Broil the pears, 6 inches from the heat source just until the cheese begins to bubble and turns golden, about 2 minutes. (Watch carefully, as it can burn easily!)

5 Meanwhile, shake the dressing, drizzle it over the salad, and toss until the leaves are coated. Mound the salad equally on 4 salad plates. Using a small spatula, carefully arrange one pear half on the top of each salad. Serve immediately while the melted cheese is warm and the greens are still crisp.

(Some More Ideas) *Nectarines grilled with Gorgonzola*: Substitute 3 ounces Gorgonzola cheese for the pecorino. Using a serrated knife, slice the cheese as thin as possible. Toss half into the salad. Place the nectarines on the baking sheet cut-side up and stuff the cavities with the remaining cheese. Broil the nectarines just until the cheese melts.

Raspberries with grilled Brie: Make the dressing with 3 tablespoons raspberry vinegar instead of balsamic. Make the salad, substituting 1/2 pint (1 cup) ripe raspberries for the grapes and 3 ounces Brie for the pecorino. Stuff the cavities of the pears with the Brie and broil cut-side up.

Exchanges

carbohydrate 1 1/2 meat (lean) 2

Each serving provides calories 313, calories from fat 181, fat 20g, saturated fat 5g, cholesterol 22mg, sodium 447mg, carbohydrate 28g, fiber 4g, sugars 21g, protein 9g. Excellent source of calcium, phosphorus, vitamin A, vitamin C. Good source of folate, potassium, riboflavin, vitamin E.

Plus Points

• This salad is a good source of calcium. The pecorino cheese contributes 78% of the total calcium content, and the watercress and arugula contribute 17%.

• Different types of grapes are grown for various purposes. Some are used for wine-making, some are dried to make raisins, and others are harvested as "table grapes" for eating. The type of grapes you purchase at the grocery store are delicious for snacking, but because of their sweet flavor they would not be ideal for making robust, full-bodied wines.

potato and zucchini tortilla

The tortilla, Spain's most famous tapa or snack, is made from the simplest of ingredients—eggs, onions, and potatoes—cooked like a flat omelet and served warm or cold, cut into wedges. All kinds of extra ingredients can be added, such as the zucchini and reduced-fat bacon used here, or asparagus, peas, and mushrooms.

Preparation time **15 minutes, plus cooling**   Cooking time **about 15 minutes**   *Serves 8*

1 1/2 pounds new potatoes, peeled and cut into 1/2-inch cubes

2 tablespoons olive oil

1 red onion, finely chopped

1 zucchini, diced

2 slices reduced-fat bacon, chopped

6 eggs

2 tablespoons chopped parsley

Pepper

1 Place the potato cubes in a saucepan and add water to cover. Bring to a boil, then lower the heat slightly and cook for 3 minutes. Drain thoroughly.

2 Heat the oil in a heavy (10 inch) non-stick skillet. Add the potatoes, onion, zucchini, and bacon, and cook over a moderate heat until the potatoes are tender and lightly golden, about 10 minutes, turning and stirring from time to time.

3 Preheat the broiler to high. In a bowl, beat the eggs with 1 tablespoon cold water. Add the parsley and pepper to taste. Pour the egg mixture over the vegetables in the skillet and cook until the egg has set on the base, about 3 to 4 minutes, lifting the edges to allow the uncooked egg mixture to run onto the pan.

4 When there is just a little uncooked egg on the top, place the pan under the hot broiler and cook for 2 minutes to set the top. Slide the tortilla out onto a plate or board and allow to cool for 2 to 3 minutes. Cut into small wedges and serve warm, or leave to cool completely before cutting and serving.

(**Some More Ideas**) Instead of zucchini, try chopped asparagus, or add chopped tomatoes or cooked peas just before pouring in the eggs. Fresh tarragon, chives, or basil can be used in place of parsley.

For a spicy tortilla, add 1/2 teaspoon crushed red pepper flakes to the beaten egg mixture.

Potato, mushroom, and Parmesan tortilla: Replace the onion, zucchini, and bacon with 1/2 cup thinly sliced mushrooms and 1 sliced leek. In Step 2, cook the potatoes with the leek for 6 minutes, then add the mushrooms, and cook until all the juices from the mushrooms have evaporated, about 4 minutes. Add 1 ounce freshly grated Parmesan cheese to the beaten eggs before pouring them into the pan.

Serve the tortilla as a light lunch for 6, with a fresh tomato salsa, leafy salad, and bread.

Plus Points

• Three cups of egg substitute can be used in place of the whole eggs in this recipe to decrease the fat and cholesterol content of the dish.

• Zucchini is a good source of vitamin B6 and niacin. The skins contain the greatest concentration of these vitamins.

Exchanges

starch 1 meat (medium fat) 1 fat 1/2

Each serving provides calories 161, calories from fat 71, fat 8g, saturated fat 2g, cholesterol 162mg, sodium 95mg, carbohydrate 16g, fiber 2g, sugars 3g, protein 7g. Good source of phosphorus, potassium, riboflavin, vitamin a, vitamin B6, vitamin B12, vitamin C.

spiced couscous-filled tomatoes

Choose ripe, well-flavored tomatoes for this dish. Hollowed out, they make the perfect container for a spicy eggplant, dried apricot, and nut couscous. The vitamin C-rich juices are squeezed out of the scooped-out tomato flesh and seeds, and whisked with a little harissa paste to make a tangy dressing. Serve with sesame breadsticks.

Preparation time **20 minutes**   Cooking time **15 minutes**   *Serves 8*

8 large beefsteak tomatoes
1 tablespoon olive oil, divided
1/2 cup sliced almonds
1 small eggplant, cut into 1/2-inch dice
1 teaspoon ground coriander
1/2 teaspoon ground cumin
Pinch ground cinnamon
1 cup boiling reduced-sodium vegetable broth
1/2 cup couscous
2 tablespoons chopped fresh mint
1/2 cup chopped dried apricots
1 teaspoon harissa paste (found in the international section of your market)
Salt and pepper

1 Cut the tops off the tomatoes and scoop out the insides using a teaspoon. Place the hollowed-out tomatoes and cut-off tops on one side. Put the seeds and scooped-out flesh in a sieve set over a small bowl and press with the back of a spoon to extract the juices; you will need about 4 tablespoons. Set aside the bowl of juice and discard the seeds and flesh.

2 Sprinkle a little salt over the insides of the hollowed-out tomatoes. Place them upside down on a plate covered with paper towel and leave to drain while making the filling.

3 Heat half the olive oil in a nonstick saucepan. Add the almonds and cook over a low heat until golden brown, about 2 to 3 minutes. Remove from the pan with a slotted spoon and set aside.

4 Add the remaining oil to the saucepan. Stir in the eggplant and cook, turning frequently, until browned and tender, about 5 minutes. Stir in the coriander, cumin, and cinnamon, and cook for a few more seconds, stirring constantly.

5 Pour in the broth and bring to a rapid boil, then add the couscous in a steady stream, stirring constantly. Remove from the heat, cover, and leave to stand for 5 minutes.

6 Uncover the pan, return to a low heat, and cook for 2 to 3 minutes, stirring with a fork to separate the couscous grains and fluff them up. Stir in the toasted almonds, mint, and dried apricots.

7 Add the harissa paste to the reserved tomato juices and stir to mix, then pour over the couscous. Season lightly with pepper and mix well. Spoon the couscous mixture into the tomatoes, replace the tops, and serve.

(Some More Ideas) Zucchini can be substituted for the eggplant.

Dried peaches and hazelnuts or pine nuts can be used in place of dried apricots and almonds.

Plus Points

• Harissa is a fiery hot condiment made from chile peppers, garlic, cumin, coriander, caraway, and olive oil. Just a tiny amount adds the perfect kick to the couscous.

• The tomatoes in this dish provide vitamin C, which improves the body's absorption of iron from the couscous and dried apricots.

• Couscous is low in fat. It has a moderate score on the Glycemic Index, which means that it is digested and absorbed relatively slowly, releasing glucose gradually into the bloodstream. This helps to keep blood sugar levels steady.

Exchanges
starch 1/2 fruit 1/2
vegetable 2 fat 1

Each serving provides calories 175, calories from fat 58, fat 6g, saturated fat 0g, cholesterol 0mg, sodium 208mg, carbohydrate 28g, fiber 5g, sugars 11g, protein 5g. Excellent source of potassium, vitamin A, vitamin C. Good source of folate, iron, magnesium, niacin, phosphorus, riboflavin, thiamine, vitamin B6.

polenta and mushroom grills

Cooked and cooled polenta can be cut into shapes and grilled to make an excellent base for a tempting topping. Here the polenta is flavored with Gruyère cheese, and the topping is a savory mixture of mushrooms, walnuts, and herbs. Serve as a sophisticated appetizer, with a few mixed salad leaves if you like.

Preparation and cooking time **45 minutes, plus 1 hour cooling**   *Serves 6 (makes 12 polenta grills)*

2 1/2 cups low-sodium vegetable broth

1 cup instant polenta

1/2 cup grated Gruyère cheese

1 ounce dried porcini mushrooms

2 tablespoons olive oil, divided

1/2 pound sliced cremini or button mushrooms

3 tablespoons dry sherry

2 tablespoons chopped fresh flat-leaf parsley, plus extra to garnish

2 teaspoons chopped fresh rosemary

1/3 cup finely chopped walnuts

Salt and pepper

1 Bring the broth to a boil in a large saucepan. Pour in the polenta in a steady stream, stirring with a wooden spoon to prevent lumps from forming. Cook over a low heat, stirring constantly, for about 5 minutes or until the mixture thickens and pulls away from the sides of the pan. Remove from the heat and stir in the Gruyère cheese. Season lightly with salt and pepper.

2 Pour the polenta onto a baking sheet coated with cooking spray and spread out into a rectangle measuring about 8 x 7 inches and about 1/2 inch thick. Allow to cool for 1 hour or until set.

3 Meanwhile, put the dried porcini mushrooms in a bowl and cover with boiling water. Leave to soak for 20 minutes. Drain, reserving 2 tablespoons of the soaking liquid. Finely chop the mushrooms.

4 Preheat the broiler to medium-high. Lightly brush the surface of the polenta with 1 tablespoon of the oil. Cut the polenta rectangle into 12 fingers, each measuring 2 x 2 1/2 inches, trimming the edges to straighten them. Separate the polenta fingers and place them on the same baking sheet. Broil for 4 minutes.

5 Turn the polenta slices over and broil for an additional 2 to 3 minutes or until lightly browned. Remove from the broiler and keep hot.

6 Heat the remaining 1 tablespoon of oil in a large nonstick skillet. Add the soaked dried mushrooms and the sliced cremini mushrooms, and sauté over medium-high heat until softened, about 3 to 4 minutes.

7 Add the sherry and the reserved mushroom soaking liquid. Cook over high heat for 1 to 2 minutes, stirring, until most of the liquid has evaporated. Add the parsley, rosemary, walnuts, and salt and pepper to taste.

8 Spoon the mushroom mixture on top of the warm polenta fingers. Garnish with a little chopped parsley and serve immediately.

(Some More Ideas) Add 2 to 3 tablespoons low-fat sour cream to the mushroom mixture with the herbs and walnuts, and heat.

Replace 1/2 cup of the broth with dry white wine for a slightly stronger flavor.

Add 1 teaspoon chili powder or cayenne pepper to the cooked polenta at the end of Step 1.

Polenta and tapenade squares: Cut the cooled and set polenta into squares (or other shapes) and broil as in the main recipe. For the tapenade topping, blend together 1/3 cup

Exchanges
starch 1 1/2 vegetable 1 fat 2

Each serving (two grills) provides calories 246, calories from fat 108, fat 12g, saturated fat 2g, cholesterol 10mg, sodium 440mg, carbohydrate 27g, fiber 3g, sugars 3g, protein 7g. Excellent source of niacin, riboflavin, thiamine. Good source of calcium, folate, iron, magnesium, phosphorus, potassium, vitamin B6.

pitted black olives, 2 tablespoons capers, 1 ounce sun-dried tomatoes packed in oil, well drained, 1 crushed garlic clove, 1 tablespoon olive oil, 2 tablespoons chopped fresh flat-leaf parsley, and salt and pepper to taste in a food processor. Alternatively, finely chop the olives, capers, and tomatoes, and mix with the garlic, oil, parsley, and seasoning.

Plus Points

• Polenta is a fine cornmeal. It provides a starchy carbohydrate alternative for those who need to avoid wheat or gluten in their diet.

• All mushrooms are a good source of copper, a mineral with many functions but particularly needed for the maintenance of healthy bones.

• Walnuts are a good source of many of the antioxidant nutrients, including selenium, zinc, copper, and vitamin E.

dinner

sirloin steaks with port sauce

In this robust dish, the juices left in the pan after cooking the steaks turn into an instant sauce with the help of a little port. A colorful stir-fry of tiny new potatoes, mushrooms, red pepper, and sugar snap peas is a perfect accompaniment.

Preparation and cooking time **30 minutes**   *Serves 4*

1 pound small new potatoes, scrubbed and any larger ones halved

1 teaspoon olive oil

1 cup large mushrooms, quartered

1 cup sugar snap peas

1 large red bell pepper, seeded and cut into thin strips

2/3 cup low-fat, reduced-sodium beef or vegetable stock, divided

1 tablespoon Worcestershire sauce

1 teaspoon Dijon mustard

1 teaspoon dark brown sugar

4 (5 ounce) thin sirloin steaks, trimmed of fat

1 teaspoon butter

1 shallot, finely chopped

2 garlic cloves, crushed

4 tablespoons port

Salt and pepper

1 Place the potatoes in a saucepan and cover with water. Bring to a boil, then reduce the heat, and simmer for 10 to 12 minutes.

2 Meanwhile, heat the oil in a nonstick wok or large skillet over medium-high heat. Add the mushrooms, peas, and pepper strips, and stir-fry for 1 minute. Mix 1/2 of the broth with the Worcestershire sauce, mustard, and sugar, and stir into the vegetables. Reduce the heat and simmer gently for 3 minutes or until the vegetables are just tender, stirring frequently.

3 Season the steaks on both sides with coarsely ground black pepper and set aside. Heat a ridged cast-iron grill pan. Meanwhile, drain the cooked potatoes and add to the vegetables. Stir gently, then cover, and leave over a very low heat until ready to serve.

4 Add the butter to the hot grill pan and turn up the heat to high. As soon as the butter sizzles and starts to foam, add the steaks. The cooking time depends on the thickness of the meat and whether you like your steaks rare, medium, or well done. Remove the steaks onto warmed dinner plates. Keep warm while making the sauce.

5 Add the shallot and garlic to the cooking juices in the pan and cook, stirring, over low heat for 1 minute. Pour in the port and increase the heat so the sauce is bubbling. Cook for about 1 minute, stirring. Pour in the remaining broth and boil 1 minute. Correct the seasoning. Spoon the sauce over the steaks and serve immediately with the vegetables.

(**Some More Ideas**) You can substitute a full-bodied red wine for the port.

For a quick and fresh vegetable stir-fry, omit the Worcestershire sauce, mustard, and sugar, and just toss the vegetables with 2 tablespoons chopped fresh chives just before serving.

Plus Points

• New potatoes are rich in vitamin C, which helps the absorption of iron from the beef in this dish. When dealing with potatoes, the preparation method makes a big difference in the amount of dietary fiber provided. Unpeeled potatoes offer one-third more fiber than peeled potatoes. Leaving potatoes unpeeled also preserves the nutrients found just under the skin.

photo, page 63

Exchanges

starch 1 1/2 vegetable 2
meat (lean) 3

Each serving provides calories 343, calories from fat 77, fat 9g, saturated fat 3g, cholesterol 83mg, sodium 235mg, carbohydrate 32g, fiber 4g, sugars 7g, protein 32g. Excellent source of iron, niacin, phosphorus, potassium, riboflavin, thiamine, vitamin A, vitamin B6, vitamin B12, vitamin C. Good source of copper, folate, magnesium.

beef-fillet salad with mustard vinaigrette

Lean roasted fillet of beef makes this a succulent salad for entertaining. Here it is combined with new potatoes and green vegetables and tossed in a mustard-flavored vinaigrette. Serve with slices of French bread.

Preparation time **35–40 minutes**   Chilling time **30 minutes**   *Serves 4*

Salad

1 pound beef fillet
1 teaspoon olive oil
3/4 pound new potatoes, scrubbed
1/4 pound haricots verts (French green beans) or regular green beans, halved
1/2 cup shelled fresh or frozen peas
1 large leek, finely chopped
2 tablespoons snipped fresh chives

Mustard Vinaigrette

1 1/2 tablespoons olive oil
1 tablespoon red wine vinegar
1 1/2 teaspoons Dijon mustard
Pinch sugar
Salt and pepper

1 Preheat the oven to 450°F. Rub the fillet with the olive oil and set on a rack in a roasting pan. Roast for 15 minutes for rare beef or up to 25 minutes for well done.

2 Meanwhile, whisk together the ingredients for the vinaigrette in a large mixing bowl.

3 Remove the beef from the oven and leave to stand for 5 minutes, then cut into thin slices against the grain. Add to the dressing and leave to cool.

4 Cook the potatoes in a saucepan of boiling water until tender, about 15 minutes. Drain well. When cool enough to handle, cut in half or into thick slices and add to the beef.

5 Drop the green beans into another pan of boiling water and cook for 1 minute. Add the peas and continue cooking until the vegetables are tender, about 3 minutes. Drain and refresh briefly under cold running water, then add to the beef and potatoes. Toss well. Cover and refrigerate for 30 minutes.

6 About 15 minutes before serving, remove the salad from the refrigerator, and stir in the leeks and chives.

(Some More Ideas) *Spicy pork-fillet salad*: Mix 1 tablespoon sugar, 1 teaspoon celery salt, 1 teaspoon garlic powder, 1/2 teaspoon ground ginger, 1/2 teaspoon ground allspice, 1/2 teaspoon paprika, and 1 teaspoon cider vinegar to make a thick, grainy paste. Spread this over a 1-pound pork tenderloin, then leave to marinate for up to 8 hours. Roast the pork in a preheated 400°F oven until cooked through, about 30 minutes. Remove from the oven and leave to cool. Meanwhile, place 1 cup basmati rice in a saucepan of boiling water and cook until tender, about 20 minutes. Drain well and set aside to cool. To assemble the salad, cut the pork into cubes and mix with the rice and 1/2 cup fresh pineapple chunks, 1 large diced mango, and 2 celery stalks, diced. Garnish with 2 tablespoons chopped parsley and 1/2 teaspoon paprika.

Plus Points

• Along with its other nutritional benefits, beef is a useful source of vitamin D, which is found in few foods. Vitamin D is essential for the absorption of calcium, and helps in forming and maintaining healthy bones.

• Peas supply good amounts of vitamins B1, B6, and niacin, along with dietary fiber, particularly the soluble variety. In addition, they provide useful amounts of folate and vitamin C.

• Many purchased salad dressings are high in sugar. When making a homemade vinaigrette like the one in this recipe, only a pinch of sugar is needed for flavor.

photo, page 63

Exchanges

starch 1 1/2 vegetable 1
meat (lean) 2 fat 1 1/2

Each serving provides calories 318, calories from fat 122, fat 14g, saturated fat 4g, cholesterol 60mg, sodium 117mg, carbohydrate 25g, fiber 4g, sugars 4g, protein 24g. Excellent source of iron, niacin, phosphorus, potassium, vitamin B6, vitamin B12, vitamin C. Good source of copper, folate, magnesium, riboflavin, thiamine.

beef waldorf

This is a fun twist on a traditional apple-and-raisin Waldorf salad. The raw fruits and vegetables in the salad are one of the richest sources of essential vitamins and minerals. We add in beef tenderloin to make this a tasty and diverse main-dish salad. A creamy mustard dressing makes it extra delicious.

Preparation time **25–30 minutes, plus 15 minutes cooling**   *Serves 4*

Salad

10 ounces beef tenderloin, trimmed of fat, cut into 2 fillets

1/4 teaspoon olive oil

1 cup radishes, thinly sliced

3 carrots, grated

1 small yellow pepper, seeded and cut into thin rings

3 celery stalks, sliced diagonally

3 scallions, sliced diagonally

2 tablespoons walnuts

1/2 cup raisins

2 small apples

2 teaspoons lemon juice

2 cups arugula leaves or other salad greens

Salt and pepper

Dressing

2 tablespoons coarse mustard

3 tablespoons low-fat mayonnaise

3 tablespoons plain low-fat yogurt

1 Brush the steaks with the oil and season with pepper. Heat a ridged grill pan or nonstick skillet over medium-high heat until hot. Add the steaks and cook for 3 minutes on each side for medium-rare or 4 minutes on each side for medium. These cooking times are for 3/4-inch steaks; adjust slightly for more or less than this thickness. Remove the steaks from the pan and leave to cool for at least 15 minutes.

2 Meanwhile, make the dressing. Combine the mustard, mayonnaise, and yogurt together in a small bowl and stir until well combined.

3 Put the radishes, carrots, yellow pepper, celery, scallions, walnuts, and raisins in a large bowl. Quarter and core the apples, then cut them into 1-inch chunks and toss in the lemon juice. Add to the bowl with half of the dressing and turn to coat everything well. Season lightly with salt and pepper.

4 To serve, pile the arugula or other salad greens on 4 plates and spoon the apple and vegetable salad alongside. Cut the steak into thin slices and arrange on top. Drizzle with the remaining dressing.

(**Some More Ideas**) Use the large white radish called daikon instead of red radishes. It is easy to grate by hand or in a food processor.

Roast beef and rice Waldorf: Mix 10 ounces cubed leftover roast beef and 1 cup cooked brown rice, cooled, into the apple and vegetable salad. This Waldorf salad is also very good when made with cooked chicken.

Plus Points

• Apples provide a good amount of soluble fiber in the form of pectin. Eating apples with their skin offers the maximum amount of fiber.

• All the sugars in this dish are in the intrinsic form, meaning they are natural sugars found in fruit (the raisins and apples) and vegetables (the radishes, carrots, yellow pepper, celery, scallions, and arugula). Fiber in the fruit and vegetables controls the rate at which these sugars are absorbed into the blood.

Exchanges

fruit 1 1/2 vegetable 3
meat (lean) 1/2

Each serving provides calories 288, calories from fat 79, fat 9g, saturated fat 2g, cholesterol 38mg, sodium 393mg, carbohydrate 39g, fiber 6g, sugars 28g, protein 17g. Excellent source of phosphorus, potassium, riboflavin, vitamin A, vitamin B6, vitamin B12, vitamin C. Good source of calcium, folate, iron, magnesium, niacin, thiamine.

beef waldorf *p62*

beef-fillet salad with mustard vinaigrette *p61*

aromatic beef
curry *p64*

sirloin steaks with port sauce *p60*

aromatic beef curry

This will satisfy even the most demanding curry addict. Lean and tender sirloin steak is quickly cooked with a vast array of spices, tomatoes, mushrooms, and spinach. Many authentic curry recipes contain a lot of oil. Here yogurt is added instead to give the sauce a rich and luxurious feel. Served with cardamom-spiced rice, it makes a really healthy and nutritious meal.

Preparation time **10 minutes**   Cooking time **20 minutes**   *Serves 4*

Beef Curry

2 teaspoons canola oil

1 large onion, thinly sliced

1/2 cup button mushrooms, sliced

1 pound sirloin steak, trimmed of fat, cut into thin strips

1 teaspoon fresh ginger, peeled and chopped

2 garlic cloves, crushed

1 teaspoon crushed red pepper flakes

2 teaspoons ground coriander

1 teaspoon ground cardamom

1 teaspoon turmeric

1 teaspoon grated nutmeg

1 can (14 ounces) chopped tomatoes

1 teaspoon flour

1 tablespoon water

1 cup plain low-fat yogurt

1 tablespoon honey

1 cup spinach leaves

Juice of 1 lime

2 tablespoons chopped cilantro

Cardamom Rice

1 cup brown or white basmati rice, well rinsed

2 1/2 cups water

1 cinnamon stick

8 whole cardamom pods, cracked

Juice of 1 lemon

Salt

1 Heat the oil in a large saucepan and add the onion and mushrooms. Cook over high heat until the onion slices begin to brown, about 2 minutes.

2 Add the beef together with the ginger, garlic, crushed red pepper flakes, ground coriander, cardamom, turmeric, and nutmeg. Cook for 2 minutes, stirring well, then add the tomatoes with their juice. Combine the flour with the water and add to the mixture. Bring to a boil, stirring. Stir in the yogurt and honey. Bring back to a boil, then reduce the heat, cover, and simmer gently for 20 minutes.

3 Meanwhile, prepare the cardamom rice. Rinse the rice in cold water. Bring the 2 1/2 cups water to a boil. Add the rice, cinnamon stick, and cardamom pods. Bring back to a boil, then cover tightly, and cook until the rice is tender, about 10 minutes. Remove the cinnamon stick, drain off any excess water, and return the rice to the saucepan. Stir in the lemon juice and keep covered until the curry is ready to serve.

4 Stir the spinach, lime juice, and chopped cilantro into the curry and allow the leaves to wilt down into the sauce. To serve, spoon the curry over the rice and garnish with additional cilantro sprigs.

(Some More Ideas) *Thai-style pork and potato curry*: Soften the onion and garlic in the oil with 1/2 pound new potatoes, washed and cut into small cubes, for 5 minutes. Stir in 3/4 pound pork tenderloin, thinly sliced, and 2 tablespoons Thai red curry paste. Cook until browned, about 2 minutes. Add the canned chopped tomatoes, 1/2 cup low-sodium vegetable broth, and 1/2 cup dried apricots, chopped. Bring to a boil, then cover and simmer until the pork is tender, about 20 minutes. Mix 1 teaspoon flour with 1 tablespoon cold water and stir into the curry with 1/2 cup plain low-fat yogurt, 1 teaspoon sugar, and the spinach. Cook until the leaves wilt down into the sauce, then serve on plain rice.

Plus Points

• Cardamom is believed to be helpful for digestive problems, such as indigestion, flatulence, and stomach cramps.

• By using dried, ground seasonings such as nutmeg, turmeric, coriander, and cardamom, food can be infused with flavor without adding salt.

• Along with its many other nutritional benefits, a small amount of beef in the diet provides vitamins from the B group and is a useful source of vitamin D, which is found in relatively few foods.

photo, page 63

Exchanges

**starch 3 1/2 vegetable 2
meat (lean) 2 fat 1/2**

Each serving provides calories 456, calories from fat 81, fat 9g, saturated fat 3g, cholesterol 69mg, sodium 303mg, carbohydrate 64g, fiber 4g, sugars 17g, protein 32g. Excellent source of iron, niacin, phosphorus, potassium, riboflavin, thiamine, vitamin B6, vitamin B12, vitamin C. Good source of calcium, folate, magnesium, vitamin A.

perfect pot roast

This long-simmered, one-pot meal is wonderfully satisfying. It can be prepared ahead, so it's perfect for family dinners as well as informal entertaining. The meat is roasted along with fresh carrots, potatoes, and celery, and the juices from the meat in combination with the wine and tomatoes create a delicious gravy to accompany the meal.

Preparation and cooking time **4 hours**   *Serves 8*

1 teaspoon olive oil

2 pounds boneless beef chuck, trimmed of fat and tied

2 large onions, finely chopped

1 celery stalk, finely chopped

3 garlic cloves, crushed

1 cup dry red or white wine

1 can (14 ounces) chopped tomatoes

1 large carrot, grated

1 teaspoon chopped fresh thyme

2 cups low-fat, reduced-sodium beef broth

1 pound new potatoes, scrubbed and quartered

1/2 medium celery root, or celeriac, peeled and cut into 1-inch cubes

4 medium carrots, sliced

Salt and pepper

Garnish

3 tablespoons chopped parsley

1 Preheat the oven to 325°F. Heat the oil in a large flameproof casserole. Add the beef and brown it over a medium-high heat until it is well browned on all sides, about 6 to 8 minutes. Remove the meat to a plate. Reduce the heat to medium. Add the onions, celery, and garlic and cook, stirring frequently, until the onions begin to soften, about 3 minutes. Add the wine and boil for about 1 minute, then add the tomatoes with their juice and the grated carrot. Cook for 2 minutes.

2 Return the beef to the casserole, together with any juices that have collected on the plate, and add the chopped thyme. Tuck a piece of foil around the top of the meat, turning back the corners so that it doesn't touch the liquid, then cover with a tight-fitting lid. Transfer the casserole to the oven and cook for 2 1/2 hours.

3 About 20 minutes before the end of the cooking time, bring the broth to a boil in a deep saucepan with a lid. Add the potatoes, celeriac, and sliced carrots. Cover and simmer gently until they are starting to become tender, about 12 to 15 minutes.

4 Meanwhile, remove the beef from the casserole and set aside. Remove any fat from the cooking liquid, either by spooning it off or by using a turkey baster, then puree the casseroled vegetables and liquid in a

blender or food processor until smooth. Season lightly with salt and pepper.

5 Drain the potatoes and other root vegetables, reserving the liquid. Make a layer of the vegetables in the casserole, put the beef on top and add the remaining root vegetables and their cooking liquid. Pour over the pureed sauce. Cover the casserole and return to the oven to cook until the root vegetables are tender, about 20 minutes.

6 Remove the beef to a cutting board, cover, and leave to rest for 10 minutes. Keep the vegetables and sauce in the oven, turned down to low. Carve the beef and arrange on warmed plates with the vegetables and sauce. Sprinkle with the parsley and serve immediately.

(Some More Ideas) Brisket or top round can be substituted for the chuck.

Any leftover beef can be chopped or shredded and mixed with the sauce and/or a freshly made tomato sauce, then served over spaghetti or other pasta.

Plus Points
• Once root vegetables are scrubbed and rinsed, the skins can usually be left on in order to add extra fiber to a meal.

photo, page 67

Exchanges		
starch 1/2	vegetable 3	
meat (lean) 3		

Each serving provides calories 267, calories from fat 54, fat 6g, saturated fat 2g, cholesterol 68mg, sodium 334mg, carbohydrate 26g, fiber 5g, sugars 10g, protein 28g. Excellent source of iron, niacin, phosphorus, potassium, riboflavin, thiamine, vitamin A, vitamin B6, vitamin B12, vitamin C, zinc. Good source of copper, folate, magnesium.

new england simmered beef

This traditional American dish is a one-pot meal of succulent beef and tender-crisp root vegetables in a nutritious and tasty broth. The tangy beet and onion relish cuts through the richness of the meat and is an inspired finishing touch. Serve with a piece of crusty bread to mop up the juices.

Preparation time **25 minutes**   Cooking time **about 2 1/2 hours**   *Serves 4*

Beef

1 pound lean chuck steak, trimmed of fat

3 sprigs fresh thyme

3 sprigs parsley

1 large bay leaf

2 large garlic cloves, sliced

10 black peppercorns, lightly crushed

1 large leek, washed and bottom part sliced

1 celery stalk, cut into 3-inch pieces

3/4 pound baby new potatoes, scrubbed

12 small shallots

1/4 teaspoon salt and pepper

1 cup peeled, cubed turnips

1 cup baby carrots

1/2 medium head Savoy cabbage, finely shredded

Finely chopped parsley to garnish

Relish

1 1/2 cups peeled diced cooked beets

6 scallions, finely chopped

3 tablespoons finely chopped parsley

1 Place the beef in a flameproof casserole. Add about 4 cups water to cover the meat very generously. Bring to a boil over a high heat, skimming the surface as necessary to remove all the gray foam.

2 As soon as the liquid comes to a boil, reduce the heat to very low. Tie the thyme, parsley, bay leaf, garlic, and peppercorns in a cheesecloth and add to the pan with the leek and celery. Partially cover the pan and simmer gently, skimming the surface when necessary, until the beef is very tender when pierced with the tip of a sharp knife, about 1 to 2 hours.

3 Meanwhile, make the beet relish. Place the beet in a bowl with the scallions and parsley. Season lightly with salt and pepper and gently stir together. Cover and chill.

4 Preheat the oven to 300°F. When the meat is tender, use 2 large spoons to transfer it to an ovenproof dish. Spoon over enough of the cooking liquid to cover the meat, then tightly cover the dish with foil. Place in the oven to keep warm.

5 Remove the cheesecloth bag from the casserole and discard. Add the potatoes and shallots to the casserole with the salt and pepper, increase the heat, and cook for 5 minutes. Add the turnips and carrots and simmer until tender, about 15 minutes. With a slotted spoon transfer them to the dish with the meat.

6 Add the cabbage to the broth in the casserole and simmer until it is tender, about 3 minutes. Remove with a slotted spoon and add to the other vegetables.

7 To serve, slice the beef against the grain and place the slices in soup plates. Top with a selection of vegetables and broth. Sprinkle with parsley and serve with the relish.

(Some More Ideas) For a different mix of vegetables, shell 1 pound fresh peas or use 8 ounces frozen peas; trim 8 ounces young asparagus tips; and cut 2 medium tender, thin leeks across into 2 inch slices. In Step 5, strain the broth, and discard the cheesecloth bag, leek, and celery. Add the asparagus to the casserole and simmer for 3 minutes, then add the peas and leeks and simmer until all the vegetables are tender, about another 3 minutes. Stir in 1 cup baby leaf spinach and cook until the spinach leaves wilt, about 2 minutes. Sprinkle with very finely sliced scallions and serve with boiled tiny new potatoes in their skins.

Plus Points
• Beets contain folate, an essential vitamin for healthy cells and the prevention of anemia, and is also believed to contain anti-carcinogens.

Exchanges
starch 2 vegetable 2
meat (lean) 3

Each serving provides calories 323, calories from fat 50, fat 6g, saturated fat 2g, cholesterol 68mg, sodium 343mg, carbohydrate 41g, fiber 8g, sugars 12g, protein 30g. Excellent source of folate, iron, magnesium, niacin, phosphorus, potassium, riboflavin, thiamine, vitamin A, vitamin B6, vitamin B12, vitamin C, zinc. Good source of calcium, copper.

new england simmered beef *p66*

perfect pot roast *p65*

one-pot steak and
pasta casserole *p69*

slow-braised beef and barley *p68*

slow-braised beef and barley

Juniper berries give this dish a distinctive flavor. The beef is slowly simmered until meltingly tender, while nourishing barley soaks up some of the juices and thickens the rich gravy to make a hearty casserole. Serve with a green vegetable such as French-cut green beans or steamed spinach.

Preparation time **20 minutes, plus 8 hours marinating**   Cooking time **2–2 1/2 hours**   *Serves 4*

1 pound beef chuck or lean braising steak, trimmed and cut into 2-inch cubes

2 garlic cloves, halved

3 bay leaves

6 juniper berries, lightly crushed

1 sprig fresh thyme

1 cup full-bodied red wine

12 pearl onions

1 tablespoon olive oil

1/2 cup pearl barley

1 1/2 cups low-fat, reduced-sodium beef broth

3 large carrots, cut into large chunks

2 celery stalks, sliced

Salt and pepper

1 Place the beef in a bowl with the garlic, bay leaves, juniper berries, and thyme. Pour over the wine, then cover, and leave to marinate in the refrigerator for 8 hours or overnight.

2 The next day, preheat the oven to 325°F. Place the pearl onions in a bowl and pour over enough boiling water to cover. Leave for 2 minutes, then drain. When cool enough to handle, peel off the skins. Set the onions aside.

3 Remove the beef from the marinade and pat dry on a paper towel. Heat the oil in a large flameproof casserole over medium heat. Add the beef and brown on all sides. Do this in batches, if necessary, so the pan is not overcrowded. Remove the beef from the casserole and set aside on a plate.

4 Add the onions to the casserole and cook gently until lightly colored all over, about 3 to 4 minutes. Add the barley and cook for 1 minute, stirring, then return the beef and any juices to the casserole. Pour in the broth and bring to a simmer.

5 Strain the marinade into the casserole, and add the bay leaves and sprig of thyme. Season lightly with salt and pepper. Cover with a tightfitting lid, transfer to the oven, and braise for 45 minutes.

6 Add the carrots and celery, stir to mix. Cover again, and braise until the beef, barley, and vegetables are tender, about 1 to 1 1/4 hours. Remove the bay leaves and thyme stalk before serving.

(**Some More Ideas**) The gravy will be quite thick. If you prefer it slightly thinner, stir in an extra 1/2 cup beef broth 20 minutes before the end of the cooking time.

Plus Points

• Juniper berries are native to America and Europe. They have a bitter taste and are often sold in a dried form. The berries are usually crushed, and used to flavor dishes containing meat.

• The barley grain contains gummy fibers called beta-glucans, which appear to have significant cholesterol-lowering properties.

• Research indicates that one glass of red wine a day can decrease the risk of elevated blood pressure and hypertension. This is due to the tannins in the wine that are found in the seeds and stems of grapes. Tannins are thought to inhibit the formation of plaque in the arteries.

photo, page 67

Exchanges

starch 1   vegetable 3
meat (lean) 3

Each serving provides calories 322, calories from fat 94, fat 10g, saturated fat 2g, cholesterol 68mg, sodium 285mg, carbohydrate 27g, fiber 5g, sugars 8g, protein 29g. Excellent source of iron, niacin, phosphorus, potassium, riboflavin, vitamin A, vitamin B6, vitamin B12. Good source of folate, magnesium, thiamine, vitamin C.

one-pot steak and pasta casserole

Thin pasta spirals called fusilli are delicious cooked in a casserole of beef and vegetables. The dried, uncooked pasta is added toward the end of the cooking time so that it retains its al dente texture while still absorbing the savory flavors of the meat, vegetables, and oregano in the rich stew.

Preparation time **20 minutes** Cooking time **about 1 1/2 hours** *Serves 4*

1 tablespoon olive oil

1 pound lean sirloin steak, cut into 1/2-inch cubes

1 onion, chopped

1 can (28 ounces) chopped tomatoes

2 tablespoons tomato puree

2 garlic cloves, crushed

3 cups reduced-sodium, low-fat beef or vegetable broth, divided

3 large carrots, sliced

4 celery stalks, sliced

1 small rutabaga, peeled and chopped

8 ounces fusilli pasta

1 tablespoon chopped fresh oregano or 1 teaspoon dried oregano

Salt and pepper

1 Heat the oil in a large Dutch oven over medium-high heat and add the beef. Brown the meat, stirring frequently. Use a slotted spoon to remove the meat from the pan and pour off any remaining grease.

2 Add the onion to the pan and cook, stirring often, until it is softened, about 5 minutes. Then add the tomatoes with their juice, the tomato puree, garlic and 2 cups of the broth. Stir well and bring to a boil.

3 Return the beef to the pan. Add the carrots, celery, and rutabaga and season lightly with salt and pepper. Cover and simmer gently until the meat is tender, about 1 hour.

4 Add the pasta and oregano with the remaining broth. Bring the mixture to a simmer, then reduce the heat and cover the pan. Cook until the pasta is tender, 20 to 25 minutes. Serve immediately.

(Some More Ideas) For a Mediterranean flavor, replace the carrots and rutabaga with 1 red bell pepper and 1 yellow or green bell pepper, seeded and chopped. Add the peppers with the onion. Also add 1 1/2 cups button mushrooms with the pasta.

Try venison steak instead of the beef, and use whole baby carrots and turnips instead of the sliced carrots and chopped rutabaga.

Plus Points

• The technique of simmering the sirloin steak in the tomato and broth mixture is called "moist cooking." Moist heat helps to tenderize even the leanest cuts of meat.

• Rutabagas are thought to be a cross between a cabbage and a turnip. They are cruciferous vegetables, meaning they are high in fiber, and they lend a delightfully sweet flavor when simmered in a stew.

photo, page 67

Exchanges

starch 3 1/2 vegetable 4
meat (lean) 2 fat 1/2

Each serving provides calories 511, calories from fat 90, fat 10g, saturated fat 2g, cholesterol 64mg, sodium 880mg, carbohydrate 71g, fiber 8g, sugars 20g, protein 35g. Excellent source of folate, iron, magnesium, niacin, phosphorus, potassium, riboflavin, thiamine, vitamin A, vitamin B6, vitamin B12, vitamin C. Good source of calcium.

chili con carne with corn bread

Slow-cooked beef and beans in a rich tomato sauce spiced with chiles and cumin makes an inviting meal on a wintry day, and warm, crumbly-moist corn bread studded with sweet corn kernels and mild green chile is the perfect accompaniment. Serve this high-protein dish with a crisp salad for a hearty, well-balanced meal.

Preparation time **25 minutes**   Cooking time **1–1 1/2 hours**   *Serves 8*

Chili con Carne

1 teaspoon olive oil

12 ounces lean stewing beef, trimmed of fat, and cut into small cubes

1 large onion, finely chopped

2 garlic cloves, crushed

1 teaspoon cumin seeds

1 teaspoon crushed dried red pepper flakes

1 tablespoon tomato puree

1 can (24 ounces) chopped tomatoes

2 cans (19 ounces) red kidney beans

1 1/2 cups low-fat, reduced-sodium beef broth

Salt and pepper

Corn Bread

Cooking spray

3/4 cup cornmeal

1/2 cup flour

2 teaspoons baking powder

1 teaspoon salt

1 large egg

1 cup fat-free milk

1/2 cup fresh or frozen corn kernels, thawed

1 small mild fresh green chile, seeded and finely chopped

1 Heat the oil in a large flameproof casserole, add the beef, and fry over a high heat, stirring occasionally, until well browned, about 3 to 4 minutes. Remove the meat with a slotted spoon.

2 Reduce the heat to low and add the onion to the pan. Stir well and cook gently for 10 minutes. Add the garlic, cumin seeds, and red pepper flakes and cook, stirring, for 1 minute, then return the meat to the pan. Add the tomato puree, the tomatoes with their juice, the beans, and broth. Stir well and bring to a boil. Reduce the heat so the chili is simmering gently, then cover with a lid, and cook for 1 to 1 1/2 hours or until the meat is tender, stirring occasionally.

3 Meanwhile, make the corn bread. Preheat the oven to 400°F and coat an 8-inch-square cake pan with cooking spray. Mix the cornmeal, flour, baking powder, and salt in a bowl. Combine the egg with the milk and stir in to make a thick batter (do not overmix or the bread will be tough). Fold in the corn and chile. Spoon into the prepared pan and bake until firm to the touch, about 20 to 25 minutes.

4 Turn the corn bread out of its pan and cut into squares. Serve the chili in warmed bowls, with the warm corn bread.

(Some More Ideas) Replace the beef with diced, boneless, lean lamb. Replace the crushed red pepper flakes with 1 seeded and finely chopped medium-hot fresh green chile, 1 teaspoon ground coriander, and 1 cinnamon stick. Instead of kidney beans, use 2 cans chickpeas, (19 ounces), drained and rinsed, adding them to the casserole after the chili has been cooking for 15 minutes. Add 2 medium zucchini, cut into 1-inch dice. Stir occasionally and add more stock if the mixture looks dry. At the end of the cooking time, stir in 3 tablespoons chopped fresh cilantro.

Plus Points

• Red kidney beans are low in fat and rich in carbohydrate. They provide good amounts of vitamins B1, niacin, and B6, and useful amounts of iron. They are also a good source of soluble fiber, which can help to reduce high cholesterol levels in the blood.

• Only a small portion of meat is needed in combination with the kidney beans, since both are high in protein. By adding more beans than meat, the saturated-fat content of the dish is decreased.

• Baked goods such as corn bread are often high in fat due to butter and shortening that are added to the recipe to make the products light and fluffy. Here one egg and skim milk are used to moisten the bread, which is quite sufficient.

photo, page 73

Exchanges

starch 2 1/2	vegetable 2
meat (very lean) 2	fat 1/2

Each serving provides calories 315, calories from fat 42, fat 5g, saturated fat 1g, cholesterol 53mg, sodium 1154mg, carbohydrate 47g, fiber 8g, sugars 10g, protein 22g. Excellent source of calcium, folate, iron, magnesium, niacin, phosphorus, potassium, riboflavin, thiamine, vitamin B6, vitamin B12, vitamin C. Good source of vitamin A. Flag: High in sodium.

goulash soup

This rich one-pot meal combines lean beef and vegetables and is crowned with tiny herbed dumplings. The soup is flavored with the three essential ingredients of an authentic goulash: paprika, onions, and caraway seeds. Serve the goulash on a bed of yolk-free egg noodles with a crisp green salad on the side.

Preparation time **30 minutes**   Cooking time **1 1/2 hours**   *Serves 6*

Soup

1 teaspoon canola oil
2 large onions, sliced
2 garlic cloves, finely chopped
1 pound lean chuck steak, trimmed of fat and cut into 3/4-inch cubes
2 large carrots, diced
1 tablespoon paprika
1/4 teaspoon caraway seeds
1 can (24 ounces) chopped tomatoes
4 cups low-fat, reduced-sodium beef broth
1 cup finely shredded green cabbage
Salt and pepper

Dumplings

1 teaspoon canola oil
1 onion, finely chopped
1 egg
3 tablespoons fat-free milk
3 tablespoons chopped parsley
1/2 cup fresh white bread crumbs

Garnish

Chopped parsley

Exchanges
vegetable 4 meat (lean) 2

1 Heat the oil in a large saucepan over medium-high heat, add the onions and garlic and cook over medium-low heat, stirring frequently, until beginning to brown, about 10 minutes.

2 Add the cubes of beef and cook, stirring, until browned all over, about 5 minutes. Add the carrots, paprika, caraway seeds, tomatoes with their juice, and beef broth. Season lightly with salt and pepper. Stir well and bring to the boil, then cover and simmer gently until the beef is just tender, about 1 hour.

3 Meanwhile, make the dumplings. Heat the oil in a nonstick skillet over medium heat. Add the onion and cook over a low heat, stirring frequently, until softened, about 10 minutes. In a bowl, beat the egg and milk together, then add the onion, parsley, and bread crumbs. Season lightly with salt and pepper and mix well.

4 Add the cabbage to the saucepan and stir to mix with the beef and other vegetables. With wet hands, shape the dumpling mixture into 12 walnut-size balls. Add to the pan, cover, and cook until the dumplings are cooked, about 15 minutes. Taste for seasoning and serve hot in warmed deep soup plates, sprinkled with chopped parsley.

(Some More Ideas) Replace the beef with 12 ounces cubed veal.

Use 1 seeded and thinly sliced red pepper instead of the cabbage.

For a spicy soup, add 1 seeded and finely chopped fresh red chile with the paprika.

Plus Points
• Because diabetes and hypertension often go hand in hand, it is recommended that diabetics restrict their sodium intake to less than 3,000mg per day. Regular canned beef broth may contain as much as 900mg of sodium, whereas the reduced-sodium variety only contains about 450mg.

photo, page 73

Each serving provides calories 227, calories from fat 58, fat 6g, saturated fat 2g, cholesterol 81mg, sodium 623mg, carbohydrate 21g, fiber 5g, sugars 14g, protein 22g. Excellent source of iron, niacin, phosphorus, potassium, riboflavin, thiamine, vitamin A, vitamin B6, vitamin B12, vitamin C, zinc. Good source of calcium, folate, magnesium.

spinach-stuffed meat loaf

Meat loaf is a versatile dish that is easy to manipulate into a very healthy entrée. In this recipe, vegetables and oats are added to increase the vitamin content and lower the fat content. The yogurt, milk, and egg help to keep the meat loaf wonderfully moist. Serve with roasted mixed vegetables such as potatoes, zucchini, and red onions.

Preparation time **45 minutes, plus 10 minutes standing**   Cooking time **50 minutes**   *Serves 8*

1 teaspoon olive oil
2 large onions, finely chopped
6 garlic cloves, crushed, or to taste
1 can (24 ounces) chopped tomatoes
2/3 cup low-fat, reduced-sodium chicken broth
1 teaspoon dried mixed herbs (use basil, oregano, and thyme)
1 pound fresh spinach leaves
2 tablespoons plain low-fat yogurt
1/2 teaspoon freshly grated nutmeg
1 pound lean (93%) ground beef
1 pound lean ground pork
1 celery stalk, finely chopped
1 large carrot, grated
1/2 cup rolled oats
2 teaspoons chopped fresh thyme
5 tablespoons 1% milk
1 egg, beaten
2 teaspoons Dijon mustard
Salt and pepper

1 Heat the oil in a saucepan over a moderate heat. Add the onions and garlic and cook until the onions are soft about 5 minutes.

2 Transfer half of the onion mixture to a large bowl and set aside. Stir the tomatoes with their juice, the broth, and mixed herbs into the onions remaining in the saucepan. Season lightly with salt and pepper. Bring to a boil, then cover, and leave to simmer very gently.

3 Preheat the oven to 350°F. Put the spinach in a large saucepan, cover with a tightfitting lid, and cook over high heat until the leaves are wilted, about 2 to 3 minutes.

4 Drain the spinach, squeeze it dry with your hands, then chop it roughly and put it into a bowl. Stir in the yogurt and season with half of the nutmeg, and salt and pepper to taste.

5 Put the beef and pork into the bowl with the reserved onion. Add the celery, carrot, oats, thyme, milk, egg, mustard, and remaining 1/4 teaspoon nutmeg. Season with salt and pepper. Mix the ingredients together with your hands.

6 Lay a large sheet of plastic wrap on the work surface and place the meat mixture in the center. With a spatula, spread the meat into a 9 x 7 inch rectangle. Spread the spinach mixture evenly over the meat, leaving a 1/2 inch border. Starting at a short end, roll up the meat and spinach. Pat the sides and place on a nonstick baking sheet, discarding the plastic wrap.

7 Place the meat loaf, uncovered, in the center of the oven and cook for 45 minutes, then remove and brush lightly with a little of the tomato sauce. Return to the oven and cook for 5 minutes to set the glaze and brown it slightly. To check if the meat loaf is cooked through, insert a skewer into the center and remove after a few seconds. It should feel very hot when lightly placed on the back of your hand. When the meat loaf is ready, remove it from the oven, cover loosely with foil, and leave to stand for 10 minutes.

(Some More Ideas) Ground beef can be used for a more traditional meat loaf, or use ground turkey, chicken, or veal. A combination of three different meats can also be used.

Leftover meat loaf is delicious sliced and served cold with salad or in sandwiches.

Plus Points

• Spinach provides good amounts of several antioxidants, including vitamins C and E. It also offers carotenoid compounds and substantial amounts of the B vitamins, including folate, niacin, and B6.
• Oats and vegetables can be added to any ground-meat dish as a filler and to lower the fat content. Try the same method for hamburgers, shepherd's pie, and meatballs.

Exchanges	
vegetable 3	meat (lean) 3

Each serving provides calories 250, calories from fat 63, fat 7g, saturated fat 2g, cholesterol 99mg, sodium 380mg, carbohydrate 17g, fiber 5g, sugars 9g, protein 30g. Excellent source of folate, iron, magnesium, niacin, phosphorus, potassium, riboflavin, thiamine, vitamin A, vitamin B6, vitamin B12, vitamin C, zinc. Good source of calcium.

spinach-stuffed meat loaf *p72*

goulash soup *p71*

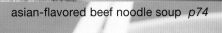
asian-flavored beef noodle soup *p74*

chili con carne with corn bread *p70*

asian-flavored beef noodle soup

Bursting with flavor, this main-course beef soup is packed with crunchy vegetables and long, thin Chinese noodles. The broth is infused with dried mushrooms and lemongrass and then finished off with creamy light coconut milk. Serve the soup with chopsticks for the noodles, beef, and vegetables, and a spoon for the delicious broth.

Preparation and cooking time **about 50 minutes**   *Serves 4*

1/2 ounces dried shiitake mushrooms

1/2 cup boiling water

3 3/4 cups low-fat, reduced-sodium beef broth

1 lemongrass stalk cut into 3 pieces, or grated zest of 1/2 lemon

1 garlic clove, crushed

1 fresh red chile, seeded and chopped

1 inch piece fresh ginger, grated

1 small bunch cilantro

1 large carrot, julienned

1 large leek, washed and bottom white part julienned

2 celery stalks, julienned

2/3 cup light coconut milk

8 ounces Chinese noodles

12 ounces lean rump steak, trimmed of fat and sliced into thin strips 1/2 inch wide

1/2 cup sugar snap peas, halved lengthwise

1/2 cup chopped bok choy

Finely grated zest and juice of 1 lime

4 teaspoons fish sauce, or to taste

1 Put the mushrooms into a small bowl, add the boiling water, and leave to soak for 20 minutes.

2 Meanwhile, pour the broth into a large saucepan and add the lemongrass or grated lemon zest, garlic, chile, and ginger. Separate the cilantro leaves from the stalks and set the leaves aside. Chop the stalks and add them to the broth. Cover the pan, and bring the broth just to a boil, then reduce the heat to very low. Let the broth simmer gently for 10 minutes while you prepare the vegetables and beef.

3 Drain the mushrooms, pouring the soaking liquid into the simmering broth. Cut each mushroom in half lengthways.

4 Remove the lemongrass (if using) from the broth. Bring the broth back to a boil, then add the carrot, leek, and celery. Cover and simmer for 3 minutes. Add in the coconut milk and increase the heat. Just as the liquid comes to a boil, add the noodles, crushing them in your hands as you drop them into the pan. Stir in the mushrooms and beef, bring back to a simmer, and cook, uncovered, for 1 minute. Stir well, then add the sugar snap peas and bok choy. Simmer until the beef, noodles, and vegetables are just

tender, about 3 minutes. Add the lime zest and juice and the fish sauce and stir well. Taste and add more fish sauce, if you like.

5 To serve, transfer the noodles, beef, and vegetables to bowls using a slotted spoon. Ladle the coconut broth over, sprinkle with the cilantro leaves, and serve immediately.

(Some More Ideas) Instead of dried mushrooms, use 1 cup sliced button mushrooms and add an extra 1/2 cup broth.

This soup is also delicious made with boneless, skinless white meat chicken strips.

Plus Points

• Celery provides potassium, a mineral that is important for the regulation of fluid balance in the body, thus helping to prevent high blood pressure.

• Coconut milk is a typical ingredient of Thai cooking. In this recipe, light coconut milk is used to decrease the amount of calories and fat while still achieving a creamy broth.

• Sugar snap peas are a good source of soluble fiber and vitamin C.

photo, page 73

Exchanges

starch 3 vegetable 2
meat (lean) 2 fat 1/2

Each serving provides calories 430, calories from fat 92, fat 10g, saturated fat 4g, cholesterol 56mg, sodium 984mg, carbohydrate 59g, fiber 4g, sugars 7g, protein 28g. Excellent source of iron, magnesium, niacin, phosphorus, potassium, riboflavin, vitamin A, vitamin B6, vitamin B12, vitamin C, zinc. Good source of copper, folate, thiamine.

beef salad with papaya

Sweet, juicy papaya, crisp leaves, and fragrant herbs are a sensational combination in this Thai-inspired salad. This is a great way to enjoy beef, while keeping the saturated-fat content of the dish low. Aromatic rice—like jasmine rice from Thailand, simmered in broth and scented with mint leaves—is the perfect complement.

Preparation time **35 minutes**   *Serves 4*

Steak

10 ounces lean sirloin steak, trimmed of fat, cut into 2 fillets

1 cup jasmine rice, rinsed

2 cups low-fat, reduced-sodium chicken broth

2 teaspoons canola oil

2 firm, ripe papayas, peeled, seeded, and sliced

1 small cucumber, halved lengthways, seeded and sliced across

20 fresh mint leaves, chopped

3 tablespoons fresh cilantro, chopped

1 red onion, thinly sliced

1 head butter (Boston or Bibb) lettuce

Dressing

2 tablespoons canola oil

1 tablespoon honey

Grated zest and juice of 1 lime

2 tablespoons Thai fish sauce

2 tablespoons light soy sauce

1 fresh red chile, or to taste, seeded, and finely chopped

2 garlic cloves, crushed

Garnish

4 tablespoons roasted peanuts, roughly chopped

Sprigs of fresh mint

1 First make the dressing. Mix all the ingredients together in a small bowl. Spoon 3 tablespoons over the steaks and set aside to marinate while you cook the rice. Reserve the remaining dressing.

2 Put the rice in a saucepan with the broth. Bring to a boil, then cover, and leave to simmer until tender, about 15 to 18 minutes.

3 While the rice is cooking, pat the steaks dry. Heat a ridged grill pan or nonstick skillet over a high heat until hot. Brush with the oil, then add the steaks and cook for 2 minutes on each side. The meat will be rare. Cook longer if you prefer it medium or well done. Remove the steaks to a chopping board and leave to rest for a few minutes.

4 Place the papayas, cucumber, mint, cilantro, and red onion in a bowl. Add all but 2 tablespoons of the remaining dressing and toss gently to mix.

5 Drain the rice well and divide among individual plates. Arrange the lettuce leaves on the plates and top with the papaya salad. Slice the beef into strips, arrange on top of the salad, and spoon the remaining dressing over it. Garnish with the peanuts and mint sprigs. Serve at room temperature.

(Some More Ideas) You can add the grated zest of 1 lime into the dressing for extra flavor.

For a Thai red curry and orange dressing, mix together 2 tablespoons canola oil, 2 tablespoons light soy sauce, 1 tablespoon light brown sugar, 1 teaspoon Thai red curry paste, 1 teaspoon grated orange zest, and tablespoons orange juice.

Plus Points

• Beef is an excellent source of zinc and a useful source of iron. The body far more easily absorbs iron from red meat than iron from vegetable sources.

• With diabetes, it is important to keep saturated fat intake to a minimum. Canola oil is an excellent choice as a fat because it contains more cholesterol-balancing monounsaturated fat than any other oil besides olive oil. It also contains polyunsaturated fat, which helps to lower cholesterol and triglycerides.

photo, page 79

Exchanges
starch 2 1/2 fruit 1 1/2
vegetable 2 meat (lean) 2 fat 2

Each serving provides calories 515, calories from fat 157, fat 17g, saturated fat 3g, cholesterol 41mg, sodium 1366mg, carbohydrate 67g, fiber 6g, sugars 20g, protein 24g. Excellent source of folate, iron, magnesium, niacin, phosphorus, potassium, riboflavin, vitamin B6, vitamin B12, vitamin C. Good source of calcium, thiamine, vitamin A. Flag: High in sodium.

veal with herbs

In this light, summery dish, the veal is pounded out until it is ultra-thin and tender. The veal is cooked in less than 5 minutes and then removed from the pan. Wine is added to the hot pan to make a sauce, and fresh herbs are added to pep up the flavor. New potatoes and wilted spinach are excellent accompaniments.

Preparation and cooking time **about 45 minutes**   *Serves 4*

Veal

1 pound baby new potatoes, scrubbed

4 (4 ounce) veal scallopini, pounded to 1/4-inch thickness

2 tablespoons flour

1 tablespoon olive oil

2 teaspoons unsalted butter

6 cups baby leaf spinach

Grated zest and juice of 1 lemon

1/3 cup dry white wine

4 tablespoons chopped mixed fresh herbs, such as parsley, chervil, chives, and tarragon

Salt and pepper

Garnish

Lemon wedges

1 First cook the potatoes. Place them in a large saucepan of boiling water and boil until tender, about 15 minutes.

2 Meanwhile, pat the veal dry with paper towels. Season the flour with a little salt and pepper. Dredge the veal in the flour to coat it lightly and evenly all over. Shake off any excess flour.

3 Heat half of the oil in a large nonstick skillet over a medium heat. Add half of the butter and heat until it starts to foam, then add the veal. Sauté until the juices run clear and not pink when the meat is pierced with a skewer or fork, about 2 to 3 minutes on each side. (You may need to cook the meat in 2 batches.) Remove the veal from the pan with a slotted spoon, place on a warmed serving dish, and keep hot.

4 Drain the potatoes in a colander. Add the remaining oil to the hot saucepan in which you cooked the potatoes and set over a low heat. Add the potatoes and toss gently until they are coated with oil. Add the spinach to the pan in 4 batches, gently tossing and stirring so that it wilts in the heat from the potatoes. Add the lemon juice, and season lightly with salt and pepper. Stir gently to mix. Cover and keep warm while you make the sauce.

5 Return the skillet to the heat and add the wine. Increase the heat so the wine boils, then stir vigorously to dislodge any browned

bits. Boil until reduced and syrupy, about 1 minute, then season lightly. Remove the pan from the heat and add the rest of the butter. Stir until it has melted.

6 Scatter the mixed herbs over the veal, then drizzle with the wine sauce. Sprinkle the lemon zest over the potatoes and spinach. Serve the vegetables alongside the veal, with lemon wedges for squeezing.

(Some More Ideas)   Lean pork or turkey fillets, pounded thin, can be cooked the same way. Remove them from the pan and keep hot. Add 2 seeded, thinly sliced green peppers and 1 cup sliced button mushrooms to the juices in the pan. Stir and toss over high heat for 2 minutes, then add 1 crushed garlic clove and the white wine. Cook until the liquid is reduced and syrupy. Season with salt and pepper to taste. Pour the wine sauce over the pork or turkey (omit the mixed herbs) and serve with boiled new potatoes.

Plus Points

• This dish is especially rich in B vitamins: B6 in the veal and the new potatoes, B3 and B12 in the veal. The veal, spinach, and new potatoes together provide an excellent source of folate.

• Unpeeled new potatoes and lemon juice are both good sources of vitamin C.

photo, page 79

Exchanges

starch 2 meat (lean) 3

Each serving provides calories 311, calories from fat 80, fat 9g, saturated fat 3g, cholesterol 82mg, sodium 102mg, carbohydrate 28g, fiber 4g, sugars 2g, protein 28g. Excellent source of folate, magnesium, niacin, phosphorus, potassium, riboflavin, vitamin A, vitamin B6, vitamin C. Good source of copper, iron, thiamine, vitamin B12.

greek lamb kebabs

Cubes of lamb flavored with a mixture of garlic, lemon, and fresh oregano are cooked on skewers and served with a Greek-style tomato and cabbage salad. By tossing the lamb in a mixture of lemon juice and a little olive oil before grilling, you keep fat to a minimum. Pita bread serves as a traditional accompaniment for a deliciously aromatic main dish.

Preparation and cooking time **30 minutes**   *Serves 4*

Kebabs

1 tablespoon olive oil

2 large garlic cloves, crushed

Juice of 1 lemon

1 tablespoon chopped a fresh oregano

1 pound boneless leg of lamb, trimmed of all fat and cut into 1-inch cubes

Salt and pepper

Salad

3 tomatoes, thickly sliced

1 small red onion, finely chopped

1/2 cup shredded green cabbage

4 tablespoons chopped fresh mint

1 cucumber, halved and thinly sliced

Juice of 1 lemon

2 teaspoons olive oil

4 white or whole-wheat pita breads, cut into triangles

1 Soak 4 wooden skewers in cold water for about 30 minutes. Drain. Preheat a grill or heat a ridged cast-iron grill pan. Put the olive oil, garlic, lemon juice, and chopped oregano in a bowl and stir to mix together. Add the cubes of lamb and turn until very well coated. Thread the cubes onto the skewers.

2 Cook the lamb on the grill or on a grill pan until tender, about 7 to 8 minutes, turning frequently. Toward the end of cooking, warm the pita bread on the grill or on the grill pan.

3 Meanwhile, make the salad. Combine all the ingredients in a salad bowl and season with salt and pepper to taste. Toss together gently.

4 Serve the kebabs with the salad, pita bread, and yogurt.

(Some More Ideas) *Beef kebabs*: Use a 1-pound sirloin steak, cut into 1-inch cubes. Mix together 1 teaspoon chili powder, 1 teaspoon ground cumin, 1 tablespoon olive oil, 2 large garlic cloves, crushed, the juice of 1 lime, and seasoning to taste. Coat the steak

cubes on all sides with the spice mixture, then thread onto 4 skewers. Meanwhile, make the salad: Mix 1 can (14 ounces) red kidney beans, drained and rinsed; 1 large diced avocado; the juice of 1 lime; 1 tablespoon olive oil; 1 red onion, very finely chopped; 1 fresh green chile, seeded and finely chopped; 1/2 cup cherry tomatoes, halved; and 2 tablespoons chopped fresh cilantro. Season to taste. Remove the steak from the skewers and divide among 8 warmed flour tortillas. Add 1 tablespoon bottled nonfat Caesar salad dressing and some of the salad to each tortilla, and roll up into wraps. Serve with the rest of the salad.

Plus Points

• Lamb is a rich source of B vitamins, needed for a healthy nervous system. It is also a good source of zinc and iron.

• Cabbage belongs to a family of vegetables that contain a number of different phytochemicals that may help to protect against breast cancer. It is also a good source of vitamin C and among the richest vegetable sources of folate.

photo, page 79

Exchanges

starch 2 1/2 vegetable 2 meat (lean) 2 fat 1

Each serving provides calories 408, calories from fat 118, fat 13g, saturated fat 3g, cholesterol 62mg, sodium 389mg, carbohydrate 46g, fiber 4g, sugars 9g, protein 27g. Excellent source of folate, iron, niacin, phosphorus, potassium, riboflavin, thiamine, vitamin B12, vitamin C. Good source of magnesium, vitamin A, vitamin B6.

lamb burgers with fruit relish

Lean ground lamb is combined with fresh vegetables and herbs to create a low-fat burger served on whole-wheat English muffins. An orange and raspberry relish adds a lovely fresh flavor and serves as a unique twist on traditional ketchup as a condiment. Serve with a green or mixed salad.

Preparation and cooking time **30 minutes**   *Serves 4*

Burgers

1 pound lean ground lamb

1 medium carrot, peeled and grated

1 small onion, finely chopped

1/2 cup fresh whole-wheat bread crumbs

Pinch freshly grated nutmeg

2 teaspoons fresh thyme leaves or 1 teaspoon dried thyme

1 large egg, beaten

2 teaspoons olive oil

4 whole-wheat English muffins

Salt and pepper

Shredded lettuce to garnish

Relish

1 orange

1/2 cup fresh or thawed frozen raspberries

2 teaspoons sugar

1 Preheat a grill or oven broiler. Put the lamb into a large bowl. Add the carrot, onion, bread crumbs, nutmeg, and thyme, and season with salt and pepper to taste. Mix well. Add the egg and use your hands to mix the ingredients together thoroughly.

2 Divide the mixture into 4 patties. Brush both sides of the burgers with oil, then put them in the grill pan. Cook for 4 to 5 minutes on each side, depending on thickness.

3 Meanwhile, make the relish. Cut the peel and pith from the orange with a sharp knife, and holding it over a bowl to catch the juice, cut between the membrane to release the segments. Roughly chop the segments and add them to the juice. Add the raspberries and sugar, lightly crushing the fruit with a fork to mix it together.

4 Split the English muffins and toast lightly. Put a lamb burger on each muffin and add some lettuce to garnish and a good spoonful of relish. Serve with the remaining relish.

(Some More Ideas) *Turkey burgers with an orange and summer fruit relish*: Use ground turkey instead of lamb, and flavor with the zest of 1 lemon and 4 tablespoons chopped parsley in place of the nutmeg and thyme; omit the bread crumbs. Serve on whole-wheat English muffins, with arugula and a relish made by simmering 1/2 cup frozen berries or peaches until thawed, about 3 minutes, and mixing with 2 teaspoons sugar and the chopped orange.

Plus Points

• Although lamb still tends to contain more fat than other meats, changes in breeding, feeding, and butchery techniques mean that lean cuts contain only about one-third of the fat that they would have 20 years ago. More of the fat is monounsaturated, which is good news for healthy hearts.

• Using whole-wheat English muffins instead of white hamburger buns increases the fiber content. The bread also provides B-complex vitamins, iron, and calcium.

• A fruit relish gives a huge bonus of protective antioxidants. It also provides useful amounts of potassium and fiber, especially from the raspberries.

Exchanges
starch 2 fruit 1/2 vegetable 1 meat (lean) 3

Each serving provides calories 370, calories from fat 110, fat 12g, saturated fat 4g, cholesterol 121mg, sodium 328mg, carbohydrate 40g, fiber 6g, sugars 13g, protein 26g. Excellent source of calcium, iron, niacin, phosphorus, riboflavin, thiamine, vitamin A, vitamin B6, vitamin B12, vitamin C, zinc. Good source of folate, magnesium, potassium.

lamb burgers with fruit relish *p78*

greek lamb kebabs *p77*

beef salad with papaya *p75*

veal with herbs *p76*

bulgur wheat salad with lamb

For this tasty dish, lamb tenderloin is quickly cooked under the grill, then cut up and mixed into a salad of bulgur wheat, red bell pepper, green olives, and fresh mint. No oil is used in the dressing for the salad, just fresh lemon and orange juices, so the fat content is kept healthfully low.

Preparation time **about 20 minutes**   Cooking time **20 minutes**   *Serves 4*

1 cup bulgur wheat

1 pound lean, boneless lamb loin, cut in half lengthways

4 shallots, finely chopped

1 large red bell pepper, seeded and chopped

1/4 cup pitted green olives

1 cucumber, chopped

4 tablespoons chopped fresh mint

Juice of 1 lemon

Grated zest and juice of 1 orange

2 heads butter (Bibb or Boston) lettuce, sliced across into shreds

Salt and pepper

1 Preheat the grill. Place the bulgur wheat in a mixing bowl, pour over enough boiling water to cover and stir well. Leave to soak for 15 to 20 minutes.

2 Meanwhile, place the lamb on the grill rack and grill for 6 to 7 minutes on each side or until browned on the outside but still slightly pink inside. Remove from the heat and leave to rest in a warm place for 5 to 10 minutes, then slice into chunky pieces.

3 Place the shallots, red bell pepper, olives, cucumber, and chopped mint in a salad bowl.

4 Drain the bulgur wheat in a sieve, pressing out excess water. Add to the salad bowl together with the lemon and orange juices, the orange zest, and salt and pepper to taste. Toss to mix everything well.

5 Add the lamb and lettuce, and toss again. Serve immediately.

(Some More Ideas) *Spicy pork and bulgur wheat salad with pineapple*: Preheat the oven to 425°F. Mix together the grated zest of half an orange, the juice of 1 orange, 1 tablespoon light soy sauce, 1 tablespoon canola oil, 2 teaspoons sugar, 1 large crushed garlic clove, and 1/2 teaspoon each ground cinnamon, ground allspice, and

pepper in a shallow ovenproof dish. Add 14 ounces pork tenderloin and turn to coat with the mixture. Roast until tender but still moist, about 25 minutes. Meanwhile, soak the bulgur wheat as in the main recipe, then mix with 1 small ripe pineapple, peeled, cored, and chopped; 1 large red bell pepper, seeded and chopped; 4 shallots, thinly sliced; the juice of 1 orange; 2 cups watercress sprigs; and 1 tablespoon chopped fresh cilantro. Season lightly with salt and pepper. Spoon onto 4 plates. Slice the pork and arrange on top of the salad. Drizzle with the cooking juices and serve immediately while still warm.

Plus Points

• Entrée salads that contain leafy greens, a carbohydrate source, and a small portion of meat make great well-balanced, low-fat meals.

• Lamb is an excellent source of zinc, which is necessary for healing wounds. Lamb also provides useful amounts of iron.

• The olive, which is native to the eastern Mediterranean region, has been cultivated since at least 3,000 B.C.—it was taken to the New World in the 15th century by the Spanish. Olives contain about 18% fat by weight, and most of this is healthy monounsaturated fat.

photo, page 83

Exchanges

starch 2 vegetable 2
meat (lean) 3

Each serving provides calories 385, calories from fat 95, fat 11g, saturated fat 3g, cholesterol 81mg, sodium 283mg, carbohydrate 43g, fiber 11g, sugars 7g, protein 33g. Excellent source of folate, iron, magnesium, niacin, phosphorus, potassium, riboflavin, thiamine, vitamin A, vitamin B6, vitamin B12, vitamin C. Good source of calcium.

spring lamb and vegetable stew

Based on a classic French dish called navarin, this delectable stew is simple and quick to prepare. In France it is made in the spring, as a celebration of the new season's lamb and the delicate young vegetables. Serve with a dish of freshly steamed green vegetables and a piece of hearty, seeded, whole-wheat bread.

Preparation time **30 minutes**   Cooking time **1–2 hours**   *Serves 6*

2 teaspoons olive oil

1 large onion, chopped

1 garlic clove, finely chopped

1 pound lean boneless leg of lamb, trimmed of fat and cut into cubes

1/2 cup dry white wine

2 cups low-fat, reduced-sodium chicken broth

1 bay leaf

1 sprig fresh thyme

2 pounds baby new potatoes, scrubbed

8 ounces baby carrots

1 cup peeled pearl onions

1 small turnip, diced

1 cup shelled fresh peas or frozen peas

2 tablespoons chopped parsley

Salt and pepper

1 Preheat the oven to 350°F. Heat the oil in a large flameproof casserole, add the chopped onion and garlic and cook, stirring, until softened, about 5 minutes. Add the cubes of lamb and cook until browned on all sides, about 5 minutes.

2 Add the wine, broth, bay leaf, thyme, potatoes, carrots, and pearl onions. Season lightly with salt and pepper. Bring to a boil, then cover with a tightfitting lid, and transfer to the oven. Cook for 1 hour.

3 Add the turnip and stir. Cover again and continue cooking until the meat and vegetables are tender, about 30 to 45 minutes, adding the peas 10 minutes before the end of the cooking time.

4 Add the parsley and stir well. Taste and add more salt and pepper if needed. Serve hot.

(Some More Ideas) For a lamb stew with a French flavor, use red wine instead of white. Omit the stock and add 1 can chopped tomatoes, (24 ounces) with the juice, and a large sprig of fresh rosemary. When you add the peas, stir in 1/2 cup pitted black olives.

French green beans can be used instead of the peas.

Plus Points

• Peas provide good amounts of the B vitamins B1, niacin, and B6. They also provide some folate and vitamin C. Frozen vegetables are just as nutritious as fresh vegetables, and in many cases they have been shown to contain higher levels of vitamin C.

• In addition to providing fiber, turnips contain the B vitamins niacin and B6, and are a useful source of vitamin C.

• Soups that are full of vegetables and simmered in a light broth provide a filling meal that is low in fat and rich in vitamins.

photo, page 83

Exchanges

starch 2 vegetable 2
meat (lean) 2

Each serving provides calories 310, calories from fat 53, fat 6g, saturated fat 2g, cholesterol 49mg, sodium 266mg, carbohydrate 43g, fiber 7g, sugars 10g, protein 21g. Excellent source of niacin, phosphorus, potassium, thiamine, vitamin A, vitamin B6, vitamin B12, vitamin C, zinc. Good source of copper, folate, iron, magnesium, riboflavin.

spanish rabbit and chickpea stew

In Spain, the home of this spicy dish, chickpeas are very popular and are often stewed with a small amount of meat and a mélange of vegetables to make hearty one-pot feasts. The stew is flavored with a unique combination of saffron, chili powder, cinnamon, and fresh herbs.

Preparation time **20 minutes**　　Cooking time **about 1 1/2 hours**　　*Serves 4*

2 teaspoons olive oil

12 ounces boneless rabbit, cut into large chunks

2 medium onions, chopped

3 garlic cloves, chopped

1 large red pepper, seeded and chopped

1 tablespoon paprika

1 teaspoon mild chili powder

1 teaspoon ground cumin

Large pinch of ground cinnamon

2 bay leaves

1 cup dry white wine

1 cup low-fat, reduced-sodium chicken stock

1 can (14 ounces) chopped tomatoes

2 tablespoons tomato puree

3 tablespoons chopped fresh flat-leaf parsley

2 pinches of saffron threads

4 tablespoons hot water

1 can chickpeas (15 ounces), drained and rinsed

1/2 pound new potatoes, scrubbed and halved

2 sprigs of fresh oregano or marjoram, leaves coarsely chopped

Grated zest and juice of 1 small orange

Salt and pepper

1 Heat the oil in a flameproof casserole, add the chunks of rabbit, and sauté until browned on all sides. Add the onions, garlic, and red pepper and sauté until the onions are softened, about 5 minutes. Add the paprika, chili powder, cumin, cinnamon, and bay leaves, stir well, and cook for 1 minute.

2 Add the wine, broth, tomatoes with their juice, tomato puree, and half of the parsley. Cover and bring to a boil, then reduce the heat to very low and simmer until the rabbit is very tender, about 40 minutes. Meanwhile, crumble the saffron into a small bowl and add the hot water. Stir, then leave to soak for 15 to 20 minutes.

3 Add the chickpeas and potatoes to the stew, together with the saffron and its soaking water, the oregano or marjoram, and orange zest and juice. Stir, then simmer until the gravy has thickened and is not too soupy, about 25 to 30 minutes. Taste and add seasoning if needed, and remove the bay leaves. Serve hot, sprinkled with the remaining parsley.

(Some More Ideas) Instead of rabbit, use lean pork tenderloin, trimmed of fat and cut into bite-size chunks.

Plus Points

• Chickpeas are an important source of vegetable protein in many parts of the world, and they are a good source of dietary fiber. Surprisingly, in this recipe the chickpeas provide a greater amount of iron per portion than the rabbit (1.5mg compared to 0.9mg). The absorption of the iron is helped by the generous amounts of vitamin C provided by the vegetables, in particular red pepper.

• Rabbit is an excellent low-fat source of protein. It can be substituted for chicken breast in many recipes because its meat looks and tastes quite similar. Nutritionally, it contains twice as much iron as chicken breast.

Exchanges

starch 2 1/2　vegetable 3　meat (lean) 3　fat 1/2

Each serving provides calories 397, calories from fat 88, fat 10g, saturated fat 2g, cholesterol 48mg, sodium 491mg, carbohydrate 50g, fiber 11g, sugars 17g, protein 28g. Excellent source of folate, iron, magnesium, niacin, phosphorus, potassium, thiamine, vitamin A, vitamin B6, vitamin B12, vitamin C. Good source of calcium, copper, riboflavin.

spanish rabbit and chickpea stew *p82*

asian pork and cabbage rolls *p84*

spring lamb and
vegetable stew *p81*

bulgur wheat salad with lamb *p80*

asian pork and cabbage rolls

Crunchy water chestnuts are combined with ground pork, soy sauce, fresh ginger, and five-spice powder to make a flavorful, Asian-style filling for green cabbage leaves. The rolls are steamed in a reduced-sodium broth, making them moist and tender. Serve with steamed brown rice and a simple romaine lettuce, red pepper, and onion salad for a quick family meal.

Preparation time 10 minutes   Cooking time 15 minutes   *Serves 4*

1 pound extra-lean ground pork

1 can (8 ounces) water chestnuts, drained and finely chopped

2 teaspoons five-spice powder

1 tablespoon finely grated fresh ginger

2 scallions, finely chopped

2 tablespoons dark soy sauce

2 garlic cloves, crushed

1 egg, beaten

8 large green cabbage leaves

2 cups hot low-fat, reduced-sodium chicken broth

2 teaspoons flour

1 teaspoon chili sauce, or to taste (optional)

Garnish

Curled strips of scallion

1 Place the pork in a bowl and add the water chestnuts, five-spice powder, ginger, scallions, soy sauce, garlic, and egg. Mix thoroughly with your hands or a fork until the ingredients are well blended, then divide into 8 equal portions.

2 Cut the tough stalk from the base of each cabbage leaf with a sharp knife. Place a portion of the pork mixture in the center of each cabbage leaf, then wrap the leaf around the filling to enclose it.

3 Pour the broth into the bottom section of a large steamer. Arrange the cabbage rolls, join side down, in one layer in the top section. Cover and steam for 15 minutes or until the cabbage is tender and the rolls are firm when pressed. Remove the top section from the steamer and keep the cabbage rolls hot.

4 Mix the flour with 2 tablespoons water, then stir this mixture into the broth in the bottom of the steamer. Bring to a boil and simmer, stirring constantly, until slightly thickened. Add the chili sauce if desired.

5 Serve the cabbage rolls with the sauce spooned over and sprinkled with curls of scallion.

(Some More Ideas) Instead of flavoring the pork filling with soy sauce, use 2 tablespoons hoisin sauce.

Ground turkey can be substituted for the ground pork.

Plus Points

• Extra-lean ground pork is lower in fat than ground beef or lamb and only slightly fattier than skinless chicken breast.

• Water chestnuts provide small amounts of potassium, iron, and fiber, but their big advantage—besides their flavor and crunch—is that they contain no fat and very few calories.

photo, page 83

Exchanges

vegetable 3   meat (lean) 3

Each serving provides calories 225, calories from fat 49, fat 5g, saturated fat 2g, cholesterol 127mg, sodium 854mg, carbohydrate 15g, fiber 4g, sugars 7g, protein 29g. Excellent source of niacin, phosphorus, potassium, riboflavin, thiamine, vitamin B6, vitamin B12, vitamin C. Good source of folate, iron, magnesium, zinc.

sesame pork and noodle salad

With its typical Asian flavors—ginger, sesame, soy sauce, and rice vinegar—this salad makes a delectable lunch or supper dish. It is very nutritious, as most of the vegetables are eaten raw. For the best effect, cut the pepper, carrot, and scallions into strips that are about the same thickness as the noodles.

Preparation time **about 25 minutes**   Cooking time **about 10 minutes**   *Serves 4*

1 pound pork tenderloin
2 teaspoons grated fresh ginger
1 large garlic clove, finely chopped
1 teaspoon toasted sesame oil
3 tablespoons light soy sauce
2 tablespoons dry sherry
2 teaspoons rice vinegar
8 ounces fine Chinese egg noodles
1 red bell pepper, seeded and cut into matchstick strips
1 large carrot, cut into matchstick strips
6 scallions, cut into matchstick strips
1 cup snow peas
1 tablespoon sesame seeds
2 teaspoons canola oil

1 Trim all visible fat from the pork. Cut the pork across into slices about 2 inches thick, then cut each slice into thin strips.

2 Combine the ginger, garlic, sesame oil, soy sauce, sherry, and vinegar in a bowl. Add the pork strips and toss to coat, then leave to marinate while you prepare the other ingredients.

3 Place the noodles in a large mixing bowl and pour over enough boiling water to cover generously. Leave to soak until tender, about 4 minutes, or according to the package instructions. Drain well and place back into the bowl. Add the red bell pepper, carrot, and scallions.

4 Drop the snow peas into a pan of boiling water and cook until just tender but still crisp, about 1 minute. Drain and refresh under cold running water. Add the snow peas to the noodle and vegetable mixture and toss to mix. Set aside.

5 Toast the sesame seeds in a large skillet over medium heat until golden, about 1 to 2 minutes, stirring constantly. Remove the seeds from the pan and set aside. Heat the oil in the skillet, increase the heat slightly, and add the pork with its marinade. Stir-fry until the pork is no longer pink, about 4 to 5 minutes.

6 Add the strips of pork and any cooking juices to the noodle and vegetable mixture, and stir gently to combine. Divide among 4 shallow bowls, sprinkle with the toasted sesame seeds, and serve.

(Some More Ideas) *Sesame pork and rice noodle salad*: Use 8 ounces rice noodles instead of egg noodles. Soak them as in the main recipe, then mix with the red bell pepper, carrot, and scallions.

Plus Points

• In the past, pork has had a reputation for being rather fatty, but this is certainly no longer the case. Over the last 20 years, in response to consumer demands, farmers have been breeding leaner pigs. Pork now contains considerably less fat, and it also contains higher levels of the "good" polyunsaturated fats. The average fat content of lean pork is less than 3%, making it very similar to skinless chicken breast.

• The vegetables in this dish are served raw to maintain the fiber and nutrient content that may be diminished during cooking.

• Sesame seeds and sesame oil are bursting with flavor. Only a small amount of these rather high-fat ingredients is needed for this salad.

photo, page 87

Exchanges
starch 3 vegetable 1
meat (lean) 3

Each serving provides calories 443, calories from fat 101, fat 11g, saturated fat 3g, cholesterol 119mg, sodium 528mg, carbohydrate 51g, fiber 4g, sugars 8g, protein 34g. Excellent source of iron, magnesium, niacin, phosphorus, potassium, riboflavin, thiamine, vitamin A, vitamin B6, vitamin C. Good Source of folate.

sweet-and-sour pork

This modern, light version allows the succulence of the meat and the fresh flavors of a colorful variety of vegetables to shine through. Instead of using a lot of oil in the preparation of the dish, add a drizzle of polyunsaturated sesame oil as the finishing touch. Steamed brown rice is all that is needed to complete the meal.

Preparation time **35 minutes** Cooking time **15 minutes** *Serves 4*

Pork

12 ounces pork fillet (tenderloin), trimmed of fat and cut into 2-inch strips

1 tablespoon light soy sauce

2 teaspoons flour

1 can (15 ounces) pineapple slices in natural juice, drained and chopped with juice reserved

8 ounces Chinese egg noodles

1 1/2 teaspoons canola oil, divided

8 baby corn, quartered lengthways

2 carrots, julienned

1 large garlic clove, finely chopped

1 tablespoon finely diced peeled ginger

1 cup bean sprouts

4 scallions, sliced diagonally

1/2 teaspoon toasted sesame oil

Pepper

Sauce

1 tablespoon flour

1 tablespoon sugar

1 tablespoon rice wine vinegar

2 tablespoons rice wine or dry sherry

2 tablespoons ketchup

3 tablespoons light soy sauce

Exchanges

starch 3 fruit 1 1/2 vegetable 2
meat (lean) 2

1 Place the pork strips in a bowl, sprinkle the soy sauce and pepper over them to taste, and stir to coat the meat. Sprinkle with the flour and stir again. Cover and set aside.

2 To make the sauce, mix together the flour, sugar, vinegar, rice wine or sherry, ketchup, soy sauce, and reserved pineapple juice in a small bowl. Set aside.

3 Cook the noodles in a saucepan of boiling water for 3 minutes, or cook or soak them according to the packet instructions. Drain well and set aside.

4 Heat a wok or heavy skillet until really hot, then add half the oil and swirl to coat the wok. Add the pork and leave for 1 minute to brown, then stir-fry over a high heat for 3 to 4 minutes. Remove the pork with a draining spoon and set aside.

5 Heat the remaining oil in the wok, then add the corn and stir-fry for 1 minute. Add the carrots, garlic, and ginger, and stir-fry for another minute. Sprinkle with 5 tablespoons water and let the vegetables steam for 2 to 3 minutes.

6 Pour in the sauce mixture, stir well, and bring to a boil. Add the meat back in the wok and add the noodles, pineapple, and bean sprouts. Heat through. Add the scallions and sesame oil and serve.

(Some More Ideas) For a hotter sauce, add 1 small fresh red chile, seeded and finely chopped.

Boneless pork shoulder can be substituted for the pork tenderloin.

Plus Points

• Over the last 20 years, farmers have been breeding leaner pigs, and pork now contains considerably less fat than it did in the past. The average fat content is only slightly higher than that of skinless chicken breast.

• Bean sprouts are rich in vitamin C and several of the B vitamins; they also provide some potassium. Adding them at the last minute preserves as much of their vitamin C content as possible.

Each serving provides calories 488, calories from fat 73, fat 8g, saturated fat 2g, cholesterol 103mg, sodium 764mg, carbohydrate 76g, fiber 5g, sugars 28g, protein 29g. Excellent source of iron, magnesium, niacin, phosphorus, potassium, riboflavin, thiamine, vitamin A, vitamin B6, vitamin C. Good source of folate.

sesame pork and noodle salad *p85*

sweet-and-sour pork *p86*

pork medallions with peppers *p89*

pork and beans *p88*

pork and beans

This dish is a specialty from New England, where the pork and beans are traditionally simmered slowly in an earthenware casserole dish. Here the beans are flavored with a little brown sugar and reduced-fat bacon to make them more healthful. Serve the beans as a side dish with homemade burgers at an outside barbecue.

Preparation time **25 minutes, plus overnight soaking**   Cooking time **about 2 hours**   *Serves 4*

1 cup dried white beans, soaked overnight in cold water

1 tablespoon canola oil

4 (4 ounce) lean bone-in pork loin chops, trimmed of fat

1 medium onion, chopped

8 ounces beer, such as dark ale

1 can (24 ounces) chopped tomatoes

2 teaspoons Worcestershire sauce, or to taste

2 tablespoons dark brown sugar

3 allspice berries

2 tablespoons Dijon mustard

2 slices reduced-fat bacon, cut into bite-size pieces

1 teaspoon cider vinegar, or to taste

1 Drain and rinse the beans, then place them in a large saucepan and pour over enough cold water to come up to about twice the depth of the beans. Cover the pan with its lid and bring to a boil. Skim off any scum, then reduce the heat, cover the pan again, and cook the beans over a low heat until they are just tender, about 45 to 60 minutes.

2 Meanwhile, heat the oil in a deep flameproof casserole, add the pork chops and onion, and sear the chops until they are browned on both sides. Pour in the beer and tomatoes with their juice, then add the Worcestershire sauce, sugar, and allspice. Reduce the heat, cover, and cook until the meat is very tender, about 1 hour. Add water if necessary to keep the pork moist.

3 Drain the beans and add to the pork chops. Add the mustard, bacon, and vinegar and stir well to mix. Cook, covered, over a low heat until both the beans and the pork are very tender, about 1 hour.

4 Before serving, taste for seasoning and add a dash or two more Worcestershire sauce or vinegar if desired.

(**Some More Ideas**) Lager or cider can be used instead of beer.

Instead of soaking and cooking dried beans, add a can of cannellini beans (15 ounces), drained and rinsed, at the beginning of Step 3.

Tuscan-style beans with sausages: Use 1 pound reduced-fat turkey sausages, cut into bite-size pieces, instead of the pork chops. Brown the sausages with the onion in a deep, nonstick frying pan; set aside. Pour off fat from the pan, then add 1/2 cup dry red wine, 1 cup chicken or vegetable stock, 1 can (24 ounces) chopped tomatoes, with the juice, 8 chopped fresh sage leaves, 2 bay leaves, 2 crushed garlic cloves, and salt and pepper to taste. Cook uncovered over a low heat for 30 minutes. Add the sausages and onion together with 1 can (15 ounces) cannellini beans, drained and rinsed, and simmer for 15 minutes.

Plus Points

• Tomatoes contain lycopene, a carotenoid compound and a valuable antioxidant that is thought to protect against prostate, bladder, and pancreatic cancers. Lycopene is enhanced by cooking and so is most readily available in processed tomato products, such as canned tomatoes, tomato puree, and tomato ketchup.

photo, page 87

Exchanges

starch 2 1/2 vegetable 2
meat (lean) 2 fat 1/2

Each serving provides calories 381, calories from fat 84, fat 9g, saturated fat 2g, cholesterol 52mg, sodium 612mg, carbohydrate 46g, fiber 9g, sugars 19g, protein 30g. Excellent source of folate, iron, magnesium, niacin, phosphorus, potassium, thiamine, vitamin B6, vitamin C. Good source of calcium, riboflavin, vitamin A.

pork medallions with peppers

This quick sauté makes an excellent dinner party dish, with its well-balanced sweet-and-sour elements coming from balsamic vinegar, oranges, and olives. In order to achieve a balanced meal, a small amount of pork is paired with a generous portion of vegetables and then served over rice. Serve the dish with steamed fresh broccoli.

Preparation and cooking time **about 50 minutes**   *Serves 4*

1 cup mixed basmati and wild rice

2 cups water

2 oranges

1 tablespoon olive oil

12 ounces pork fillet (tenderloin), sliced across into medallions 1/2-inch thick

1 large sweet onion (Vidalia) or red onion, halved lengthways and thinly sliced into half rings

1 red pepper, seeded and sliced into strips

1 yellow pepper, seeded and sliced into strips

1 large carrot, grated

1 garlic clove, finely chopped

1/2 cup orange juice

3 tablespoons balsamic vinegar

1/4 cup pitted chopped black olives

10 basil leaves

Salt and pepper

1 Put the rice and water in a saucepan. Bring to a boil, then reduce the heat to low. Cover and simmer according to the packet instructions, until the rice is tender and all the water has been absorbed, about 15 minutes.

2 Meanwhile, peel the oranges and cut them crossways into slices about 1/2-inch thick. Stack the slices 3 or 4 at a time and cut into quarters. Set the orange slices aside.

3 Heat the oil in a large nonstick skillet over medium-high heat. Cook the pork medallions, in batches, for 2 to 3 minutes on each side. Remove the meat with a slotted spoon and set aside.

4 Reduce the heat to medium and add the onion, pepper strips, carrot, and garlic to the pan. Cover and cook, stirring frequently, until the vegetables start to soften, about 5 to 6 minutes. Add 2 tablespoons water, orange juice, and the balsamic vinegar. Stir well to mix. Cover and cook until the vegetables are tender, about 3 to 4 minutes.

5 Return the pork to the pan. Add the olives, orange slices and their juice, and the basil leaves. Cook for 1 minute to reheat the pork, stirring well. Taste and add salt and pepper, if needed.

6 To serve, divide the rice among 4 warmed plates and place the pork medallions and vegetables on top. Drizzle over any juices remaining in the pan and serve immediately.

(**Some More Ideas**) For lamb with peppers, use lean lamb neck fillets or boneless lean lamb leg steaks, pounded thin, instead of pork fillet. Omit the basil and flavor the lamb with 1/2 teaspoon chopped fresh rosemary.

Plus Points

• Wild rice comes from North America. It is not a true rice, but the seeds of a wild aquatic grass. It is gluten-free, like the basmati rice it is mixed with here, and contains useful amounts of B vitamins, particularly niacin.

• Peppers contain high levels of beta-carotene and other members of the carotene family, such as capsanthin and zeaxanthin. All of these work as antioxidants, helping to prevent cancers, heart disease, strokes, and cataracts.

photo, page 87

Exchanges

starch 2 1/2 fruit 1 vegetable 2 meat (lean) 2

Each serving provides calories 415, calories from fat 74, fat 8g, saturated fat 2g, cholesterol 49mg, sodium 124mg, carbohydrate 63g, fiber 7g, sugars 19g, protein 25g. Excellent source of folate, magnesium, niacin, phosphorus, potassium, riboflavin, thiamine, vitamin A, vitamin B6, vitamin C. Good source of iron.

five-spice pork

The simple Asian technique of stir-frying is perfect for preparing meals in a hurry. It is also a great healthy-cooking method because it uses just a small amount of oil and cooks vegetables quickly so that most of their beneficial vitamins and minerals are preserved.

Preparation and cooking time **30 minutes**   *Serves 4*

1 pound pork tenderloin, trimmed of fat, cut into 2-inch strips

8 ounces medium Chinese egg noodles

1 teaspoon canola oil

1 large onion, finely chopped

1 large garlic clove, crushed

1 tablespoon five-spice powder

1 cup sugar snap peas

2 large red peppers (or 1 red and 1 yellow or orange), seeded and thinly sliced

1/2 cup hot reduced-sodium vegetable broth

Salt and pepper

Garnish

Fresh cilantro leaves

1 Cook the noodles in a saucepan of boiling water for 4 minutes, or cook or soak them according to the packet instructions. Drain the noodles well and set aside.

2 While the noodles are cooking, heat a wok or a large heavy-based frying pan until hot. Add the oil and swirl to coat the wok, then add the onion and garlic and stir-fry for 1 minute. Add the five-spice powder and stir-fry for another minute.

3 Add the pork strips to the wok and stir-fry for 3 minutes. Add the sugar snap peas and the peppers and stir-fry for a further 2 minutes. Pour in the broth, stir well and bring to a boil.

4 Add the noodles to the wok and stir and toss until all the ingredients are well combined, about 2 to 3 minutes. Season to taste, sprinkle with coriander leaves, and serve immediately.

(**Some More Ideas**) To reduce the fat content of this dish even further, use just 1/2 pound pork and add 1/2 pound firm light tofu. Drain the tofu well and cut it into 1-inch cubes, then add in Step 3 with the sugar snap peas and peppers. Add 2 tablespoons light soy sauce with the stock.

For a vegetarian dish, replace the pork with 1 pound drained and diced firm light tofu and add 1 cup broccoli florets. Add the tofu and broccoli with the sugar snap peas and peppers in Step 3, and add 1/4 cup bean sprouts with the noodles in Step 4.

Plus Points

• Peppers have a naturally waxy skin that helps to protect them against oxidation and prevents loss of vitamin C during storage. As a result, their vitamin C content remains high even several weeks after harvesting.

• Heating the pan until hot before adding any oil not only helps to prevent ingredients from sticking, but also means less oil is needed.

• Chinese egg noodles are a low-fat source of carbohydrate. When they are eaten with ingredients high in vitamin C, such as the peppers in this recipe, the body is able to absorb the iron they contain.

Exchanges

starch 2 1/2 vegetable 3
meat (lean) 3

Each serving provides calories 427, calories from fat 73, fat 8g, saturated fat 3g, cholesterol 119mg, sodium 188mg, carbohydrate 55g, fiber 6g, sugars 9g, protein 34g. Excellent source of iron, magnesium, niacin, phosphorus, potassium, riboflavin, thiamine, vitamin A, vitamin B6, vitamin C. Good source of folate.

japanese chicken salad

In true Japanese style, the presentation of juicy steamed chicken and clusters of fresh vegetables is a work of art. This dish is a good choice for a dinner party because the sauce is served on the side and guests can adjust their meal to taste. Try cutting the vegetables into various shapes and lengths to make the presentation even more appealing.

Preparation time **45 minutes**   Cooking time **10 minutes**   *Serves 8*

Salad

1 1/2 pounds boneless, skinless chicken breasts

2 tablespoons rice wine (mirin or sake)

1/2 teaspoon freshly ground white pepper

1 large cucumber, unpeeled

4 large carrots, peeled

2 large red bell peppers

1 large head Bibb lettuce

1/2 cup finely shredded basil leaves

1/4 cup finely shredded mint leaves

8 scallions, cut in half lengthwise

6 ounces button mushrooms, thinly sliced

Dressing

3 tablespoons fresh lemon juice

2 tablespoons rice wine (mirin or sake)

2 tablespoons light soy sauce

2 tablespoons tahini (sesame-seed paste)

1 large garlic clove, minced

Pinch chili powder

1 In a small bowl, whisk all of the dressing ingredients together. Pour into a small serving dish.

2 To steam the chicken, place the chicken breasts over boiling water in a steamer or on a rack in a shallow skillet with a cover. Sprinkle with the mirin and pepper. Cover and steam until the juices of the chicken run clear when a breast is pierced with a fork, about 10 minutes. Transfer to a plate to cool.

3 Cut the cucumber (do not peel) and the carrots into thin 3-inch matchsticks. Remove the stem, seeds, and membranes from the red peppers and cut into thin 3-inch matchsticks. Separate the lettuce into leaves and arrange at one end of a large platter. Scatter the shredded basil and mint over the lettuce and the rest of the platter.

4 Cut the chicken into thin slices and place on the lettuce. Arrange the cucumber, carrots, peppers, onions, and mushrooms attractively on the platter. Serve with the dressing in a small bowl.

(Some More Ideas) *Asian chicken salad with plum dressing*: Reduce the carrots to 2. Add a mound of 4 cups fresh bean sprouts on the platter, plus a cluster of 1 cup sliced water chestnuts, and another cluster of 1 cup drained canned baby corn. To make the dressing, substitute 1 cup bottled plum sauce for the mirin and 2 teaspoons toasted sesame oil for the tahini. Top with 2 tablespoons toasted sesame seeds.

Tahini tip: Popular in Middle Eastern cooking, this thick, oily paste is made from crushed sesame seeds. If you are not able to find it in your market, toast 1 cup sesame seeds in a small skillet over high heat for a few minutes, stirring constantly and watching them closely so they do not burn. Then process the seeds with a little sesame oil in a food processor (or mash in a mortar with a pestle) until a paste forms.

Plus Points

• Because all of the vegetables are eaten raw, this salad offers excellent amounts of vitamin C, which helps the body absorb the iron from the chicken.

• Rice wine is made from steamed rice that is fermented. It is used most often in Japanese cooking for sauces and marinades. Just a small amount of the wine adds a wonderful, full-bodied flavor to Asian dishes.

photo, page 95

Exchanges

vegetable 3 meat (very lean) 3

Each serving provides calories 179, calories from fat 33, fat 4g, saturated fat 1g, cholesterol 48mg, sodium 237mg, carbohydrate 14g, fiber 5g, sugars 7g, protein 23g. Excellent source of niacin, phosphorus, potassium, riboflavin, vitamin A, vitamin B6, vitamin C. Good source of folate, iron, magnesium, thiamine.

roasted chicken salad with ginger

This creamy, light chicken salad is ideal for a summer luncheon. The slightly tart flavor from the lime juice and green apples is balanced by pieces of sweet apricot. The low-fat dressing is made with reduced-fat sour cream and mayonnaise. Don't be tempted to omit the fresh ginger—its subtle flavor makes all the difference.

Preparation time **25 minutes**   *Serves 8*

Salad

1 broiler-fryer chicken, roasted (3 1/2 pounds) or 1 1/2 pounds cooked boneless, skinless chicken breasts

3 tablespoons fresh lime juice

2 large green apples, such as Granny Smith, unpeeled and cut into 1/2-inch dice

4 celery stalks, thinly sliced

1 cup quartered dried apricots

Dressing

1 cup reduced-fat sour cream

1/2 cup reduced-fat mayonnaise

1 tablespoon grated peeled ginger

1 teaspoon salt

1 teaspoon freshly ground black pepper

1/4 cup minced white onion

Garnish

1/3 cup toasted chopped walnuts

Sprigs of watercress

1. If using a whole roasted chicken, remove the meat from the bones and discard the skin and bones. Cut the chicken into bite-size pieces and place in a large serving bowl.

2. Squeeze the lime juice into a medium-size bowl. Add the apples to the juice. Toss until all of the pieces are well coated.

3. To the chicken, add the apples and any lime juice remaining in the bowl, the celery, and the apricots. Toss gently until well mixed.

4. In a small bowl, stir together the sour cream, mayonnaise, ginger, salt, and pepper. Fold in the onion. Spoon this dressing over the chicken mixture and toss gently until all the pieces are coated well. Sprinkle the toasted walnuts on top of the salad and garnish with the sprigs of watercress.

(Some More Ideas) *Smoked turkey salad*: Substitute 1 1/2 pounds cooked boneless, skinless smoked turkey breast, cut into bite-size pieces, for the chicken. Substitute 1 cup dried pitted cherries for the apricots.

Chicken and grape salad: Add 1 cup red or purple seedless grapes, cut in half, with the apples, celery, and apricots. Substitute 1/3 cup toasted slivered almonds for the walnuts.

Chicken and pineapple salad: Add 2 cups fresh pineapple wedges with the apples, celery, and apricots.

Chicken and melon salad: Substitute 2 cups honeydew melon balls for the apricots.

Plus Points

• This recipe offers a good source of dietary fiber, thanks to the unpeeled apples, celery, and dried apricots. Fiber is essential to keep the digestive tract healthy. The soluble fiber pectin, found mostly in the peels of fruits and vegetables, can also lower blood cholesterol levels.

• Dried apricots provide a good source of beta-carotene. They are also one of the best fruit sources of iron.

• When nuts are added to a meal in small amounts, they help to maintain satiety due to their high fat content.

photo, page 95

Exchanges

fruit 1 1/2 meat (lean) 4 fat 1/2

Each serving provides calories 336, calories from fat 125, fat 14g, saturated fat 3g, cholesterol 87mg, sodium 521mg, carbohydrate 24g, fiber 4g, sugars 15g, protein 30g. Excellent source of niacin, phosphorus, vitamin A, vitamin B6. Good source of iron, magnesium, potassium, riboflavin, vitamin C.

stir-fried chicken and avocado salad with hot balsamic dressing

In this recipe, juicy strips of chicken are quickly stir-fried with bits of turkey bacon, then tossed with a warm dressing. Serve on top of a fresh green salad tossed with rich avocado slices, fresh cherry tomatoes, and slivered red onion.

Preparation time **20 minutes**　Cooking time **7 minutes**　*Serves 8*

Chicken

1 pound boneless, skinless chicken breasts

2 teaspoons olive oil

2 large garlic cloves, cut into slivers

2 tablespoons honey

1 tablespoon whole-grain Dijon mustard

1 tablespoon balsamic vinegar

6 strips reduced-fat turkey bacon, diced

Salad

2 heads Boston lettuce, separated into leaves

1 bunch watercress

2 large ripe avocados

3 tablespoons fresh lemon juice

1 pint cherry tomatoes

1 small red onion

1 First, prepare the salad. In a large salad bowl, place the lettuce leaves. Trim the tips of the watercress and toss with the lettuce (you will have about 9 cups of greens). Peel the avocados, cut in half, and discard the seeds. Slice the avocados lengthwise, 1/2 inch thick, and toss with the lemon juice. Cut the tomatoes in half and the onion into thin slivers. Scatter the avocados, tomatoes, and red onion on top of the salad and refrigerate.

2 Cut the chicken into 3- to 4-inch strips, 1 inch wide. In a large skillet or wok, heat the oil over medium-high heat. Add the chicken strips and garlic and stir-fry until the chicken turns opaque, about 3 minutes.

3 Add the honey, mustard, and vinegar, and stir to mix well. Add the diced turkey bacon and stir-fry until the bacon is cooked and the chicken is tender and moist (do not overcook), about 3 minutes.

4 Spoon the stir-fried chicken strips, bacon, and any liquid remaining in the skillet on top of the salad. Serve with wedges of warm, crusty bread.

(Some More Ideas) *Cobb salad with stir-fried chicken*: Substitute 1 cup sliced green onions for the red onion. Before serving, sprinkle the salad with 1/2 cup crumbled Roquefort cheese.

Chicken, spinach, and orange salad: Substitute 5 cups fresh baby spinach leaves and 2 cups orange sections for the Boston lettuce and tomatoes.

Turkey-artichoke salad: Substitute one 10-ounce jar well-drained marinated artichokes for the avocados. In the salad, omit the 3 tablespoons fresh lemon juice, but add them to the skillet instead with the honey, vinegar, and mustard. Use 1 pound boneless, skinless turkey breast for the chicken breasts.

Plus Points

• Ounce for ounce, turkey bacon contains one-third less fat than pork bacon and one-third fewer calories.

• Balsamic vinegar is made from fermented grape juice that is aged in barrels for several years. It is a wonderful sodium-free ingredient to use in vinaigrette dressings and sauces.

Exchanges

carbohydrate 1/2　vegetable 1
meat (lean) 2　fat 1

Each serving provides calories 222, calories from fat 112, fat 12g, saturated fat 3g, cholesterol 42mg, sodium 220mg, carbohydrate 14g, fiber 4g, sugars 8g, protein 17g. Excellent source of niacin, vitamin A, vitamin B6, vitamin C. Good source of folate, iron, magnesium, phosphorus, potassium, riboflavin, thiamine.

japanese chicken salad *p92*

stir-fried chicken and avocado salad
with hot balsamic dressing *p94*

chicken and artichoke sauté *p96*

roasted chicken salad with ginger *p93*

chicken and artichoke sauté

On the Mediterranean coast, artichokes, peppers, and olives often team up in the same dish to create traditional fare. Simmer them in a lemony white wine sauce as the perfect accompaniment for sautéed chicken thighs.

Preparation time **20 minutes**   Cooking time **25 minutes**   *Serves 6*

Chicken

1/4 cup all-purpose flour

1 tablespoon chopped fresh thyme leaves

1 teaspoon salt

1 teaspoon freshly ground black pepper

12 (3 ounce) small boneless, skinless chicken thighs

1 tablespoon olive oil

Sauté

1 can (15 ounces) artichoke hearts

2 large red bell peppers

1 large garlic clove, minced

1/2 cup pitted black olives, cut in half

1/4 cup dry white wine

1 cup low-fat, reduced-sodium chicken broth

2 teaspoons grated lemon zest

Garnish

Sprigs of fresh thyme

2 large lemons, cut into 4 wedges each

1 Preheat the oven to 300°F. In a large zippered plastic bag, shake the flour, thyme, salt, and pepper. Add the chicken thighs to the bag and shake until they are lightly coated. Remove the chicken to a plate, shaking off and discarding any excess flour.

2 Heat the oil in a large skillet over medium-high heat. Add the chicken thighs and sauté for 3 minutes on each side until golden brown.

3 Reduce the heat to medium and cook until the juices of the chicken run clear when a thigh is pierced with a fork, about 12 minutes more. Transfer the thighs to a heatproof platter and place in the oven to keep warm.

4 Drain the artichokes well and cut in half. Remove the stems, seeds, and membranes of the bell peppers, then cut the peppers into thin strips. Add the garlic to the same skillet and cook over medium-high heat just until soft. Add the artichokes and red peppers, and sauté just until the peppers are crisp-tender, about 5 minutes. Stir in the black olives.

5 Add the wine and let the vegetables simmer until the wine has almost evaporated. Stir in the broth and lemon zest, bring to a boil, and let boil, uncovered, until the liquid has reduced by about one-half.

6 Transfer the chicken thighs from the oven to a large serving platter and spoon the rtichoke and pepper mixture alongside.

(Some More Ideas) *Chicken breast sauté*: Substitute 1 pound boneless, skinless chicken breasts for the chicken thighs. Reduce the sautéing time to 6 to 8 minutes, depending upon the thickness of the chicken breasts.

Chicken and zucchini sauté: Omit the artichokes. Sauté 2 cups sliced mushrooms with the garlic, then add 2 cups zucchini slices with the red pepper strips. Decorate with 1/4 cup fresh basil leaves instead of the sprigs of fresh thyme.

Chicken and asparagus sauté: Substitute 2 cups fresh asparagus tips for the artichokes.

Plus Points

• Artichokes are not only low in calories and fat, but are also a good source of vitamin C and folate. Look for artichokes that feel heavy and that do not have browning on the leaves. The leaves should squeak when rubbed together.

• Although olives have a high fat content, most of this fat is monounsaturated. This is why olive oil is preferred over butter, margarine, and some oils.

• Invest in a good-quality nonstick skillet. It allows you to sauté poultry and vegetables with very little oil.

photo, page 95

Exchanges

vegetable 2 meat (lean) 4 fat 1

Each serving provides calories 311, calories from fat 135, fat 15g, saturated fat 3g, cholesterol 99mg, sodium 780mg, carbohydrate 13g, fiber 2g, sugars 3g, protein 31g. Excellent source of folate, niacin, phosphorus, riboflavin, vitamin A, vitamin B6, vitamin C. Good source of iron, magnesium, potassium, thiamine.

chicken fajitas with tomato salsa

The original Mexican fajitas are made by marinating strips of beef for 24 hours, then grilling the meat and wrapping it in warm tortillas with peppers and onions, and serving with spicy salsa. Here sizzling chicken strips replace the beef for a lower-fat variation of this Southwestern favorite. A fresh tomato salsa tops it all off.

Preparation time **45 minutes**   Marinating time **30 minutes**   Cooking time **20 minutes**   *Serves 8*

Fajitas

1 1/2 pounds boneless, skinless chicken breasts

1 teaspoon lime zest

3 large limes

1/2 cup chopped fresh cilantro leaves

3 large garlic cloves, minced

2 to 3 teaspoons mild chili powder

1 teaspoon ground cumin

1 teaspoon paprika

2 tablespoons canola oil, divided

3 large green or red bell peppers

2 large yellow onions

8 flour tortillas (8 inches in diameter)

1/2 cup reduced-fat sour cream

Fresh cilantro sprigs

Salsa

1 cup chopped ripe tomatoes,

1/2 cup thinly sliced green onions

1 medium-hot fresh green chile pepper, seeded and minced

2 tablespoons fresh lemon juice

2 tablespoons tomato paste

1 tablespoon chopped fresh cilantro leaves

2 large garlic cloves, minced

1/2 teaspoon ground cumin

Hot pepper sauce (optional)

1 In a large, shallow dish, arrange the chicken breasts in a single layer. In a small bowl, whisk 1 teaspoon lime zest, the juice of the 3 limes, cilantro, garlic, chili powder, cumin, paprika, and half the oil. Pour this mixture over the chicken, cover with plastic wrap, and let marinate in the refrigerator for at least 30 minutes.

2 Prepare the salsa. In a medium bowl, toss the tomatoes, green onions, minced chile pepper, lemon juice, tomato paste, cilantro, garlic, and cumin.

3 Preheat the grill to high and preheat the oven to 350°F. Peel the onions and seed the peppers and slice into thin strips. Heat a large skillet over high heat and brush with the remaining oil. Add the peppers and onions and sauté until the onions are brown, about 8 minutes. Remove the skillet from the heat.

4 Wrap the tortillas in foil and keep warm in the oven for 10 minutes. Grill the chicken 6 inches from the heat for about 10 minutes until the juices of the chicken run clear when a breast is pierced with a fork. Cut the chicken into long strips, 1 inch wide.

5 To serve, divide the chicken, onions, and peppers among the warm tortillas and roll up. Garnish with sprigs of cilantro and serve with the fresh salsa and sour cream.

(Some More Ideas) *Chicken-cheddar quesadillas*: Prepare chicken, peppers, and onions as directed through Step 4. Use 9 tortillas. Preheat the oven to 350°F but do not warm the tortillas. Instead, on an ungreased baking sheet, make 3 stacked quesadillas. For each stack: top a tortilla with one-sixth each of the grilled chicken and the sautéed bell peppers and onions; sprinkle with 2 heaping tablespoons shredded sharp reduced-fat cheddar cheese. Cover with a second tortilla and repeat with one-sixth more of the chicken, bell peppers, and onions and 2 more heaping tablespoons cheddar. Top with a third tortilla, pressing down lightly. Bake the quesadilla stacks until the cheese melts and the tortillas are slightly crisp, about 5 minutes. Cut each stack in half and serve with the salsa and sour cream.

Plus Points

• Garlic has been used throughout history as a cure-all. Recent research has found that it can help lower blood lipids, thus reducing the risk of heart disease. Garlic can also act as an antioxidant and lengthens blood-clotting times.

photo, page 101

Exchanges

starch 2 vegetable 2 meat (very lean) 2 fat 1/2

Each serving provides calories 357, calories from fat 89, fat 10g, saturated fat 2g, cholesterol 56mg, sodium 304mg, carbohydrate 42g, fiber 5g, sugars 9g, protein 26g. Excellent source of folate, niacin, phosphorus, thiamine, vitamin A, vitamin B6, vitamin C. Good source of calcium, iron, magnesium, potassium, riboflavin.

mexican tostadas

Tostada comes from the Spanish word meaning "toasted." In Mexico it refers to flat, crisply fried corn tortillas, topped with beans, shredded chicken, lettuce, and cheese, diced tomatoes, and sour cream. Here spicy tomato sauce and pinto beans replace the traditional refried beans. The tortillas are toasted with a little oil and served with low-fat condiments.

Preparation time **30 minutes**   Cooking time **50 minutes**   *Serves 8*

Tostadas

2 pounds boneless, skinless chicken breasts

2 tablespoons canola oil

2 large red or green bell peppers, seeded and coarsely chopped

2 large yellow onions, chopped

2 large garlic cloves, thinly sliced

1 tablespoon chili powder

2 teaspoons paprika

1 teaspoon ground cumin

1/2 teaspoon freshly ground black pepper

1/4 teaspoon salt

1 can (14 ounces) chopped tomatoes with juice, no salt added

1/2 teaspoon sugar

1 can (15 ounces) pinto beans

8 (6 inch) soft corn tortillas

Toppings

2 large tomatoes, cut into 1-inch dice

2 cups shredded iceberg lettuce

4 pickled jalapeño chiles, coarsely chopped

1 cup shredded reduced-fat cheddar cheese

1/2 cup low-fat sour cream

2 radishes, sliced

Bottled chunky tomato salsa

1 Cook the chicken. In a large saucepan, place the chicken breasts; add enough cold water to cover. Bring to a boil over high heat, then reduce the heat to medium-low and simmer, uncovered, for 20 minutes. Using a slotted spoon, transfer the chicken to a rack to cool. Shred the meat and set aside.

2 Cook the vegetables. Heat 1 tablespoon of the oil in a large skillet over medium-high heat. Add the peppers, onions, and garlic. Sauté until softened, about 8 minutes. Stir in the chili powder, paprika, cumin, pepper, and salt; cook 2 minutes more. Stir in the tomatoes with their juice and the sugar. Simmer, uncovered, until the sauce thickens, about 8 minutes more. Remove from the heat and keep warm. Meanwhile, in a small saucepan, heat the beans over medium heat in their liquid; drain well.

3 In a heavy skillet (use a cast-iron skillet if you have one), heat the remaining oil and toast the tortillas, one at a time, over high heat, until slightly crisp and lightly browned, about 1 minute on each side. Keep hot in foil.

4 To assemble each of the 8 tostadas, divide the tomato sauce, beans, chicken, diced tomato, and lettuce among all 8 tostadas. Sprinkle with a few jalapeños. Top with 1 tablespoon each of the cheddar cheese and sour cream, plus a radish slice and some salsa, if desired.

(Some More Ideas) Substitute 2 cups fresh or frozen corn kernels (cooked and drained) for the beans (end of Step 2).

Plus Points
• Dried beans, peas, and lentils are an excellent source of protein and a good source of soluble dietary fiber. They are an even better source when they are eaten with grains, such as the corn found in these tortillas.

photo, page 101

Exchanges
starch 1 1/2 vegetable 2
meat (very lean) 3 fat 1

Each serving (one tostada) provides calories 329, calories from fat 70, fat 8g, saturated fat 1g, cholesterol 67mg, sodium 435mg, carbohydrate 34g, fiber 8g, sugars 10g, protein 32g. Excellent source of folate, niacin, phosphorus, potassium, vitamin A, vitamin B6, vitamin C. Good source of calcium, iron, magnesium, riboflavin, thiamine.

chicken and broccoli chapatis

These mouthwatering, pancake-like breads are one of the simplest and most healthful breads found in India. Chapatis are made from whole-wheat flour and water, then baked on a dry griddle without any fat. Fill the bread with this warm chicken, broccoli, and cashew mixture, and top the sandwiches with a traditional Indian yogurt and cucumber sauce called raita.

Preparation time **30 minutes**   Cooking time **18 minutes**   *Serves 4*

Chapatis

12 ounces cooked boneless, skinless chicken breasts

2 teaspoons canola oil

3 cups coarsely chopped fresh broccoli florets

1/3 cup coarsely chopped unsalted cashews

2 teaspoons grated fresh ginger

1 large garlic clove, minced

1/3 cup bottled mango chutney

1/2 teaspoon freshly ground black pepper

4 (10 inch) whole-wheat chapatis or 4 (8 inch) whole-wheat pitas

Raita

1 cup plain low-fat yogurt

1 cucumber, peeled and chopped

2 tomatoes, seeded and very finely chopped

1/2 teaspoon dried coriander

1/2 teaspoon cumin

Pinch cayenne pepper

Salt and pepper

1 Combine all ingredients for the raita in a serving bowl. Cover and refrigerate.

2 Prepare the chapati filling. Cut the chicken into bite-size pieces. Heat the oil in a large skillet over medium-high heat. Add the broccoli, cashews, ginger, and garlic and stir-fry just until the broccoli is crisp-tender, about 4 minutes.

3 Add the chicken, chutney, and pepper to the broccoli mixture. Stir-fry until the chicken is cooked and turns opaque, about 3 minutes more.

4 Meanwhile, coat a nonstick griddle or a medium nonstick skillet with cooking spray and heat until hot. Sprinkle the chapatis with a little water and heat for 2 minutes on each side or until hot. Keep hot.

5 For each chapati, spoon one-fourth of the chicken-broccoli mixture across one end of the chapati, stopping within 1 inch of the edge, then roll it up. (Or stuff into pitas.) Serve the chapatis hot with the raita on the side.

(Some More Ideas) *Chicken-chili enchiladas*: Replace the chicken-broccoli filling with Mexican chicken: Preheat the oven to 350°F. In a large nonstick skillet, heat 1 tablespoon canola oil. Add 1 1/2 pounds uncooked skinless chicken breast strips (4 inches long and 1 inch wide), 1 cup yellow onion strips, and 1 teaspoon each of chili powder, cumin seeds, and coriander. Sauté until the chicken turns opaque, about 5 minutes. Stir in 2 cups each of green bell pepper strips and red bell pepper strips and continue sautéing until the peppers are tender, about 8 minutes more; remove from the heat. Meanwhile, heat 8 (10 inch) flour tortillas instead of chapatis, according to the directions in Step 4. For each enchilada, use 1/8 of the chicken-chili mixture and roll up as in Step 5. Place all 8 enchiladas seam side down in a baking dish, sprinkle with 1 cup reduced-fat shredded cheddar cheese, and bake until piping hot, about 15 minutes. Serve with chunky tomato salsa. Makes 4 servings.

Plus Points

• Broccoli is packed with vitamins. It is an excellent source of the antioxidants beta-carotene and vitamin C. Just 1 cup of cooked broccoli provides over 100% of the Daily Value (DV) for vitamin C and 20% of the DV for vitamin A, folate, and fiber.

• Like other members of the cruciferous family of vegetables (such as cauliflower, Brussels sprouts, cabbage, and kale), broccoli contains a number of different phytochemicals. One of these, indoles, may help to protect against breast cancer by inhibiting the action of the estrogens that trigger the growth of tumors.

photo, page 101

Exchanges

starch 2 carbohydrate 1 1/2 vegetable 2
meat (very lean) 3 fat 1 1/2

Each serving provides calories 525, calories from fat 123, fat 14g, saturated fat 3g, cholesterol 77mg, sodium 486mg, carbohydrate 65g, fiber 5g, sugars 23g, protein 40g. Excellent source of folate, iron, magnesium, niacin, phosphorus, potassium, riboflavin, thiamine, vitamin A, vitamin B6, vitamin C. Good source of calcium, vitamin B12.

chicken and vegetable phyllo rolls

Start with thin sheets of pastry made from a flour-and-water mixture, called phyllo (the Greek word for leaf). Cut the pastry sheets into strips and fill them with a chicken and vegetable filling seasoned with herbs and a little smoked ham. The phyllo rolls are served on a bed of salad greens and topped with a colorful cranberry mustard.

Preparation time **45 minutes**   Baking time **30 minutes**   *Serves 8*

Phyllo Rolls

2 large carrots, peeled and cut into julienne strips

2 cups Savoy cabbage with curly dark green leaves, shredded

3 slivered green onions

1/2 pound ground uncooked chicken breast

1 cup lean cooked smoked ham, minced

1 cup finely chopped yellow onion

2 tablespoons dry plain bread crumbs

2 tablespoons chopped fresh sage leaves

2 teaspoons chopped fresh thyme leaves

1 teaspoon freshly ground black pepper

1/2 teaspoon salt

8 large sheets phyllo pastry (18 x 14 inches)

Butter-flavored cooking spray

2 teaspoons sesame seeds

2 cups mesclun salad greens

Cranberry Mustard

1 cup canned jellied cranberry sauce

2 tablespoons red wine vinegar

1 tablespoon olive oil

1 teaspoon Dijon mustard

Exchanges
starch 1 vegetable 1
meat (lean) 1

1 First, make the filling. Half-fill a medium-size saucepan with water and bring to a boil over high heat. Add the carrots, cabbage, and green onions, then blanch for 1 minute. Transfer to a colander and rinse immediately with cold running water. Pat the vegetables dry with paper towels and place in a large bowl. Mix in the chicken, ham, yellow onion, bread crumbs, sage, thyme, pepper, and salt; set aside.

2 Preheat the oven to 375°F and set out a nonstick baking sheet. On a flat surface, cut the 8 phyllo sheets in half lengthwise, making 16 pieces. Trim each into a thin strip, 15 x 6 inches, and cover quickly, first with plastic wrap then with a damp towel (phyllo dries in a couple of minutes if left uncovered). Work fast!

3 For each phyllo roll, use 2 pastry strips. Spray one pastry strip lightly with butter-flavored spray, then top with a second strip. Repeat with spray. Place 1/8 of the filling across one end of this pastry strip. Roll up the filling inside the pastry, folding in the long sides as you go and making a closed parcel, about 5 inches long and 2 inches in diameter. Place the parcels on a baking sheet, seam side down, and spray again. Repeat, making a total of 8 rolls.

4 Using a serrated knife, make 3 shallow diagonal slashes across the top of each parcel. Spray again. Sprinkle with sesame seeds. Bake until golden, about 30 minutes.

5 Meanwhile, shake all of the cranberry mustard ingredients in a screw-top jar until well blended. Drizzle a little cranberry mustard around the edge of each plate, mound some salad greens in the center, and place a phyllo roll on top.

(**Some More Ideas**) *Greek spinach and chicken phyllo pockets*: Substitute 2 cups slivered fresh spinach leaves for the cabbage. Omit the ham, bread crumbs, and sage. To the vegetables add the chicken, onion, thyme, pepper, and salt, plus 1 cup cooked white rice and 3 tablespoons fresh lemon juice. Cut the 8 phyllo sheets into 16 (6 inch) squares. For each phyllo parcel, spray with butter-flavored cooking spray, cover with a second square, and spray again. Place 1/8 of the filling in a triangular shape, slightly off-center, near one corner. Fold the pastry over the filling to make a triangular parcel, matching up the opposite corner and sealing the sides. Sprinkle with 2 teaspoons poppy seeds instead of the sesame seeds. Bake for 30 minutes as directed and serve on a bed of salad leaves. Omit the cranberry mustard.

Plus Points
• Unlike butter pastry, phyllo is low in fat and calories. One sheet (18 x 14 inches, about 1 ounce) contains 2 grams fat and just 85 calories.

Each serving (one phyllo roll) provides calories 178, calories from fat 29, fat 3g, saturated fat 1g, cholesterol 26mg, sodium 521mg, carbohydrate 23g, fiber 2g, sugars 10g, protein 14g. Excellent source of niacin, vitamin A, vitamin C. Good source of folate, phosphorus, riboflavin, thiamine, vitamin B6.

chicken and vegetable phyllo rolls p100

chicken and broccoli chapatis p99

mexican tostadas p98

chicken fajitas with tomato salsa p97

herbed chicken and apple burgers

This recipe will lighten up your burgers and add new flavor at the same time. First, use ground chicken instead of beef. Then, to boost the fiber and flavor, add grated apples, as well as fresh sage and thyme. Serve the burgers on whole-wheat buns spread with the sweet honey mustard sauce.

Preparation time **20 minutes**   Chilling time **1 hour**   Grilling or broiling time **20 minutes**   *Serves 4*

Burgers

1 pound ground chicken

1 large red onion, finely chopped

1/4 cup plain dry bread crumbs

2 large green apples, such as Granny Smith (for a tart taste) or Golden Delicious (for a sweet taste), peeled and coarsely grated

1 tablespoon chopped fresh sage leaves

1 tablespoon fresh thyme leaves

1/4 teaspoon salt

1/4 teaspoon freshly ground black pepper

To serve

1/4 cup Dijon mustard

1 tablespoon honey

4 whole-wheat hamburger buns, split

3 ounces watercress sprigs, large stalks discarded

1 In a large bowl, place the chicken, onion, bread crumbs, apples, sage, thyme, salt, and pepper. Using your hands, mix the ingredients together until the ingredients are distributed evenly throughout. Wet your hands, then divide the mixture into 4 equal portions and shape each into a burger about 4 inches in diameter and 1 1/2 inches thick. Chill the burgers for 1 hour to firm up the meat and make it easier to hold together while it cooks.

2 Preheat the grill or broiler to high. Place burgers on a rack about 6 inches from the source of heat. Grill or broil the burgers, turning them once, until they are golden brown on both sides and just until they are still juicy but cooked through completely.

3 While the burgers cook, mix the mustard and honey in a small cup. On a flat surface, open the 4 buns with the soft cut sides up. Spread the cut sides of both the tops and bottoms of the buns with the honey mustard. Pile one-fourth of the watercress on the bottom of each bun.

4 When the burgers are ready, transfer a burger to the bottom of each bun, placing it on top of the watercress. Cover with the top of the bun and serve immediately.

(Some More Ideas) *Barbecued chicken burgers*: Add 1/4 cup bottled barbecue sauce (choose the hotness you like) to the chicken mixture (beginning of Step 1). If the mixture is too moist to shape, add an extra tablespoon of bread crumbs. Omit the honey mustard (Step 3), and spread the rolls with a little extra barbecue sauce instead.

Burgers in a skillet: Instead of grilling or broiling the burgers (Step 2), heat 1 tablespoon canola oil in a large skillet over medium-high heat. Add the burgers and cook until brown, about 3 to 4 minutes on each side, turning each burger once. Reduce the heat to medium and cook the burgers until they are cooked through completely, about 12 to 14 minutes more.

Plus Points
• Apples provide good amounts of vitamin C and pectin, a soluble fiber. When you eat apples with their skins still on, you get even more fiber—one-third more, to be exact.
• Ounce for ounce, ground chicken has 48% less fat than lean ground beef.

photo, page 107

Exchanges
starch 2 fruit 1 vegetable 1 meat (very lean) 4

Each serving (one burger) provides calories 364, calories from fat 43, fat 5g, saturated fat 1g, cholesterol 64mg, sodium 872mg, carbohydrate 49g, fiber 6g, sugars 23g, protein 34g. Excellent source of magnesium, niacin, phosphorus, potassium, thiamine, vitamin B6, vitamin C. Good source of calcium, folate, iron, riboflavin, vitamin A.

chicken fingers with spicy mustard dip

Fried chicken fingers are an American favorite. Here chicken breasts are cut into strips and baked in the oven instead of deep-fat frying. The bread-crumb topping becomes crisp in the oven. Serve the chicken fingers with a spicy dip made with reduced-fat sour cream and mustard. Oven-baked potato fries can be prepared as a side dish.

Preparation time **30 minutes**   Chilling time **30 minutes**   Cooking time **15 minutes**   *Serves 6*

Chicken Fingers

1 1/2 pounds boneless, skinless chicken breasts

1/2 teaspoon salt

1/4 teaspoon freshly ground black pepper

1/2 cup all-purpose flour

2 large eggs

2 tablespoons water

2 cups plain dry bread crumbs

1/4 cup whole-grain Dijon mustard

1 large garlic clove, minced

1 tablespoon paprika

Dip

1 cup reduced-fat sour cream

2 tablespoons whole-grain Dijon mustard

2 tablespoons snipped fresh chives

1 Make the spicy dip. Blend the sour cream, mustard, and chives. Spoon into a small serving bowl, cover with plastic wrap, and refrigerate.

2 Prepare the chicken. Cut the chicken lengthwise into strips, about 3 inches long and 1 inch wide, and sprinkle all over with all of the salt and half of the pepper.

3 Place the flour in a zippered plastic bag. In a pie plate, whisk the eggs and water until frothy. In a large, shallow dish, mix the bread crumbs, mustard, garlic, paprika, and the rest of the pepper until blended.

4 Drop the chicken strips, a few at a time, into the bag of flour and shake until they are well coated. Shake off any excess flour. Dip the strips, first into the beaten eggs, then into the bread-crumb mixture, gently pressing the crumbs onto the chicken so they adhere. Arrange the strips on a large nonstick baking sheet and refrigerate for 30 minutes.

5 Meanwhile, preheat the oven to 400°F. Bake the chicken strips until they are golden brown and crisp, about 15 minutes, turning once or twice. Serve hot or at room temperature with the chilled mustard dip.

(Some More Ideas) *Chicken fingers Indian style*: For the spicy dip, use only 1 tablespoon Dijon mustard and stir in 1 teaspoon curry powder (Step 1). In the bread-crumb mixture, omit the mustard (Step 3). Add 2 teaspoons ground coriander, 1 teaspoon ground cumin, 1/2 teaspoon ground cardamom, and 1/2 teaspoon ground cinnamon to the crumbs.

Oven potato fries: Preheat the oven to 375°F. Peel 2 pounds russet baking potatoes and cut into thick sticks, about 4 inches long and 1 inch thick. Soak in ice water for 15 minutes, then dry thoroughly on paper towels. Brush with 2 teaspoons olive oil. Bake in a single layer on a nonstick baking sheet for 1 hour, turning 2 or 3 times. Season with salt, to taste.

Oven potato chips: Follow directions for potato fries (above), except cut potatoes crosswise into thin slices, 1/4 inch thick. Bake at 400°F for 25 to 30 minutes, tossing frequently.

Plus Points

• One tablespoon of reduced-fat sour cream has 1 gram of fat and 20 calories compared with 3 grams of fat and 30 calories for regular.

photo, page 107

Exchanges

starch 2 1/2 meat (very lean) 4
fat 1

Each serving provides calories 394, calories from fat 85, fat 9g, saturated fat 3g, cholesterol 148mg, sodium 980mg, carbohydrate 39g, fiber 1g, sugars 5g, protein 38g. Excellent source of iron, niacin, phosphorus, riboflavin, thiamine, vitamin B6. Good source of calcium, folate, magnesium, potassium, vitamin A, vitamin B12.

spicy drumsticks with creole rice

These chicken drumsticks, coated in a mixture of dried herbs and spices, can be cooked under the grill in next to no time. Serve the drumsticks with steamed green vegetables and a moderate portion of the Creole red beans and rice.

Preparation and cooking time **30 minutes**   *Serves 4*

Drumsticks

1 tablespoon flour
1 teaspoon paprika
1 teaspoon ground black pepper
1 teaspoon garlic powder
1 teaspoon crushed red pepper
1 teaspoon dried thyme
8 chicken drumsticks, skinned (about 1 pound)
1 tablespoon olive oil
Salt and pepper

Rice

1 teaspoon olive oil
1 onion, chopped
1 red bell pepper, seeded and diced
2 celery stalks, diced
1 cup long-grain rice
2 cups low-sodium vegetable broth
1 cup canned red kidney beans, drained and rinsed
2 tablespoons chopped parsley

Garnish

Sprigs of fresh parsley

1 Preheat a grill to medium heat. Put the flour, paprika, pepper, garlic, red pepper, thyme, and a pinch of salt in a plastic zippered bag and shake to mix. Make 2 slashes in each chicken drumstick and rub with the olive oil. Toss them one at a time in the bag to coat with the spice mixture. Shake off any excess mixture and place the chicken on the grill rack. Grill until golden and cooked through, about 20 to 25 minutes, turning often.

2 Meanwhile, make Creole rice. Heat the oil in a large saucepan, add the onion, pepper, and celery, and cook until softened, about 2 minutes. Stir in the rice, then add the broth and kidney beans. Bring to a boil. Cover, and simmer gently until all the broth has been absorbed and the rice is tender, about 15 to 20 minutes.

3 Stir the chopped parsley into the rice and season with salt and pepper to taste. Spoon the rice onto 4 plates and place 2 drumsticks on top of each portion. Serve hot, garnished with sprigs of parsley.

(Some More Ideas) *Sticky chili drumsticks*: Mix 2 tablespoons low-sodium ketchup with 1 tablespoon light soy sauce and 2 tablespoons sweet chili sauce or paste. Rub onto the chicken drumsticks and grill as in the main recipe. Meanwhile, place 1 cup bulgur wheat in a heatproof bowl, pour over enough boiling water to cover, and soak for 15 to 20 minutes. Squeeze out any excess water, then mix with 1 cup canned red kidney beans, drained and rinsed; 1 small diced cucumber; 2 chopped tomatoes; 2 tablespoons chopped fresh mint; and 2 tablespoons chopped parsley. Add 1 tablespoon lemon juice and 1 tablespoon olive oil and season to taste. Toss to mix. Serve with the sticky chili drumsticks.

Plus Points

• In diabetes it is important to maintain an appropriate blood pressure level. Celery contains a compound called phthalide, which is believed to help lower high blood pressure.
• Canned and dried beans and legumes are very high in fiber, containing approximately 8 grams per 1/2 cup serving. They are also a low-fat protein source.

Exchanges
starch 3 1/2 vegetable 1
meat (lean) 2 fat 1/2

Each serving provides calories 444, calories from fat 88, fat 10g, saturated fat 2g, cholesterol 69mg, sodium 659mg, carbohydrate 58g, fiber 6g, sugars 6g, protein 29g. Excellent source of folate, iron, niacin, phosphorus, potassium, riboflavin, thiamine, vitamin A, vitamin B6, vitamin C. Good source of magnesium, zinc.

spicy drumsticks with creole rice p106

chicken and sweet potato salad
with pineapple salsa p104

herbed chicken and
apple burgers p102

chicken fingers with
spicy mustard dip p103

chicken and sausage jambalaya

The name of the famous Cajun-Creole dish probably comes from the French word *jambon* (ham), which often appeared in the early jambalayas in the late 19th century. Here ham teams up with chicken, sausage, vegetables, and traditional Cajun seasonings. Rice is added to the dish as it simmers to create a complete meal.

Preparation time **30 minutes**   Cooking time **50 minutes**   *Serves 10*

1 pound chorizo sausage
12 ounces cooked smoked ham
1 pound boneless, skinless chicken breasts
4 teaspoons Cajun seasoning
2 large yellow onions
2 large green bell peppers
3 celery stalks
2 tablespoons canola oil
2 large garlic cloves, minced
3 tablespoons all-purpose flour
1 tablespoon chopped fresh sage leaves
1 tablespoon chopped fresh thyme leaves
2 large bay leaves
2 cups uncooked long-grain white rice
3 cups low-fat, reduced-sodium chicken broth
1 can (14 ounces) whole tomatoes in juice
Hot pepper sauce
6 scallions, trimmed and sliced
1/2 cup chopped parsley

1 Slice the chorizo 1/4 inch thick and dice the ham. Cut the chicken into bite-size pieces and coat all sides of the chicken with 2 teaspoons of the Cajun seasoning. Coarsely chop the yellow onions. Remove the stems, membranes, and seeds from the bell peppers and coarsely chop them. Thinly slice the celery.

2 In a 6-quart Dutch oven or saucepot, heat 1 tablespoon oil over medium-high heat. Add the chorizo and ham and sauté for 3 minutes. Add the chicken and sauté until the chicken is brown on all sides, about 5 minutes more. Using a slotted spoon, transfer the mixture to a plate and keep warm.

3 Add the remaining oil to the hot Dutch oven. Stir in the onions, peppers, celery, and garlic, and sauté until the vegetables soften, about 5 minutes. Stir in the flour, sage, thyme, bay leaves, and the remaining Cajun seasoning; cook and stir constantly until the flour browns, about 5 minutes. Add the rice and sauté 2 minutes more. Return the chicken mixture, and any juices that have collected, to the pan.

4 Pour in the broth and the tomatoes with their juice. Bring to a full boil. Lower the heat to medium-low, cover, and simmer until the rice has absorbed almost all the liquid. Discard the bay leaves and season to taste with the hot pepper sauce. Top with the scallions and parsley.

(Some More Ideas) Smoked turkey sausage can be substituted for the chorizo, making the recipe lower in fat.

If your grocer does not have ready-made Cajun seasoning, use a mixture of 1 tablespoon paprika and 1 teaspoon cayenne pepper.

Bayou jambalaya: Omit the chorizo sausage. At the beginning, shell and devein 1 1/2 pounds large shrimp; cook in boiling water just until they turn opaque, about 3 minutes. Transfer the shrimp to a colander and rinse with cold water; set aside. Add the shrimp to the jambalaya during the last 5 minutes of cooking.

Plus Points

• This recipe for jambalaya is a hearty one-pot meal. One serving contains 2 starch exchanges from the rice, 3 lean meat exchanges, 2 vegetable exchanges, and 1 fat exchange. When cooking for people with diabetes it is important to look at the exchange breakdown to determine if a meal is well balanced.

• Scallions are actually immature onions and are commonly referred to as "green onions." They impart wonderful flavor to low-fat meals and work nicely sprinkled on top of a dish as a garnish.

photo, page 113

Exchanges

starch 2   vegetable 2
meat (lean) 3   fat 1

Each serving provides calories 413, calories from fat 129, fat 14g, saturated fat 4g, cholesterol 65mg, sodium 1297mg, carbohydrate 43g, fiber 3g, sugars 6g, protein 28g. Excellent source of ion, niacin, phosphorus, potassium, riboflavin, thiamine, vitamin B6, vitamin C. Good source of folate, magnesium, vitamin B12. Flag: High in sodium.

indian-style tandoori grilled chicken breasts

In India, the tandoor oven is a barrel-shaped clay oven, heated by hot coals to such a high temperature that it cooks meats in seconds. At home, a grill works fine too. Here breasts of chicken are seasoned with Indian spices from curry powder and garam masala. Serve raita, the creamy yogurt-vegetable salad, alongside.

Preparation time **30 minutes**   Marinating time **30 minutes or overnight**   Cooking time **15 minutes**   *Serves 6*

6 (5 ounce) boneless, skinless chicken breast halves
Canola oil for brushing grill

Marinade

1 cup plain low-fat yogurt
2 tablespoons tomato paste
1 tablespoon peeled and grated ginger
1 tablespoon curry powder
2 teaspoons garam masala
1 large garlic clove, minced

Raita

1 large cucumber
1 1/2 cups plain low-fat yogurt
1 large tomato, finely chopped
1 teaspoon ground coriander
1 teaspoon ground cumin
Pinch cayenne pepper
Pinch salt

Garnish

2 large lemons or limes, cut in wedges
Sprigs of fresh coriander

1 To make the marinade, process all of the marinade ingredients in a food processor or blender until blended, about 30 seconds. Or simply whisk together all of the ingredients in a small bowl. Transfer to a large, shallow bowl that is big enough to hold the chicken breasts in a single layer.

2 Score 2 slits on each side of the chicken breasts. Place them in the marinade, turning to coat and rubbing the marinade into the slits. Cover with plastic wrap and let marinate in the refrigerator for 30 minutes (or, if you have time, marinate overnight).

3 Meanwhile, make the raita. Cut the cucumber in half lengthwise (do not peel) and remove the seeds with a spoon. Grate the cucumber into a medium bowl and squeeze out as much juice as possible with your hands (discard the juice). Add the remaining ingredients for the raita and mix well; transfer to a serving bowl and keep cold in the refrigerator.

4 To cook the chicken, preheat the grill or broiler to high. Remove the chicken from the marinade. Discard the marinade. Brush the grill rack with oil, then place the chicken breasts on top. Grill or broil 6 inches from the heat, turning several times, until the juices of the chicken run clear when a breast is pierced with a fork, about 12 minutes (the outsides of the chicken breasts may look slightly charred).

5 Transfer the chicken breasts to a serving plate. Decorate with the lemon or lime wedges and the sprigs of coriander. Serve with the raita in a separate serving dish, on the side.

(Some More Ideas) *Tandoori chicken kebabs*: First, cut the chicken breasts into 1 1/4-inch cubes, then place them in the marinade. Soak 8 bamboo skewers in cold water. Cut 1 large zucchini (do not peel) in circles, 1 inch thick. Cut 1 large red bell pepper and 1 large yellow bell pepper into 1 1/4-inch cubes. Parboil the vegetables in boiling water just until crisp-tender, about 3 minutes. Alternately thread the chicken and vegetables on the 8 skewers. Grill or broil the kebabs for only 8 to 10 minutes.

Plus Points

• The marinade used in this recipe does not contain oil, making it very low in fat. The acidity from the yogurt tenderizes the chicken in as little as 30 minutes.

• The yogurt-based raita sauce is also very low in fat and contributes a cooling effect to contrast with the spicy marinated chicken.

• Using aromatic ingredients such as fresh herbs, ginger, and garlic creates a healthy and highly flavorful dish.

photo, page 113

Exchanges

carbohydrate 1/2	meat (very lean) 5	fat 1/2

Each serving provides calories 236, calories from fat 46, fat 5g, saturated fat 2g, cholesterol 92mg, sodium 139mg, carbohydrate 10g, fiber 1g, sugars 8g, protein 37g. Excellent source of niacin, phosphorus, vitamin B6. Good source of calcium, magnesium, potassium, riboflavin, thiamine, vitamin B12, vitamin C.

chicken and fresh corn chowder

Here's a chowder that tastes rich and creamy, but is made with low-fat milk instead of cream. Use fresh corn and flavor with fresh tarragon and black pepper. Crumbled turkey bacon can be used as a garnish instead of incorporating it into the soup. Serve with a crisp vegetable salad.

Preparation time **30 minutes**   Cooking time **25 minutes**   *Serves 6*

Chowder

4 large ears yellow corn on the cob

2 teaspoons canola oil

1 large onion, finely chopped

2 large potatoes, peeled and cut into 1/2-inch chunks

2 1/2 cups low-fat, reduced-sodium chicken broth

2 cups 1% milk

1 pound cooked boneless, skinless chicken breasts, cut into bite-size pieces

2 teaspoons chopped fresh tarragon or 1/2 teaspoon dried

1/4 teaspoon freshly ground black pepper

Garnish

4 slices turkey bacon

Fresh tarragon leaves

1 Remove the green husks and all the silk from the corn. Stand each cob on the wide stem end on a chopping board, at an angle. Cut the corn kernels off the cob with a serrated knife (you need 2 cups kernels). Set aside.

2 Heat the oil in a large saucepan over medium-high heat. Add the onion and sauté until tender, but not brown, about 5 minutes. Stir in the potatoes and corn kernels and cook 5 minutes, stirring frequently. Pour in the chicken broth and bring to a boil. Lower the heat to medium-low and simmer gently until the potatoes are tender, but not breaking apart, about 5 minutes.

3 Stir in the milk, one-third of the chicken, the chopped tarragon, and pepper. Cook, stirring gently, until hot, about 3 minutes.

4 Pour one-third of the mixture into a food processor or blender and blend to a coarse texture, not to a puree. Return to the pan. Stir in the rest of the chicken and heat the chowder until hot.

5 In a medium skillet, cook the bacon over medium-high heat until golden brown and crisp. Drain on paper towels, then crumble. Ladle the chowder into 4 bowls. Sprinkle each bowl with 1/4 of the bacon and a few tarragon leaves. Serve steaming hot.

(Some More Ideas) *Chicken and mushroom chowder*: After preparing the corn, slice 8 ounces trimmed white mushrooms (you need 3 cups). In a large skillet, sauté the mushrooms in 2 teaspoons unsalted butter over medium-high heat for 5 minutes; add 2 tablespoons Madeira wine and continue cooking until most of the liquid evaporates. Add mushrooms with the potatoes and corn.

Wintertime chowder: When fresh corn is not in the market, substitute 10 ounces frozen corn kernels for the corn on the cob. Omit Step 1. After sautéing potatoes, add frozen kernels (no need to thaw) with the chicken broth.

Plus Points

• Corn contains some protein, but it is an incomplete protein because it lacks two essential amino acids (tryptophan and lysine). When eaten with beans or other legumes, it provides a complete protein.

• Turkey bacon is lower in fat than pork bacon and can be substituted in any recipe. The sodium content of the turkey bacon is still high, however, so it should be used in moderation in your diet.

photo, page 113

Exchanges

starch 2 1/2 milk (fat-free) 1/2
meat (very lean) 3 fat 1/2

Each serving provides calories 357, calories from fat 68, fat 8g, saturated fat 2g, cholesterol 74mg, sodium 427mg, carbohydrate 42g, fiber 5g, sugars 9g, protein 33g. Excellent source of magnesium, niacin, phosphorus, potassium, riboflavin, thiamine, vitamin B6, vitamin C. Good source of calcium, folate, iron, vitamin B12.

greek-style lemon chicken soup

This delicate yet rich-tasting soup is packed with good things, and makes a warming and sustaining main course. Chicken breasts are poached with vegetables and then rice is cooked in the flavorful broth. At the last minute, the soup is enriched with eggs and fresh lemon juice in traditional Greek fashion.

Preparation time **15 minutes**   Cooking time **30 minutes**   *Serves 4*

1 Place the chicken breasts, onion, celery, carrot, black peppercorns, lemon zest, and dill or parsley into a large saucepan. Add 4 cups water and bring to a boil over medium heat, skimming off any foam that rises to the surface. Reduce the heat, and half-cover the pan with a lid, so the water just bubbles gently. Simmer until the chicken is cooked through, about 15 minutes.

2 Remove the chicken from the pan with a slotted spoon and set aside. Strain the broth through a large sieve into a clean pan, discarding the vegetables and flavorings.

3 Reheat the broth until boiling, then stir in the rice. Simmer gently until the rice is almost tender, about 8 to 10 minutes. Meanwhile, cut or tear the chicken into thin shreds, and mix the lemon juice with the beaten eggs.

4 Add the shredded chicken to the soup. Heat over medium heat until the soup almost starts to boil again. Remove the pan from the heat, and pour in the lemon juice mixture, stirring constantly. Season lightly with salt and pepper. Serve immediately, garnished with sprigs of dill or parsley.

Soup

12 ounces boneless, skinless chicken breasts
1 large onion, thinly sliced
2 celery stalks, chopped
1 large carrot, thinly sliced
6 black peppercorns
Strip of lemon zest
1 small bunch fresh dill or flat-leaf parsley
1/2 cup long-grain white rice
Juice of 1 lemon
2 eggs, beaten
Salt and pepper

Garnish

Sprigs of fresh dill or flat-leaf parsley

Exchanges
starch 1 1/2 meat (very lean) 3

(Some More Ideas) Any assortment of vegetables can be added to the soup in addition to the carrot, onion, and celery. Try adding sliced zucchini, summer squash, and green peas.

To increase the iron content of the soup, add 2 cups of washed, trimmed spinach along with the chicken in Step 4.

Plus Points
• The combination of rice, lean chicken, and vegetables keeps this soup low in fat, while providing good amounts of protein and carbohydrate.
• Although eggs contain cholesterol, it is now generally agreed that, for most people, eating them in moderation has little effect on blood cholesterol levels. Rather, it is the intake of saturated fat, as well as other factors, that can increase blood cholesterol. As eggs are an excellent source of protein, they can make a valuable contribution to a healthy diet.

Each serving provides calories 225, calories from fat 42, fat 5g, saturated fat 2g, cholesterol 157mg, sodium 78mg, carbohydrate 20g, fiber 0g, sugars 1g, protein 24g. Excellent source of niacin. Good source of iron, phosphorus, riboflavin, thiamine, vitamin B6, vitamin B12.

french-style chicken

In the French countryside, braised meats are traditionally simmered in robust red Burgundy wine, usually with mushrooms, onions, and bacon. For this healthier version, chicken breasts are substituted for the whole chicken and turkey bacon is used. You save on both fat and calories, without sacrificing flavor. Serve with sautéed new potatoes and steamed broccoli.

Preparation time **30 minutes** Cooking time **about 1 hour** *Serves 6*

Chicken

2 pounds (about 16) small white onions

6 slices lean turkey bacon

1 tablespoon garlic-flavored olive oil

2 pounds boneless, skinless chicken breasts

1 teaspoon salt

1 teaspoon black pepper

1/2 pound white mushrooms

12 sprigs parsley, 5 inches long

8 sprigs fresh thyme, 5 inches long

1 large bay leaf

2 cups low-fat, reduced-sodium chicken broth

1 1/2 cups full-bodied red Burgundy wine

2 cups bite-size peeled carrot chunks

1 teaspoon sugar

2 tablespoons cornstarch

1/4 cup cold water

Garnish

1/2 cup minced fresh parsley

1 Place the onions in a heatproof bowl. Pour boiling water over to cover, let stand about 1 minute, transfer to a colander, and cool under cold running water. Peel, cut any large ones in half lengthwise, and set aside.

2 Cut the bacon crosswise, on a slant, into thin strips, 1/4 inch wide. In a 6-quart flameproof Dutch oven or casserole, heat 1 tablespoon of the oil over medium-high heat. Add the onions and bacon and stir until the onions are golden brown and the bacon is crispy, about 5 minutes. Using a slotted spoon, transfer the mixture to a platter lined with paper towels.

3 Cut the chicken breasts into fillets and season with half of the salt and pepper. Drizzle 1 more tablespoon of the oil into the Dutch oven; add the chicken. Sauté until golden brown all over, turning each piece one time, about 7 minutes. Using the slotted spoon, transfer to the plate with the bacon and onions.

4 Wash the mushrooms and quarter them. Heat the remaining oil in the Dutch oven, add the mushrooms, and sprinkle with the rest of the salt and pepper. Sauté until golden brown, about 5 minutes.

5 Return the chicken, onions, and bacon to the Dutch oven with the mushrooms and stir to distribute the ingredients. Add the parsley, thyme, and bay leaf. Pour in the stock and wine.

6 Increase the heat to high, bring to a boil, and add the carrots. Lower the heat to medium-low, cover, and simmer until the carrots are tender and the juices of the chicken run clear when a breast is pierced with a fork, about 35 minutes. Discard the bay leaf. Using a slotted spoon, arrange all of the ingredients on a serving platter.

7 Increase the heat to high, add the sugar to the pan juices, and boil, uncovered, until reduced to about 2 cups. In a cup, dissolve the cornstarch in the water; whisk into the pan juices. Return to a boil and cook until the gravy thickens, about 2 minutes. Spoon the sauce over the chicken and vegetables and sprinkle with the parsley.

Plus Points

• Ounce for ounce, cooked chicken breast without its skin has 16% fewer calories and 54% less fat than cooked chicken breast with its skin. Cooking the chicken with the skin on keeps the moisture in, and the skin can be easily removed before serving.

Exchanges
vegetable 4 meat (lean) 4

Each serving provides calories 341, calories from fat 82, fat 9g, saturated fat 2g, cholesterol 102mg, sodium 830mg, carbohydrate 22g, fiber 5g, sugars 13g, protein 39g. Excellent source of niacin, phosphorus, potassium, riboflavin, vitamin A, vitamin B6, vitamin C. Good source of folate, iron, magnesium, thiamine.

chicken and fresh corn chowder *p110*

french-style chicken *p112*

indian-style tandoori grilled chicken breasts *p109*

chicken and sausage jambalaya *p108*

chicken livers sautéed with sage

Liver is loaded with iron, making it a highly nutritious meat. Here chicken livers are quickly sautéed with fresh mushrooms. The dish is sparked up with a splash of balsamic vinegar, shreds of fresh sage leaves, and a little dry sherry. Spoon the livers over a piece of toasted French bread for a fast, but unique, evening meal.

Preparation time **25 minutes**   Cooking time **20 minutes**   *Serves 4*

Liver

1 tablespoon unsalted butter

1 tablespoon extra-virgin olive oil

4 slices French bread, 1 inch thick

1 small red onion, finely chopped

2 garlic cloves, minced

1 pound chicken livers, well trimmed

1/2 pound white mushrooms, quartered

3 tablespoons balsamic vinegar

2 tablespoons shredded fresh sage leaves

1/4 teaspoon salt

1/4 teaspoon freshly ground black pepper

2 tablespoons dry sherry

Garnish

Sprigs of fresh sage

1 Preheat the oven to 350°F. In a large skillet, melt the butter and heat the oil over medium heat; remove the skillet from the heat. Brush both sides of the bread slices with about half the butter-oil mixture. Place on a baking sheet. Bake until golden brown, about 10 minutes, turning the bread slices over about halfway through.

2 Meanwhile, reheat the remaining butter-oil mixture over medium-high heat in the same skillet. Add the onion and garlic and sauté until softened, about 5 minutes.

3 Add the chicken livers and sauté for 3 minutes. Add the mushrooms and continue sautéing until both the livers and the mushrooms are brown, about 5 minutes more (the livers may break up a little as they cook).

4 Add the vinegar, sage, salt, and pepper to the liver mixture in the skillet. Reduce the heat to medium-low and cook until the livers are just cooked through, about 3 minutes more. Stir in the sherry and remove from the heat.

5 Place a slice of bread on each of 4 individual plates. Spoon the chicken livers on top and decorate with sprigs of fresh sage.

(Some More Ideas) *Sautéed chicken livers over homemade mashed potatoes*: Instead of toasting French bread, mash 2 medium cooked russet potatoes with 1 tablespoon unsalted butter and 1/2 cup fat-free milk, adding a little more milk if necessary to make the potatoes extra fluffy. Fold in 2 tablespoons minced chives. Spoon the chicken livers on top of the potatoes.

Chicken livers Provençal: Substitute 1/4 cup dry red wine for the balsamic vinegar and 1 teaspoon dried herbes de Provence for the slivered sage leaves. Serve with a mixture of cooked long-grain and wild rice.

Sautéed chicken livers with fresh marjoram: Substitute 3 tablespoons chopped fresh marjoram leaves for the chopped sage. Garnish with sprigs of fresh marjoram.

Plus Points

• Like all liver, chicken livers are a rich source of iron, which helps to prevent anemia. It is also high in protein and vitamin A.

• Garlic (along with leeks, onions, and chives) contains allicin, which reduces blood cholesterol levels. It also lowers blood pressure, possibly reducing the risk of heart attacks and strokes. Garlic contains other compounds that may reduce the risk of colon cancer.

photo, page 117

Exchanges
starch 1 1/2   vegetable 1
meat (lean) 2   fat 1

Each serving provides calories 295, calories from fat 94, fat 10g, saturated fat 2g, cholesterol 466mg, sodium 396mg, carbohydrate 26g, fiber 2g, sugars 5g, protein 23g. Excellent source of folate, iron, niacin, phosphorus, riboflavin, thiamine, vitamin A, vitamin B6, vitamin B12, vitamin C. Good source of potassium.

chicken marsala with fennel

From the Sicilian city of Marsala comes this famous fortified wine with a deep amber color. Choose the dry superior type for this dish. Begin with your favorite parts of the chicken, then sauté with leeks, fennel, green peas, and Marsala. Another day, try substituting tomatoes and red bell peppers for the fennel.

Preparation time **30 minutes**   Cooking time **1 hour**   *Serves 10*

4 pounds chicken parts on the bone (breasts, legs, and thighs)
1/4 cup all-purpose flour
1/2 teaspoon freshly ground black pepper
1/4 teaspoon salt
2 tablespoons olive oil
1 large leek or 2 extra-large yellow onions
2 tablespoons slivered basil leaves
1 teaspoon fennel seeds
1 cup dry Marsala wine
2 cups low-fat reduced-sodium chicken broth
2 large fennel bulbs, trimmed and cut into bite-size chunks
2 cups fresh or frozen peas
1 large lemon
1 tablespoon cornstarch
1/4 cup finely chopped parsley

1 Remove the skin from the chicken. Shake the flour and half the pepper and salt in a zippered plastic bag. Add the chicken, a few pieces at a time, seal, and shake until well coated.

2 In a large skillet or sauté pan, heat 1 tablespoon of the oil over medium-high heat. Add the leek, basil, and fennel seeds and sauté until the leek softens, 5 minutes. Using a slotted spoon, transfer the leek mixture to a large plate and set aside.

3 Add the remaining oil to the skillet and sauté the chicken until golden brown all over, about 7 minutes. Transfer the chicken to the plate with the leek mixture and keep warm.

4 Pour 1/2 cup of the Marsala into the hot skillet and let it simmer until it reduces to about half. Stir in the stock and bring to a simmer. Return the leek mixture and pieces of dark chicken meat to the skillet (wait to add the breasts, as they can overcook). Stir in the fennel.

5 Reduce the heat to medium-low, cover, and simmer the chicken mixture for 15 minutes. Add the chicken breasts, cover, and simmer 10 minutes more. Then stir in the peas and continue to cook until the juices of the chicken run clear when a thigh is pierced with a fork, about 5 minutes more. Using a slotted spoon, transfer the chicken and the vegetables to a serving platter and keep warm.

6 Remove several strips of lemon zest from the lemon and set aside. Squeeze the juice into the skillet. In a cup, dissolve the cornstarch in the remaining 1/2 cup Marsala, whisk into the pan juices, and boil until the sauce thickens, about 2 minutes. Spoon the sauce over the chicken and vegetables. Sprinkle with the lemon zest and parsley and serve immediately.

(Some More Ideas)   *Chicken Italiano*: Sauté 2 cups red bell pepper strips, 1/2 inch thick, with the leek and basil; omit the fennel seeds. Add 2 cups tomato wedges with the peas. Substitute 1/2 cup additional slivered basil leaves for the parsley.

Chicken breast Marsala: Substitute 1 1/2 pounds boneless, skinless chicken breasts for the chicken parts. Cook the breasts for only 10 minutes, then add the peas and cook 5 minutes more.

Plus Points

• Fennel, a member of the parsley plant family, is very high in fiber and low in calories. It is also a good source of vitamin C and potassium.
• The dark meat of chicken contains 80% more vitamin A and almost 50% more zinc than the llight meat.

photo, page 117

Exchanges
starch 1/2 vegetable 2
meat (lean) 4

Each serving provides calories 311, calories from fat 87, fat 10g, saturated fat 2g, cholesterol 90mg, sodium 311mg, carbohydrate 18g, fiber 5g, sugars 5g, protein 33g. Excellent source of niacin, phosphorus, potassium, riboflavin, vitamin B6, vitamin C. Good source of folate, iron, magnesium, thiamine.

roasted herb and garlic chicken

In this recipe, a reduced-fat cream cheese and fresh herb seasoning paste is pushed underneath the skin to keep the meat moist. For more flavor, a large fresh lemon is stuffed in the cavity of the bird and dry white wine is used for basting. The skin of the chicken is removed and slices of the moist meat are served with a lovely gravy made from the pan drippings.

Preparation time **30 minutes**   Roasting time **2 hours**   *Serves 8*

Chicken

1 whole roasting chicken (about 5 pounds)

1 teaspoon freshly ground black pepper

1 teaspoon salt

2 teaspoons grated lemon zest

1 large lemon

1 cup fresh cilantro leaves

1 cup fresh parsley

2 large garlic cloves, peeled

1/2 cup reduced-fat cream cheese (Neufchâtel)

3 tablespoons reduced-fat sour cream

1 cup dry white wine

1 cup low-fat, reduced-sodium chicken broth

2 tablespoons cornstarch

1/4 cup cold water

Garnish

Lemon slices

Sprigs of fresh cilantro and parsley

1 Preheat the oven to 425°F and set out a roasting pan and rack. Wash the chicken inside and out with cold running water; discard the giblets and neck. Sprinkle the large cavity with half the pepper and salt. Grate the zest from the lemon and sprinkle 1 teaspoon zest into the cavity. Cut the lemon in half. Holding the chicken on a slant, squeeze the lemon juice inside the cavity. Stuff the 2 lemon halves inside.

2 Place the chicken breast side up. Starting at the neck end, ease your fingers gently under the skin to loosen the skin over the breasts and thighs (be careful not to tear the skin).

3 In a food processor or blender, process the cilantro, parsley, and garlic until finely chopped. Add the cream cheese and sour cream, and the remaining pepper, salt, and lemon zest; process a few seconds more to mix. Push the herb cheese under the skin, easing it along so that it covers the breasts and thighs evenly in a thin layer.

4 Truss the chicken and insert a roasting thermometer in its thigh, then place on the rack in the pan. Pour the wine over the chicken and roast at 425°F for 30 minutes. Lower the oven temperature to 350°F and continue roasting the chicken, without covering, basting frequently with the pan juices, until the thermometer registers 180°F and the juices of the chicken run clear when a thigh is pierced with a fork, about 1 1/2 hours.

5 Carefully lift the chicken in the roasting pan, tilting it so the juices run out of the cavity into the pan; let it stand on a carving board 10 minutes.

6 Meanwhile, pour the pan drippings into a heatproof measuring cup and skim off the fat. Add enough chicken stock to make 2 cups liquid and pour back into the roasting pan. In a cup, dissolve the cornstarch in the water and whisk into the drippings. Bring to a boil over high heat, scraping up the browned bits from the bottom of the pan. Boil until the gravy thickens, about 2 minutes.

7 Carve the chicken. Serve skinless slices. Decorate with lemon slices and sprigs of coriander and parsley. Serve with the pan gravy.

(**Some More Ideas**) *Roasted chicken with wild-rice stuffing*: Cook a 6-ounce package of long-grain white and wild-rice mix, according to package directions; toss in 1/2 cup toasted chopped pecans. Then, prepare the chicken, substituting orange zest and juice for the lemon zest and juice; discard the orange halves. Stuff the cavity with the cooked rice mixture. Prepare and roast the chicken as in Steps 2 through 7.

Exchanges

meat (lean) 5 fat 1 1/2

Each serving provides calories 354, calories from fat 191, fat 21g, saturated fat 7g, cholesterol 112mg, sodium 521mg, carbohydrate 4g, fiber 0g, sugars 1g, protein 34g. Excellent source of niacin, phosphorus, vitamin B6, vitamin C. Good source of iron, potassium, riboflavin, vitamin A, zinc.

chicken livers sautéed
with sage *p114*

roasted herb and
garlic chicken *p116*

turkey, chestnut, and
barley soup *p118*

chicken marsala with fennel *p115*

turkey, chestnut, and barley soup

One of the best parts of roasting a turkey is making a big pot of soup from the rest of the bird. If you're not roasting a bird, use low-sodium canned chicken broth instead of the homemade stock. Add winter vegetables and chestnuts for a satisfying, healthy meal.

Preparation time **45 minutes**   Cooking time **2 hours**   *Serves 8*

Soup

2 pounds cooked turkey breast (boneless)

3 large carrots, peeled and chopped

4 large turnips, peeled and chopped

4 large celery stalks, chopped

6 ounces pearl onions, peeled

1 cup pearl barley

8 ounces Brussels sprouts, halved or chopped

1 cup coarsely chopped chestnuts

1/4 cup chopped fresh parsley

Stock

1 turkey carcass (from at least a 12-pound bird) or 5 pounds turkey parts, on bone

1 large yellow onion, peeled and quartered

2 large celery stalks, coarsely chopped

10 sprigs each fresh parsley and thyme

1 large bay leaf

12 black peppercorns

1 teaspoon salt

1 Begin by making the stock. Break up the turkey carcass, discarding any skin, and place in an 8-quart stockpot. Add enough cold water to cover (about 12 cups), and bring to a boil over high heat; skim off any foam with a slotted spoon. Add the remaining ingredients for the stock and return to a full boil.

2 Lower the heat and simmer the stock gently, uncovered, for 1 1/2 hours. Strain and discard the bones and vegetables (you need 9 cups stock). Skim off any fat and return the stock to the stockpot.

3 To make the soup, return the stock to a boil. Remove the skin from the turkey breast and cut the turkey into bite-size pieces (you need 6 cups). Add the turkey to the stockpot, along with the carrots, turnips, celery, onions, and barley. Simmer the soup, uncovered, until the barley is tender, about 30 minutes.

4 Add the sprouts and chestnuts and simmer just until the sprouts are crisp-tender, about 5 minutes. Sprinkle with the parsley and serve steaming hot.

(Some More Ideas) *In-a-hurry turkey soup*: Substitute 9 cups canned low-sodium chicken broth for the homemade turkey stock. Pour the broth into the stockpot and bring to a boil over high heat. Proceed by adding and cooking the vegetables.

Vegetable garden turkey soup: Substitute 1 cup uncooked white rice for the barley. Omit the sprouts and chestnuts; add 2 cups fresh or frozen green peas and 1 cup chopped tomatoes. Simmer 10 minutes more if using fresh peas (only 5 minutes more for frozen peas).

Turkey noodle soup: Omit the barley, sprouts, and chestnuts. Decrease the cooking time from 30 minutes to 15 minutes. Add 1 cup uncooked angel hair pasta and 1 cup chopped red bell pepper. Return to a boil and cook until pasta is tender, about 3 to 5 minutes. Sprinkle with the parsley, then top with 1/4 cup chopped dry roasted peanuts.

Plus Points

• Barley is believed to be the world's oldest cultivated grain. It is low in fat and rich in carbohydrates. Like many other cereals, it is also a good source of B vitamins, which are essential for a healthy nervous system and helping the body transform food into energy. Pearl barley has had the outer husk and the bran removed and has been steamed and polished.

photo, page 117

Exchanges
starch 1 1/2 vegetable 2
meat (very lean) 4

Each serving provides calories 302, calories from fat 16, fat 2g, saturated fat 0g, cholesterol 95mg, sodium 347mg, carbohydrate 33g, fiber 6g, sugars 8g, protein 39g. Excellent source of niacin, phosphorus, potassium, vitamin A, vitamin B6, vitamin C. Good source of folate, iron, magnesium, riboflavin, thiamine.

turkey with lemon couscous

Frozen turkeys, and often fresh ones too, are available year-round. The smaller 10- to 12-pound turkey hens are exceptionally juicy and tender—ideal for serving ten people. For this meal, the spiced couscous is served in lemon halves for an interesting and colorful presentation.

Preparation time **30 minutes**   Roasting time **3 1/2 hours**   *Serves 10*

Turkey

1 (10–12 pounds) whole turkey, fresh or frozen and thawed
1 teaspoon salt
1 teaspoon freshly ground black pepper
1/2 cup dry white wine
3 tablespoons cornstarch
1/4 cup cold water

Stuffing

5 large lemons
2 1/2 cups hot reduced-sodium, low-fat chicken or turkey broth
1 cup boiling water
1 cup chopped apricots
1/2 cup slivered fresh mint leaves, plus sprigs
1 teaspoon ground cinnamon
1 teaspoon ground cumin
1 teaspoon ground turmeric
2 packages (10 ounces each) instant couscous

1 Preheat the oven to 325°F and set out a roasting pan and rack. Cut the lemons in half lengthwise. Gently squeeze the juice into a measuring cup; discard the seeds and the membranes. Cut a thin slice off the base of each lemon shell so that it stands firmly. Set aside the 10 shells.

2 In a medium saucepan, mix 1 1/2 cups broth, the boiling water, 1/4 cup lemon juice, the apricots, the slivered mint leaves (save sprigs for garnish), the cinnamon, cumin, and turmeric; bring to a boil over high heat. Stir in the couscous. Remove from the heat, cover, and let stand until the couscous has absorbed all the liquid, about 5 minutes.

3 Wash the turkey inside and out with cold running water; discard the giblets and neck. Sprinkle both the small and large cavities with the salt and pepper. Stuff both cavities with the couscous and truss the turkey.

4 Insert a roasting thermometer into a thigh of the turkey, then place on the rack in the pan. Pour the wine and the remaining lemon juice over the turkey, cover with the top to the roasting pan or with foil. Roast the bird, basting frequently with the pan juices, for 3 hours. Uncover the pan. Continue roasting the turkey until it is

golden brown, a thermometer registers 180°F, and the juices run clear when a thigh is pierced with a fork, about 30 minutes more. Transfer the bird to a carving board and let it stand for 10 minutes.

5 Meanwhile, pour the pan drippings into a heatproof measuring cup and skim off the fat. Add the remaining 1 cup chicken broth, plus water if necessary, to make 3 cups of liquid, then return the mixture to the roasting pan. In a cup, dissolve the cornstarch in the 1/4 cup cold water and whisk into the drippings. Bring to a boil over high heat, scraping up the browned bits from the bottom of the pan, and boil until the gravy thickens, about 2 minutes.

6 Stuff the lemon shells with some of the couscous. Carve the turkey, discarding the skin. Garnish with the lemon shells, any extra couscous, and sprigs of mint. Serve with pan gravy.

Plus Points

• Couscous is low in fat. It scores low on the Glycemic Index, which means that it breaks down slowly in the body, releasing energy gradually into the bloodstream and maintaining blood sugars at an even level.

photo, page 123

Exchanges
starch 3 fruit 1/2
meat (very lean) 9

Each serving provides calories 654, calories from fat 107, fat 12g, saturated fat 4g, cholesterol 174mg, sodium 530mg, carbohydrate 57g, fiber 5g, sugars 7g, protein 76g. Excellent source of iron, magnesium, niacin, phosphorus, potassium, riboflavin, vitamin B6, zinc. Good source of copper, thiamine, vitamin A, vitamin B12, vitamin C.

turkey kebabs with fennel and red pepper relish

Marinate small pieces of turkey breast in white wine and fresh herbs. Then skewer with small onions and grill until golden brown. Serve with fennel and red pepper relish, and a side of whole-wheat couscous or wild rice.

Preparation time **20 minutes**   Marinating time **30 minutes**   Cooking time **15 minutes**   *Serves 4*

Kebabs

8 stalks fresh rosemary or 8 wooden skewers
1 pound boneless, skinless turkey breast fillets
1/2 teaspoon salt
1/4 teaspoon freshly ground black pepper
1/2 cup dry white wine
3 tablespoons fresh lemon juice
2 large garlic cloves, minced
1 tablespoon chopped fresh rosemary leaves
1 tablespoon chopped fresh sage leaves
1 tablespoon fresh thyme leaves
1 teaspoon fennel seeds, lightly crushed
1 tablespoon extra-virgin olive oil
16 small white onions, peeled

Relish

2 large red bell peppers
1 fennel bulb, trimmed
1/4 cup pitted kalamata olives
1 tablespoon fresh lemon juice
1 tablespoon extra-virgin olive oil
1 large garlic clove, minced
1/2 teaspoon freshly ground black pepper

Exchanges

vegetable 4 meat (very lean) 3
fat 1 1/2

1 If using the rosemary stalks, pull off and reserve the leaves from the bottom end of each stalk, keeping a cluster of about 2 inches of leaves at the top. Soak the rosemary stalks (or the wooden skewers if using instead) in water while you marinate the turkey.

2 Cut the turkey into 24 cubes, about 1 1/2 inches each. Sprinkle the turkey with the salt and pepper and spread in a single layer in a shallow baking dish. In a small bowl, whisk the wine, lemon juice, garlic, rosemary, sage, thyme, and fennel seeds; whisk in the oil. Drizzle the marinade over the turkey and toss until all of the pieces are coated. Cover with plastic wrap and marinate in the refrigerator for 30 minutes, turning once.

3 Meanwhile, make the relish. Seed the red peppers and cut into 1/4-inch dice. Trim the fennel bulb and cut into 1/4-inch dice. Cut the olives into 1/4-inch dice. In a medium bowl, mix the diced peppers, fennel, and olives with the lemon juice, oil, garlic, and pepper.

4 Preheat the grill or broiler to high. Thread the marinated turkey pieces and the onions onto the soaked rosemary stalks or skewers. In a small saucepan, bring the remaining marinade to a boil over high heat.

5 Grill or broil the kebabs until the turkey is golden brown, about 12 minutes, basting often with the marinade.

(**Some More Ideas**) *Turkey-vegetable kebabs*: Increase the rosemary stalks or wooden skewers to 12 (Step 1). Increase the turkey to 1 1/2 pounds and cut into 36 cubes (Step 2). Alternately thread additional vegetables with the turkey and onions on the kebabs: 2 cups zucchini slices (1 inch thick); 2 cups fresh or frozen and thawed corn-on-the-cob pieces (1 inch thick); 2 cups cherry tomatoes (Step 4). Cook as directed in Step 5 until the turkey is cooked throughout and the corn and zucchini are tender, about 12 to 14 minutes. This recipe makes 6 servings, 2 kebabs per person.

Tomato and roasted pepper relish: Use roasted red peppers instead of fresh, and 1 cup chopped tomatoes instead of fennel (Step 3). To roast the peppers, cut into quarters, then grill or broil for 6 minutes or until the skins are charred. Let cool in a closed plastic bag, then peel off the skin. Finely dice and stir into relish.

Plus Points

• This vegetable relish is a low-fat condiment that is high in vitamin C from the red peppers.
• If rosemary stalks are used in place of wooden skewers, the turkey meat absorbs a wonderful herb flavor as the kebabs cook.

photo, page 123

Each serving (two kebabs) provides calories 290, calories from fat 80, fat 9g, saturated fat 1g, cholesterol 73mg, sodium 452mg, carbohydrate 22g, fiber 6g, sugars 11g, protein 30g. Excellent source of niacin, phosphorus, potassium, vitamin A, vitamin B6, vitamin C. Good source of folate, iron, magnesium, riboflavin, thiamine.

turkey and lentil pâté

This coarse-textured pâté, deliciously flavored with garlic and fresh cilantro, combines ground turkey and turkey livers with lentils for an appetizer that has considerably less fat than a traditional pâté. Serve with toasted slices of French baguette, plus some crisp vegetable sticks and crunchy radishes.

Preparation time **1 hour**   Chilling time **2 hours**   *Serves 6*

Pâté

2 ounces green lentils
2 teaspoons canola oil
4 shallots, finely chopped
1 garlic clove, crushed
1 pound ground turkey
1/4 pound turkey livers, chopped
3 tablespoons dry Marsala wine
1/4 cup fresh cilantro
Salt and pepper

Garnish

Sprigs of fresh cilantro

1 Place the lentils in a saucepan, cover generously with water, and bring to a boil. Simmer until tender, about 45 minutes. Drain well and set aside to cool.

2 Heat the oil in a large skillet and sauté the shallots and garlic over medium-high heat until they have softened, about 2 minutes. Reduce the heat to medium and add the turkey and the livers. Cook, stirring, for 8 to 10 minutes.

3 Pour in the Marsala, bring to a boil, and allow the mixture to boil for 1 to 2 minutes. Season lightly with salt and pepper.

4 Transfer the mixture to a food processor. Add the cilantro and cooked lentils, and process for a few seconds to form a coarse paste consistency.

5 Spoon into 6 ramekins, pressing down well with the back of the spoon. Cover with plastic wrap and chill for 2 hours before serving, garnished with fresh cilantro sprigs.

(**Some More Ideas**) Chicken livers can be substituted for the turkey livers, or a mixture of the two.

Try replacing the Marsala with dry sherry.

Plus Points

• Turkey livers are a rich source of iron, zinc, vitamin A, and many of the B vitamins, especially B12. The iron present in the livers is in a form that is easily absorbed by the human body.

• Lentils can be used as a substitute for meat in many recipes such as hamburgers and meat loaf. Simply replace about half of the meat with cooked lentils and proceed as usual with the recipe. This will cut the amount of fat and cholesterol in the recipe and increase the fiber content.

photo, page 123

Exchanges

starch 1/2 meat (very lean) 3
fat 1/2

Each serving provides calories 167, calories from fat 25, fat 3g, saturated fat 0g, cholesterol 123mg, sodium 47mg, carbohydrate 9g, fiber 3g, sugars 2g, protein 24g. Excellent source of folate, niacin, phosphorus, vitamin A, vitamin B6, vitamin B12. Good source of iron, potassium, riboflavin.

turkey sausage and bean hot pot

Healthy eating doesn't mean giving up favorite family meals. Simple ingredient substitutions are often difficult to detect in the final product and they can make a meal much more nutritious. Here lean turkey sausages replace the more traditional pork in a hearty hot pot, with a spicy bean sauce and a covering of thinly sliced root vegetables.

Preparation time **about 1 hour** Cooking time **30–35 minutes** *Serves 6*

1 1/2 pounds potatoes, peeled and thinly sliced

1 large carrot, thinly sliced diagonally

1 medium parsnip, thinly sliced diagonally

Cooking spray

8 reduced-fat turkey sausages, (about 1 pound)

1 onion, finely chopped

2 teaspoons paprika

2 tablespoons flour

1 3/4 cups low-fat, reduced-sodium chicken broth

1 tablespoon Worcestershire sauce

3 teaspoons coarse mustard

1 teaspoon light brown sugar

1 can (15 ounces) red kidney beans, drained and rinsed

1 tablespoon butter, melted

Salt and pepper

1 Preheat the oven to 375F. Cook the potato, carrot, and parsnip slices in a saucepan of boiling water until just tender, about 3 to 4 minutes. Drain and set aside.

2 Coat a large nonstick skillet with cooking spray. Add the sausages and cook over medium heat for 10 minutes, turning to brown them evenly. Remove the sausages from the pan and reserve.

3 Add the onion to the pan and sauté, stirring until soft and golden, about 5 minutes. Stir in the paprika and flour, then gradually mix in the broth. Bring to a boil, stirring, then reduce the heat to medium and simmer until thickened and smooth. Stir in the Worcestershire sauce, 2 teaspoons of the mustard, and the sugar. Season lightly to taste with salt and pepper. Add the beans. Cut the sausages into slices and stir into the sauce. Bring back to a boil.

4 Spoon the sausage and bean mixture into a 4-cup shallow baking dish. Arrange the sliced root vegetables over the top, starting in the center and working out in overlapping rings to cover the surface completely. Mix the remaining 1 teaspoon mustard with the melted butter and brush over the vegetables.

5 Bake until the sauce is bubbling and the vegetable topping is golden brown, about 30 to 35 minutes. Serve hot.

(Some More Ideas) The hot pot can be prepared in advance and kept in the fridge until ready to bake. Allow 40 to 45 minutes cooking time, covering the top of the dish with foil after 20 minutes.

Vegetarian version: Use meat-free sausages and vegetable broth. Replace the Worcestershire sauce with mild chili sauce.

Use 2 sliced leeks instead of the onion, and omit the paprika. Use cannellini beans and 1/2 cup halved pitted prunes.

Plus Points

• Red kidney beans are a good source of dietary fiber, particularly soluble fiber, which can help to reduce high blood cholesterol levels. Using the canned variety instead of dried beans makes dinner preparation fast and easy.

• Both parsnips and potatoes provide useful amounts of potassium. Parsnips also contain some of the B vitamins, particularly folate and thiamine.

Exchanges

starch 2 vegetable 2
meat (lean) 1 fat 1

Each serving provides calories 327, calories from fat 83, fat 9g, saturated fat 3g, cholesterol 53mg, sodium 1486mg, carbohydrate 42g, fiber 6g, sugars 10g, protein 18g. Excellent source of folate, iron, niacin, phosphorus, potassium, riboflavin, vitamin A, vitamin B6, vitamin C. Good source of magnesium, thiamine. Flag: High in sodium.

turkey sausage and bean hot pot *p122*

turkey kebabs with fennel and red pepper relish *p120*

turkey with lemon couscous *p119*

turkey and lentil pâté *p121*

turkey drumsticks braised with baby vegetables

In this recipe, the drumsticks are lightly browned, then herb-seasoned broth is added to the pan and it is placed in the oven. The long, slow cooking helps to develop flavor in the dish and tenderizes the meat. Tiny baby vegetables are added toward the end of cooking and braised until just tender.

Preparation time **15 minutes**   Cooking time **1 1/2 hours**   *Serves 4*

Drumsticks

2 (1 1/2 pound) large turkey drumsticks on the bone

1 teaspoon freshly ground black pepper

1/2 teaspoon salt

2 teaspoons canola oil

1 1/2 cups turkey stock or low-fat, reduced-sodium chicken broth

2 sprigs each fresh rosemary and thyme

1 bay leaf

Vegetables

2 pounds yellow onions, sliced 1/2 inch thick

2 cups baby zucchini, trimmed

2 cups peeled baby carrots

2 cups drained canned baby corn

1 Preheat the oven to 350°F. Season the turkey drumsticks all over with the pepper and salt. In a large flameproof Dutch oven, heat the oil over a medium-high heat. Add the drumsticks and cook until brown, turning them frequently. Pour the stock or broth over the drumsticks; add the rosemary and thyme sprigs, and the bay leaf.

2 Cover the Dutch oven and transfer the drumsticks to the oven; cook, covered, for 1 hour.

3 Sprinkle the vegetables around the drumsticks and continue to cook, still covered, until the vegetables are tender, about 30 minutes. When ready to serve, the turkey will be golden brown and the juices of the drumsticks will run clear when pierced with a fork; the vegetables should be tender, but not overcooked. Discard the bay leaf.

4 To serve, slice the meat off the turkey drumsticks and serve with the vegetables. Drizzle a little of the pan juices over both the meat and the vegetables.

(Some More Ideas) *Braised chicken drumsticks*: Substitute 8 chicken drumsticks (a total of 2 pounds) for the turkey

drumsticks. Continue with Step 2, braising for only 30 minutes, instead of 1 hour, before adding the vegetables.

Roasted turkey breast: Substitute 1 whole turkey breast, on the bone (about 5 pounds), for the turkey drumsticks. Continue with Step 2, braising the turkey breast for 1 1/2 hours, instead of 1 hour, before adding double the amount of vegetables. If you wish, use chunks of peeled carrots and zucchini instead of the baby ones.

Substitute 1 1/2 cups dry white wine for the turkey stock.

Plus Points

• Preparing an assortment of vegetables can be quite laborious due to the peeling and chopping. Fortunately, grocery stores now offer a wide variety of products that make prep time easier. Fresh baby vegetables or low-sodium canned vegetables can be used when you are pinched for time and can be added to recipes whole instead of cut up.

• The baby corn in this recipe provides some vitamin A (from beta-carotene) and fiber. The tiny vegetable enhances the appearance of the dish as well.

photo, page 127

Exchanges

vegetable 6 meat (lean) 3
fat 1/2

Each serving provides calories 327, calories from fat 96, fat 11g, saturated fat 3g, cholesterol 83mg, sodium 604mg, carbohydrate 31g, fiber 8g, sugars 20g, protein 29g. Excellent source of folate, iron, magnesium, niacin, phosphorus, potassium, riboflavin, thiamine, vitamin A, vitamin B6, vitamin C, zinc.

turkey cutlets with citrus and sweet onion sauce

Here boneless turkey breast fillets are pounded out into cutlets (better known as *escalopes* in France) and then sautéed quickly on each side. Serve the turkey with bright green beans and a zesty citrus sauce.

Preparation time **15 minutes**   Cooking time **13 minutes**   *Serves 4*

Cutlets

4 (4 ounce) small boneless, skinless turkey breast fillets

1 teaspoon salt

1 pound green beans or haricots verts (French green beans)

Sauce

2 tablespoons grated orange zest

1 cup fresh orange juice

2 teaspoons grated lemon zest

1/4 cup fresh lemon juice

3 tablespoons honey

1/4 teaspoon freshly ground black pepper

1 tablespoon unsalted butter

1 large yellow onion, sliced thin

2 large shallots, sliced

2 large garlic cloves, minced

1 In a small bowl, whisk the orange zest and juice, the lemon zest and juice, the honey, and pepper; set aside.

2 In a medium nonstick skillet, melt the butter over medium-high heat. Add the onion, shallots, and garlic; sauté just until the onion is transparent, but not brown, about 2 minutes. Pour the citrus sauce over the onion mixture, bring to a boil, and cook for 2 minutes. Remove from heat, cover, and keep hot.

3 Place the turkey fillets between 2 sheets of plastic wrap and pound them with a meat mallet to 1/4 inch thick. Sprinkle steaks with 1/2 teaspoon of the salt.

4 To cook the green beans, half-fill a medium saucepan with water, add the remaining salt, and bring to a boil over medium-high heat. Add the beans and cook just until the beans turn bright green, about 3 minutes. Drain, transfer to a platter, and keep warm.

5 Spray a large nonstick skillet with cooking spray and heat 1 minute over medium-high heat. Add the turkey steaks and sauté for 3 minutes on each side. Arrange turkey escalopes on top of the beans. Reheat the sauce until bubbly; spoon over escalopes.

(**Some More Ideas**) *Sautéed duck breasts with raspberry-citrus sauce*: Make the sauce as directed. Substitute 4 boneless, skinless duck breasts for the turkey fillets, but do not flatten them. For duck breasts with pink centers, sauté for 3 minutes on each side; for well-done duck, 1 or 2 minutes longer on each side. Arrange duck breasts on top of the beans. Stir 1 cup fresh raspberries into the prepared sauce. Reheat the sauce until bubbly and spoon over duck breasts.

Turkey cutlets with honey-glazed vegetables: In Step 4, cook 1 cup peeled baby carrots (cut in half lengthwise) with the green beans; drain. Toss with 2 tablespoons honey and lemon juice, and 1 tablespoon butter.

Plus Points

• Turkey contains even less fat than chicken, making it one of the leanest meats available.

• In this recipe, only a touch of butter is used to finish off the sauce, making it smooth and glossy. The healthy citrus fruits are allowed to contribute most of the flavor in the zesty reduced-fat sauce.

• All citrus fruits are an excellent source of vitamin C. This vitamin helps reduce the risk of cataracts, and is essential for healthy gums and teeth.

photo, page 127

Exchanges

fruit 1/2 carbohydrate 1
vegetable 3 meat (very lean) 3
fat 1/2

Each serving provides calories 327, calories from fat 96, fat 11g, saturated fat 3g, cholesterol 83mg, sodium 604mg, carbohydrate 31g, fiber 8g, sugars 20g, protein 29g. Excellent source of folate, iron, magnesium, niacin, phosphorus, potassium, riboflavin, thiamine, vitamin A, vitamin B6, vitamin C, zinc.

turkey mole

Derived from the word *molli* (concoction), this spicy Mexican sauce is a rich blend of onions, garlic, and chile peppers. Traditionally, mole is made with Mexican chocolate, but in America, bitter chocolate is used. Cooked turkey, tomatoes, raisins, and almonds are tossed in the sauce, making a delicious meal.

Preparation time **30 minutes**   Cooking time **30 minutes**   *Serves 4*

Turkey

2 teaspoons canola oil

2 large onions, chopped

2 large garlic cloves, minced

1 1/2 tablespoons chili powder, or more to taste

1 tablespoon sesame seeds

1 small red chile pepper, seeded and minced

1 pound boneless, skinless turkey-breast fillets, cut into 1-inch-wide strips

1/2 teaspoon salt

1 can (14 ounces) whole tomatoes in juice

1 cup dark raisins

1/2 teaspoon ground cloves

1 cup low-fat, reduced-sodium chicken broth

3 tablespoons chopped bittersweet chocolate

1/4 cup toasted sliced almonds

2 tablespoons chopped fresh cilantro

Garnish

Sprigs of fresh cilantro

1 Heat the oil in a large skillet over medium-high heat. Add the onions, garlic, chili powder, sesame seeds, and chile pepper. Sauté until the onions are soft and the sesame seeds are fragrant and toasted, about 10 minutes.

2 Season the strips of turkey with the salt. Add the turkey to the skillet and toss with the onion mixture. Stir in the canned tomatoes with their juice and the raisins. Sprinkle in the cloves.

3 Pour in the broth and bring to a full boil. Reduce the heat to medium-low, cover the skillet, and simmer gently for 10 minutes.

4 Add the chocolate, almonds, and chopped cilantro, and stir until the chocolate has melted. Spoon into a serving dish and decorate with sprigs of cilantro.

(Some More Ideas) *Turkey mole tacos*: At the end of Step 3, dissolve 2 teaspoons cornstarch in 1/4 cup cold water, then whisk into the turkey mixture. Bring to a boil and cook until the sauce thickens, about 2 minutes. Then add the chocolate, almonds, and cilantro, and stir until the chocolate melts and the sauce bubbles and thickens. Preheat the oven to 350°F. Toss 4 cups shredded leaf or iceberg

lettuce, 1/2 cup thin avocado slices, 1 cup slivered yellow onions, 1 cup chopped tomatoes, and 1/4 cup fresh cilantro leaves. Heat 12 flour tortillas. To make the tacos, stuff each taco shell about half full with 1/3 cup of the mole mixture. Spoon the salad on top of the mole mixture and wrap up the tortilla.

Quick mole: Omit the uncooked turkey breast and the salt. Instead, stir 3 cups cooked bite-size pieces of turkey into the onion mixture and proceed with the addition of the tomatoes and the rest of the ingredients. Simmer gently for 7 minutes.

Plus Points

• Turkey is an excellent source of protein and provides many B vitamins, in particular niacin. The dark meat contains twice as much iron and zinc as the light meat. Eaten without the skin, turkey is low in fat and what fat it does contain is mostly unsaturated.

• Raisins are a good source of potassium and a fair source of iron and fiber. As grapes are dried to make raisins, the natural sugars are concentrated. For this reason, dried fruits should be used in moderation for people with diabetes, serving as a complement to a dish for color and flavor. Raisins make a great snack mixed into trail mix or cereal.

Exchanges
fruit 2 1/2 vegetable 3
meat (very lean) 4 fat 1

Each serving provides calories 412, calories from fat 95, fat 11g, saturated fat 2g, cholesterol 70mg, sodium 708mg, carbohydrate 51g, fiber 7g, sugars 38g, protein 34g. Excellent source of iron, magnesium, niacin, phosphorus, potassium, riboflavin, thiamine, vitamin A, vitamin B6, vitamin C. Good source of calcium, copper, folate, zinc.

spiced stir-fried duck *p128*

turkey mole *p126*

turkey cutlets with citrus and sweet onion sauce *p125*

turkey drumsticks braised
with baby vegetables *p124*

spiced stir-fried duck

In this dish, strips of duck are stir-fried in the Chinese tradition with onions, water chestnuts, bok choy, and bean sprouts. For an unusual sweet touch, some chunks of juicy fresh pear are added. Five-spice powder—which contains equal parts of cinnamon, cloves, fennel seed, star anise, and peppercorns—serves as the seasoning.

Preparation time **30 minutes**   Cooking time **10 minutes**   *Serves 6*

1 1/2 pounds boneless duck breasts

2 teaspoons five-spice powder

4 celery stalks, few leaves to decorate

8 ounces small white onions

2 large juicy pears

1 cup sliced canned water chestnuts, drained

1/2 pound bok choy

1 1/2 cups bean sprouts

2 tablespoons canola oil

3 tablespoons rice vinegar or sherry vinegar

3 tablespoons light soy sauce

2 tablespoons honey

6 cups cooked Chinese noodles or spaghetti (optional)

1 Remove the skin and all fat from the duck breasts, then cut them across the grain into long strips, 1 inch wide. Sprinkle with the five-spice powder and toss to coat. Set aside.

2 Thinly slice the celery. Peel and thinly slice the onions. Peel, core, and cut the pears into bite-size pieces. Shred the bok choy. Wash and drain the bean sprouts.

3 Heat a wok or heavy skillet over high heat until hot. Add the oil, swirling the wok to coat the bottom and sides. Add the duck breasts and stir-fry for 2 minutes. Then add the celery and onions and continue to stir-fry until the celery and onions have softened, about 3 minutes. Add the pears and water chestnuts and stir just to mix.

4 In a cup, whisk the vinegar, soy sauce, and honey and add to the wok. Heat until the liquid is bubbling and stir-fry 2 minutes more. Add the bok choy and bean sprouts and stir-fry just until the bok choy and sprouts wilt, about 1 minute more. Decorate with the celery leaves and serve with the Chinese noodles, if desired.

(Some More Ideas) *Orange stir-fried duck*: Use 1 teaspoon ground anise instead of the five-star powder. Substitute 2 cups fresh orange sections for the pears. Stir 2 tablespoons fresh orange juice into the sauce with the vinegar.

Spiced duck in plum sauce: Substitute 2 cups peeled ripe plum slices for the pears. Stir 2 tablespoons bottled plum sauce into the sauce with the vinegar.

Spicy stir-fried chicken: Substitute 1 1/2 pounds boneless, skinless chicken breasts (cut into strips) for the duck breasts.

Plus Points

• Removing the skin and fat from duck lowers the fat content substantially. Ounce for ounce, a skinless duck breast contains 77% less fat than one with both its skin and fat intact. In this recipe, the duck is combined with plenty of vegetables so the flavor is retained but less meat is needed to create the meal.

• Dark green leafy vegetables, such as bok choy, provide a good source of vitamin C, as well as vitamin B6, folate, and niacin.

• Bean sprouts are a good source of vitamin C and also offer B vitamins.

photo, page 127

Exchanges

fruit 1   vegetable 2   meat (lean) 2   fat 1/2

Each serving provides calories 251, calories from fat 62, fat 7g, saturated fat 1g, cholesterol 108mg, sodium 441mg, carbohydrate 26g, fiber 4g, sugars 18g, protein 23g. Excellent source of iron, niacin, vitamin C. Good source of folate, potassium, vitamin A, vitamin B6.

piquant pasta and tuna salad

This salad is a great alternative to the traditional tuna casserole. Using canned tuna fish makes it inexpensive and easy to prepare. The dressing has a sweet-and-sour flavor, which perfectly complements the lightly cooked zucchini, tuna, tomatoes, and al dente pasta. Serve the salad cool or while it is still warm, accompanied by wedges of juicy cantaloupe.

Preparation time **20–25 minutes, plus cooling**   *Serves 4*

Salad

8 ounces pasta twists or spirals, such as cavatappi, fusilli, or rotini

2 tablespoons olive oil

1 onion, chopped

1 garlic clove, chopped

2 zucchini, thinly sliced

2 teaspoons sugar

2 tablespoons commercially prepared red or green pesto sauce

1 tablespoon white or red wine vinegar

1 tablespoon capers

6 tomatoes, halved and cut into thin wedges

1 can (7 ounces) water-packed solid white tuna, drained and roughly flaked

6 black olives, pitted and halved

Garnish

Fresh flat-leaf parsley

1 Cook the pasta in boiling water for 10 to 12 minutes, or according to package instructions, until al dente. Drain well, rinse with cold water, and drain again.

2 While the pasta is cooking, heat 1 tablespoon of the oil in a saucepan. Add the onion and garlic, and sauté for 3 minutes, stirring often. Add the remaining oil and the zucchini and cook, stirring occasionally, for 3 minutes.

3 Add the sugar, pesto, vinegar, and capers to the onion and zucchini. Heat for a few seconds, stirring until the ingredients have combined to form a dressing. Stir in the tomatoes, then transfer the mixture to a large mixing bowl and set aside to cool.

4 Add the drained pasta to the bowl, then gently mix in the tuna fish and olives. Divide among 4 plates or transfer to a large serving bowl. Serve garnished with flat-leaf parsley leaves, if desired.

(Some More Ideas) To increase the fiber content and make a more substantial meal, add 1 can (15 ounces) red kidney beans or cannellini beans, drained and rinsed, with the pasta. Omit the tuna for a vegetarian dish.

Try using 8 ounces small pattypan squash instead of the zucchini. Trim their tops and bases, then slice them in half.

Plus Points

• Using tuna canned in water, rather than in oil, keeps the fat content of the dish low.

• Both the tomatoes and zucchini ensure that this simple salad provides an excellent supply of vitamin C.

Exchanges

**starch 3 vegetable 3
meat (very lean) 1 fat 2**

Each serving provides calories 435, calories from fat 106, fat 12g, saturated fat 1g, cholesterol 13mg, sodium 400mg, carbohydrate 62g, fiber 6g, sugars 14g, protein 22g. Excellent source of folate, iron, magnesium, niacin, phosphorus, potassium, riboflavin, thiamine, vitamin A, vitamin B6, vitamin B12, vitamin C.

tuna and pepper salad

Chunks of tuna, wedges of potato, crisp green beans, and tangy tomatoes are combined with colorful peppers to create a salad that will make you feel like you are dining in Provence. The eggs and tuna serve as a good source of lean protein, while the rest of the salad contributes several servings of vegetables.

Preparation time **45 minutes**   *Serves 6*

Salad

1 pound new potatoes

1 cup haricots verts (French green beans) or green beans

6 eggs

3 cups mixed salad leaves

1 tablespoon chopped parsley

1 tablespoon snipped fresh chives

1 small red onion, thinly sliced

1 tablespoon tapenade (black-olive paste)

2 garlic cloves, chopped

2 tablespoons olive oil

1 tablespoon red wine vinegar

1 teaspoon balsamic vinegar

10 to 15 radishes, thinly sliced

1 can (7 ounces) tuna in spring water, drained

1/2 cup cherry tomatoes

1 red pepper, seeded and thinly sliced

1 yellow pepper, seeded and thinly sliced

1 green pepper, seeded and thinly sliced

8 black olives

Garnish

Fresh basil leaves

1 Place the potatoes in a saucepan and cover with boiling water. Cook over medium heat for 10 minutes. Add the beans and cook until the potatoes are tender and the beans are just cooked, about 5 minutes. Drain well and set aside to cool.

2 Place the eggs in a saucepan with cold water to cover and bring to a boil. Reduce the heat and cook at a low simmer for 3 minutes. Rinse well in cold water. Peel the eggs carefully and place in cold water.

3 Toss the salad leaves with the parsley, chives, and red onion in a large, shallow bowl.

4 To make the dressing, mix the tapenade with the garlic, olive oil, red wine vinegar, and balsamic vinegar, and lightly season with salt and pepper. Pour 2/3 of the dressing over the salad leaves and toss well to mix.

5 Halve the potatoes and arrange them on top of the leaves with the green beans, radishes, chunks of tuna, tomatoes, peppers, and olives. Halve the eggs and add them to the salad. Pour over the remaining dressing, garnish with basil leaves, and serve.

(Some More Ideas) *Classic Italian cannellini bean and tuna salad*: Omit the potatoes and eggs and add 1 can (15 ounces) cannellini beans, well drained, to the salad leaves. Use the juice of 1 lemon in the dressing instead of balsamic vinegar.

Try this salad using different varieties of tomatoes, such as yellow cherry tomatoes, baby plum tomatoes, or quartered vine-ripened plum tomatoes.

Plus Points

• Canned tuna retains a high vitamin content, particularly vitamins B12 and D.
• In common with many other salad ingredients, radishes are a useful source of vitamin C and are very low in calories. The radish has a very hot flavor due to an enzyme in the skin that reacts with another substance to form a mustard type of oil.
• Green beans are a good source of dietary fiber and provide valuable amounts of folate.

photo, page 133

Exchanges

starch 1 1/2   vegetable 1
meat (very lean) 1   fat 2

Each serving provides calories 270, calories from fat 101, fat 11g, saturated fat 3g, cholesterol 221mg, sodium 255mg, carbohydrate 26g, fiber 5g, sugars 7g, protein 17g. Excellent source o folate, niacin, phosphorus, potassium, riboflavin, vitamin A, vitamin B6, vitamin B12, vitamin C. Good source of iron, magnesium, thiamine.

grilled salmon salad

Conjure up the flavors of a tropical island excursion with this unusual warm salad. The rich flavor of salmon is perfectly balanced by the gentle acidity of orange and the sweetness of mango and papaya. Serve with an accompanying salad of mixed long-grain and wild rice or a piece of crusty French bread.

Preparation and cooking time **30 minutes, plus 30 minutes marinating**   *Serves 4*

8 cardamom pods, crushed

1 teaspoon cumin seeds

Finely grated zest and juice of 1 lime

Juice of 1 large orange

1 tablespoon light soy sauce

1 tablespoon honey

4 (4 ounce) pieces of skinless salmon fillet

4 cups mixed salad leaves, such as oak leaf, red leaf lettuce, and baby chard, or use romaine

1 mango, peeled and cut into 1-inch cubes

1 papaya, peeled, seeded, and cut into 1-inch cubes

1 orange, peeled and segmented

Salt and pepper

1 Heat a small nonstick skillet over medium heat. Scrape the seeds from the cardamom pods, and add them to the hot pan with the cumin seeds. Toast for a few seconds to release the aromas, and remove the seeds to a shallow nonmetallic dish.

2 Add the lime zest and juice, orange juice, soy sauce, and honey to the seeds, and season lightly with salt and pepper. Lay the pieces of salmon in the dish. Turn them over to coat both sides. Cover and leave to marinate for about 30 minutes.

3 Preheat a grill or oven broiler. Lift the salmon out of the marinade, place on the grill rack or broiler pan, and grill or broil for 4 to 5 minutes on one side only; the salmon fillets should still be slightly translucent in the center. Meanwhile, pour the marinade into a small saucepan and bring just to a boil.

4 Arrange the salad leaves in the middle of 4 plates. Scatter the mango and papaya cubes and orange segments over the salad. Place the cooked salmon on top of the salad and drizzle with the warm marinade. Serve immediately.

(Some More Ideas) *Asian-style halibut salad*: Use 4 (4 ounce) pieces of skinless halibut fillet instead of the salmon. Make a marinade with 2 garlic cloves, crushed, 1 teaspoon grated ginger, 1 teaspoon ground cumin, 1 teaspoon ground coriander, 2 tablespoons rice wine or dry sherry, 1 tablespoon fish sauce, the grated zest of 1 lime, the juice of 2 limes, and salt to taste. Marinate the halibut for at least 30 minutes, then grill for 5 to 6 minutes. Strain the marinade and bring just to a boil. Serve the fish on a crunchy salad of bean sprouts, shredded Chinese cabbage, carrot, red pepper, and thinly sliced mushrooms, with the warm marinade drizzled on top.

Serve the salmon on a bed of stir-fried or steamed zucchini and carrots.

Plus Points

• Salmon is a useful source of potassium, which is needed for the regulation of fluid balance in the body, to help prevent high blood pressure.

• Papaya is a useful source of vitamin A, in the form of beta-carotene, which helps to maintain good vision. The papaya has a vital role to play in preventing blindness in many parts of the world where few other foods that are high in vitamin A content are eaten regularly.

photo, page 133

Exchanges

fruit 2 meat (lean) 4

Each serving provides calories 313, calories from fat 93, fat 10g, saturated fat 2g, cholesterol 77mg, sodium 223mg, carbohydrate 30g, fiber 4g, sugars 24g, protein 26g. Excellent source of folate, niacin, phosphorus, potassium, riboflavin, thiamine, vitamin A, vitamin B12, vitamin C. Good source of magnesium, vitamin B6.

crab and avocado salad

Fresh crab is a real summertime treat. It is rich in flavor and combines well in a salad with crunchy apples and bean sprouts, chunks of perfectly ripe avocado, and nutty-flavored bulgur wheat. The avocados in this salad are rich and succulent, due to their high and healthful monounsaturated fat content.

Preparation time **40 minutes, plus cooling**   *Serves 6*

Salad

12 ounces fresh white crabmeat

2 avocados

2 crisp green apples

1/2 cup bean sprouts

3 tablespoons low-fat mayonnaise

3 tablespoons plain low-fat yogurt

1 tablespoon lemon juice

Small pinch cayenne pepper

1 head butter (Bibb or Boston) lettuce, separated into leaves

1/4 cup walnut halves, toasted and roughly chopped

Bulgur Wheat

1 cup bulgur wheat

2 1/2 cups boiling water

1 tablespoon olive oil

3 tablespoons lemon juice

3 tablespoons chopped fresh flat-leaf parsley

1 tablespoon snipped fresh chives

2 medium tomatoes, diced

Salt and pepper

1 Put the bulgur wheat in a large saucepan with the water. Bring to a boil over high heat, then reduce the heat and simmer for 10 to 15 minutes or until the grains are just tender. Drain in a large sieve, pressing down well to squeeze out all the excess water. Leave to cool.

2 Combine the oil, lemon juice, parsley, chives, and diced tomatoes in a large mixing bowl. Add the bulgur wheat and mix thoroughly, then season with salt and pepper to taste. Leave to stand at room temperature while preparing the crab salad.

3 Pick over and flake the crabmeat, discarding any fragments of shell. Halve, pit, and peel the avocados, then chop the flesh. Add to the crab. Quarter and core the apples, then thinly slice them. Add to the crabmeat with the bean sprouts.

4 Mix the mayonnaise with the yogurt until smooth. Add the lemon juice and cayenne pepper. Spoon onto the crab mixture and toss very gently until just combined.

5 Pile the bulgur onto a serving platter and arrange the lettuce leaves on top. Spoon the crab salad onto the leaves and scatter over the walnuts. Serve immediately.

(Some More Ideas) Canned crabmeat is less expensive than fresh and can be used as a substitute in this recipe. Use 2 cans, about 7 ounces each, well drained, instead of the fresh crab.

Use 1 cup basmati rice instead of the bulgur wheat. Cook the rice in boiling water according to the packet instructions, until tender, about 10 to 12 minutes. Drain, rinse with cold water, and drain again, then leave to dry before mixing with the dressing and tomatoes.

Plus Points

• Although yogurt has been used for its nutritional and medicinal properties for hundreds of years in the Middle East, the Far East, and Eastern Europe, it has only become popular in this country in the past few decades. Like other dairy products, yogurt is a good source of calcium. This mineral is recognized mainly for its involvement with maintaining healthy bones, but it is also vital for the proper functioning of muscles and nerves and for blood clotting.

• Walnuts are a good source of the antioxidant nutrients selenium, zinc, copper, and vitamin E. Nuts should be used in moderation in diabetic cooking for their beneficial monounsaturated fat.

Exchanges

starch 1 1/2 fruit 1
meat (very lean) 2 fat 2

Each serving provides calories 341, calories from fat 133, fat 15g, saturated fat 2g, cholesterol 57mg, sodium 254mg, carbohydrate 39g, fiber 10g, sugars 12g, protein 18g. Excellent source of folate, magnesium, niacin, phosphorus, potassium, vitamin B6, vitamin B12, vitamin C. Good source of calcium, copper, iron, riboflavin, thiamine, vitamin A.

tuna and pepper salad *p130*

crab and avocado salad *p132*

shrimp, melon, and mango salad *p134*

grilled salmon salad *p131*

shrimp, melon, and mango salad

A very pretty salad, this combines shrimp with colorful, juicy fruits tossed in a light dressing flavored with honey and fresh mint. The shrimp is left to marinate in the dressing so the flavors develop and infuse. This dish is perfect for a light summer meal, out on the patio with a glass of refreshing lemonade.

Preparation time **20 minutes, plus at least 30 minutes marinating**   *Serves 6*

Salad

1 pound cooked peeled
large shrimp

1 mango

1 honeydew melon,
peeled and cubed

8 cherry tomatoes, halved

3 cups arugula leaves

1 medium cucumber, sliced

Salt and pepper

Dressing

2 tablespoons olive oil

Juice of 1 lemon

1 tablespoon honey

2 tablespoons chopped
fresh mint

Garnish

Fresh mint leaves

1 Whisk together all the ingredients for the dressing in a large bowl and season lightly with salt and pepper. Add the shrimp to the dressing, cover, and leave to marinate in the refrigerator for 30 minutes to 1 hour.

2 Halve the mango lengthways, cutting down each side of the pit. Cut the flesh on each half in a criss-cross fashion to make cubes, then cut the cubes away from the skin.

3 Remove the shrimp from the fridge. Add the mango, melon, and tomatoes and gently stir together. Arrange the arugula leaves and cucumber slices around the edge of a shallow serving dish, and spoon the shrimp into the center. Garnish with sprigs of mint and serve.

(Some More Ideas) Use mixed seafood instead of the shrimp.

To add a slightly spicy note to the salad, add 1 (1 inch) slice of fresh ginger, cut into very fine strips, to the dressing.

Other fruits can be used in place of the melon and mango. Good combinations include chopped nectarine and halved, seedless white grapes or sliced kiwifruit with cubes of fresh pineapple.

To vary the dressing, use the juice of 1 orange in place of the lemon juice and 2 tablespoons chopped fresh cilantro instead of mint.

Presentation: Serve the salad in halved honeydew or cantaloupe melon shells.

Plus Points

• Melons are made up of approximately 90% water, which makes them very refreshing. The varieties with orange flesh, like cantaloupe, contain beta-carotene as well.

• Lemon juice is a wonderful flavoring for fish and poultry. Sprinkling the fish or poultry with lemon juice before grilling or baking adds flavor to the meal without using salt or condiments that are high in fat.

photo, page 133

Exchanges

fruit 2 meat (very lean) 2 fat 1

Each serving provides calories 242, calories from fat 53, fat 6g, saturated fat 1g, cholesterol 147mg, sodium 198mg, carbohydrate 33g, fiber 3g, sugars 29g, protein 18g. Excellent source of potassium, vitamin A, vitamin C. Good source of iron, magnesium, niacin, phosphorus, thiamine, vitamin B6.

lobster salad with lime dressing

Precooked lobster meat makes a luxurious salad for two people to share. Here the firm, sweet-flavored lobster meat is served on a bed of peppery salad leaves with snow peas, grapes, and tiny new potatoes. The salad is tossed with a creamy dressing spiked with lime zest. Serve the salad with small whole-wheat dinner rolls for a well-balanced meal.

Preparation time **1 hour**   *Serves 4*

1 Put the potatoes in a saucepan and cover with boiling water. Cook until just tender, about 15 minutes. Drain and leave to cool, then cut the potatoes in half.

2 While the potatoes are cooling, mix together the mayonnaise, yogurt, and lime zest, and season with salt and pepper to taste. Set aside.

3 Toss the potatoes with the shallots, snow peas, grapes, and lime dressing. Arrange the arugula on large plates and add the watercress and potato salad. Scatter the lobster meat on top and serve.

Plus Points
• Lobster is an excellent source of the antioxidant selenium, which helps to protect cells from damage by free radicals from the environment.
• Some varieties of grapes are cultivated for wine, others for drying to become raisins and currants, and others for just eating. The nutrient content of different-colored grapes is very similar. And they are a good source of potassium and can be incorporated into the diabetic diet as a carbohydrate-fruit exchange.

1/2 pound baby red-skinned new potatoes, scrubbed
2 tablespoons low-fat mayonnaise
2 tablespoons low-fat yogurt
Finely grated zest of 1 lime
2 small shallots, thinly sliced
1/2 cup snow peas, sliced
1/2 cup halved seedless red grapes
1/2 cup halved seedless green grapes
1 cup watercress, washed
2 cups arugula, washed
Salt and pepper
1 pound cooked lobster meat

(Some More Ideas) *Curried lime and honey dressing*: Mix 2 tablespoons canola oil with 1 tablespoon lemon juice, 1 teaspoon curry paste, and 1 teaspoon honey.

Lobster and papaya salad: Instead of the snow peas and grapes, toss 1 large ripe papaya, seeded and sliced, and 1 chopped avocado with the potatoes, watercress, and shallots. Pile the papaya salad onto salad leaves (combine romaine and leaf lettuce) rather than arugula. Drizzle with the curried lime and honey dressing, above, and scatter the lobster meat over it.

Exchanges
starch 1 fruit 1/2
meat (very lean) 3

Each serving provides calories 219, calories from fat 16, fat 2g, saturated fat 0g, cholesterol 81mg, sodium 518mg, carbohydrate 25g, fiber 2g, sugars 11g, protein 26g. Excellent source of phosphorus, potassium, vitamin A, vitamin B12, vitamin C. Good source of calcium, magnesium, niacin, riboflavin, vitamin B6.

italian seafood stew

Any fish or shellfish is delicious in this Italian fisherman's stew—make the bubbling tomato mixture and add whatever seafood is in season. The stew also contains an array of fresh vegetables such as peas, peppers, zucchini, and leafy greens that are an excellent source of vitamins, fiber, and antioxidants. Serve with triangles of polenta grilled at the last minute.

Preparation time **20 minutes**   Cooking time **1 hour**   *Serves 4*

Stew

1 tablespoon olive oil

1 medium leek, coarsely chopped

1 onion, chopped

4 garlic cloves, chopped

1 green pepper, seeded and chopped

1 medium bulb of fennel, diced

1 1/2 cups dry white wine

1 1/4 cups fish, chicken, or vegetable broth

1 can (32 ounces) chopped tomatoes

2 tablespoons tomato puree

1 teaspoon dried herbes de Provence

1 medium zucchini, sliced

3 tablespoons coarsely chopped parsley

1/2 cup shelled fresh or frozen peas

1/2 cup baby chard or spinach leaves

1/2 pound skinless cod fillet, cut into chunks

1 pound peeled or shelled mixed shellfish, such as shrimp, scallops, squid rings, and mussels

Polenta

Cooking spray

1 cup instant polenta

2 teaspoons olive oil

Exchanges

starch 2 vegetable 5
meat (very lean) 4 fat 1 1/2

1 Heat the oil in a large saucepan, add the leek and onion, and cook until starting to soften, about 2 minutes. Add the garlic, pepper, and fennel, and cook until softened, about 5 to 10 minutes.

2 Add the wine, broth, and tomatoes with their juice, and season lightly with salt and pepper. Simmer until the mixture has thickened slightly, about 30 minutes. Stir in the tomato puree, herbes de Provence, and zucchini, and continue simmering for 10 minutes, adding a little water if the mixture becomes too thick.

3 Meanwhile, cook the polenta according to the packet instructions until it is thick. Season lightly with salt and pepper. Pour the polenta into a 7 x 11-inch shallow pan coated with cooking spray. Leave until cool and firm, then cut the polenta into triangles. Preheat the oven broiler or grill to high.

4 Stir the parsley, peas, chard or spinach, fish, and shellfish into the tomato mixture. Cover and simmer gently over medium heat until all the seafood is just cooked, about 5 minutes.

5 Lightly brush the polenta triangles with the oil and place directly on grill rack or place on a broiler pan. Grill or broil until lightly browned. Serve the fish stew in bowls with the polenta triangles.

(Some More Ideas) *Italian clam stew with asparagus*: Use 3 medium onions, chopped, and omit the leek and green pepper. In Step 2, omit the broth. Replace the fish and shellfish with 2 pounds clams in their shells. After adding them to the tomato mixture, cover, and bring to a boil, then reduce the heat and simmer over a low heat for about 2 minutes or until the shells start to pop open. Add 1/4 pound thin asparagus spears, cut into bite-size pieces, cover again, and cook until all the clams have opened (discard any that remain shut) and the asparagus is just tender, about 5 minutes. Serve the stew with the polenta triangles or with steamed rice.

Plus Points

• Cod provides excellent quantities of iodine. Fish is a reliable source of this essential mineral because of the consistent iodine content of sea water. Other foods depend on the iodine content of soil, which can vary considerably.

• Polenta, which is finely milled corn meal, is a good gluten-free source of carbohydrate.

• Fresh peas have a relatively short season, but frozen peas can be enjoyed year-round. The nutritional content of frozen peas is very similar to that of fresh if the recommended cooking instructions are followed. Boiling the peas too long can reduce the vitamin content.

photo, page 139

Each serving provides calories 487, calories from fat 89, fat 10g, saturated fat 1g, cholesterol 111mg, sodium 760mg, carbohydrate 58g, fiber 11g, sugars 16g, protein 39g. Excellent source of folate, iron, magnesium, niacin, phosphorus, potassium, riboflavin, thiamine, vitamin A, vitamin B6, vitamin B12, vitamin C. Good source of calcium.

chunky fish soup

Although this soup contains starchy root vegetables such as potatoes and parsnips, it still fits nicely into a well-rounded meal plan for diabetes. Fish soup makes an appealing first course any time of the year, but especially on a cold winter day. Rich in B-complex vitamins, it is also low in fat and contains a good amount of fiber.

Preparation time **15 minutes**   Cooking time **about 20 minutes**   *Serves 4*

Soup

Pinch saffron threads

2 teaspoons olive oil

2 slices reduced-fat bacon, chopped

3 ounces red potatoes, washed and finely diced

2 parsnips, peeled and finely diced

2 celery stalks, finely chopped

1/2 cup finely chopped onions

1 bay leaf

1 strip of finely pared lemon zest

4 cups low-sodium vegetable broth

1/2 pound skinless haddock fillet, cut into bite-size pieces

Salt and pepper

Garnish

4 scallions, finely chopped

1 Place the saffron threads in a small non-stick skillet over medium heat and stir until they just begin to give off their aroma. Remove the saffron to a small plate and set aside.

2 Heat the oil in a large nonstick saucepan, add the bacon, and cook over a moderate heat, stirring, for about 2 minutes. Add the potatoes, parsnips, celery, and onion, and cook gently for about 1 minute, stirring frequently.

3 Add the saffron threads, bay leaf, and lemon zest, and season with salt and pepper to taste. Pour in the broth and slowly bring to a boil. Reduce the heat to medium low, half cover the pan, and simmer, stirring occasionally, until the vegetables are almost tender when pierced with the tip of a knife, about 8 minutes.

4 Lay the pieces of haddock on top of the vegetables. Reduce the heat to low and cover the pan tightly. Simmer until the fish will flake easily and all the vegetables are tender, about 7 to 8 minutes. Remove and discard the bay leaf and lemon zest.

5 Ladle the soup into bowls, sprinkle with the chopped scallions, and serve immediately.

(Some More Ideas) Vary the vegetables to use what is in season. Green beans are an excellent alternative to the celery, and turnips can replace the parsnips. Other suitable vegetables include carrots, zucchini, fennel, and peppers.

Monkfish and cod also work well in this recipe.

Main-dish soup: Increase or double the amount of vegetables, use 6 cups of broth, and increase the amount of fish to 1 pound.

Plus Points

• On an ounce-for-ounce basis, white fish provides similar amounts of protein to that found in lean meat.
• Celery was originally grown as a medicinal herb, only being used as a cooked vegetable and salad ingredient in the late 17th century. Celery contains beta-carotene, which the body converts into vitamin A.

photo, page 139

Exchanges
starch 1 vegetable 1
meat (very lean) 1 fat 1/2

Each serving provides calories 178, calories from fat 42, fat 5g, saturated fat 1g, cholesterol 38mg, sodium 1,127 mg, carbohydrate 20g, fiber 4g, sugars 7g, protein 14g. Excellent source of folate, iron, niacin, phosphorus, potassium, vitamin B6, vitamin C. Good source of calcium, magnesium, riboflavin, thiamine, vitamin B12. Flag: High in sodium.

mixed seafood and noodle broth

Here reduced-sodium chicken broth and light soy sauce are used to lower the sodium content of the soup. The fresh ginger and sherry add incredible flavor. You can prepare part of this soup ahead of time, then add the scallops, vegetables, and noodles just before serving.

Preparation and cooking time **25 minutes**   *Serves 6*

Broth

2 ounces fine stir-fry rice noodles, broken into 4-inch lengths

2 teaspoons dark sesame oil

1 (1 inch) piece fresh ginger, peeled and finely chopped

1 cup shiitake mushrooms, stemmed, caps thinly sliced

4 cups reduced-sodium low-fat chicken broth

1 tablespoon dry sherry

2 tablespoons light soy sauce

1/2 pound cooked mixed seafood, shrimp, squid, and scallops (any combination)

1 cup shredded bok choy

4 scallions, thinly sliced

1/2 cup fresh bean sprouts

Garnish

Sprigs of fresh cilantro

Chili sauce, optional

1 Put the noodles in a bowl and pour over boiling water to cover. Set aside to soak for 4 minutes.

2 Meanwhile, heat the sesame oil in a large saucepan, add the ginger and mushrooms, and cook for about 2 minutes to soften slightly. Add the broth, sherry, and soy sauce, and bring to a boil.

3 Halve the scallops if they are large. Add the mixed seafood to the boiling broth together with the bok choy, scallions, and bean sprouts. Bring back to a boil and cook until the seafood is heated through, about 1 minute.

4 Drain the noodles and add to the soup. Bring back to a boil, then ladle into large soup bowls. Scatter over a few cilantro sprigs and serve with chili sauce if desired.

(Some More Ideas) *Crab and noodle broth*: Use 1 can (12 ounces) white crabmeat, drained, instead of the mixed seafood. Replace the mushrooms with 1/2 cup thinly sliced canned baby corn and 1 diced zucchini, cooking them with the ginger for 1 minute. In Step 3, omit the bok choy. After adding the rice noodles in Step 4, bring to a boil and season with 1 tablespoon fish sauce.

Plus Points

• Scallops are an excellent source of selenium and B12, and a useful source of phosphorus and potassium. Shrimp provides calcium, while squid is an excellent source of B12.

• Shiitake mushrooms contain the B vitamins B2, niacin, and pantothenic acid. They also provide potassium and good quantities of copper.

• Rice noodles are gluten-free and wheat-free, making them useful for people with gluten intolerances or wheat allergies.

Exchanges
starch 1/2 vegetable 1
meat (very lean) 1 fat 1/2

Each serving provides calories 120, calories from fat 22, fat 2g, saturated fat 0g, cholesterol 43mg, sodium 640mg, carbohydrate 14g, fiber 1g, sugars 3g, protein 10g. Good source of niacin, phosphorus, vitamin C.

mixed seafood and noodle broth *p138*

seafood jambalaya *p140*

italian seafood stew *p136*

chunky fish soup *p137*

seafood jambalaya

Mixed with rice and plenty of vegetables, a small amount of succulent salmon and shrimp goes a long way, making a good balance of protein and carbohydrate in this temptingly spicy Louisiana-style dish. As an added bonus for the busy cook, it is prepared in just one pan and makes a complete meal on its own.

Preparation and cooking time **30 minutes**   *Serves 4*

1 tablespoon olive oil

1 onion, chopped

2 celery stalks, sliced

1 green or red pepper, seeded and cut into strips

2 garlic cloves, crushed

1 teaspoon ground ginger

1/2 teaspoon cayenne pepper

1 teaspoon mild chili powder

1 cup long-grain white rice

2 cups hot vegetable or low-fat, reduced-sodium chicken broth

1 can (14 ounces) chopped tomatoes

3 tablespoons coarsely chopped parsley

1/2 pound large raw shrimp, peeled and deveined

1/2 pound skinned salmon fillet, cut into 1-inch cubes

Dash hot red pepper sauce (optional)

Salt and pepper

1 Heat the oil in a large, wide pan over medium heat. Add the onion and cook, stirring, for about 3 minutes. Add the celery, green or red pepper, garlic, ginger, cayenne, chili powder, and rice, and cook, stirring, for 2 minutes.

2 Pour in the hot broth and stir well, then reduce the heat so that the broth is simmering gently. Cover the pan with a tightfitting lid and simmer for 15 minutes.

3 Stir in the chopped tomatoes with their juice and 2 tablespoons of the parsley, then add the shrimp and salmon. Cover again, and simmer until the seafood is just cooked and the rice has absorbed most of the liquid and is tender, about 3 to 4 minutes.

4 Add the hot sauce, if using, and season lightly with salt and pepper. Sprinkle with the remaining 1 tablespoon parsley and serve hot.

(Some More Ideas) Brown rice can be substituted for the white rice. It will take 30 to 40 minutes to cook and will need about 1/2 cup more broth.

Pork and turkey sausage jambalaya: Cut 1/2 pound pork tenderloin into thin strips and brown in 2 teaspoons olive oil, then remove from the pan and set aside. Add 1 chopped red onion to the pan and cook until almost soft, about 5 minutes. Stir in the rice and cook for 2 to 3 minutes, then pour in 2 cups low-sodium vegetable broth. Cover and simmer for 10 minutes. Stir in 1 can (14 ounces) tomatoes with the juice, and 2 medium zucchini, sliced. Cover and cook for 5 minutes. Return the pork to the pan together with 1/4 pound sliced reduced-fat turkey sausage and cook, covered, until all the liquid has been absorbed and the rice is tender, about 5 minutes. Serve sprinkled with 2 tablespoons chopped parsley.

Plus Points

• Salmon is rich in vitamins B6 and B12 and the minerals selenium and potassium.

• Rice requires more water for growing than any other cereal crop. However, the main purpose of the standing water in paddy fields is to drown the weed competition that the rice seedlings face.

photo, page 143

Exchanges	
starch 2 1/2	vegetable 2
meat (very lean) 3	

Each serving provides calories 416, calories from fat 91, fat 10g, saturated fat 1g, cholesterol 121mg, sodium 595mg, carbohydrate 50g, fiber 4g, sugars 8g, protein 30g. Excellent source of iron, niacin, phosphorus, potassium, thiamine, vitamin A, vitamin B6, vitamin B12, vitamin C. Good source of calcium, folate, magnesium, riboflavin.

cod with gremolata crust

This is a delicious recipe for jazzing up plain cod fillets. Gremolata is an Italian mixture of parsley, lemon zest, and garlic (and sometimes chopped anchovy). This recipe uses the gremolata with bread crumbs to make a tasty topping for the fish, which is baked with a blend of juicy tomatoes and zucchini and served with saffron mashed potatoes.

Preparation time **20 minutes**   Cooking time **25 minutes**   *Serves 4*

2 lemons
1/2 cup white bread crumbs
3 tablespoons chopped parsley
2 garlic cloves, crushed
4 (4 ounce) pieces of skinless cod fillet
Cooking spray
2 teaspoons coarse mustard
3 plum tomatoes, quartered
1 large zucchini, thinly sliced diagonally
1 tablespoon olive oil
1 pound potatoes, peeled and cut into chunks
1 teaspoon saffron threads
3 tablespoons 1% milk
Salt and pepper

1 Preheat the oven to 400°F. Finely grate the zest and squeeze the juice from one of the lemons. Mix the zest with the bread crumbs, parsley, and garlic, and season lightly with salt and pepper.

2 Place the cod fillets in a large ovenproof dish coated with cooking spray. Spread the mustard evenly over the top of the fish, then sprinkle on the lemon juice. Arrange the tomatoes and zucchini around the fish. Cut the remaining lemon into 4 wedges and put them into the dish.

3 Spoon the bread-crumb mixture over the fish and press down lightly. Drizzle with the olive oil. Bake the fish until it will flake easily and the topping is crisp, about 25 minutes.

4 Meanwhile, place the potatoes in a saucepan, cover with boiling water, and add the saffron. Cook the potatoes until tender, about 15 to 20 minutes. Drain the potatoes and mash with the milk. Season lightly with salt and pepper. Serve the fish with the potatoes, tomatoes, and zucchini.

(Some More Ideas) *Special occasions*: Bake the cod in individual ovenproof dishes. Slice the tomatoes, and replace the zucchini with 1 red or yellow pepper, seeded and chopped. Put a piece of fish in each dish and arrange the sliced tomatoes on top. Scatter over the pepper and then the bread-crumb mixture, and bake for 20 minutes. Garnish with wedges of lemon.

Pieces of skinless salmon fillet can be used instead of cod. Replace the lemon zest with orange zest and add some snipped fresh chives to the bread-crumb topping.

Plus Points

• Garlic has long been credited with prolonging physical strength. It was fed to the Egyptian slaves who built the pyramids.
• Crushing garlic releases more of its essential oils and results in a sharper flavor than slicing the cloves or leaving them whole.
• Saffron is the world's most expensive spice. Fortunately, a little of the spice goes a long way. Thousands of years ago, saffron was used as a flavoring, to dye cloth, and to make medicines. Today it is an integral seasoning in many dishes from Spain and France.

photo, page 143

Exchanges
starch 1 1/2 vegetable 1
meat (very lean) 2 fat 1/2

Each serving provides calories 251, calories from fat 45, fat 5g, saturated fat 1g, cholesterol 49mg, sodium 174mg, carbohydrate 28g, fiber 4g, sugars 6g, protein 24g. Excellent source of magnesium, niacin, phosphorus, potassium, thiamine, vitamin B6, vitamin B12, vitamin C. Good source of folate, iron, riboflavin, vitamin A.

cod with spicy lentils

Dark green Puy lentils, grown in the south of France, have a unique, peppery flavor that is enhanced by chile. They hold their shape during cooking and their texture is a perfect complement for the flakiness of fresh cod. The thin, papery skins that encase lentils are also high in fiber. Serve this satisfying dish with a mixed salad.

Preparation and cooking time **about 35 minutes**   *Serves 4*

1 tablespoon olive oil, divided
1 onion, chopped
2 celery stalks, chopped
2 medium leeks, chopped
1 to 2 fresh red chiles, seeded and finely chopped
1 cup small lentils, rinsed and drained
4 cups reduced-sodium vegetable broth
1 sprig fresh thyme
1 bay leaf
Juice of 1 lemon
Pinch cayenne pepper
4 (4 ounce) skinless cod fillets or cod steaks
Salt and pepper
Lemon wedges to serve

1 Preheat the grill to medium-high heat. Heat half of the olive oil in a saucepan, add the onion, celery, leeks, and chiles, and cook gently for 2 minutes. Stir in the lentils. Add the vegetable broth, thyme, and bay leaf, and bring to a boil. Lower the heat and simmer until the lentils are tender, about 20 minutes. If at the end of this time the lentils have not absorbed all the broth, drain them (you can use the excess stock to make a soup).

2 While the lentils are cooking, mix together the remaining oil, the lemon juice, and cayenne pepper. Lay the cod on a ridged grill pan or broiler pan, skinned side up, season lightly with salt and pepper, and brush with the oil mixture. Grill over high heat or oven broil until the fish will flake easily, about 6 to 7 minutes. There is no need to turn the fish over.

3 Spread the lentils in a warmed serving dish and arrange the pieces of cod on top. Serve immediately, with lemon wedges.

(Some More Ideas) Halibut or salmon can be substituted for the cod.

Plus Points

• "Fish and chips" containing fried cod is an all-time American favorite. Frying the cod in batter more than doubles the calorie content, whereas brushing it with a little oil and grilling it keeps the fat, and therefore calories, at healthy levels.
• Lentils, which are small seeds from a variety of leguminous plants, do not need to be soaked before cooking. Lentils are a good source of iron. Iron absorption from lentils is poor, however, but vitamin C–rich foods, such as the lemon juice in this recipe, can improve this process considerably.
• Thyme has been used as an antiseptic since Greek and Roman times.

Exchanges
starch 2 vegetable 2
meat (very lean) 3 fat 1/2

Each serving provides calories 328, calories from fat 47, fat 5g, saturated fat 0g, cholesterol 50mg, sodium 1074mg, carbohydrate 38g, fiber 12g, sugars 9g, protein 33g. Excellent source of folate, iron, magnesium, niacin, phosphorus, potassium, thiamine, vitamin B6, vitamin C. Good source of calcium, riboflavin, vitamin A, vitamin B12. Flag: High in sodium.

cod with gremolata crust *p141*

cod with spicy lentils *p142*

baked trout with
cucumber sauce *p144*

swordfish with salsa dressing *p145*

baked trout with cucumber sauce

Orange and lemon slices add a great citrus flavor to this recipe for baked fish, and a cucumber and yogurt sauce provides a refreshing contrast. New potatoes are roasted with the fish, cutting down on preparation time. Serving the dish with potatoes as the starch and eliminating a crumb topping on the fish lower the total carbohydrate content of the meal.

Preparation and cooking time **40 minute**   *Serves 4*

Trout

1 pound new potatoes, quartered lengthways

2 teaspoons olive oil

4 (10 ounce) small trout, cleaned

4 sprigs fresh tarragon

1 orange, cut into 8 slices

1 lemon, cut into 8 slices

4 tablespoons orange juice

Sauce

1 large cucumber, peeled and seeded

2/3 cup plain low-fat yogurt

2 tablespoons chopped fresh mint

Salt and pepper

Garnish

1 cup watercress

1 Preheat the oven to 400°F and put 2 baking sheets in the oven to heat up. Place the potatoes in a large saucepan and pour over enough boiling water to cover them. Bring back to a boil, then simmer for 5 minutes. Drain and return to the pan.

2 Drizzle the oil over the potatoes and toss them quickly to coat. Spread them out on one of the hot baking sheets and roast for 10 minutes. Turn the potatoes over and roast for another 10 minutes, then turn them again and roast until crisp and tender, about another 5 minutes.

3 Meanwhile, season inside the fish and tuck in the sprigs of tarragon. Cut out 4 squares of foil, each large enough to wrap up a fish. Cut the orange and lemon slices in half. Divide half the orange and lemon slices among the foil squares, lay the fish on top, and cover with the remaining fruit slices. Sprinkle 1 tablespoon orange juice over each fish.

4 Wrap up the fish, completely enclosing it in the foil, twisting the ends to seal. Lay the parcels on the second hot baking sheet and bake for 20 minutes.

5 While the fish and potatoes are cooking, make the sauce. Grate the cucumber, put it into a sieve, and press to squeeze out the water. Mix together the cucumber, yogurt, and mint, and season lightly with salt and pepper. Arrange the fish, orange, and lemon slices, and roasted potatoes on warm plates. Add a garnish of watercress and serve with the cucumber sauce.

(Some More Ideas) *A very speedy trout dish*: Buy trout fillets, 2 per person. Sprinkle with a little extra-virgin olive oil and grill, skin side down, for 2 to 4 minutes, depending on the thickness. Serve with boiled small new potatoes.

Vary the flavor of the sauce by adding 1 teaspoon prepared horseradish. Or, instead of mint, use 1 tablespoon chopped fresh chives or green olives.

Mackerel can be substituted for the trout.

Plus Points

• Like other oily fish, trout contains beneficial fats from the omega-3 family of essential fatty acids. These help to protect the body against strokes and heart disease.

• Plain yogurt is often used in recipes as an alternative to heavy cream. This has the advantage of helping to lower the fat content of a recipe. In addition, yogurt provides more calcium than cream on a ounce for ounce basis.

photo, page 143

Exchanges

starch 1 1/2 fruit 1/2
meat (lean) 3

Each serving provides calories 320, calories from fat 79, fat 9g, saturated fat 2g, cholesterol 65mg, sodium 73mg, carbohydrate 34g, fiber 4g, sugars 11g, protein 27g. Excellent source of niacin, phosphorus, potassium, thiamine, vitamin B6, vitamin B12, vitamin C. Good source of calcium, copper, folate, magnesium, riboflavin, vitamin A.

swordfish with salsa dressing

Orange juice adds a refreshing note to the salsa-style tomato-and-pepper dressing for this vibrant-looking salad. As the dressing can be made well in advance and the swordfish steaks take only minutes to cook, this is a very quick dish to prepare—ideal when you are entertaining. Serve with thin sesame breadsticks on the side.

Preparation time **30 minutes**   Marinating time **20 minutes**   Cooking time **5–6 minutes**   *Serves 4*

Swordfish

4 (5 ounce) swordfish steaks, 1/2 inch thick
1 teaspoon olive oil
2 cups baby spinach leaves
2 zucchini, coarsely grated
1 tablespoon chopped parsley

Dressing

1 large orange
1 pound ripe tomatoes, seeded and cut into 1/4-inch dice
4 large scallions, green parts only, finely chopped
1 orange bell pepper, seeded and cut into 1/4-inch dice
1 yellow bell pepper, seeded and cut into 1/4-inch dice
1 teaspoon ground cumin, or to taste
2 teaspoons olive oil
1 fresh green chile pepper, seeded and finely chopped
Salt and pepper
2 tablespoons finely chopped fresh cilantro

1 Prepare the salsa dressing at least 20 minutes (or up to 8 hours) before serving. Finely grate the zest from the orange and squeeze out 4 tablespoons juice. Place the zest and juice in a large mixing bowl and add the tomatoes, scallions, peppers, cumin, olive oil, and chile. Season lightly with salt and pepper. Stir, then cover and refrigerate.

2 Preheat the grill to high. Lightly brush the swordfish steaks with some of the olive oil and place on the grill rack. Grill, about 3 inches from the heat, for 2 1/2 minutes. Turn the swordfish steaks over, brush with the rest of the olive oil, and grill until the edges are lightly charred and the flesh is just firm, about another 2 to 3 minutes. Don't overcook or the swordfish will be tough and dry. Remove from the heat and set aside to cool slightly.

3 Meanwhile, put the spinach leaves, zucchini, and parsley in a bowl and toss to mix. Divide among 4 plates.

4 Stir the cilantro into the dressing. Break the swordfish into bite-size pieces, add to the dressing, and gently mix in, taking care not to break up the fish. Spoon the dressed fish on top of the spinach salad and serve.

(Some More Ideas) Skinless salmon fillets can be substituted for the swordfish.

Warm Mediterranean tuna salad: Using 4 tuna steaks, 1 inch thick, about 5 ounces each. Grill the steaks, basting with a mixture of 1 teaspoon extra-virgin olive oil and 1 tablespoon orange juice, for 2 to 3 minutes on each side, according to how well done you like tuna. Instead of using the tomatoes in the salsa dressing, slice them. Make the salsa dressing omitting the cumin, chile, and cilantro, and toss with 2 cups shredded radicchio and 1 cup arugula. Arrange the tomato slices and salsa salad on 4 plates, top with the tuna, broken into pieces, and scatter some shredded fresh basil over it.

Plus Points

• Swordfish is a good low-fat source of protein and is very nutritious, providing excellent amounts of vitamin B12, niacin, and selenium, as well as useful quantities of potassium.
• Zucchini provide the B vitamins B6, folate, and niacin. The greatest concentration of these nutrients is found in the skin, which is also rich in the antioxidant beta-carotene.

photo, page 143

Exchanges

vegetable 3 meat (lean) 4

Each serving provides calories 280, calories from fat 90, fat 10g, saturated fat 0g, cholesterol 54mg, sodium 158mg, carbohydrate 18g, fiber 5g, sugars 9g, protein 32g. Excellent source of folate, magnesium, niacin, phosphorus, potassium, vitamin A, vitamin B6, vitamin B12, vitamin C. Good source of iron, riboflavin, thiamine.

salmon with tarragon mayonnaise

Salmon is not a mild-tasting fish, so a creamy sauce made of low-fat yogurt, mayonnaise, and herbs balances the flavors and makes the dish cool and refreshing. Here the fish is served on a bed of couscous flavored with the light, wine-based poaching liquid from the fish, eliminating the need for store-bought broth, which is usually high in sodium.

Preparation and cooking time **35 minutes**   *Serves 4*

Salmon

4 (4 ounce) salmon steaks or fillets
1/2 cup dry white wine
1 to 2 bay leaves
Strip of pared lemon zest

Mayonnaise

4 tablespoons low-fat mayonnaise
1/2 cup plain low-fat yogurt
Finely grated zest of 1 lemon
2 tablespoons chopped fresh tarragon

Couscous

1 cup couscous
4 tomatoes, roughly chopped
3 scallions, chopped
2 cups watercress, roughly chopped
1 tablespoon olive oil
Juice of 1 lemon
Salt and pepper

1 Place the salmon in a deep-sided, non-stick skillet. Pour the wine over it and add the bay leaves, lemon zest, and seasoning to taste. Bring to a boil, then reduce the heat, cover, and poach the salmon until just cooked, about 5 to 6 minutes. It should still be very slightly translucent in the center.

2 Meanwhile, stir together the mayonnaise, yogurt, grated lemon zest, and tarragon. Season lightly with salt and pepper and spoon the mixture into a serving bowl.

3 When the fish is cooked, drain off most of the cooking liquid into a measuring cup, and add enough boiling water to make 1 1/2 cups. Cover the pan with a lid to keep the salmon warm, off the heat.

4 Pour the diluted fish broth over the couscous in a bowl and leave for 3 to 4 minutes for the liquid to be absorbed. Fluff up the couscous with a fork and stir in the chopped tomatoes, scallions, and watercress. Drizzle the olive oil and lemon juice over it, and stir to blend everything together. Season slightly with salt and pepper.

5 Serve the warm salmon with the couscous salad and the tarragon mayonnaise.

(Some More Ideas) Low-fat sour cream can be used for making the sauce in place of the yogurt and mayonnaise.

For a watercress sauce, replace the tarragon with 1/4 cup chopped watercress.

Special occasions: Cook a whole salmon and serve it garnished with twists of lemon and sprigs of fresh tarragon. To cook salmon, season and wrap loosely in a large sheet of foil coated with cooking spray, then bake in a preheated 350°F oven until fish flakes easily with a fork, allowing 10 minutes per pound.

Plus Points

• Combining mayonnaise with plain low-fat yogurt makes a lighter sauce that is lower in calories and fat than mayonnaise alone.
• Incorporating low-fat dairy products into sauces and soups is a good way to increase calcium and protein intake.

photo, page 149

Exchanges	
starch 2 1/2	vegetable 2
meat (lean) 3	fat 1

Each serving provides calories 463, calories from fat 138, fat 15g, saturated fat 3g, cholesterol 73mg, sodium 247mg, carbohydrate 46g, fiber 4g, sugars 11g, protein 33g. Excellent source of niacin, phosphorus, potassium, riboflavin, thiamine, vitamin A, vitamin B6, vitamin B12, vitamin C.

grilled halibut steaks with tomato and red pepper salsa

Halibut is a white, low-fat, mild-flavored fish and is well suited to cooking on a grill or in a metal-ridged grill pan. A vibrant salsa transforms this fish into an exciting dish. Serve with steamed brown rice and a mixed leaf salad.

Preparation time **15 minutes**   Cooking time **4–6 minutes**   *Serves 4*

Steaks

4 (4 ounce) halibut steaks,
1 tablespoon extra-virgin olive oil
Juice of 1 small orange
1 garlic clove, crushed
Cooking spray

Salsa

1/2 pound ripe plum tomatoes, diced
1 red pepper, seeded and diced
1 small red onion, finely chopped
Juice of 1 small orange
2 tablespoons chopped fresh basil
1 tablespoon balsamic vinegar
1 teaspoon sugar
Salt and pepper

Garnish

1 orange, cut into wedges

1 Place the halibut steaks in a shallow nonmetallic dish. Mix together the oil, orange juice, and garlic and season lightly with salt and pepper. Spoon the mixture over the fish steaks.

2 Combine all the salsa ingredients and season lightly with salt and pepper. Spoon into a serving bowl.

3 Heat ridged grill pan or heavy skillet coated with cooking spray over high heat. Place the fish steaks on the grill pan or in the skillet and cook until the fish flakes easily, about 2 to 3 minutes on each side, basting from time to time with the oil mixture.

4 Place the fish steaks on warm serving plates and sprinkle with freshly ground black pepper. Garnish with wedges of orange and serve with the salsa.

(Some More Ideas) Other white fish steaks, such as cod, haddock, swordfish, or monkfish fillets, can be cooked in the same way.

Tomato and olive salsa: Combine the diced tomatoes with 1 diced cucumber, 4 chopped scallions, 2 tablespoons pitted chopped green or black olives, and 2 tablespoons chopped fresh basil. Or use 1 tablespoon drained and rinsed capers instead of olives.

In summer, the fish can be cooked outdoors on a barbecue. Lay the steaks on a sheet of foil to prevent the delicate flesh slipping through the grill.

Plus Points

• Halibut is a good source of niacin, which has an important role to play in the release of energy inside cells. Niacin is one of the most stable vitamins, and there are little or no losses during preparation or cooking.

• In restaurants, fish is often pan-fried in a good amount of oil. This contributes added fat to the dish. When grilling fish at home, limit cooking fat for a much healthier meal.

photo, page 149

Exchanges

fruit 1/2 vegetable 2
meat (very lean) 3 fat 1

Each serving provides calories 225, calories from fat 56, fat 6g, saturated fat 0g, cholesterol 37mg, sodium 69mg, carbohydrate 17g, fiber 3g, sugars 12g, protein 25g. Excellent source of magnesium, niacin, phosphorus, potassium, vitamin A, vitamin B6, vitamin C. Good source of folate, riboflavin, thiamine.

haddock with parsley sauce

The mild-flavored haddock is served with mashed potatoes mixed with leeks and zucchini. The fish is poached in a milk-based cooking liquid richly flavored with parsley, onion, carrots, and pepper. To finish the dish, the cooking liquid is used to create a lovely, creamy sauce that is drizzled over the fish and mashed potatoes.

Preparation and cooking time **45–50 minutes**   *Serves 4*

Haddock

4 (4 ounce) pieces of haddock fillet
Cooking spray
1 large bunch of parsley
1 small onion, thinly sliced
1 carrot, thinly sliced
6 black peppercorns
1 1/4 cups 1% milk
1 pound potatoes, peeled and cut into chunks
1 large leek, thinly sliced
2 zucchini, cut into thin sticks
1 tablespoon butter
1 tablespoon flour
Finely grated zest and juice of 1/2 lemon
Salt and pepper

Garnish

Chopped fresh parsley
Lemon wedges to serve

1 Place the fish in a large nonstick skillet coated with cooking spray. Tear the leaves from the parsley stalks and add the stalks to the pan with the onion, carrot, peppercorns, and milk. Bring just to a boil, then cover, and simmer very gently for 5 minutes. Remove the pan from the heat and leave for 5 minutes to complete the cooking.

2 Meanwhile, put the potatoes in a saucepan, cover with boiling water, and simmer until tender, about 15 minutes. About 5 minutes before the end of the cooking time, add the white part of the leek to the potatoes. Set a colander on top of the pan and steam the zucchini with the green part of the leek over the potatoes.

3 Transfer the fish to a plate and remove the skin. Keep warm. Strain the cooking liquid and reserve.

4 Melt the butter in a medium saucepan, stir in the flour, and cook for 1 minute. Gradually stir in the cooking liquid and bring to a boil, stirring until the sauce is thickened and smooth. Finely chop the parsley leaves and stir into the sauce with the lemon zest. Season to taste and keep hot.

5 Drain the potatoes and white leeks and mash with the lemon juice and seasoning. Stir in the green leek tops and zucchini.

Transfer the fish fillets to serving plates and spoon the sauce over them. Garnish with parsley and serve with the mashed potatoes and lemon wedges.

(**Some More Ideas**) *Haddock and spinach gratin*: Cook the fish and potatoes as above. Slice 3 tomatoes and arrange in a shallow 6-cup oven-safe dish. Steam 3 cups spinach leaves until wilted, then squeeze dry and sprinkle with 1 tablespoon lemon juice. Spread over the tomatoes and arrange the fish on top. Pour the parsley sauce over it and spread the mashed potatoes on top. Sprinkle with 3 tablespoons grated reduced-fat cheddar cheese and broil until the top is golden, about 5 minutes.

Plus Points

• Zucchini provides niacin and vitamin B6. It is the tender skins that contain the greatest concentration of these nutrients.
• Parsley was used in Greek times for its medicinal purposes, but the Romans used it as an herb. Parsley is rich in nutrients, particularly vitamin C. Just a teaspoon of chopped parsley can make a significant contribution to the daily requirement for vitamin C.

Exchanges

starch 1 1/2 vegetable 2
meat (very lean) 3 fat 1/2

Each serving provides calories 290, calories from fat 45, fat 5g, saturated fat 3g, cholesterol 75mg, sodium 173mg, carbohydrate 34g, fiber 5g, sugars 9g, protein 28g. Excellent source of folate, magnesium, niacin, phosphorus, potassium, thiamine, vitamin A, vitamin B6, vitamin B12, vitamin C. Good source of calcium, iron, riboflavin.

grilled halibut steaks with tomato and red pepper salsa *p147*

haddock with parsley sauce *p148*

linguine and salmon with creamy lemon-dill sauce *p150*

salmon with tarragon mayonnaise *p146*

linguine and salmon with creamy lemon-dill sauce

For this dish, the ingredients are quickly assembled and cooked, and the result is truly delicious as well as visually impressive. Simply cut the vegetables and marinate the salmon ahead of time. Serve this light, zesty dish with bread and salad for a refreshing, healthy meal.

Preparation time **10 minutes, plus optional marinating**   Cooking time **15 minutes**   *Serves 4*

Salmon

1 pound skinned salmon fillet

Grated zest and juice of 1 lemon

2 tablespoons chopped fresh dill

8 ounces linguine

2 large carrots, peeled and cut into matchstick strips

2 large zucchini, unpeeled and cut into matchstick strips

1 teaspoon canola oil

1/3 cup reduced-fat crème fraîche or sour cream

Salt and pepper

Garnish

Sprigs of fresh dill

1 lemon, cut into wedges

1 Cut the salmon into chunks and place in a dish. Add the lemon zest and juice, and the dill. Turn the pieces of salmon to coat them evenly. If time permits, cover and marinate in the refrigerator for at least 10 minutes.

2 Cook the linguine in boiling water for 10 minutes, or according to the package instructions, until al dente. Add the carrots to the pasta after 8 minutes of cooking, then add the zucchini 1 minute later.

3 Meanwhile, brush a nonstick or heavy-based skillet with the oil and heat thoroughly. Drain the salmon, reserving the lemon-juice marinade. Add the salmon to the hot skillet and cook, turning the pieces occasionally, until the fish is firm and just cooked, 3 or 4 minutes.

4 Add the reserved marinade and the crème fraîche or sour cream to the salmon, and cook for a few seconds. Remove from the heat and season lightly with salt and pepper.

5 Drain the pasta and vegetables, and transfer them to a serving dish or to 4 individual plates. Add the salmon mixture, garnish with fresh dill if desired, and serve with lemon wedges.

(**Some More Ideas**) Trout fillets, asparagus tips, and fava beans are an excellent alternative combination to the salmon, carrot, and zucchini. Add the asparagus tips and beans to the pasta for the last 4 to 5 minutes of cooking.

A quick, healthy supper dish: Add frozen green beans and corn to the pasta, and use a can of well-drained salmon instead of the fresh fish. There is no need to marinate or cook the canned salmon: The heat of the pasta will bring out its flavor beautifully.

Plus Points

• Using low-fat crème fraîche or sour cream makes a deceivingly creamy lemon sauce for the fish that tastes simply decadent.

• Cutting the zucchini and carrots into thin strips and mixing them with pasta creates a colorful base and appealing presentation for the salmon.

photo, page 149

Exchanges

starch 3 vegetable 2
meat (lean) 3 fat 1/2

Each serving provides calories 483, calories from fat 125, fat 14g, saturated fat 3g, cholesterol 84mg, sodium 99mg, carbohydrate 55g, fiber 6g, sugars 9g, protein 35g. Excellent source of folate, magnesium, niacin, phosphorus, potassium, riboflavin, thiamine, vitamin A, vitamin B6, vitamin B12, vitamin C. Good source of copper, iron.

spaghetti with clams

This popular trattoria dish is easily made at home. A classic tomato sauce, flavored with chile and fresh herbs in true Italian style, is delicious with clams, especially if tossed with perfectly cooked spaghetti. Serve with a green salad—and a glass of red wine.

Preparation time **15 minutes**   Cooking time **20 minutes**   *Serves 4*

1 tablespoon olive oil

1 onion, chopped

2 garlic cloves, chopped

1 small fresh red chile, seeded and chopped

1/2 cup chopped cremini or white button mushrooms

1 can (24 ounces) plum tomatoes

1 tablespoon chopped fresh basil

1 tablespoon chopped parsley

1 teaspoon sugar

8 ounces spaghetti

48 clams (about 2 pounds) in their shells

4 tablespoons red or white wine

1 Heat the oil in a medium saucepan, add the onion, garlic, and chile, and cook over medium heat for 5 minutes. Stir in the mushrooms and cook for 2 minutes, then add the tomatoes and their juice, crushing them down with a wooden spoon. Sprinkle in the basil, parsley, and sugar and stir. Cover and simmer for 10 minutes.

2 Meanwhile, cook the spaghetti in boiling water according to the packet instructions, until al dente, about 10 to 12 minutes. Drain the pasta in a colander.

3 Place the empty pasta pan back on the heat, add the clams and wine. Add the pasta back in. Cover, and cook for 3 minutes, shaking the pan occasionally. All the shells should have opened; discard any clams that remain shut.

4 Pour the tomato sauce into the spaghetti and clam mixture. Stir and toss over the heat until it is all bubbling, about 1 to 2 minutes. Season lightly with salt and pepper, then serve.

(Some More Ideas) If fresh clams are not available, make a tomato, olive, and caper sauce with canned clams. Heat 2 teaspoons extra-virgin olive oil in a saucepan. Add 1 chopped onion, 1 small red pepper, seeded and chopped, and 1 chopped garlic clove. Cook for 5 minutes, then add 1 can (24 ounces) of tomatoes, with the juice, crushing them down. Cover and cook for 10 minutes. Stir a can of baby clams (10 ounces) into the tomato sauce and add 8 black olives, roughly chopped, 1 tablespoon capers, and a handful of freshly torn basil leaves. Taste and season with black pepper. Simmer for 2 minutes, then serve the sauce over the spaghetti.

Use spinach or whole-wheat pasta instead of traditional thin spaghetti.

Plus Points

• One glass of red wine per day has been shown to decrease the incidence of heart disease. For people with diabetes, alcohol should be limited and it is counted as a carbohydrate exchange.

• Clams are an excellent source of phosphorus.

• Contrary to popular belief, pasta eaten in moderation is not a fattening food. It is only when excessive amounts of oil, cream, or butter are added to the accompanying sauces that the calories are considerably increased.

• All mushrooms are a good source of copper, which has many important functions in the body, including maintaining healthy bones and helping to prevent anemia by improving the absorption of iron from food.

photo, page 155

Exchanges

starch 3 vegetable 3
meat (very lean) 3 fat 1/2

Each serving provides calories 449, calories from fat 61, fat 7g, saturated fat 1g, cholesterol 64mg, sodium 369mg, carbohydrate 61g, fiber 4g, sugars 16g, protein 34g. Excellent source of ilron, niacin, phosphorus, potassium, riboflavin, thiamine, vitamin A, vitamin B6, vitamin B12, vitamin C. Good source of calcium, folate, magnesium.

151

parmesan-topped mussels

Make this dish when you can buy large mussels, such as the green-lipped mussels from New Zealand, and buy a few extra because some might have to be discarded. After the mussels are cooked in a flavorful wine-based broth, they are crowned with a cheese and bread crumb topping and broiled to perfection.

Preparation and cooking time **30 minutes**   Serves 4

1/2 cup white wine or low-sodium vegetable broth

1 large onion, very finely chopped

3 large garlic cloves, crushed

About 30 large mussels, scrubbed and beards removed

1 slice (1 ounce) fresh whole-wheat bread

1/4 cup chopped parsley

1/4 cup grated Parmesan cheese

1 tablespoon finely grated lemon zest

Pinch cayenne pepper

2 teaspoons olive oil

Lemon wedges to serve

1 Pour the wine or broth into a large saucepan, add the onion and garlic, and bring to a boil over high heat. Boil rapidly for 1 minute. Add the mussels, cover the pan tightly, and cook for 2 to 3 minutes, shaking the pan occasionally. Uncover the pan and give the mussels a good stir. Using tongs, remove the mussels from the pan as soon as they open and set them aside. Discard any mussels that remain shut.

2 When the mussels are cool enough to handle, remove and discard the top shell. Place 24 mussels on the half shell in a single layer in a shallow flameproof dish, loosening the mussels from the shells but leaving them in place. Set the dish aside.

3 Preheat an oven broiler. Put the bread in a food processor or blender and process to fine crumbs. Add the parsley, Parmesan, lemon zest, cayenne pepper, and olive oil, and process again until well blended.

4 Using your fingers, put a mound of the cheese and crumb mixture on each mussel and pack it down firmly so the mussel is completely covered. Put the dish under the broiler and cook until the crumb topping is crisp and lightly browned, about 2 to 3 minutes. Divide the mussels among individual plates and serve with lemon wedges.

(Some More Ideas) Oysters can be substituted for the mussels.

To use large, peeled shrimp in place of the mussels: Poach the shrimp in the broth and then remove from the pan with a slotted spoon. Lay the shrimp on their sides on a foil-lined baking sheet. Place a spoonful of the topping mixture on each shrimp and then broil as directed above.

Plus Points

• Mussels are available year-round, but get used less frequently than clams and oysters. They have a delightfully sweet flavor that is often under recognized.

• Cayenne pepper, made from one of the smallest and hottest chiles, is often used in herbal medicine to stimulate circulation.

photo, page 155

Exchanges

carbohydrate 1/2 vegetable 1 meat (lean) 2 fat 1/2

Each serving provides calories 190, calories from fat 69, fat 8g, saturated fat 2g, cholesterol 41mg, sodium 408mg, carbohydrate 12g, fiber 1g, sugars 9g, protein 19g. Excellent source of iron, phosphorus, vitamin B12, vitamin C. Good source of calcium, folate, niacin, riboflavin, thiamine, vitamin A.

shrimp with pepper salsa

A salsa is a Mexican-style vegetable or fruit sauce with a fresh and zingy flavor. A tomato, pepper, and chile salsa makes a wonderful accompaniment for grilled shrimp kebabs, skewered with sweet melon. Serve the kabobs with brown rice or a piece of crusty bread.

Preparation and cooking time **30 minutes**   *Serves 8*

Shrimp

32 large shrimp, peeled, deveined, tails left on

1 medium cantaloupe, seeded and cut into 2 inch cubes

Marinade

2 tablespoons lime juice

1 teaspoon chopped garlic

1 teaspoon chopped, peeled ginger

Salsa

6 medium tomatoes, chopped

1 small red onion, finely chopped

1 red pepper, seeded and chopped

1 teaspoon chopped garlic

1 fresh green chile, seeded and finely, chopped

2 tablespoons lime juice

2 tablespoons chopped fresh cilantro

Salt and pepper

Chopped scallions to garnish

1 Soak 8 bamboo skewers in cold water (this will prevent them from burning under the grill) for 30 minutes. Combine all of the ingredients for the marinade in a shallow dish. Add the shrimp and stir to coat them with the marinade. Cover and refrigerate while preparing the salsa.

2 Mix together all the salsa ingredients and season with salt and pepper to taste. Pile into a serving bowl. Thread the cubes of melon onto 8 unsoaked wooden skewers and place on a serving dish. Set aside.

3 Thread 4 shrimp onto each of the soaked skewers, piercing them through both ends (this will help to keep them flat). Place on the grill or oven-broiler rack and cook until they are pink, about 3 to 4 minutes, turning them once. Do not overcook or they will become tough.

4 Garnish the salsa with the shredded scallions. Place the shrimp kebabs on the serving dish with the melon and serve immediately, with the salsa alongside.

(Some More Ideas) *Grilled chicken kebabs with a fresh citrus salsa*: Cut 2 skinless boneless chicken breasts into cubes and marinate as described in the main recipe. Grill the chicken on skewers until tender and cooked through, about 10 minutes. For the salsa, chop the flesh from 1 pink grapefruit, 1 orange, and 1 crisp apple (such as Jonagold), and mix with 2 chopped scallions, 1 finely chopped fresh green chile, and 1 tablespoon chopped fresh mint.

Many fruits can be substituted for the melon in this recipe. Try cubes of fresh pineapple, or fresh apricot halves.

Plus Points
• The raw fruit and vegetables in the salsa are packed with vitamins. The tomatoes and red peppers are excellent sources of the antioxidants beta-carotene and vitamin C.
• Shrimp is a high-protein, low-fat food.

photo, page 155

Exchanges
fruit 1/2 vegetable 1
meat (very lean) 1

Each serving provides calories 86, calories from fat 8, fat 1g, saturated fat 0g, cholesterol 47mg, sodium 72mg, carbohydrate 15g, fiber 3g, sugars 10g, protein 7g. Excellent source of vitamin A, vitamin C. Good source of potassium, vitamin B6.

153

shrimp gumbo

A bowl of steaming gumbo—a thick and spicy cross between a soup and a stew, full of peppers, tomatoes, okra, herbs, and shrimp—brings you all the good tastes of the Louisiana bayou. In this version, butter is eliminated and the soup is thickened with a mix of flour and broth. Serve the gumbo over steamed brown rice to soak up the sauce.

Preparation time **25 minutes**   Cooking time **40 minutes**   *Serves 4*

Gumbo

1 tablespoon olive oil

2 onions, chopped

1 red pepper, seeded and chopped

2 celery stalks, chopped

3 garlic cloves, chopped

2 slices reduced-fat bacon, diced

1 tablespoon flour

1 tablespoon paprika

3 cups reduced-sodium low-fat chicken or vegetable broth

1 teaspoon chopped fresh thyme

1 can (14 ounces) chopped tomatoes

2 tablespoons chopped parsley

2 bay leaves

2 teaspoons Worcestershire sauce

Hot red pepper sauce to taste

1/2 cup okra, sliced crossways

12 ounces large shrimp, peeled and deveined

1 cup haricots verts (French green beans) or green beans, cut into bite-size pieces

Salt and pepper

Garnish

Thinly sliced scallions

1 Heat the oil in a large saucepan, add the onions, pepper, and celery, and cook until lightly browned, about 5 to 6 minutes. Stir in the garlic and bacon and cook for 3 to 4 minutes. Stir in the flour, increase the heat slightly, and cook for 2 minutes, stirring. Stir in the paprika and cook for 2 more minutes. Gradually add the broth, stirring well to dissolve the flour mixture.

2 Add the thyme, tomatoes with their juice, parsley, bay leaves, and Worcestershire sauce. Bring to a boil, then reduce the heat to a simmer and add hot sauce to taste. Add the okra and simmer until the okra is tender and the gumbo mixture has thickened, about 15 minutes.

3 Add the shrimp and green beans and cook until the shrimp turn pink and the beans are tender, about 3 minutes. Remove the bay leaves and season the gumbo lightly with salt and pepper. Serve in bowls, sprinkled with scallions.

(Some More Ideas) Use a mixture of 1/2 pound shrimp and 1/2 pound canned crab-meat, adding the crab to the gumbo at the very end, with the final seasoning.

Plus Points
• Okra contains a mucilaginous substance that is useful to thicken the liquid in dishes such as gumbo (the name gumbo comes from the African word for okra). The nutrient content of okra is very similar to other green vegetables in that it provides useful amounts of dietary fiber, potassium, calcium, folate, and vitamin C.
• Brown rice still contains the husk of the rice kernel, which contains the majority of the fiber in the grain. White rice goes through a process that removes this outer husk, making it lower in fiber and less nutritious.

Exchanges

vegetable 4 meat (very lean) 3 fat 1

Each serving provides calories 255, calories from fat 70, fat 8g, saturated fat 1g, cholesterol 172mg, sodium 808mg, carbohydrate 21g, fiber 5g, sugars 12g, protein 27g. Excellent source of folate, iron, magnesium, niacin, phosphorus, potassium, riboflavin, thiamine, vitamin A, vitamin B6, vitamin B12, vitamin C. Good source of calcium.

spaghetti with clams *p151*

shrimp gumbo *p154*

parmesan-topped mussels *p152*

shrimp with pepper salsa *p153*

shrimp provençal

In this dish, light, licorice-flavored fennel contrasts beautifully with chopped tomatoes and garlic. The ideal accompaniment to this stylish main dish is a simple salad of sliced tomatoes drizzled with a little vinaigrette and served on a bed of fresh baby spinach leaves—perfect for a quick supper.

Preparation and cooking time **30 minutes**   *Serves 4*

Shrimp Provençal

1 tablespoon olive oil

1 large onion, chopped

1 bulb of fennel, chopped

1 large garlic clove, crushed

1 can (14 ounces) chopped tomatoes

1/2 cup reduced-sodium vegetable broth

1 tablespoon fennel seeds

Finely grated zest and juice of 1 orange

Pinch saffron threads

1 cup long-grain rice

2 cups water

1 pound large shrimp, peeled and deveined

Salt and pepper

Garnish

Fresh basil leaves

1 Heat the oil in a large nonstick skillet with a tight fitting lid. Add the onion, fennel, and garlic and cook over medium heat, stirring occasionally, until softened but not browned, about 5 minutes. Add the tomatoes with their juice, the broth, fennel seeds, and orange zest and juice, and season lightly with salt and pepper. Bring to a boil, stirring, then reduce the heat to low and half cover the pan. Simmer for 12 minutes.

2 Meanwhile, crumble the saffron threads into the 2 cups water. Bring to a boil. Add the rice and boil until tender, about 15 to 20 minutes.

3 Bring the tomato sauce back to a boil. Place the shrimp on top of the sauce, cover the pan tightly, and cook over a low heat until the shrimp are cooked through and opaque, about 3 to 4 minutes. Do not boil the mixture or the shrimp may toughen.

4 Drain the rice and divide among serving bowls. Top with the shrimp and tomato sauce. Sprinkle with basil and serve immediately.

(Some More Ideas) This combination of seafood and tomatoes also makes a delicious sauce on a bed of whole-wheat spaghetti. A light seafood-based sauce is lower in saturated fat than a meat-based sauce.

Tuna Provençal: Make the tomato sauce and, just before serving, stir in 2 cans (3 ounces each) tuna in spring water, drained and flaked. This makes a great sauce for cooked pasta shells. Serve garnished with fresh dill.

Use 2 chopped small zucchini instead of the fennel. Chopped green beans and red, yellow, orange, or green peppers also work well in the sauce.

Plus Points

• Called scampi in Italy, but known in the United States as shrimp, this crustacean is a rich source of vitamin E. Vitamin E is actually a group of several related compounds that have powerful antioxidant properties.

• The vitamin C in tomatoes is concentrated in the jellylike substance surrounding the seeds. Vitamin C is an important nutrient for maintaining immunity and healthy skin.

• Fennel seeds are thought to aid digestion, and fennel tea is often recommended to ease flatulence.

photo, page 159

Exchanges

starch 2 1/2 vegetable 3
meat (very lean) 2 fat 1/2

Each serving provides calories 369, calories from fat 50, fat 6g, saturated fat 1g, cholesterol 176mg, sodium 487mg, carbohydrate 54g, fiber 6g, sugars 11g, protein 26g. Excellent source of iron, magnesium, niacin, phosphorus, potassium, thiamine, vitamin B6, vitamin C. Good source of calcium, folate, vitamin A.

seafood with watercress dressing

Scallops and strips of salmon fillet are briefly poached in a little wine and seafood broth, then served atop a colorful crunchy salad. The poaching liquid is used as the base for a creamy dressing made with low-fat yogurt, watercress, lemon, and chives. Serve the salad with a piece of crusty whole-wheat bread.

Preparation time **about 30 minutes**   Cooking time **20 minutes**   *Serves 4*

Seafood

1/2 pound piece of skinless salmon fillet, cut into 4 strips

1/2 pound bay scallops

3 tablespoons dry white wine

1 cup fish stock or bottled clam juice

Thin slice of fresh ginger, unpeeled

1/2 pound sugar snap peas

8 radishes

4 cups mixed salad leaves, including baby spinach, watercress, romaine, and oak leaf lettuces

Dressing

1 1/2 cups watercress, chopped

1 shallot, chopped

Thin strip of lemon zest

2 tablespoons snipped fresh chives

1 teaspoon lemon juice

2 tablespoons plain low-fat yogurt

Salt and pepper

1 Place the strips of salmon into a non-aluminum saucepan or sauté pan with a tight-fitting lid—the pan should be just big enough for the salmon to fit in one layer. Arrange the scallops on top of the salmon. Pour the wine and fish stockover them, and add the slice of ginger. Bring to a boil over a medium heat, then lower the heat until the liquid is simmering very gently. Cover and poach until the salmon and scallops are cooked and feel just firm to the touch, about 5 to 8 minutes.

2 While the seafood is cooking, drop the sugar snap peas into a pan of boiling water and cook until just tender but still crunchy, about 3 to 4 minutes. Drain, then refresh under cold running water. Set aside.

3 To make radish flowers, cut 5 slits on each radish, cutting down from the top almost to the base. Put into a bowl of iced water and leave until the "petals" open slightly. Alternatively, simply slice the radishes.

4 Put the mixed leaves into a salad bowl. Add the sugar snap peas and the drained radishes and mix well.

5 With a slotted spoon, lift the seafood out of the pan onto a plate. Reserve the poaching liquid. Cut each strip of salmon in half, or flake into large chunks. Arrange the salmon and scallops on top of the salad.

6 To make the dressing, remove the tough stalks from the watercress and reserve. Drop the leaves into a pan of boiling water and bring back to a boil. Immediately drain and refresh under cold running water. Squeeze out excess water, then chop very finely.

7 Put the reserved watercress stalks in a pan with the shallot, lemon zest, and 1/2 cup seafood poaching liquid. Half-cover the pan and simmer for 5 minutes. Strain the liquid, discarding the zest and vegetables. Stir in the chopped watercress, chives, lemon juice, and yogurt, and season with salt and pepper to taste. Spoon the warm dressing over the salad and serve.

Plus Points

• Scallops are an excellent source of selenium, a powerful antioxidant that protects the body against disease, and of vitamin B12. They also provide useful amounts of phosphorus and potassium.

• Watercress is a positive powerhouse of disease-fighting nutrients. It contains phytochemicals that help to protect against cancer. It is also an excellent source of vitamin C and beta-carotene.

photo, page 159

Exchanges

vegetable 1 meat (lean) 3

Each serving provides calories 188, calories from fat 59, fat 7g, saturated fat 1g, cholesterol 50mg, sodium 198mg, carbohydrate 9g, fiber 2g, sugars 4g, protein 22g. Excellent source of folate, niacin, phosphorus, vitamin A, vitamin B12, vitamin C. Good source of iron, magnesium, potassium, riboflavin, thiamine, vitamin B6.

steamed sea bass fillets with spring vegetables

Oriental steamer baskets are handy for this dish because you can stack them so that everything is steamed together. The moist heat from steaming ensures that the fish doesn't dry out. Steaming is a fat-free cooking method, since no added fat is needed to prevent sticking. Vegetables remain crisp and retain their vibrant color and vitamin content.

Preparation and cooking time **30 minutes**   *Serves 4*

Fillets

4 sea bass fillets,
(about 5 ounces each)
3 cups reduced-sodium
vegetable broth
1 cup couscous
1 strip of lemon zest
2 cups baby carrots
12 scallions, trimmed to about
4 inches long
2 cups asparagus tips
2 tablespoons chopped parsley
Salt and pepper

Marinade

1 teaspoon grated fresh
root ginger
1 tablespoon light soy sauce
1 teaspoon toasted sesame oil
1 garlic clove, finely chopped
1 tablespoon dry sherry,
dry white wine, or vermouth

1 First make the marinade. Combine the ginger, soy sauce, sesame oil, garlic, and sherry, wine, or vermouth in a bowl. Add the fish and turn to coat in the marinade. Set aside.

2 Bring 1 cup of the broth to a boil in a saucepan that will accommodate the steamer basket(s). Put the couscous in a bowl and pour the boiling broth over it. Cover and leave to stand until the couscous has swelled and absorbed the liquid, about 15 minutes.

3 Pour the remaining broth into the saucepan. Add the lemon zest and bring to a boil. Add the carrots. Reduce the heat so the broth simmers.

4 Place the fish, skin side down, in a single layer in a steamer basket. Add the scallions and asparagus, or put them in a second stacking steamer basket. Place the steamer basket(s) over the gently boiling broth and cover. Steam until the fish is opaque throughout and begins to flake, and the vegetables are tender, about 10 to 12 minutes.

5 When the couscous is ready, add the parsley and fluff the grains with a fork to mix the couscous and parsley. Season lightly with salt and pepper.

6 Lift the steamer basket(s) off the pan. Drain the carrots, reserving the cooking liquid. Arrange the fish, carrots, and steamed vegetables on warm plates with the couscous. Discard the lemon zest from the cooking liquid. Moisten the fish, vegetables, and couscous with a little of the liquid, and serve with any remaining liquid as a sauce.

Plus Points

• White fish such as sea bass is low in fat and calories and offers many B-complex vitamins. Sea bass is also a good source of calcium, an essential mineral with many important functions in the body, including keeping bones and teeth strong.

• The active ingredient in asparagus, called asparagine, has a strong diuretic effect. Herbalists recommend eating asparagus as a treatment for rheumatism, arthritis, and the bloating associated with PMS.

Exchanges
starch 2 vegetable 2
meat (very lean) 3 fat 1

Each serving provides calories 412, calories from fat 53, fat 6g, saturated fat 1g, cholesterol 60mg, sodium 557mg, carbohydrate 49g, fiber 6g, sugars 7g, protein 39g. Excellent source of folate, magnesium, niacin, phosphorus, potassium, riboflavin, Thiamine, vitamin A, vitamin B6, vitamin B12, vitamin C. Good source of iron.

steamed sea bass fillets
with spring vegetables *p158*

shrimp provençal *p156*

winter vegetable casserole *p160*

seafood with watercress dressing *p157*

winter vegetable casserole

This simple casserole is made without exotic ingredients or hours of precise slicing and chopping. Use everyday vegetables from the refrigerator for a warming and heart-healthy meal. After the casserole is made, it is placed in the oven to bake for an hour.

Preparation time **15 minutes**   Cooking time **1 hour**   *Serves 4*

Casserole

2 onions, each cut into 6 wedges

3 carrots, cut into 1/2-inch chunks

3 celery stalks, cut into chunks

2 medium or 1 large sweet potato, cut into 1/2 inch chunks

2 1/2 cups hot reduced-sodium, low-fat chicken or vegetable broth

2 garlic cloves, finely chopped

3 small leeks, washed and thickly sliced

1/2 cup pearl barley

2 teaspoons dried sage

Salt and pepper

Garnish

3 tablespoons coarsely chopped fresh flat-leaf parsley

1 Preheat the oven to 350°F. Place the onions, carrots, celery, and sweet potato in a large Dutch oven. Pour in the broth and bring to a boil.

2 Add the garlic, leeks, pearl barley, and sage. Season lightly with salt and pepper and stir to mix the vegetables together. Cover and transfer to the oven to cook until the vegetables are just soft and the barley is tender, about 1 hour. Sprinkle with the parsley and serve.

(**Some More Ideas**) A combination of lentils and barley works well in this casserole. Try using 1/3 cup pearl barley with 1/2 cup brown or green lentils.

Add parsnips, turnips, and peeled chunks of butternut squash for interesting variations.

One small, cored, sliced apple or 1/2 cup ready-to-eat chopped, dried pears can be added to the casserole for a hint of sweetness.

The casserole can be simmered gently on the stovetop for 45 to 50 minutes, instead of cooking in the oven. Stir occasionally.

Plus Points
• A well-stocked pantry allows you to prepare hearty meals without a lot of planning. Root vegetables keep for quite a while when kept in a cool, dark place and are good ingredients for last-minute casseroles, soups, and stews.
• Instead of sautéing the vegetables in oil, you simmer them in broth. This makes the dish extremely low in fat. With some bread to accompany it, the meal also offers a healthy balance of starchy carbohydrates.

photo, page 159

Exchanges
starch 2 1/2 vegetable 2

Each serving provides calories 229, calories from fat 9, fat 1g, saturated fat 0g, cholesterol 0mg, sodium 341mg, carbohydrate 51g, fiber 8g, sugars 14g, protein 7g. Excellent source of potassium, vitamin A, vitamin B6, vitamin C. Good source of calcium, folate, iron, magnesium, niacin, phosphorus, riboflavin, thiamine.

caribbean butternut squash and corn stew

Butternut squash has a lovely, firm texture, ideal for cooking in stews. Combined with black-eyed peas, corn, and red bell pepper, it makes a nutritious family supper dish that is perfect for cold winter days. Serve the stew with steamed rice or warm naan bread.

Preparation time **10 minutes**   Cooking time **30 minutes**   *Serves 4*

Stew

1 tablespoon olive oil

1 onion, sliced

2 garlic cloves, crushed

1 medium butternut squash, peeled and cut into 1/2 inch cubes

1 red bell pepper, seeded and sliced

1 bay leaf

1 can (28 ounces) chopped tomatoes

1 can (15 ounces) black-eyed peas

1 cup frozen corn, thawed

1 1/4 cups reduced-sodium vegetable broth

1 tablespoon Worcestershire sauce, or to taste

1 teaspoon hot red pepper sauce, or to taste

1 tablespoon dark brown sugar

1–2 teaspoons balsamic vinegar

Garnish

Chopped parsley

1 Heat the oil in a large saucepan and add the onion, garlic, butternut squash, red pepper, and bay leaf. Stir well, then cover the pan and allow the vegetables to cook for 5 minutes, stirring occasionally.

2 Add the tomatoes with their juice, the black-eyed peas and corn, and stir to mix. Add the broth, Worcestershire sauce, hot sauce, sugar, and vinegar and stir again. Cover and simmer until the squash is tender, about 15 minutes.

3 Sprinkle the parsley over the stew and serve at once.

(Some More Ideas) *Authentic Indian-flavor stew*: Soften the sliced onion and garlic in the olive oil for 2 to 3 minutes, then stir in 1 teaspoon curry powder and 1/2 teaspoon ground turmeric. Add the butternut squash with 1 cup thickly sliced baby corn. Cover and cook for 5 to 6 minutes. Replace the black-eyed peas with chickpeas, adding them with the canned tomatoes and broth (omit the corn kernels). Garnish with 2 tablespoons chopped fresh cilantro instead of parsley, and serve with steamed jasmine rice or warm naan bread.

Cubed, fresh pumpkin can be substituted for the butternut squash.

Plus Points

• There are over 25 species of pumpkin and squash, some of which have been cultivated for 9,000 years. All varieties are rich in beta-carotene and contain useful amounts of vitamin C.

• Research has shown that leaving freshly crushed garlic cloves to stand for 10 minutes before cooking maximizes the formation and retention of cancer-fighting compounds.

Exchanges
starch 2 1/2 vegetable 3 fat 1/2

Each serving provides calories 272, calories from fat 44, fat 5g, saturated fat 0g, cholesterol 0mg, sodium 1023mg, carbohydrate 53g, fiber 9g, sugars 21g, protein 10g. Excellent source of folate, iron, magnesium, niacin, phosphorus, potassium, thiamine, vitamin A, vitamin B6, vitamin C. Good source of calcium, riboflavin.

roast vegetable and bean stew

This easy, one-pot dish of root vegetables and pinto beans makes a nourishing winter main course, and needs no accompaniments. It's particularly enjoyable with a glass of cider or apple juice.

Preparation time **20 minutes**   Cooking time **50–55 minutes**   *Serves 4*

1 medium acorn squash

1 pound new potatoes, scrubbed and cut into 1 1/2-inch chunks

2 carrots, cut into 1 1/2-inch chunks

2 parsnips, cut into 1 1/2-inch chunks

2 large zucchini, cut into 1 1/2-inch chunks

2 teaspoons olive oil

1 garlic clove, finely chopped

4 large sprigs of fresh rosemary, plus extra sprigs to garnish

2 cans (15 ounces) pinto beans, drained and rinsed

1 cup cider

1 cup hot low-sodium vegetable broth

Salt and pepper

1 Preheat the oven to 400°F. Halve the squash and remove the seeds, then peel the skin, and cut the flesh into 1 1/2-inch chunks.

2 Put the squash in a bowl and add the potatoes, carrots, parsnips, and zucchini. Drizzle over the olive oil and toss to coat the vegetables evenly. Stir in the garlic and season lightly with salt and pepper.

3 Lay the rosemary sprigs on the bottom of a large roasting pan and spread the vegetables on top in a single layer. Roast until lightly browned, about 30 minutes, turning once.

4 Remove from the oven and stir in the pinto beans, cider, and broth. Cover the pan tightly with foil, then return to the oven and cook until the vegetables are tender, about 20 to 25 minutes. Before serving, remove the rosemary stalks and garnish with fresh rosemary sprigs.

(Some More Ideas) You can also cook the stew on top of the stove. Heat the oil in a large saucepan, add the vegetables, and sauté for 4 to 5 minutes, stirring, then add the garlic, rosemary, and seasoning. Stir in the beans, cider, and broth, and bring to a boil. Cover and simmer until tender, about 30 to 35 minutes.

Butternut squash can be substituted for the acorn squash.

Plus Points

• Parsnips are a very nutritious starchy vegetable, providing useful amounts of potassium, the B vitamins thiamine and folate, and vitamin C.

• Apple cider is made from pressed apples and is sometimes fermented to make vinegar and brandy. It is usually more concentrated than apple juice, so it lends a nice sweet flavor to this casserole.

Exchanges

starch 5 1/2 fruit 1/2 vegetable 1

Each serving provides calories 478, calories from fat 34, fat 4g, saturated fat 0g, cholesterol 0mg, sodium 484mg, carbohydrate 98g, fiber 24g, sugars 24g, protein 19g. Excellent source of folate, iron, magnesium, niacin, phosphorus, potassium, riboflavin, thiamine, vitamin A, vitamin B6, vitamin C. Good source of calcium.

roast vegetable and bean stew *p162*

black-eyed pea soup *p164*

chickpea and pita salad *p165*

rustic grilled vegetable
and rigatoni salad *p166*

black-eyed pea soup

The creamy texture of black-eyed peas works particularly well in warming spicy soups. This one is filling enough to make a hearty main course and is easy to prepare. A sprinkling of low-fat grated cheese melting into the soup is the finishing touch. Serve with toasted tortillas on the side, cut into wedges, if you wish.

Preparation time **20 minutes**   Cooking time **20 minutes**   *Serves 6*

1 teaspoon canola oil

1 large fresh green chile, seeded and finely chopped

2 green peppers, seeded and chopped

1 teaspoon ground cumin

1 can (14 ounces) chopped tomatoes

1 teaspoon sun-dried tomato paste

3 cups low-fat chicken or vegetable broth

1 bay leaf

2 cans (15 ounces) black-eyed peas, drained and rinsed

1 cup frozen corn

3 tablespoons chopped fresh cilantro

Salt and pepper

To serve

6 (8 inch) flour tortillas

1/2 cup reduced-fat coarsely grated Monterey Jack cheese

Sprigs of fresh cilantro (optional)

Thinly sliced fresh green chile (optional)

1 Heat the oil in a large saucepan, add the chile and green peppers, and cook gently until almost soft, about 5 minutes, stirring frequently. Stir in the ground cumin and cook for a few seconds.

2 Add the canned tomatoes with their juice, the tomato paste, 2 cups of the broth, the bay leaf, and 1 can of peas. Bring to a boil slowly, then turn down the heat, cover, and simmer gently for 15 minutes. Discard the bay leaf.

3 Puree the soup, either in batches in a blender or food processor, or by using a handheld blender directly in the pan. Stir in the remaining peas, plus the corn, and chopped cilantro. Add the remaining broth. Season lightly with salt and pepper, then heat through gently until hot.

4 Meanwhile, heat the tortillas in the oven or microwave, according to the package instructions.

5 Ladle the soup into bowls and sprinkle with the cheese. Garnish with cilantro sprigs and green chile, if desired. Serve with the tortillas.

(Some More Ideas) Reduced-fat cheddar cheese can be substituted for the Monterey Jack.

Canned pinto or black beans can be substituted for the black-eyed peas.

Plus Points

• The black-eyed pea is a legume related to the bean family. Using canned beans rather than dried beans has little effect on the nutritional value of a dish, and it certainly saves time.

• Bean-based soups are extremely high in fiber and make a great vegetarian alternative. This soup is perfect to serve for a mixed crowd at a casual dinner party.

• For people with diabetes, it is beneficial to have several meat-free meals a week to limit cholesterol and saturated-fat intake. Soy-based products and beans make delicious low-fat protein sources.

photo, page 163

Exchanges

starch 3 1/2 vegetable 1 meat (very lean) 1 fat 1

Each serving provides calories 370, calories from fat 59, fat 7g, saturated fat 2g, cholesterol 7mg, sodium 803mg, carbohydrate 61g, fiber 12g, sugars 8g, protein 19g. Excellent source of folate, iron, magnesium, niacin, phosphorus, potassium, thiamine, vitamin C. Good source of calcium, riboflavin, vitamin A, vitamin B6.

chickpea and pita salad

This dish is based on fattoush, the popular salad enjoyed in Lebanon and Syria, and it makes a satisfying main dish that is high in fiber. It's important to grill the pita bread until it is really crisp and golden or it will quickly become soggy when mixed with the other ingredients. The dressing adds the distinctive flavors of olives, anchovy, and garlic.

Preparation and cooking time **20 minutes**   *Serves 8*

Salad

4 sesame pita breads

2 cans (15 ounces) chickpeas, rinsed and drained

1 cucumber, diced

4 large beefsteak tomatoes

6 scallions, chopped

1/2 cup pitted black olives, preferably kalamata olives

Dressing

1 1/2 tablespoons olive oil

1 tablespoon balsamic vinegar

2 teaspoons olive tapenade

1 tablespoon chopped fresh mint

Pepper

Garnish

Sprigs of fresh mint

1 Preheat the oven broiler. Split the pita breads in half by carefully cutting them open with a sharp knife. Place them on a baking sheet. Toast under the broiler until golden brown and crisp, turning once, then allow to cool. Tear into bite-size pieces.

2 Put the chickpeas, cucumber, tomatoes, scallions, and olives in a serving bowl. For the dressing, whisk together the olive oil, vinegar, tapenade, mint, and pepper to taste. Drizzle over the vegetables and toss together.

3 Just before serving, add the pieces of pita bread and mix well. Serve garnished with sprigs of fresh mint.

(**Some More Ideas**) If you cannot find sesame pita bread, you can substitute whole-wheat pita breads.

Chickpea and eggplant salad: Cut 1 small eggplant into 1/2-inch cubes and gently sauté in 2 teaspoons olive oil for 5 minutes. Stir in 1 teaspoon cumin seeds, and continue cooking until the eggplant is lightly browned and tender. Remove from the heat and mix with 2 cans (15 ounces) chickpeas, drained and rinsed, 1 thinly sliced red onion, 1 1/2 cups baby spinach leaves, and 1 seeded and thinly sliced yellow pepper. For the dressing, whisk together 1 tablespoon olive oil, 2 teaspoons lemon juice, 2 tablespoons chopped fresh cilantro, and pepper to taste.

Plus Points

• Tapenade is a thick paste made from capers, anchovies, olives, lemon juice, and seasonings. Just a little of this potent condiment goes a long way in flavoring a dish.

• Both the white bulb and the green leaves of scallions can be eaten. Using the green leaves increases the amount of beta-carotene that is consumed.

photo, page 163

Exchanges

starch 2 1/2 vegetable 1 fat 1

Each serving provides calories 269, calories from fat 58, fat 6g, saturated fat 1g, cholesterol 0mg, sodium 365mg, carbohydrate 44g, fiber 8g, sugars 8g, protein 11g. Excellent source of folate, iron, thiamine, vitamin C. Good source of magnesium, niacin, phosphorus, potassium, riboflavin, vitamin A, vitamin B6.

rustic grilled vegetable and rigatoni salad

Grilled vegetables are delicious with chunky pasta in a tangy dressing. Serve this salad as a light lunch or offer it as an accompaniment for grilled poultry or meat, when it will serve 6 or 8.

Preparation time **35 minutes, plus cooling and 30 minutes marinating**   Cooking time **25 minutes**   *Serves 4*

8 ounces rigatoni

1 large red pepper, seeded and halved

2 medium tomatoes, cut into wedges

1 medium eggplant, trimmed and sliced lengthways

2 tablespoons balsamic vinegar or lemon juice

2 tablespoons olive oil

2 tablespoons chopped fresh basil

1 tablespoon chopped capers

1 large garlic clove, crushed (optional)

1/4 cup grated Parmesan cheese

Salt and pepper

1 Cook the rigatoni in boiling water for 10 to 12 minutes, or according to package directions, until al dente. Drain and rinse under cold running water, then drain thoroughly and set aside to cool.

2 Preheat the broiler or a grill to high. Broil or grill the pepper halves, skin side up, until blistered and blackened, 5 to 10 minutes. Place in a plastic zippered bag, then leave until cool enough to handle.

3 Broil or grill the tomatoes and eggplant for about 5 minutes. Turn the vegetables so that they cook evenly, and remove the pieces as they are ready. Place the tomato wedges in a large salad bowl. Set the eggplant slices aside on a plate to cool slightly.

4 Cut the eggplant slices into 1-inch strips and add to the tomatoes. Peel the peppers and cut them into 1-inch strips, then add to the salad bowl. Mix in the pasta.

5 In a small bowl, mix the balsamic vinegar or lemon juice with the olive oil, basil, capers, garlic, if using, and Parmesan cheese. Lightly toss this dressing into the salad. Season lightly with salt and pepper. Set the salad aside to marinate for about 30 minutes so that the flavors can infuse before serving.

(Some More Ideas) For a hearty vegetarian main-course salad, stir in 1 can (15 ounces) cannellini or red kidney beans, drained and rinsed.

Add grilled zucchini and asparagus. Slice the zucchini lengthways. Grill alongside the eggplant and tomatoes.

Replace the eggplant with well-drained, bottled artichokes.

Plus Points

• Grilling or baking is a healthy cooking method for vegetables like eggplant, which can absorb large amounts of fat when they are fried or sautéed in oil.

• Adding a little Parmesan cheese to pasta dishes contributes calcium as well as a wonderful flavor.

photo, page 163

Exchanges

starch 2 vegetable 2
fat 1

Each serving provides calories 242, calories from fat 63, fat 7g, saturated fat 2g, cholesterol 5mg, sodium 137mg, carbohydrate 38g, fiber 4g, sugars 7g, protein 8g. Excellent source of folate, thiamine, vitamin A, vitamin C. Good source of iron, magnesium, niacin, phosphorus, potassium, riboflavin, vitamin B6.

tagliatelle with green sauce

This simple vegetable and yogurt sauce is ready in as little time as it takes to cook and drain the fresh pasta. It is irresistibly creamy, but does not have the heaviness of a classic cream sauce. The fresh vegetables and herbs add a burst of flavor to the sauce as well as iron and vitamins.

Preparation time **10 minutes**   Cooking time **8–10 minutes**   *Serves 4*

3 cups baby spinach, thick stalks discarded

2 cups watercress, thick stalks discarded

1 cup frozen peas

12 ounces fresh or boxed tagliatelle

2 teaspoons cornmeal

1 cup plain low-fat yogurt

4 tablespoons chopped parsley

6 sprigs of fresh basil, torn into pieces

Salt and pepper

1 Rinse the spinach and watercress and place in a large saucepan while still wet. Cover and cook over medium heat, stirring the vegetables occasionally, until they have wilted, about 2 minutes.

2 Add the peas and heat through, uncovered, for 2 minutes—there should be enough liquid in the pan to cook the peas. Place the greens and their liquid into a bowl. Set aside.

3 Cook the pasta in a large saucepan of boiling water for 3 minutes, or according to the package instructions, until al dente.

4 Meanwhile, blend the cornmeal to a smooth paste with the yogurt, and place in the pan used for cooking the vegetables. Stir over medium heat until just bubbling. Add the vegetables, parsley, basil, and salt and pepper to taste and stir well. Cook the sauce until heated through, then remove the pan from the heat.

5 Drain the pasta and add to the sauce. Toss to mix with the sauce and serve.

(Some More Ideas) When fresh peas are in season, use them instead of frozen. Add to the spinach and watercress in Step 1 and cook for 4 minutes.

Creamy broccoli and pea sauce: Replace the spinach and watercress with 5 cups of small broccoli florets. Cook the broccoli in a little boiling water for 5 to 8 minutes, then drain, refresh in cold running water, drain well again, and return to the pan. Mash the broccoli with a potato masher, then add the yogurt mixed with the cornmeal and 5 tablespoons fat-free milk. Stir in 1 cup frozen peas and 2 scallions, finely chopped. Bring to a boil, stirring, and cook for 1 to 2 minutes to thicken. Season lightly with salt and pepper and add a dash of lemon juice if you like. Toss with the freshly cooked pasta, then sprinkle with chopped parsley.

Plus Points

• Cream-based sauces are always popular for pasta dishes. Traditionally, the sauces are made with heavy cream and cheese. This recipe uses low-fat yogurt to create a creamy sauce that is much lower in fat.

• Heat can destroy vitamin C. The best way to cook leafy green vegetables, such as spinach and watercress, and still retain the maximum vitamin C, is to wilt them quickly and serve them immediately.

• Peas provide protein. They are also rich in fiber, some of it soluble, and this helps to keep blood sugar levels and cholesterol under control.

photo, page 169

Exchanges

starch 4

Each serving provides calories 322, calories from fat 27, fat 3g, saturated fat 1g, cholesterol 5mg, sodium 273mg, carbohydrate 58g, fiber 6g, sugars 8g, protein 16g. Excellent source of folate, iron, magnesium, niacin, phosphorus, riboflavin, thiamine, vitamin A, vitamin C. Good source of calcium, potassium, vitamin B6.

penne rigati with sesame-and-orange dressing

This fresh-flavored pasta salad is wonderful on its own or as a side dish with grilled chicken or firm fish. The Asian-style dressing combines citrus flavors with sesame, soy sauce, and ginger. Any type of pasta can be used in this recipe, including rice noodles or orzo.

Preparation time **25–30 minutes, plus cooling**   *Serves 4*

Pasta

8 ounces penne noodles

2 large oranges

6 scallions, cut into short fine strips

1/2 cup bean sprouts (optional)

2 tablespoons sesame seeds, toasted

Dressing

Grated zest and juice of 1 orange

1 tablespoon toasted sesame oil

2 tablespoons light soy sauce

1 garlic clove, crushed

1 tablespoon finely grated peeled fresh ginger

Salt and pepper

1 Cook the pasta in boiling water for 10 to 12 minutes, or according to the package instructions, until al dente.

2 While the pasta is cooking, peel the oranges, removing all the pith. Holding the oranges over a bowl to catch any juice, cut out the segments from their surrounding membrane. Set the segments aside, and reserve the juice in the bowl.

3 Place the scallion strips in a bowl of cold water and set them aside until they curl.

4 To make the dressing, add the orange zest and juice to the juices reserved from segmenting the oranges. Add the sesame oil, soy sauce, garlic, grated fresh ginger, and salt and pepper to taste. Whisk lightly to mix.

5 Drain the pasta and add to the dressing. Mix well, then cover and set aside to cool.

6 When ready to serve, thoroughly drain the scallions; reserve a few for garnish and add the remainder to the salad together with the orange segments, bean sprouts, and toasted sesame seeds. Gently toss the ingredients together, then serve the salad immediately, sprinkled with the reserved scallions.

(Some More Ideas) Use Japanese soba noodles, made from buckwheat flour instead of penne, and cook them for 5 to 7 minutes. Use canola oil in the dressing instead of the sesame oil and omit the sesame seeds. Stir in 1 tablespoon Thai red curry paste instead of the fresh ginger. Add 2 tablespoons finely chopped fresh cilantro with the orange segments, if desired.

To increase the vegetable content of the salad, finely shred 1/2 fennel bulb and add it to the salad; sprinkle with the feathery leaves from the fennel to garnish.

Plus Points

• Oranges are an excellent source of vitamin C, and 1 orange provides more than twice the recommended daily intake of vitamin A.

• Oranges, and other citrus fruit, also contain coumarins, compounds that are believed to help thin the blood and thus prevent stroke and heart attacks.

Exchanges

starch 3 fruit 1 fat 1

Each serving provides calories 334, calories from fat 62, fat 7g, saturated fat 1g, cholesterol 0mg, sodium 311mg, carbohydrate 58g, fiber 6g, sugars 14g, protein 12g. Excellent source of folate, niacin, riboflavin, thiamine, vitamin C. Good source of calcium, iron, magnesium, phosphorus, potassium, vitamin B6.

penne rigati with sesame-and-orange dressing *p168*

chickpea and rice balls *p171*

cheese-baked peppers with linguine *p170*

tagliatelle with green sauce *p167*

cheese-baked peppers with linguine

Traditionally, stuffed peppers are often prepared with rice. In this unique recipe, noodles are used and baked in the pepper shells with a cheesy custard dotted with fresh tomatoes and herbs. The stuffed peppers can be served as an appetizer for four or as a vegetarian lunch for two.

Preparation time **about 40 minutes**   Cooking time **20–25 minutes**   *Serves 4*

Peppers

2 large red, orange, or yellow bell peppers

2 ounces linguine

2 eggs, beaten

2/3 cup reduced-fat cheddar cheese

1 teaspoon dry mustard

3 tablespoons fat-free milk

3 tablespoons chopped fresh chives

1/2 teaspoon dried marjoram or oregano

2 tomatoes, peeled, seeded, and diced

Salt and pepper

Garnish

Salad leaves

1 Preheat the oven to 350°F. Halve the peppers lengthways, carefully cutting through the stem. Remove the membrane and seeds. Cook the pepper shells in boiling water until tender, 6 to 8 minutes. Drain thoroughly and place on a paper towel.

2 Cook the linguine in boiling water for 10 minutes, or according to the package instructions, until al dente. Drain well and set aside.

3 Beat the eggs with the cheese, mustard, milk, chives, and marjoram or oregano. Stir in the tomatoes and season lightly with salt and pepper.

4 Place the peppers in a shallow oven-proof dish or roasting pan, supporting them with pieces of crumpled foil, if necessary, to ensure that they are level (otherwise the filling will spill out). Fill each pepper halfway full with linguine, then spoon the egg and cheese mixture over the pasta.

5 Bake until the filling is set and beginning to turn golden, 20 to 25 minutes. Serve garnished with whole chives, with an accompaniment of mixed salad leaves, if desired.

(Some More Ideas) Use 2 ounces fresh linguine instead of dried. Fresh linguine will only need to be cooked for 2 to 3 minutes.

For a more substantial dish, cook an additional 5 ounces of linguine while the peppers are baking and toss it with 1 table-spoon snipped fresh chives. Serve this pasta as a base for the peppers.

Tasty supper for two: Thoroughly drain and flake 1 can (7 ounces) tuna packed in water, and add it to the egg mixture. Serve 2 pepper halves per person.

Stir 4 pitted green olives, finely chopped, into the egg mixture for a more complex flavor.

Plus Points

• These peppers make an elegant vegetarian meal. They serve as a complete meal, since they contain a starch component, protein from the milk and cheese, and several servings of vegetables.

• Red, yellow, or orange bell peppers are used in this recipe not only for a bright presentation, but because they have a sweeter flavor than green bell peppers.

photo, page 169

Exchanges

starch 1   vegetable 1
meat (medium fat) 1

Each serving provides calories 185, calories from fat 65, fat 7g, saturated fat 3g, cholesterol 120mg, sodium 207mg, carbohydrate 21g, fiber 3g, sugars 6g, protein 11g. Excellent source of calcium, phosphorus, riboflavin, vitamin A, vitamin C. Good source of folate, iron, potassium, thiamine, vitamin B6.

chickpea and rice balls

These tasty chickpea-based balls, flavored with garlic, chile, and lots of fresh cilantro, make a delicious alternative to plain rice or potatoes. They go especially well with Indian food and other spicy dishes. The chickpea balls are high in protein and can be paired with an assortment of grilled fresh vegetables to create a balanced vegetarian meal.

Preparation time **50 minutes**   Cooking time **30 minutes**   *Serves 4 (makes 12)*

1/2 cup long-grain white rice
1 cup water
2 teaspoons canola oil
1 small onion, finely chopped
1 garlic clove, crushed
1 fresh red chile, seeded and finely chopped
2 tomatoes, skinned, seeded and very finely chopped
1 can (15 ounces) chickpeas, drained and rinsed
1 egg yolk
3 tablespoons chopped fresh cilantro
1 teaspoon paprika
Salt and pepper

1 Put the rice in a saucepan, add the water, and bring to a boil. Cover and simmer very gently until the rice is tender and has absorbed all the water, about 10 to 15 minutes. Remove from the heat and leave to cool for a few minutes.

2 Meanwhile, preheat the oven to 350°F. Heat the oil in a saucepan, add the onion, and sauté until soft, about 5 minutes, stirring frequently. Stir in the garlic and chile, and cook for 2 minutes. Remove from the heat and stir in the chopped tomatoes.

3 Put the chickpeas in a bowl and mash with a potato masher until fairly smooth, or puree them in a food processor. Add the onion mixture, rice, egg yolk, cilantro, paprika, and salt and pepper to taste. Mix well. Divide the mixture into 12 equal portions and shape each into a ball.

4 Place the chickpea and rice balls on a sprayed baking sheet and bake until beginning to brown, about 30 minutes, turning them over carefully halfway through the cooking. Serve hot.

(Some More Ideas) Try varying the fresh herb according to the food you're serving with the chickpea and rice balls: mint with lamb, or sage and parsley with pork.

Plus Points
• Eating onions regularly can have several beneficial effects, particularly in helping to reduce blood cholesterol levels and lessen the risk of blood clots forming.
• Garlic contains a phytochemical called allicin, which has both antifungal and antibiotic properties. For this reason, garlic is thought to help clear cold symptoms and chest infections.

photo, page 169

Exchanges
starch 2 1/2 vegetable 1
fat 1

Each serving provides calories 269, calories from fat 53, fat 6g, saturated fat 1g, cholesterol 53mg, sodium 117mg, carbohydrate 45g, fiber 7g, sugars 8g, protein 10g. Excellent source of folate, iron, phosphorus, thiamine, vitamin C. Good source of magnesium, niacin, potassium, vitamin A, vitamin B6.

greek stuffed grape leaves

Here's a new, healthy twist on these delicious and popular little Greek parcels. To boost the fiber and nutrient content, brown rice is used instead of the traditional white rice. The filling for the grape leaves is flavored with garlic and fresh herbs, with a hint of sweetness from the raisins and crunch from the walnuts.

Preparation time **1 hour**   Cooking time **10–15 minutes**   *Serves 8*

Grape Leaves

1 cup long-grain brown rice

24 large grape leaves preserved in brine, drained

2 teaspoons olive oil, divided

1 onion, finely chopped

1 large garlic clove, finely chopped

1 tablespoon chopped parsley

1 tablespoon chopped fresh mint

1 tablespoon chopped fresh dill

Grated zest and juice of 1 lemon

1/2 cup raisins

1/4 cup chopped walnuts

Salt and pepper

Garnish

Lemon wedges

Sprigs of fresh dill, parsley, or mint

1 Bring 2 cups of water to a boil. Add the rice and return to a boil. Lower the heat, cover, and simmer until rice is tender, about 40 minutes. Remove from the heat.

2 While the rice is cooking, drain the grape leaves, rinse with cold water, and pat dry with a paper towel.

3 Heat 1 teaspoon of the oil in a saucepan over medium heat. Add the onion and garlic, and cook until soft but not browned, stirring occasionally, for 5 to 8 minutes. Remove from the heat and stir in the parsley, mint, dill, lemon zest, and raisins.

4 Place the walnuts in a small skillet and toast them over medium heat until lightly browned and fragrant, stirring constantly. Add the toasted walnuts to the onion mixture. Stir in the cooked rice and add the lemon juice (you may not need all of it), and season lightly with salt and pepper. Mix well.

5 Spread one of the grape leaves flat on a work surface and place about 2 spoonfuls of the rice mixture in the center. Fold over the stalk end, then fold in the sides. Roll up the leaf into the shape of a cylinder. Repeat with the remaining grape leaves and filling.

6 Place the rolls seam side down in a steamer and brush the tops with the remaining 1 teaspoon of oil. Cover and steam until piping hot, about 10 to 15 minutes. Serve hot or at room temperature, garnished with lemon wedges, and sprigs of fresh herbs.

Plus Points

• Brown rice has only the outer husk removed and therefore contains all the nutrients in the germ and outer layers of the grain. Raw brown rice contains 1.9 grams fiber per 1/2 cup compared with 0.4 grams fiber for the same weight of raw white rice. It also contains more B vitamins.

• Toasting raw nuts before adding them to a dish helps to make the nuts more flavorful and aromatic.

• When using grape leaves that are preserved in brine, always rinse them first. The brine is extremely high in sodium.

photo, page 175

Exchanges

starch 1 1/2 fruit 1/2 fat 1/2

Each serving (three grape leaves) provides calories 165, calories from fat 40, fat 4g, saturated fat 0g, cholesterol 0mg, sodium 119mg, carbohydrate 29g, fiber 2g, sugars 8g, protein 3g. Good source of copper, magnesium, phosphorus, vitamin A, vitamin B6.

minted barley and beans

The mild, sweet flavor and slightly chewy texture of pearl barley is combined here with black-eyed peas and lots of colorful vegetables. A fresh-tasting sun-dried tomato and mint dressing adds a summery feel to this wholesome salad. Serve on its own for lunch or supper, with a fresh fruit salad on the side.

Preparation and cooking time **1 1/2 hours**   *Serves 8*

Salad

4 cups vegetable broth

1 teaspoon lemon zest

1 bay leaf

1 large leek, bottom half washed and sliced

1 teaspoon canola oil

1 cup pearl barley

1 can (14 ounces) black-eyed peas, drained

6 ripe plum tomatoes, cut into thin wedges

2 cups shredded baby spinach

1 bunch scallions, halved lengthwise and shredded

Dressing

2 sun-dried tomatoes, packed in oil, drained and finely chopped

2 tablespoons oil from the sun-dried tomatoes

1 tablespoon red wine vinegar

1 garlic clove, crushed

2 tablespoons chopped fresh mint

1 tablespoon chopped fresh parsley

Garnish

Fresh mint leaves

1 Pour the broth into a saucepan and add the lemon zest and bay leaf. Bring to a rapid boil and add the leek. Cook for 2 to 3 minutes. Remove the leek with a slotted spoon and rinse under cold water.

2 Add the oil to the broth and bring back to a boil. Add the barley, cover, and simmer until tender, about 30 to 40 minutes.

3 Spoon out 2 tablespoons of the broth and then drain the barley. Discard the bay leaf. Pour the barley in a bowl and set aside to cool.

4 Add the leek, black-eyed peas, tomatoes, spinach, and scallions to the barley and mix well.

5 To make the dressing, combine the sun-dried tomatoes, oil, vinegar, garlic, mint, parsley, and the reserved broth. Season lightly with salt and pepper and mix well.

6 Drizzle the dressing over the barley and vegetables and toss to coat thoroughly. Serve at room temperature. Garnish with mint leaves.

(Some More Ideas) *Dilled barley and smoked salmon salad:* Use 6 ounces smoked salmon, cut into strips, instead of the black-eyed peas. Replace the leeks with fine asparagus spears, preparing them in the same way. Add the cooked barley together with the smoked salmon, scallions, 1 halved and very thinly sliced bulb of fennel, and 1 1/2 cups halved red and yellow cherry tomatoes. For the dressing, whisk 2 table-spoons canola oil with 2 teaspoons lemon juice, 1/2 teaspoon Dijon mustard, 3 table-spoons chopped fresh dill, and salt and pepper to taste. Toss into the salad with 1 tablespoon drained capers. Serve cool, garnished with sprigs of fresh dill.

Plus Points

• Barley is believed to be the world's oldest cultivated grain. It is low in fat and rich in complex carbohydrates, and like other cereals, it is a good source of B vitamins.

• Although highly refined, ounce for ounce pearl barley provides more dietary fiber than brown rice.

• Spinach contains oxalic acid, which binds with iron, making most of it unavailable to the body. Eating spinach with something that is a good source of vitamin C, such as tomatoes, can increase iron uptake.

photo, page 175

Exchanges

starch 1 1/2 vegetable 1 fat 1/2

Each serving provides calories 167, calories from fat 42, fat 5g, saturated fat 0g, cholesterol 0mg, sodium 555mg, carbohydrate 27g, fiber 5g, sugars 5g, protein 6g. Excellent source of folate, vitamin C. Good source of iron, magnesium, niacin, phosphorus, potassium, riboflavin, thiamine, vitamin A, vitamin B6.

quinoa with grilled eggplant

Quinoa, a nutritious grain from South America, has a texture similar to split lentils when cooked. It contains more protein than any other grain and is also lower in carbohydrate content. Here it is combined with grilled zucchini, peppers, cherry tomatoes, and onions, and then baked with tangy goat cheese on the top. Serve with a mixed leaf salad.

Preparation time **35 minutes**   Cooking time **35 minutes**   *Serves 4*

1 cup quinoa

3 or 4 sprigs fresh thyme

2 1/2 cups low-sodium vegetable broth

2 baby eggplants, cut lengthways into quarters

1 red pepper, seeded and cut into chunks

1 red onion, cut into chunks

2 teaspoons olive oil

1 cup cherry tomatoes

2 garlic cloves, crushed

1 1/4 cups tomato juice

7 ounces low-fat goat-cheese log with herbs, cut into 8 slices

Salt and pepper

1 Preheat the oven to 375°F. Put the quinoa in a sieve and rinse thoroughly under cold running water. Place in a saucepan with the thyme sprigs and broth, and bring to a boil. Cover and simmer gently until all the broth has been absorbed and the quinoa is tender, about 20 minutes.

2 Meanwhile, heat a ridged grill pan. Brush the eggplants, red pepper, and onion with the olive oil, then cook them on the grill pan (in batches if necessary) until softened and lightly charred on both sides, about 4 to 5 minutes. Transfer to a plate.

3 Put the whole tomatoes on the grill pan and cook until they are just beginning to burst their skins, about 2 minutes. Remove from the heat.

4 When the quinoa is cooked, place it in an ovenproof dish. Add the grilled vegetables, garlic, and tomato juice, and season lightly with salt and pepper. Fold together gently.

5 Arrange the slices of goat cheese on top of the quinoa mixture. Cover with foil and bake until the vegetables are tender, about 35 minutes. Serve hot.

(Some More Ideas) *Quinoa with fresh tuna*: Marinate 2 fresh tuna steaks in 1 tablespoon olive oil, the grated zest of 1 lemon, and 1/4 teaspoon crushed dried chiles. Meanwhile, brush 1/2 cup asparagus tips, and 2 zucchini, sliced on the diagonal, with 2 teaspoons olive oil, and cook on the grill pan for about 30 seconds on each side. Grill the cherry tomatoes as in the main recipe. Place the tuna on the grill pan and cook for 2 minutes on each side. Combine the quinoa, vegetables, garlic, and tomato juice in an ovenproof dish, adding a handful of torn fresh basil leaves. Break the tuna into pieces and scatter over the top, pushing it down slightly. Cover with foil, and bake for 25 minutes.

Plus Points

• Quinoa is not a typical cereal—it produces large quantities of small seeds—but it is used like other grains. Because it is actually lower in carbohydrates than other grains, it works well for people with diabetes.

• Eggplant is filling and satisfying without adding many calories—there are just 15 calories in a 1/2-cup serving of cooked eggplant.

Exchanges

starch 2 vegetable 3
meat (lean) 1 fat 1 1/2

Each serving provides calories 346, calories from fat 111, fat 12g, saturated fat 6g, cholesterol 35mg, sodium 1121mg, carbohydrate 44g, fiber 8g, sugars 13g, protein 17g. Excellent source of copper, folate, iron, magnesium, niacin, phosphorus, potassium, riboflavin, thiamine, vitamin A, vitamin B6, vitamin C. Good source of calcium, zinc.

minted barley and beans *p173*

quinoa with grilled eggplant *p174*

greek stuffed grape leaves *p172*

spinach and potato frittata *p177*

rice-stuffed squash

Here's an attractive and fun way to serve small winter squashes—filled with a mixture of wild and white rice, chestnuts, dried cranberries, and mozzarella cheese. Individual squashes, such as acorn or even small pumpkins, work well in this recipe and they make an impressive vegetarian main course for a winter dinner.

Preparation time **25 minutes**   Cooking time **45 minutes**   *Serves 4*

1 cup mixed basmati and
wild rice

3 cups water

4 small acorn squashes

3/4 cup cooked chestnuts
(canned or vacuum packed),
roughly chopped

1/2 cup dried cranberries

1 small red onion,
finely chopped

2 tablespoons chopped
fresh thyme

2 tablespoons chopped parsley

1/2 cup grated
mozzarella cheese

Salt and pepper

1 Put the rice in a saucepan, add the 3 cups water, and bring to a boil. Cover, and simmer very gently until the rice is just tender, about 20 minutes. Drain off any excess water.

2 Meanwhile, preheat the oven to 350°F. Using a large, sharp knife, slice off the top quarter (stalk end) of each squash. Set aside these little hats, then scoop out the seeds and fiber from the center of the squashes using a small spoon. Trim the bases to make them level, if necessary. Season the cavity of each squash lightly with salt and pepper, then place them in a large ovenproof dish or roasting pan.

3 Mix together the rice, chestnuts, cranberries, onion, thyme, parsley, and mozzarella in a large bowl. Season lightly with salt and pepper.

4 Spoon the rice stuffing into the squashes, pressing it down, and mounding it up neatly on top. Replace the reserved "hats" on top. Bake until the flesh of the squash is tender when pierced with a small, sharp knife, about 45 minutes. Serve hot.

(Some More Ideas) Use other winter squashes such as small pumpkins instead of acorn squash. The cooking time can vary from 45 to 60 minutes, depending on the type of squash and its size.

Replace the mozzarella with other cheeses, such as Gruyère.

Plus Points

• Acorn squash is a winter variety of squash. Winter squashes are allowed to mature into hard, starchy vegetable fruits with very good keeping properties, while varieties such as zucchini are eaten while immature and the skins are still edible. Acorn squash is a good source of beta-carotene, which the body can convert to vitamin A.

• Unlike other nuts, chestnuts are low in fat—other nuts have up to 20 times as much fat. Chestnuts are also a good source of thiamine and potassium, and a valuable source of dietary fiber.

• Both dried and fresh cranberries are a good source of vitamin C. Cranberries also have the reputation of helping to control urinary tract infections such as cystitis.

Exchanges

starch 5 fruit 1/2

Each serving provides calories 415, calories from fat 34, fat 4g, saturated fat 2g, cholesterol 8mg, sodium 85mg, carbohydrate 89g, fiber 14g, sugars 25g, protein 12g. Excellent source of calcium, folate, iron, magnesium, niacin, phosphorus, potassium, thiamine, vitamin B6, vitamin C. Good source of copper, riboflavin, vitamin A.

spinach and potato frittata

This flat omelet makes a delicious vegetarian main course, and can be eaten hot or at room temperature. It is a very versatile recipe, as almost anything can be added to it—a handy way of using up leftovers. Serve with sliced tomatoes and a mixed green salad or fruit for a quick supper.

Preparation time **10 minutes**   Cooking time **25 minutes**   *Serves 4*

1 pound russet potatoes, washed and cut into 1/2-inch cubes

3 cups baby spinach leaves, trimmed of any large stalks

1 tablespoon olive oil

1 red bell pepper, quartered lengthways, seeded and thinly sliced

5–6 scallions, thinly sliced

3 egg whites

2 whole eggs

2 tablespoons freshly grated Parmesan cheese

Salt and pepper

1 Cook the potatoes in a saucepan of boiling water until almost tender, 5 to 6 minutes. Place the spinach in a steamer or colander over the potatoes and cook until the potatoes are tender and the spinach has wilted, another 5 minutes. Drain the potatoes. Press the spinach with the back of a spoon to extract excess moisture, then chop.

2 Heat the oil in a nonstick skillet about 10 inches in diameter. Add the pepper slices and sauté over medium heat for 2 minutes. Stir in the potatoes and scallions and continue cooking for 2 minutes.

3 Beat the egg whites and whole eggs in a large bowl, season lightly with salt and pepper, and mix in the spinach. With a slotted spoon, remove the vegetables from the skillet and add to the egg mixture, leaving any remaining oil in the pan. Stir the egg and vegetables briefly to mix, then pour into the skillet. Cover and cook, without stirring, until the omelet is almost set but still a little soft on top, about 6 minutes. Meanwhile, preheat the broiler.

4 Dust the top of the frittata with the Parmesan cheese and place under the broiler. Cook until browned and puffed around the edges, 3 to 4 minutes. Cut into quarters or wedges and serve.

(Some More Ideas) *Zucchini and potato frittata*: Replace the spinach with 1 large or 2 small zucchini, quartered lengthways and sliced, and use 1 thinly sliced small leek instead of scallions. Sauté the leek and zucchini with the pepper slices for 3 to 4 minutes. Add the potatoes and stir. Mix a handful of torn fresh basil leaves with the beaten eggs, and cook the omelet as in the main recipe.

Smoked-salmon frittata: Omit the potatoes and red pepper, and sauté a zucchini, quartered lengthways and sliced, with the scallions. Add 2 1/2 ounces slivered smoked salmon to the eggs with the spinach. Finish the frittata under the broiler without the Parmesan.

Plus Points

• This frittata also works well when made with an egg substitute. You can replace the whole eggs and egg whites with 1 1/4 cups egg substitute and proceed with the recipe as directed above.

• Frittatas are an excellent way to incorporate vegetables into the diet. Any leftover cooked vegetables can be tossed into the mix along with or in place of the ones listed above.

photo, page 175

Exchanges

starch 1 1/2 vegetable 1
meat (lean) 1 fat 1/2

Each serving provides calories 209, calories from fat 64, fat 7g, saturated fat 2g, cholesterol 109mg, sodium 122mg, carbohydrate 27g, fiber 4g, sugars 4g, protein 10g. Excellent source of folate, potassium, riboflavin, vitamin A, vitamin B6, vitamin C. Good source of calcium, iron, magnesium, niacin, phosphorus, thiamine.

salads and sides

garlicky tomato salad

When tomatoes are at the peak of their sweetness, this salad is particularly delicious. It's eye-catching, too, if you make it with a mixture of different-colored tomatoes. New varieties are coming on the market all the time—look for yellow cherry tomatoes as well as small red or yellow pear-shaped plum tomatoes. Your local farmers' market is also a great place to find unique types of heirloom tomatoes.

Preparation time **15 minutes**   *Serves 4*

Salad

1 large butter (Bibb or Boston) lettuce, large leaves torn into smaller pieces

4 large or 6 small ripe plum tomatoes, sliced

20 cherry tomatoes, halved

16 fresh basil leaves

1 tablespoon toasted pumpkin seeds

1 tablespoon toasted sunflower seeds

Vinaigrette

1 small garlic clove, very finely chopped

1 teaspoon red wine vinegar

1 tablespoon olive oil

Salt and pepper

1 To make the garlic vinaigrette, whisk together the garlic, vinegar, oil, and salt and pepper to taste in a small mixing bowl.

2 Place a layer of lettuce leaves on a serving platter or on 4 plates and arrange the sliced tomatoes and then the cherry tomatoes on top. Drizzle over the vinaigrette.

3 Scatter the basil leaves and the pumpkin and sunflower seeds over the tomatoes, and serve at once.

(Some More Ideas) *Tomato and black olive salad*: Slice about 1 pound ripe tomatoes, preferably beefsteak, and arrange on a serving platter. Top with 4 thinly sliced scallions and drizzle over 1 tablespoon olive oil and the juice of 1/2 lemon. Arrange 8 black olives, halved and pitted, on top and sprinkle with 2 tablespoons chopped parsley.

Fresh and sun-dried tomato salad: Cut 6 ripe plum tomatoes into thin wedges and place them in a mixing bowl. Thinly slice 3 sun-dried tomatoes and add to the bowl. Make a vinaigrette by whisking 1 tablespoon of the oil from the jar of sun-dried tomatoes with 1 teaspoon wine vinegar and seasoning to taste. Drizzle over the tomatoes and marinate briefly. Arrange 4 cups arugula on 4 plates and divide the tomatoes

among them. Sprinkle with 2 tablespoons toasted pine nuts and serve.

Cherry tomato and sugar snap pea salad: Trim 1 cup sugar snap peas and steam until tender but still crisp, about 3 minutes. Rinse the peas under cold running water, then cool. Mix with 1 pint cherry tomatoes, halved if large, and 6 thinly sliced scallions. Make the garlic vinaigrette as in the main recipe and drizzle it over the tomatoes and peas. Add 3 tablespoons chopped fresh mint, or 1 tablespoon each chopped fresh tarragon and parsley, and toss to mix.

Plus Points

• Pumpkin seeds are one of the richest vegetarian sources of zinc, a mineral that is essential for the functioning of the immune system and for growth and wound healing. They are a good source of protein and unsaturated fat and a useful source of iron, magnesium, and fiber.

• Fresh basil and a light drizzle of dressing are all that is needed to enhance the flavor of sweet, fresh tomatoes. The tomatoes can be marinated in the dressing overnight and then used in sandwiches, paired with fresh basil and mozzarella cheese.

photo, page 183

Exchanges

vegetable 2 fat 1

Each serving provides calories 106, calories from fat 59, fat 7g, saturated fat 1g, cholesterol 0mg, sodium 20mg, carbohydrate 11g, fiber 3g, sugars 6g, protein 4g. Excellent source of vitamin A, vitamin C. Good source of folate, iron, magnesium, phosphorus, potassium, riboflavin.

roasted-pepper salad

This colorful salad makes a tasty accompaniment to seafood, chicken, or lamb, or it can be served as part of a Mediterranean appetizer selection, with ciabatta bread or baguettes. Bell peppers are an excellent source of vitamin C, and when roasted, they still retain substantial amounts of this important vitamin.

Preparation time **45 minutes, plus cooling**   *Serves 6*

Salad

2 large red bell peppers
2 large yellow or orange bell peppers
2 large green bell peppers
2 tablespoons olive oil
2 teaspoons balsamic vinegar
1 small garlic clove, very finely chopped or crushed
Salt and pepper

Garnish

12 black olives, pitted
A handful of small fresh basil leaves

1 Preheat the oven to 400°F. Brush the peppers with 1 tablespoon of the olive oil and arrange them in a shallow roasting pan. Roast until the pepper skins are evenly darkened, about 35 minutes, turning them 3 or 4 times. Place the peppers in a plastic bag and leave until they are cool enough to handle.

2 Working over a bowl to catch the juice, peel the peppers. Cut them in half and discard the cores and seeds (strain out any seeds that fall into the juice), then cut into thick slices.

3 Measure 1 1/2 tablespoons of the pepper juice into a small bowl (discard the remainder). Add the vinegar, garlic, and salt and pepper to taste, and whisk in the remaining 1 tablespoon olive oil.

4 Arrange the peppers on a serving platter or on individual salad plates. Drizzle over the dressing and garnish with the olives and basil leaves.

(Some More Ideas) *Roasted red pepper and onion salad*: Quarter and seed 4 red bell peppers and put them in a baking dish with 4 small red onions, quartered. Drizzle over 1 tablespoon olive oil and season to taste.

Roast in a 400°F oven until the vegetables are tender and browned around the edges, about 35 minutes, turning once. Cool, then peel the peppers, if desired, holding them over the baking dish. Whisk 2 teaspoons lemon juice with 1 tablespoon olive oil in a salad bowl and season to taste. Add 2 cups mixed red salad leaves and toss to coat. Pile the peppers and onions on top and drizzle with their cooking juices. Serves 4.

Asian-style pepper and Chinese leaf salad: Seed and thinly slice 2 red bell peppers (or 1 red and 1 yellow bell pepper). Mix in a salad bowl with 2 cups shredded bok choy. For the dressing, whisk together 1 tablespoon rice vinegar, 1 teaspoon toasted sesame oil, and 1 teaspoon soy sauce. Drizzle over the vegetables and toss to coat. Sprinkle with 1 tablespoon toasted sesame seeds. Serves 4.

Plus Points

• Yellow, orange, and red bell peppers have much more vitamin C than green ones do.
• Roasted red bell peppers have incredible flavor and are softer to chew and easier to digest than raw peppers. For this dish, they can be roasted ahead of time, peeled, and then stored in an airtight container in the refrigerator for several days.

photo, page 183

Exchanges

vegetable 2 fat 1

Each serving provides calories 85, calories from fat 42, fat 5g, saturated fat 0g, cholesterol 0mg, sodium 80mg, carbohydrate 11g, fiber 3g, sugars 4g, protein 2g. Excellent source of vitamin A, vitamin C. Good source of vitamin B6.

warm potato salad

Here tender new potatoes, cooked in their jackets, are combined with crunchy celery, scallions, and walnuts in a nutty dressing, then served warm. The salad is a delightful alternative to potato salads in creamy mayonnaise-based dressings, and goes well with cold meats or grilled fish, poultry, meat, or vegetables.

Preparation time **10–20 minutes**   Cooking time **20–25 minutes**   *Serves 4*

Salad

1 pound small new potatoes
1/3 cup walnut pieces
3 celery stalks, thinly sliced
6 scallions, thinly sliced
4 tablespoons chopped parsley

Dressing

1 1/2 tablespoons walnut oil
1 tablespoon balsamic vinegar
1 garlic clove, crushed (optional)
1/4 teaspoon sugar
Salt and pepper

Garnish

Sprigs of fresh flat-leaf parsley

1 Cut any large potatoes in half. Put the potatoes in a saucepan, cover with water, and bring to a boil. Reduce the heat and simmer until the potatoes are just tender, about 15 to 20 minutes.

2 Meanwhile, make the dressing: Whisk together the oil, vinegar, garlic, sugar, salt, and pepper.

3 Drain the potatoes and put them into a serving bowl. Add the walnuts, celery, scallions, and chopped parsley. Drizzle on the dressing and toss the ingredients together gently. Allow to cool slightly until just warm, then serve garnished with parsley.

(Some More Ideas) Add a peppery flavor with watercress or arugula leaves. Fresh cilantro or basil can be used instead of parsley.

Replace half the quantity of potatoes with an equal weight of other root vegetables, such as young carrots and baby turnips. Cook the carrots and turnips with the potatoes.

Other oils can be used instead of walnut oil. For a creamy dressing, use 4 tablespoons plain nonfat yogurt instead of the oil.

Plus Points

• The preparation method makes a big difference to the amount of fiber provided: New potatoes cooked in their skins offer one-third more fiber than peeled potatoes. Cooking potatoes in their skins also preserves the nutrients found just under the skin.
• It's what you put on potatoes that makes them fattening. An average small potato only contains 90 calories and no fat. And by using an olive oil–based dressing instead of mayonnaise in this recipe, you'll get more monounsaturated fat.

photo, page 183

Exchanges

starch 1 1/2   vegetable 1
fat 2

Each serving provides calories 222, calories from fat 103, fat 11g, saturated fat 0g, cholesterol 0mg, sodium 48mg, carbohydrate 28g, fiber 4g, sugars 4g, protein 4g. Excellent source of vitamin B6, vitamin C. Good source of folate, magnesium, phosphorus, potassium, thiamine.

garlicky tomato salad *p180*

creamy vegetable salad *p185*

warm potato salad *p182*

roasted-pepper salad *p181*

zesty tomato salad

Seek out the most delicious tomatoes available, preferably sun-ripened on the vine, and you will be rewarded with an incomparable flavor. Lemon, fresh cilantro, and mint add freshness and zest to the tomatoes in this tangy salad, which can easily be varied with other fresh herbs and flavorings such as onion and garlic.

Preparation time **10 minutes**   *Serves 4*

Salad

1 pound ripe tomatoes, sliced

1/4 teaspoon sugar

1 lemon

3 scallions, thinly sliced

1 tablespoon chopped fresh cilantro

1 tablespoon chopped fresh mint

Garnish

Sprigs of fresh mint

1 Place the tomatoes in a large, shallow dish and sprinkle with the sugar. Cut the lemon in half lengthways. Set one half aside, then cut the other half lengthways into 4 wedges. Holding the wedges firmly together on a board, skin side up, thinly slice them across, including the peel.

2 Arrange the pieces of thinly sliced lemon over the top of the tomatoes, then sprinkle with the scallions, cilantro, and mint. Squeeze the juice from the remaining lemon half and sprinkle it over the salad. Serve immediately or cover and refrigerate until ready to serve. Garnish with sprigs of mint just before serving.

(**Some More Ideas**) *Tomato salad with rosemary and basil*: Make a dressing by mixing together 1 tablespoon each chopped fresh rosemary and basil, 1 to 2 garlic cloves, finely chopped, and 2 teaspoons raspberry vinegar or balsamic vinegar. Scatter thinly sliced red onion over the tomatoes. Sprinkle the dressing evenly over the tomatoes. Serve at once or cover and refrigerate until ready to serve.

A tomato salad makes a delicious filling for hot baked potatoes, particularly baked sweet potatoes. Bake 4 large potatoes until crisp and golden outside, then split and fill with the tomato salad. Top each potato with a spoonful of nonfat plain yogurt and serve immediately.

Tomato salad omelet filling: For each serving, make a plain omelet by lightly beating 2 eggs with 2 tablespoons cold water and a little seasoning, then cooking in the minimum of olive oil in a very hot omelet pan until just set, lifting the edges to allow unset egg to run onto the hot pan. Spoon one-quarter of the tomato salad over half of the set omelet and fold the other half over. Slide the omelet onto a warmed plate. Serve with a mixed green salad and crusty bread.

Plus Points

• Tomatoes have an abundance of vitamin C. It is thought that vitamin C as an antioxidant may help to protect against cancer.

• Refresh your breath with fresh no-calorie mint flavor in this dish as opposed to eating sugary candy mints.

Exchanges

vegetable 1

Each serving provides calories 28, calories from fat 3, fat 0g, saturated fat 0g, cholesterol 0mg, sodium 12mg, carbohydrate 6g, fiber 2g, sugars 4g, protein 1g. Excellent source of vitamin C.

creamy vegetable salad

It is easy to overlook root vegetables as a salad ingredient. Try this colorful mixture, tossed in a creamy, reduced-fat dressing, and discover a satisfying alternative to the ubiquitous mayonnaise-dressed potato salad. It makes a tempting light lunch or a delicious accompaniment to grilled meat or fish.

Preparation time **45 minutes**   Chilling time **2–3 hours**   *Serves 4*

Salad

10 ounces small new or salad potatoes, cut into 1-inch cubes

1 small celeriac, or celery root, cut into 1-inch cubes

1 medium sweet potato, peeled and cut into 1-inch cubes

Juice of 1 lemon

4 medium carrots

4 tablespoons currants

3 tablespoons pumpkin seeds

1 tablespoon orange juice

2 teaspoons olive oil

Dressing

2 tablespoons low-fat mayonnaise

2 tablespoons plain low-fat yogurt

1 teaspoon coarse mustard

2 tablespoons snipped fresh chives

1 tablespoon chopped fresh dill

Freshly ground black pepper

Garnish

Snipped fresh chives

Chopped fresh dill

1 Place the potatoes and celeriac in a saucepan. Add boiling water to cover and bring back to the boil. Reduce the heat and simmer until tender, about 10 minutes.

2 Meanwhile, place the sweet potato in another pan. Cover with boiling water, bring back to the boil, and simmer for 3 minutes.

3 Make the dressing: Mix the mayonnaise, yogurt, and mustard together. Stir in the chives, dill, and black pepper to taste.

4 Drain all the vegetables well and put them in a large mixing bowl. Add the lemon juice and the dressing, and toss lightly. Set the vegetables aside to cool, then cover and refrigerate them for 2 to 3 hours.

5 To finish the salad, use a vegetable peeler to cut ribbon strips from the carrots. Mix the carrot strips with the currants and pumpkin seeds. Stir in the orange juice and oil. Spread the carrot mixture in a large shallow serving bowl or place on individual plates.

6 Pile the chilled root vegetable salad on top of the carrot mixture. Garnish with a scattering of snipped chives and chopped dill, and serve.

(Some More Ideas) To vary the dressing for the root vegetables, replace the dill, chives, and coarse mustard with 1 tablespoon chopped fresh tarragon, 1 tablespoon chopped parsley, and 1 teaspoon Dijon mustard.

Plus Points

• Root vegetables are generally good sources of fiber.

• Carrots offer vitamin A as beta-carotene, which is essential for good night vision.

• Pumpkin seeds are rich in fiber and minerals, such as iron, zinc, and copper.

photo, page 183

Exchanges

starch 2 vegetable 1
fat 1

Each serving provides calories 231, calories from fat 69, fat 8g, saturated fat 1g, cholesterol 1mg, sodium 173mg, carbohydrate 37g, fiber 6g, sugars 12g, protein 7g. Excellent source of magnesium, phosphorus, potassium, vitamin A, vitamin B6, vitamin C. Good source of Iron, niacin, thiamine.

melon, feta, and orange salad

This recipe is based on the classic combination of melon and prosciutto (a delicious but fatty cured ham from Parma, Italy), but transformed into a healthy main-dish salad. Using lean ham and just enough feta cheese for flavor lessens the fat content of the dish. Cherry tomatoes, cucumber, and oranges add color to the salad, and a zesty citrus and herb dressing contrasts perfectly with the flavor of the ham.

Preparation time **20–25 minutes**   *Serves 6*

Salad

2 oranges

1 medium honeydew melon, peeled, seeded, and sliced

1/2 cup cherry tomatoes, halved

1/3 cup pitted black olives

1 small cucumber, diced

4 scallions, thinly sliced

6 (1 ounce) slices lean ham, trimmed of all fat and cut into strips

1/3 cup feta cheese, crumbled into large pieces

Dressing

1 teaspoon grated orange zest

4 tablespoons orange juice

1 tablespoon olive oil

1 teaspoon toasted sesame oil

6 fresh basil leaves, chopped

Salt and pepper

1 Make the dressing. Mix the orange zest and juice with the olive oil, sesame oil, and basil in a large salad bowl. Season with salt and pepper to taste. Set aside.

2 Cut the peel and pith away from the oranges with a sharp knife. Holding them over the salad bowl to catch the juice, cut between the membrane to release the orange segments. Add the segments to the bowl.

3 Add the melon, tomatoes, olives, cucumber, scallions, and ham. Toss until the ingredients are well blended and coated in dressing. Scatter the feta cheese over the top and serve.

(**Some More Ideas**) *Melon and fresh pineapple salad*: Mix cottage cheese, the melon, tomato, and cucumber with 2 cups of fresh pineapple (peeled, cored and chopped), and 3 shallots, thinly sliced. Make a lime dressing by mixing 1 teaspoon grated lime zest and 2 tablespoons lime juice with 1 tablespoon canola oil and 1 teaspoon honey. Season lightly with salt and pepper. Stir the dressing into the melon mixture and arrange on 6 plates. Spoon 1/4 cup low-fat cottage cheese on top of each salad.

Plus Points

• Feta cheese is rather high in fat and salt, but its strong flavor makes a little go a long way. Instead of stirring feta into dishes, just use it to crown the final presentation.

• Foods that have a high water content, such as melon, cucumber, and celery, help fill you up but with fewer calories.

Exchanges

fruit 2 meat (lean) 1
fat 1

Each serving provides calories 220, calories from fat 68, fat 8g, saturated fat 2g, cholesterol 23mg, sodium 560mg, carbohydrate 31g, fiber 4g, sugars 26g, protein 10g. Excellent source of potassium, thiamine, vitamin C. Good source of folate, niacin, phosphorus, riboflavin, vitamin B6.

mango and greens salad

This mixture of salad leaves and herbs, with their robust flavor, marries well with the sweetness and smooth texture of mango. The result is a salad that is colorful and refreshing, ideal as a light appetizer or side dish. Serve with warm mixed-grain bread or rolls.

Preparation time **15 minutes**   *Serves 4*

Salad

1 large ripe mango

4 cups mixed baby spinach leaves, watercress and arugula or frisée

12 fresh basil leaves, coarsely shredded or torn

1/3 cup cashews or peanuts, toasted and coarsely chopped

Dressing

Grated zest of 1 lime

2 tablespoons lime juice

2 teaspoons finely chopped or grated fresh ginger

2 teaspoons toasted sesame oil

2 teaspoons canola oil

Salt and pepper

1 Peel the mango. Cut the flesh from both sides of the pit and slice it thinly into lengthwise strips.

2 Mix the salad leaves and the basil together and place on a platter. Arrange the mango slices on and between the salad leaves.

3 Whisk the ingredients for the dressing together and spoon it over the salad. Sprinkle with the chopped cashews or peanuts and serve.

(Some More Ideas) Thin strips of peeled cooked beets and cooked or raw celery root are delicious additions to this salad.

Instead of mango, use seedless green grapes, halved if large, thinly sliced apple, or diced avocado.

Toasted pumpkin seeds, sesame seeds, or pine nuts can be used instead of the cashews or peanuts.

Completely fat-free dressing: Mix 1 tablespoon seasoned rice vinegar with the ginger and lime zest and juice. Add 2 tablespoons fresh orange juice. Or mix 2 tablespoons each of orange juice, dry sherry, and low-sodium soy sauce for a punchy dressing.

Plus Points

• Mango supplies iron, potassium, magnesium, and vitamins B, C, and E.
• All the salad leaves provide minerals, such as potassium, calcium, and iron, which help to protect against cancer. Raw spinach provides folate.

Exchanges

fruit 1 fat 2

Each serving provides calories 156, calories from fat 91, fat 10g, saturated fat 2g, cholesterol 0mg, sodium 84mg, carbohydrate 16g, fiber 2g, sugars 11g, protein 3g. Excellent source of vitamin A, vitamin C. Good source of folate.

mediterranean marinated salad

Inspired by Mediterranean cooking methods, this salad of roasted vegetables has a rich flavor cut by a piquant dressing. It is ideal for a healthy mid-week meal with crusty bread, some pasta, or couscous. It is also good as a dinner-party appetizer and delicious with grilled fish, poultry, or meat.

Preparation time **about 1 hour**   Marinating time **4 hours**   *Serves 4*

Salad

1 small eggplant, cut into 1-inch-thick slices

1 red pepper, cored, seeded, and cut into 2-inch squares

1 yellow pepper, cored, seeded, and cut into 2-inch squares

4 baby zucchini, halved lengthways

1 tablespoon olive oil

1 garlic clove, crushed

4 canned anchovy fillets, drained and finely chopped (optional)

2 tablespoons finely chopped fresh rosemary

Salt and pepper

Dressing

1 tablespoon olive oil

1 tablespoon red wine vinegar

1 teaspoon honey

1 teaspoon Dijon mustard

Garnish

Sprigs of fresh rosemary (optional)

1 Preheat the oven to 400°F. Lay the eggplant slices in a single layer in a large roasting pan. Arrange the red and yellow peppers and zucchini around the eggplant, placing them cut sides up.

2 Brush the vegetables lightly with the oil. Scatter the garlic, anchovies (if using) and chopped rosemary over the vegetables, and add salt and pepper to taste. Roast the vegetables for 25 to 30 minutes.

3 Cover the vegetables with foil and roast until they are tender, about 10 to 15 minutes. Transfer the cooked vegetables to a large dish and drizzle the cooking juices over them.

4 Whisk the dressing ingredients together and pour over the vegetables. Cover and leave to cool completely, then put the vegetable salad in the refrigerator to marinate for at least 4 hours.

5 Remove the salad from the refrigerator 1 hour before serving so it can return to cool room temperature if desired. Garnish with sprigs of rosemary, if desired.

(Some More Ideas) Replace the zucchini with 1/2 pound plum tomatoes, halved, and use fresh thyme instead of rosemary. Roast the eggplant and peppers for 30 minutes, then add the tomatoes, and roast for a further 15 minutes without covering with foil.

For a vegetarian version, omit the anchovies and add 2 tablespoons chopped capers.

Plus Points

• Eggplant is satisfyingly filling but low in calories. Three ounces contains just 15 calories. It is renowned for absorbing oil when fried, but cooking it this way keeps the fat content very low.

• Roasting brings out all the natural flavors of the vegetables. Serve this to people who typically do not like vegetables and watch them enjoy this dish!

• All of the vegetables in this dish are good sources of fiber and they provide lots of vitamins and minerals.

photo, page 191

Exchanges

fruit 1 fat 2

Each serving provides calories 109, calories from fat 64, fat 7g, saturated fat 1g, cholesterol 0mg, sodium 34mg, carbohydrate 12g, fiber 3g, sugars 7g, protein 2g. Excellent source of vitamin A, vitamin C. Good source of vitamin B6.

mixed salad leaves with flowers and blueberries

This pretty summer salad is a delightful combination of edible flowers, salad leaves, alfalfa sprouts, and juicy fresh blueberries. Some large supermarkets sell packages of edible flowers. Or you can pick them from your garden—just be sure to choose those that have not been sprayed with pesticides.

Preparation time **10–15 minutes**   *Serves 4*

Salad

1 small oak leaf lettuce or other desired lettuce, torn into bite-size pieces

2 cups arugula

1 cup alfalfa sprouts

1 cup blueberries

1/2 cup mixed edible flowers (nasturtiums, borage, violas, or pansies; herb flowers like sage and rosemary)

Dressing

2 tablespoons grapeseed or olive oil

Juice of 1 small lemon

1 teaspoon Dijon mustard

1 teaspoon honey

Salt and pepper

1 To make the dressing, whisk the oil with the lemon juice, mustard, honey, and salt and pepper to taste in a large shallow salad bowl.

2 Add the lettuce and arugula and toss to coat with the dressing. Sprinkle the salad with the alfalfa sprouts and blueberries. Arrange the flowers on top and serve at once.

(Some More Ideas) *Flowery carrot salad*: Tear the lettuce into bite-size pieces and put into a shallow salad bowl. Add 2 carrots, cut into long thin ribbons with a vegetable peeler, 2 oranges, peeled and divided into segments, and 1 cup blueberries. Make the honey-mustard dressing as in the main recipe, using orange juice instead of lemon. Drizzle it over the salad and garnish with mixed orange and yellow nasturtium flowers.

Plus Points

• Naturally sweet blueberries are rich in vitamin C and also contain antibacterial compounds thought to be effective against some gastrointestinal disorders and urinary infections such as cystitis.

• The nutritional value of petals and flower heads is very small, as they are used in such tiny quantities, but you will get some essential oils and phytochemicals, particularly antioxidants, from some flowers, especially herb flowers.

Exchanges

fruit 1/2 vegetable 1

fat 1

Each serving provides calories 108, calories from fat 66, fat 7g, saturated fat 1g, cholesterol 0mg, sodium 45mg, carbohydrate 11g, fiber 3g, sugars 6g, protein 2g. Excellent source of vitamin A, vitamin C. Good source of folate, riboflavin.

mixed salad leaves with flowers and blueberries *p190*

papaya and avocado salad *p192*

basil-scented sautéed vegetables *p193*

mediterranean marinated salad *p189*

sesame greens and bean sprouts

With a little inspiration and the easy availability of international ingredients, even the most humble vegetables can be elevated to new heights. This succulent stir-fry is full of flavor and crunch. It is delicious with grilled fish, poultry, or meat.

Preparation time **10 minutes**   Cooking time **4–6 minutes**   *Serves 6*

1 tablespoon sesame seeds
2 teaspoons canola oil
1 onion, chopped
2 garlic cloves, chopped
1 small Savoy cabbage, finely shredded
1 small head bok choy, finely shredded
1 cup bean sprouts
4 tablespoons oyster sauce
2 tablespoons water
Salt and pepper

1 Heat a small saucepan and dry-roast the sesame seeds, shaking the pan frequently over medium heat, until they are just beginning to brown. Turn the seeds out into a small bowl and set aside.

2 Heat the oil in a wok or large frying pan. Add the onion and garlic, and stir-fry until softened slightly, about 2 to 3 minutes. Add the cabbage and bok choy and stir-fry over high heat until the vegetables are just beginning to soften, about 2 to 3 minutes. Add the bean sprouts and continue cooking for a few seconds.

3 Make a space in the center of the pan. Add in the oyster sauce and water, and stir until hot, then toss the vegetables into the sauce. Taste and add pepper, with salt if necessary (this will depend on the saltiness of the oyster sauce). Serve immediately, sprinkled with the toasted sesame seeds.

(**Some More Ideas**) Use 1/2 head red cabbage, finely shredded, instead of the Savoy cabbage, and add 3 cooked beets, chopped, with the bean sprouts. Red cabbage will require 2 minutes additional stir-frying, so add to the wok before the bok choy. Use 1 tablespoon honey with 2 tablespoons soy sauce instead of the oyster sauce.

Finely shredded Brussels sprouts are crisp and full-flavored when stir-fried. Use them instead of the Savoy cabbage. Slice the sprouts thinly, then shake the slices to loosen the shreds.

Toasted almonds can be sprinkled over the vegetables instead of the sesame seeds.

Plus Points
• As well as contributing distinctive flavor, sesame seeds are a good source of calcium. Bear in mind they do contain fat, and you would not want to eat sesame seeds in very large quantities.
• The oyster sauce provides an abundance of flavor. Even though this product is salty, the sodium content per serving is not as high as some of the typical dishes served in Asian restaurants. You'll have the control to add even less oyster sauce if desired.

Exchanges
vegetable 2 fat 1/2

Each serving provides calories 68, calories from fat 23, fat 3g, saturated fat 0g, cholesterol 0mg, sodium 336mg, carbohydrate 10g, fiber 4g, sugars 6g, protein 3g. Excellent source of folate, vitamin A, vitamin C. Good source of calcium, magnesium, potassium, vitamin B6.

roasted vegetables with herbs

Use this recipe as a basic guide for roasting single vegetables, such as potatoes or parsnips, as well as for a superb dish of mixed root vegetables. Serve them with roast poultry or meat, but also remember that they are delicious with vegetarian main dishes and with lightly baked fish.

Preparation time **15–20 minutes**   Cooking time **30–35 minutes**   *Serves 8*

Vegetables

2 pounds root vegetables, such as potatoes, sweet potatoes, carrots, and parsnips

1/2 pound shallots

2 tablespoons olive oil

1 teaspoon coarse sea salt

1 teaspoon cracked black peppercorns

Few sprigs of fresh thyme

Few sprigs of fresh rosemary

Garnish

Sprigs of fresh thyme or rosemary (optional)

1 Preheat the oven to 425°F. Scrub or peel the vegetables, according to type and your taste. Halve or quarter large potatoes. Cut large carrots and parsnips in half lengthways, then cut the pieces across in half again. Peel and leave shallots or onions whole.

2 Place the vegetables in a saucepan and pour in enough boiling water to cover them. Bring back to the boil, then reduce the heat and simmer until the vegetables are lightly cooked, but not yet tender, about 5 to 7 minutes.

3 Drain the vegetables and place them in a roasting pan. Brush with the oil and sprinkle with the salt and peppercorns. Add the herb sprigs to the pan and place in the oven.

4 Roast until the vegetables are golden brown, crisp, and tender, about 30 to 35 minutes. Turn the vegetables over halfway through the cooking. Serve hot, garnished with sprigs of thyme or rosemary, if desired.

(**Some More Ideas**) Baby new vegetables can also be roasted. For example, try new potatoes, carrots, beets, and turnips. As well as root vegetables, pattypan squash and asparagus are delicious roasted. Sprinkle with herbs and a little balsamic vinegar or lemon juice.

Quartered acorn squash is good roasted with mixed root vegetables.

Plus Points
• Combining different root vegetables instead of serving roast potatoes alone provides a good mix of flavors and nutrients.
• All these vegetables provide plenty of fiber, so portions of meat can be modest.

Exchanges

starch 1 1/2 fat 1/2

Each serving provides calories 123, calories from fat 32, fat 4g, saturated fat 0g, cholesterol 0mg, sodium 314mg, carbohydrate 22g, fiber 4g, sugars 5g, protein 2g. Excellent source of vitamin A, vitamin C. Good source of potassium, vitamin B6.

196

sweet potato and celery root puree

Mashed or pureed vegetables are so easy to fix and eat, and they provide yet another interesting way to eat your vegetables. Here silky-smooth sweet potatoes and slightly strong-flavored celery root are deliciously flavored with apple and spices.

Preparation time **15 minutes**   Cooking time **15–20 minutes**   *Serves 6*

1 pound sweet potato, peeled and cut into 1-inch cubes

1 medium celeriac, or celery root, peeled and cut into 1-inch cubes

Juice of 1 lemon

1 tablespoon olive oil

2 garlic cloves, finely chopped

1 tablespoon coarsely grated fresh ginger

1 teaspoon ground cumin

1 Golden Delicious apple, peeled, cored, and finely chopped

1 tablespoon coriander seeds, roughly crushed

1 Cut the sweet potato and celeriac into similar-sized chunks and place in a large saucepan. Add half the lemon juice, and water to cover the vegetables, bring to a boil. Reduce the heat and simmer gently until the vegetables are tender, about 15 to 20 minutes.

2 Meanwhile, heat the oil in a small saucepan. Add the garlic, ginger, and cumin, and cook for 30 seconds. Stir in the apple and remaining lemon juice and cook until the apple begins to soften, about 5 minutes.

3 Toast the crushed coriander seeds in a small, dry pan, stirring occasionally, until they are fragrant.

4 Drain the vegetables well, then mash them. Stir in the apple mixture and sprinkle with the toasted coriander seeds. Serve hot.

(Some More Ideas) For a creamy puree, add 5 tablespoons low-fat plain yogurt or low-fat sour cream to the mashed vegetables before you add the apple mixture.

Plus Points

• Remember to keep sweet potatoes on your list when you are choosing your starches. Sweet potatoes provide excellent fiber and are very high in vitamin A. Choose more starchy vegetables in place of refined starches such as white flour and white grains. Sweet potatoes also provide good amounts of vitamin C and potassium, and contain more vitamin E than any other vegetable.

Exchanges

starch 1 vegetable 1
fat 1/2

Each serving provides calories 113, calories from fat 25, fat 3g, saturated fat 0g, cholesterol 0mg, sodium 46mg, carbohydrate 22g, fiber 3g, sugars 11g, protein 2g. Excellent source of vitamin A, vitamin C. Good source of potassium, vitamin B6.

pork and pear salad with pecans

This is a simple yet substantial salad of new potatoes, crunchy red and white radishes, peppery watercress, and juicy pears, topped with slices of lean roast pork and finished with a sprinkling of toasted pecans. The dressing is delicately flavored with ginger juice, squeezed from fresh ginger root.

Preparation time **35 minutes**   *Serves 6*

Salad

1/3 cup halved pecans

1 1/2 pounds even-sized new potatoes, washed

1 small daikon radish (Japanese white radish), peeled and thinly sliced

8 red radishes, cut into quarters

2 firm ripe pears

1 oak leaf lettuce or other greens, separated into leaves

1 bunch watercress, tough stalks discarded

12 ounces cooked roast pork loin, trimmed of fat and thinly sliced

Dressing

2 tablespoons finely minced fresh ginger

2 teaspoons coarse mustard

2 teaspoons white wine vinegar

2 tablespoons canola oil

2 teaspoons hazelnut oil

Salt and pepper

1 Heat a small skillet over medium-high heat and toast the pecans for 6 to 7 minutes. Cool, then chop roughly. Set aside.

2 Cook the potatoes in a saucepan of boiling water until tender, about 15 minutes. Drain. When cool enough to handle, cut into quarters and place in a mixing bowl.

3 To make the dressing, first put the ginger in a garlic crusher and press to squeeze out the juice (this will have to be done in 3 or 4 batches). You need 2 teaspoons of this ginger juice. Place the ginger juice, mustard, vinegar, canola and hazelnut oils, and salt and pepper to taste, in a small jar or container with a tightfitting lid. Shake well to mix. Pour about 1/3 of the dressing over the warm potatoes and toss gently to coat. Leave to cool.

4 Meanwhile, in another bowl, toss the daikon and red radishes with half of the remaining dressing, to prevent them from browning. Halve the pears lengthways and scoop out the cores, then cut into long wedges. Toss with the radishes.

5 Arrange the lettuce leaves and watercress in a shallow salad bowl. Add the radish mixture to the potatoes and gently

mix together. Pile onto the middle of the salad leaves, and arrange the pork slices on top.

6 Stir the toasted pecans into the remaining dressing and drizzle over the top of the salad. Serve immediately.

(Some More Ideas) Instead of pears, use other fresh fruits such as 2 peaches or 4 apricots.

Pork and apple salad with hazelnuts: Replace the pears with red-skinned dessert apples. Instead of daikon and red radishes, cut 1 1/2 cups each celeriac and carrots into 2-inch-long matchstick strips. Finish with toasted hazelnuts instead of pecans.

Plus Points

• The flavor of hazelnut oil is highly concentrated. Just one teaspoon adds a special note to the ginger dressing.

• Most of the enzymes responsible for the hot taste of radishes are found in the skin—if you find the taste overpowering, peeling will help to reduce the heat.

Exchanges

starch 1 1/2 fruit 1/2
meat (lean) 2 fat 2

Each serving provides calories 355, calories from fat 145, fat 16g, saturated fat 3g, cholesterol 48mg, sodium 93mg, carbohydrate 34g, fiber 5g, sugars 10g, protein 21g. Excellent source of niacin, potassium, riboflavin, thiamine, vitamin A, vitamin B6, vitamin C. Good source of copper, folate, iron, magnesium, phosphorus.

soups and stews

chicken stock

After roasting a chicken, the bones can be used to make a flavorful stock. The flavor from the bones seeps into the simmering stock, creating a rich homemade base for soups or meat dishes. Small bits of meat may come off the bones, flavoring the stock even more.

Preparation time **10 minutes**   Cooking time **about 2 hours**   *Makes about 5 cups*

1 chicken carcass or the bones from 4 chicken pieces, cooked

1 onion, coarsely chopped

1 large carrot, coarsely chopped

1 celery stalk, coarsely chopped

1 bay leaf

2 tablespoons fresh parsley, chopped, or 2 teaspoons dried parsley

1 tablespoon fresh thyme, chopped, or 1 teaspoon dried thyme

1/2 teaspoon salt

1/4 teaspoon black pepper

1 Break up the chicken carcass or bones and place them in a large saucepan or stockpot. Add the onion, carrot, and celery. Pour in 7 cups water and bring to a boil over high heat, skimming off any scum from the surface.

2 Add the bay leaf, parsley, thyme, salt, and pepper. Reduce the heat to low, cover, and simmer for 2 hours.

3 Strain the stock into a large, heatproof bowl, discarding the bones and vegetables. Use immediately or cool and then refrigerate until needed. After cooling, skim the fat that sets on the surface before using.

(Some More Ideas) To make turkey stock, use a turkey carcass. For game stock, use the carcass from 1 large or 2 small cooked game birds. Each type of meat will lend a different and unique flavor to the stock.

Plus Points

• Canned chicken broth and chicken bouillon are very high in sodium. By making your own natural stock, the amount of salt added can be controlled. Even though it may take a little time to prepare the homemade stock, it is a much healthier choice.

• Canned chicken broth and bouillon powder also may contain monosodium glutamate (MSG), which is a powdered flavor enhancer derived from glutamic acid. Many people are sensitive to MSG and experience headaches and dizziness after consuming the additive.

Exchanges

free food

Each serving provides calories 16, calories from fat 7, fat 1g, saturated fat 0g, cholesterol 5mg, sodium 159mg, carbohydrate 1g, fiber 0g, sugars 0g, protein 2g.

quick chicken soup

This lively recipe is perfect for a quick lunch or supper. Red bell pepper, corn, and a sprinkling of fresh herbs bring color and texture to a simple chicken-soup base, and adding a little sherry takes it to the next level. Leftover cubed chicken can be used, making the preparation time even shorter.

Preparation time **10 minutes**   Cooking time **about 20 minutes**   *Serves 4*

4 cups boiling water

2 reduced-sodium chicken bouillon cubes, crumbled

1 red bell pepper, seeded and cut into thin strips

3/4 cup frozen corn, thawed

8 ounces skinless, boneless chicken breast, cut into 1/2-inch strips

2 cups fresh broccoli, cut into small florets

2 tablespoons dry sherry

3 tablespoons snipped fresh chives or 3 teaspoons dried chives

3 tablespoons chopped fresh tarragon or 3 teaspoons dried tarragon

Salt and pepper

1 Pour the water into a large saucepan. Add the bouillon cubes and stir over high heat until the broth boils. Add the red bell pepper strips and corn. Bring back to a boil, then add the chicken and immediately reduce the heat to low. Cover and simmer gently for 5 minutes.

2 Uncover the pan and bring the soup back to a boil. Add the broccoli florets to the soup, but do not stir them in. Leave the broccoli to cook on the surface of the soup, uncovered, until just tender, about 3 to 4 minutes.

3 Remove the pan from the heat. Stir in the sherry, chives, tarragon, and salt and pepper. Serve immediately.

(**Some More Ideas**) A generous amount of fresh tarragon gives this soup a powerful flavor. For a delicate result, reduce the quantity of tarragon to 1 tablespoon or use chervil instead.

Savoy cabbage or curly kale can be substituted for the broccoli. Trim off any thick stalks before shredding the cabbage or kale.

To give the soup a Chinese flair, marinate the chicken strips in a mixture of 2 tablespoons low-sodium soy sauce, 2 tablespoons rice wine or dry sherry, and 2 teaspoons grated fresh ginger for 10 minutes while you prepare the vegetables. Use bok choy instead of the broccoli. Slice the thick white stalks lengthways and the green tops across into ribbon strips. Add the white strips in Step 2 and cook for 1 minute before adding the green tops. Add 2 chopped scallions with the shredded bok-choy tops. Cook for 2 to 3 minutes.

Thin strips of lean, boneless pork can be used instead of chicken.

Add 3/4 cup dried thin egg noodles to make the soup more substantial. Crush the noodles and stir them into the soup in Step 2. Bring the soup to a boil before adding the vegetables.

Plus Points

• Corn adds carbohydrate and dietary fiber to the soup. Green vegetables are also a good source of fiber, which is thought to reduce the risk of colon cancer.

• In this fast recipe, cutting fresh broccoli in small pieces means it will cook quickly to retain as much of its vitamin C as possible.

• This recipe is great to prepare on a cold winter day or to treat a sudden cold. The common ingredients are ones that are usually kept on hand, making the soup a quick and healthy meal option.

photo, page 205

Exchanges

starch 1/2 vegetable 1
meat (very lean) 2

Each serving provides calories 125, calories from fat 10, fat 1g, saturated fat 0g, cholesterol 32mg, sodium 52mg, carbohydrate 13g, fiber 3g, sugars 4g, protein 15g. Excellent source of niacin, vitamin A, vitamin B6, vitamin C. Good source of folate, phosphorus, potassium.

chicken and potato chowder

The simple, delicious flavors of this soup make it popular with the entire family. Here fat-free milk and turkey bacon are used to create a nutritious alternative to the classic version served in pub-style restaurants. Prepare the chowder for lunch on the weekend, served with a piece of crusty bread and a fresh fruit salad.

Preparation time **15 minutes**   Cooking time **about 50 minutes**   *Serves 4*

Chowder

Cooking spray

2 strips low-fat turkey bacon, finely chopped

5 ounces boneless, skinless chicken breasts, cubed

2 small onions, finely chopped

1 pound potatoes, peeled and diced

3 cups low-fat, reduced-sodium chicken broth

Leaves from 4 sprigs fresh thyme or 1/2 teaspoon dried thyme

Salt and pepper

1 1/2 cups fat-free milk

Garnish

Chopped fresh parsley

1 Heat a large saucepan, coated with cooking spray, over medium heat. Add the bacon, chicken, and onions, and cook, stirring occasionally, until the chicken is golden, about 8 minutes.

2 Add the potatoes and cook for 2 minutes, stirring constantly. Pour in the broth and then add the thyme, salt, and pepper. Bring to a boil. Reduce the heat to low, cover the pan, and simmer for 30 minutes.

3 Stir in the milk and reheat the soup over medium heat without boiling.

4 Ladle the soup into bowls and garnish with chopped parsley. Serve immediately.

(Some More Ideas) For a smooth result, puree the soup in a blender or food processor.

Garlic is delicious in potato soups. Add 2 to 3 chopped garlic cloves with the potatoes. Add a pinch of grated nutmeg instead of the thyme.

Winter vegetable soup: Use 1 1/2 pounds diced leeks (white and pale green parts) and carrots instead of the onions and potatoes.

Boost the vitamin C and iron content of the chowder by adding watercress. Add 2 cups watercress sprigs and the juice of 1 lemon with the chopped, cooked chicken and puree the soup until smooth. Stir in the milk, adding an extra 1/2 cup. Reheat the soup if necessary.

Add 1 cup chickpeas or cannellini beans, drained, and halve the quantity of potatoes.

Plus Points

• Potatoes undeservedly have a reputation for being fattening. In fact, they are rich in complex carbohydrate and low in fat, making them satisfying without being high in calories. They also provide useful amounts of vitamin C and potassium, and good amounts of fiber.

• Cream-based soups made with fat-free milk or fat-free evaporated milk are a healthier way to satisfy a craving for chowder—a popular comfort food.

Exchanges

starch 1 1/2 vegetable 1
meat (very lean) 1 fat 1/2

Each serving provides calories 214, calories from fat 42, fat 5g, saturated fat 2g, cholesterol 30mg, sodium 532mg, carbohydrate 27g, fiber 3g, sugars 9g, protein 16g. Excellent source of niacin, phosphorus, potassium, vitamin B6. Good source of calcium, magnesium, riboflavin, thiamine, vitamin B12, vitamin C.

chicken and potato chowder *p204*

quick chicken soup *p203*

turkey-chili soup with salsa *p206*

herb-scented ham and pea soup *p207*

turkey-chili soup with salsa

This colorful soup is inspired by the spicy and complex flavors of chili con carne. Full of delicious vegetables and served with tortillas and a refreshing salsa, it makes a healthy main course that is fun to eat. The ground turkey makes the soup lower in fat than traditional beef-based chilies, and the kidney beans add a valuable amount of fiber.

Preparation time **20 minutes**   Cooking time **about 45 minutes**   *Serves 6*

Soup

Cooking spray

1 pound ground turkey

1 onion, finely chopped

2 celery stalks, finely chopped

1 red or yellow bell pepper, seeded and finely chopped

3 garlic cloves, finely chopped

1 can (14 1/2 ounces) diced tomatoes

4 cups low-fat, reduced-sodium chicken broth

2 cups water

1/2 teaspoon ground coriander

1/2 teaspoon ground cumin

1/2 teaspoon dried oregano

1/2 teaspoon chili powder, or to taste

1 cup diced zucchini

1/2 cup frozen corn, thawed

1 can (15 ounces) kidney beans, drained and rinsed

Salt and pepper

Avocado Salsa

1 tablespoon fresh lime juice

1 avocado

1/2 cup cherry tomatoes, quartered

2 scallions, finely chopped

1 Heat a large saucepan coated with cooking spray over medium-high heat. Add the turkey and cook, stirring occasionally, until lightly browned, about 4 minutes. Reduce the heat to medium and add the onion, celery, pepper, and garlic. Continue cooking, stirring frequently, until the onion begins to soften, about 2 minutes. Stir in the tomatoes with juices, the broth, water, coriander, cumin, oregano, and chili powder. Bring to a boil, then reduce the heat to low, cover the pan, and simmer for 20 minutes.

2 Add the zucchini, corn, and kidney beans to the soup. Bring back to a boil, then reduce the heat to low and cover the pan. Simmer the soup until the zucchini is tender, about 10 minutes.

3 To make the salsa: Place the lime juice in a bowl. Halve, pit, peel, and dice the avocado, then add to the bowl and toss with the lime juice. Gently stir in the tomatoes and scallions.

4 Season the soup lightly with salt and pepper. Ladle the soup into bowls, serve topped with the avocado salsa and with the tortillas.

(**Some More Ideas**) *Vegetarian chili bean soup*: Omit the turkey and replace the chicken broth with low-sodium vegetable broth. Thickly slice 1 eggplant and brush the slices very lightly on both sides with 2 teaspoons olive oil. Lightly brown the eggplant slices on both sides in a nonstick skillet over medium-high heat, or under the broiler. Remove the eggplant from the pan or broiler and cut into cubes, then add to the soup with the tomatoes, broth, and spices.

Plus Points

• Beans are a good source of dietary fiber, particularly soluble fiber, which can help to reduce high blood cholesterol levels. They also provide useful amounts of vitamin B1 and iron.

• Vitamin C from the salsa will help the body absorb iron from the beans.

• Avocados are rich in vitamin B6, which is vital for making the "feel good" hormone serotonin. They also provide the antioxidant vitamin E, which can help to protect against heart disease.

photo, page 205

Exchanges

starch 1 vegetable 2
meat (very lean) 3 fat 1

Each serving provides calories 271, calories from fat 72, fat 8g, saturated fat 2g, cholesterol 49mg, sodium 630mg, carbohydrate 27g, fiber 8g, sugars 8g, protein 25g. Excellent source of folate, iron, magnesium, niacin, phosphorus, potassium, riboflavin, thiamine, vitamin A, vitamin B6, vitamin C. Good source of zinc.

herb-scented ham and pea soup

When they are available, fresh, shelled peas make this green soup taste delightfully indulgent, but frozen peas can be used as well. The high proportion of peas fills the soup with vitamins and fiber, while a modest amount of lean cooked ham adds protein and depth of flavor. The soup can be served as a satisfying appetizer or paired with half a sandwich for a light lunch.

Preparation time **15 minutes**   Cooking time **about 1 hour**   *Serves 4*

Cooking spray
1 onion, chopped
1 carrot, chopped
2 garlic cloves, chopped
1 leek, chopped
1 celery stalk, chopped
2 tablespoons fresh parsley, chopped, or 2 teaspoons dried parsley
1 potato, peeled and diced
3 ounces low-sodium, lean cooked ham, diced
1 pound shelled fresh or frozen peas
1/2 teaspoon dried herbes de Provence
4 cups reduced-sodium vegetable broth
2 cups water
3 large lettuce leaves, finely shredded
2 tablespoons fat-free half-and-half
Salt and pepper

1 Heat a large saucepan coated with cooking spray over medium-high heat. Add the onion, carrot, garlic, leek, celery, parsley, potato, and ham. Stir well, then cover the pan, reduce the heat to low, and cook the vegetables until they are softened, stirring occasionally, about 30 minutes.

2 Add the peas, herbes de Provence, broth, and water. Bring to a boil, then reduce the heat to medium and cook until the peas are just tender—allow about 10 minutes for fresh peas or 5 minutes for frozen. Add the lettuce and cook for 5 minutes.

3 Puree two-thirds of the soup in a blender, then stir the puree back into the rest of the soup. Alternatively, use a handheld blender to partly puree the soup in the pan. Reheat the soup if necessary and then ladle into bowls. Swirl a little half-and-half into each portion and serve immediately.

(Some More Ideas) *Split-pea soup:* Use 1 cup dried split peas (yellow or green) instead of fresh or frozen peas. Add 1 cup peeled, diced celery root, 1/2 teaspoon ground cumin, and a few shakes of chili sauce, such as Tabasco, to the vegetables and ham in Step 1. Increase the amount of broth to 5 cups, and simmer until the peas are tender, about 1 to 1 1/2 hours. Omit the lettuce and fat-free half-and-half. Puree all of the soup until smooth. Season lightly with salt and pepper and reheat.

Plus Points

• Throughout history garlic has been used to treat everything from athlete's foot to colds and flu. Scientific facts now give credence to the folklore—for example, allicin, the compound that gives garlic its characteristic smell and taste, is known to act as a powerful antibiotic, and it also has antiviral and antifungal properties.
• Peas are a good source of vitamins B1, B6, and niacin, and they provide useful amounts of folate and vitamin C. As a source of soluble fiber, they are helpful for anyone with high cholesterol levels.

photo, page 205

Exchanges
starch 1 1/2 vegetable 2

Each serving provides calories 182, calories from fat 17, fat 2g, saturated fat 0g, cholesterol 12mg, sodium 537mg, carbohydrate 30g, fiber 8g, sugars 11g, protein 13g. Excellent source of folate, thiamine, vitamin A, vitamin B6, vitamin C. Good source of iron, magnesium, niacin, phosphorus, potassium, riboflavin.

207

fish soup with pepper polenta

Good broth provides the flavor base for this delicate soup. Clam juice, garlic, chile pepper, and fennel are added to the low-sodium chicken broth to complement the mild monkfish that is added. The polenta accompaniment is prepared in advance, so the soup is simple to cook at the last minute—ideal when friends come to lunch.

Preparation time **30 minutes**   Cooking time **about 1 1/2 hours**   Standing time **10-20 minutes**   *Serves 4*

Soup

4 cups low-fat, low-sodium chicken broth

1 cup clam juice

1 bay leaf

1 sprig fresh parsley

1 sprig fresh thyme

2 celery stalks, thinly sliced

1 fennel bulb, thinly sliced (reserve the leaves)

2 carrots, halved lengthways and thinly sliced

Zest of 1 lemon

1 shallot, finely chopped

1 garlic clove, finely chopped

1 red chile pepper, halved, and seeded (optional)

1/2 pound monkfish fillet, cut into bite-size pieces

1/2 pound skinless white fish fillet, such as cod or haddock, cut into bite-size pieces

Salt and pepper

Pepper Polenta Sticks

2 red bell peppers, halved lengthways and seeded

1 cup instant polenta

1/2 teaspoon salt

Cooking spray

2 tablespoons freshly grated Parmesan cheese

Garnish

Fresh fennel leaves

1 Prepare the polenta sticks in advance: Preheat the broiler. Place the pepper halves on a broiler pan, cut sides down, and broil until the skin is charred and bubbly, about 10 minutes. To make the peppers easy to peel, place them in a plastic freezer bag and let stand until cool enough to handle, about 15 minutes. Peel the peppers and cut lengthways into 1/4-inch-wide strips. Set aside.

2 Cook the polenta with the salt according to the instructions on the package. Continue to cook, stirring constantly, until thick.

3 Place a piece of wax paper on a cutting board. Use a wet spatula to spread the polenta into a rectangle about 1/2 inch thick on the wax paper. Arrange the strips of pepper diagonally on top, gently pressing them into the polenta. Wet a sharp knife and use it to trim the edges of the polenta rectangle. Allow to cool.

4 Preheat the oven to 400°F and coat a baking sheet with cooking spray. Sprinkle the Parmesan cheese over the polenta rectangle and cut it into 16 sticks. Transfer the polenta sticks to the baking sheet and bake until the cheese is melted, about 15 minutes. Remove from the oven and allow to cool for 2 minutes, then transfer to a wire rack and cool completely.

5 For the soup: Pour the broth and clam juice into a large saucepan. Place the bay leaf, parsley, and thyme on a small piece of cheesecloth, gather the top, and tie with a piece of string. Place the herb bundle in the pan and add the celery, fennel, carrots, lemon zest, shallot, garlic, and chile pepper, if using (wear gloves when handling red chiles; they burn). Heat gently over medium-high heat until boiling, then reduce the heat to low and

Exchanges

**starch 2 vegetable 3
meat (very lean) 2**

Each serving provides calories 308, calories from fat 28, fat 3g, saturated fat 1g, cholesterol 42mg, sodium 1054mg, carbohydrate 43g, fiber 8g, sugars 7g, protein 27g. Excellent source of folate, magnesium, niacin, phosphorus, potassium, riboflavin, thiamine, vitamin A, vitamin B6, vitamin B12, vitamin C. Good source of calcium, iron. Flag: High in sodium.

simmer until the vegetables are slightly tender, about 5 minutes. Cover the pan and remove it from the heat. Let stand 10 to 20 minutes to allow the flavors to infuse into the liquid.

6 Remove and discard the herb bundle and chile halves. Bring the liquid back to a boil. Reduce the heat to low, add the monkfish and white fish, and cook until the fish is opaque and will flake easily, about 4 minutes. Season lightly with salt and pepper.

7 Transfer the polenta sticks to a serving plate. Ladle the soup into bowls and sprinkle with the fennel leaves. Serve immediately with the polenta sticks.

(Some More Ideas) *Mushroom polenta*: Cook 6 ounces sliced mushrooms with 1 crushed garlic clove and 1 tablespoon chopped shallot in 1 tablespoon olive oil for about 5 minutes. Add 1 tablespoon snipped fresh chives and spread over the polenta sticks. Sprinkle 2 tablespoons freshly grated Parmesan cheese over the mushrooms and brown under the broiler instead of baking.

Plus Points
• Celery and fennel are good sources of potassium.
• Cod, haddock, and monkfish—like other white fish—are very low in fat and calories.
• Polenta is a combination of cornmeal and liquid, usually water or broth. Here, the polenta is cooked, spread thinly, and then sprinkled with cheese and baked. It serves as an interesting, low fat starch in place of regular bread.

hearty mussel soup

This soup tastes fabulous. The diced potatoes absorb the flavors from the herbs and vegetables to make a mellow complement to the mussels. Warm whole-wheat bread is an ideal partner, delicious for dunking and mopping up the last of the soup. To complete the meal, serve a light, fruity dessert for a refreshing, vitamin-packed finale.

Preparation time **30 minutes**   Cooking time **40–50 minutes**   *Serves 4*

Soup

2 1/2 pounds mussels in their shells, scrubbed
Cooking spray
1 onion, finely chopped
2 garlic cloves, finely chopped
2 leeks, thinly sliced
3 celery stalks, thinly sliced
2 carrots, chopped
12 ounces potatoes, peeled and diced
3 cups reduced-sodium vegetable broth
2 cups water
3/4 cup dry white wine
1 tablespoon lemon juice
1 bay leaf
1 sprig fresh thyme
Salt and pepper
4 tablespoons chopped parsley or 4 teaspoons dried parsley
2 tablespoons snipped fresh chives or 2 teaspoons dried chives

Garnish

Reserved mussels

1 To prepare the mussels: Discard any broken shells or shells that do not close when tapped. Put the wet mussels into a clean saucepan and cover tightly. Cook over medium heat for 4 minutes, shaking the pan occasionally. Check that the mussels have opened—if not, cover and cook for 1 to 2 minutes longer. Drain the mussels, reserving the juices that have come from the shells. Reserve a few mussels in their shells for garnish; remove the remainder from their shells and set aside. Discard the shells and any unopened mussels.

2 Heat a large saucepan coated with cooking spray over medium heat. Add the onion, garlic, leeks, celery and carrots, and cook for 5 to 10 minutes, stirring frequently, until the vegetables are softened but not browned. Add the potatoes, broth, water, wine, reserved juices from the mussels, lemon juice, bay leaf, thyme, and salt and pepper. Bring to a boil, then reduce the heat to low. Cover the pan and simmer the soup gently until all the vegetables are tender, about 20 to 30 minutes.

3 Remove the bay leaf and thyme, then add the shelled mussels, parsley, and chives to the pan. Heat gently for about 1 minute.

Do not allow the soup to boil or cook for any longer than 1 minute or the mussels will become tough.

4 Ladle the soup into bowls and garnish with the reserved mussels in shells. Serve immediately while piping hot.

(Some More Ideas) Cooked fresh mussels are available in most supermarkets, usually vacuum packed and displayed in the refrigerated section near the seafood counter. For this soup, you need 10 ounces shelled weight of mussels. Alternatively, 2 cans of mussels packed in brine (each about 9 ounces) can be used. Drain the canned mussels thoroughly and pat dry before adding them to the soup.

Plus Points

• Like other shellfish, mussels are a good low-fat source of protein. They are an extremely good source of vitamin B12 and provide useful amounts of copper, iodine, iron, phosphorus, and zinc.
• Vitamin C from the potatoes, parsley, and chives aids the absorption of iron from the mussels.

photo, page 213

Exchanges

starch 1 vegetable 3
meat (very lean) 1

Each serving provides calories 192, calories from fat 19, fat 2g, saturated fat 0g, cholesterol 25mg, sodium 511mg, carbohydrate 29g, fiber 4g, sugars 10g, protein 13g. Excellent source of folate, iron, phosphorus, potassium, riboflavin, thiamine, vitamin A, vitamin B6, vitamin B12, vitamin C. Good source of magnesium, niacin.

shrimp bisque

Thick and creamy bisques are often prepared with pureed seafood and heavy cream. In this healthy version, a flavorful seafood stock is prepared with the shells of the shrimp and serves as a fat-free base. Dry white wine, fennel, and shallots are added to the soup, and chopped red bell pepper adds flavor, texture, and extra vitamins instead of the traditional cream.

Preparation time **30 minutes**   Cooking time **about 1 hour**   *Serves 6*

Bisque

1 pound raw shrimp, heads removed

4 tablespoons dry white wine

4 slices lemon

4 black peppercorns, lightly crushed

2 tablespoons fresh parsley, chopped, or 2 teaspoons dried parsley

Cooking spray

1 fennel bulb, finely sliced (reserve the leaves)

1 shallot, finely chopped

1/4 cup white bread crumbs

Pinch paprika

1 red bell pepper, seeded and finely chopped

Salt and pepper

Garnish

Chopped fennel leaves

1 Peel the shrimp and set them aside. Place the shells in a large saucepan. Add 6 cups cold water, the wine, lemon slices, peppercorns, and parsley to the pan. Bring to a boil, then reduce the heat to low and simmer for 20 minutes. Skim off any scum that rises to the surface during cooking.

2 Meanwhile, under running water, use a small, sharp knife to make a shallow slit along the curved back of each shrimp. With the tip of the knife, remove the black vein and discard it. Cover and chill the shrimp until needed.

3 Allow the shrimp-shell broth to cool slightly and then strain through a fine sieve into a large bowl.

4 Heat the same saucepan coated with cooking spray over medium heat. Add the fennel and the shallot and cook, stirring frequently, until the vegetables are soft but not brown, about 8 minutes. Stir in the bread crumbs, paprika, and stock. Bring to a boil, then reduce the heat and simmer. Add the shrimp and continue simmering for 3 minutes.

5 Use a slotted spoon to remove 6 shrimp for garnishing the soup. Set them aside. Lightly season the soup with salt and pepper and simmer for 15 minutes.

6 Puree the soup in a blender or food processor until smooth. Return to the pan and add the red bell pepper. Reheat the soup until piping hot. Serve garnished with the reserved shrimp and chopped fennel leaves.

(Some More Ideas) To add extra fiber, sprinkle the soup with garlic-flavored rye-bread croutons just before serving. Cut 2 slices light rye bread into 1/2-inch cubes and toss them with 2 teaspoons garlic-flavored olive oil. Transfer to a baking sheet and bake at 350°F until crisp, about 10 minutes.

To serve the soup as a filling main course, make the stock with 5 cups water and add 1 cup frozen corn with the red bell pepper and fennel. Serve with a simple side salad of mixed greens, cucumber, and green bell pepper.

A variety of other vegetables can be added with or instead of the red bell pepper. For example, try a mixture of small broccoli florets, finely chopped celery, and frozen peas.

Plus Points
• Bread crumbs, instead of the cream used in the traditional recipe, act as a thickener in the bisque.
• Simmering the shrimp shells in the broth gives the bisque a full flavor and boosts its calcium content.

photo, page 213

Exchanges

vegetable 1 meat (very lean) 1

Each serving provides calories 79, calories from fat 7, fat 1g, saturated fat 0g, cholesterol 97mg, sodium 143mg, carbohydrate 6g, fiber 2g, sugars 2g, protein 11g. Excellent source of vitamin A, vitamin C. Good source of iron.

211

piquant cod chowder

A variety of vegetables ensures that this wonderful soup is as healthy as it is delicious. The broth can be prepared a day in advance, ready for adding the fish at the last minute, which is useful when cooking mid-week meals. Planning ahead like this means a healthy homemade dinner can be on the table in minutes.

Preparation time **20 minutes**   Cooking time **about 50 minutes**   *Serves 4*

Chowder

2 sprigs fresh parsley

2 sprigs fresh thyme

1 bay leaf

1 celery stalk

1 can (14 1/2 ounces) diced tomatoes

4 cups low-fat, low-sodium chicken broth

1 cup clam juice

1 large onion, chopped

12 ounces red potatoes, cut into large pieces

1/2 pound carrots, thickly sliced

1 cup zucchini, thickly sliced

1 cup green beans, cut into short pieces

1 yellow or red bell pepper, seeded and sliced

1 pound cod fillet, skinned and cut into large pieces

Salt and pepper

Garnish

2 tablespoons finely chopped fresh parsley

1 tablespoon snipped fresh chives

Zest of 1 lemon

1 Place the parsley, thyme, and bay leaf on a small piece of cheesecloth, gather the top, and tie with a piece of string. Place the herb bundle in a large saucepan. Add the tomatoes and their juice, the broth, water, and onion, stir and bring to a boil. Reduce the heat to low, cover the pan, and simmer for 15 minutes.

2 Add the potatoes and carrots. Increase the heat to medium and cook, covered, until the vegetables are almost tender, about 15 minutes. Stir in the zucchini, green beans, and yellow or red bell pepper and continue simmering, covered, until all the vegetables are tender, about 5 minutes. Discard the herb bundle.

3 Add the cod to the gently simmering broth and season lightly with salt and pepper. Cover and cook until the fish is opaque and flakes easily, about 3 to 5 minutes. Do not allow the broth to boil rapidly or the fish will overcook and start to break into pieces.

4 For the garnish: Mix the parsley, chives, and lemon zest together. Ladle the fish and vegetables into bowls, then add the broth. Sprinkle the chowder with the herb mixture and serve immediately.

(Some More Ideas) Try using different vegetables in the chowder, such as broccoli florets, sliced leeks, corn, peas, and green bell peppers. Add them instead of the zucchini, green beans, and yellow pepper in Step 2.

Smoked haddock is delicious in this dish. It can be used on its own or used to replace half of the white fish.

Plus Points

• Serving whole-wheat rolls with the soup will add to the dietary fiber provided by all the vegetables.

• Green beans are a good source of fiber, and they also provide valuable amounts of folate.

• When a bundle of fresh herbs is prepared and used to flavor a simmering broth, only a small amount of salt is needed to adjust the taste at the end of cooking.

Exchanges

starch 1   vegetable 4
meat (very lean) 2

Each serving provides calories 271, calories from fat 13, fat 1g, saturated fat 0g, cholesterol 50mg, sodium 931mg, carbohydrate 38g, fiber 7g, sugars 14g, protein 28g. Excellent source of folate, magnesium, niacin, phosphorus, potassium, riboflavin, thiamine, vitamin A, vitamin B6, vitamin B12, vitamin C. Good source of calcium, iron.

hearty mussel soup *p210*

piquant cod chowder *p212*

rich vegetable stock *p215*

shrimp bisque *p211*

light vegetable stock

This light stock is suitable for vegetarian dishes and for fish, poultry, or meat recipes when a delicate flavor is desired. The stock is easy to prepare and can be stored in the refrigerator for several days for use in multiple recipes.

Preparation time **15 minutes**   Cooking time **about 1 hour**   *Makes about 6 cups*

Cooking spray
2 leeks, chopped
1 large onion, chopped
1 bay leaf
2 tablespoons fresh thyme, chopped, or 2 teaspoons dried thyme
2 tablespoons fresh parsley, chopped, or 2 teaspoons dried parsley
3 carrots, diced
3 celery stalks with leaves, diced
1/2 teaspoon salt
1/4 teaspoon black pepper

1 Heat a large saucepan or stockpot coated with cooking spray over medium heat. Add the leeks and onion, stir well, and reduce the heat to low. Cover and leave the vegetables to cook for about 20 minutes, shaking the pan occasionally without lifting the lid.

2 Add the bay leaf, thyme, parsley, carrots, celery, salt, and pepper. Pour in 7 cups cold water and increase the heat to high. Bring to a boil, skimming the surface of the stock to remove any scum.

3 As soon as the water boils and all the scum has been removed, reduce the heat to low. Cover and simmer for 35 minutes.

4 Strain the stock into a large, heatproof bowl and set it aside to cool. Use at once or cool and then refrigerate until needed.

(**Some More Ideas**) Because this stock is mild and has a light flavor, it works well when used as a cooking liquid for rice and pasta.

Plus Points
• This vegetable stock counts as a "free food" on the diabetic exchange list. It can easily be turned into a satisfying meal by adding some more vegetables and pairing it with bread or crackers and low-fat cheese.

Exchanges

free food   **Each serving provides** calories 2, calories from fat 0, fat 0g, saturated fat 0g, cholesterol 0mg, sodium 130mg, carbohydrate 1g, fiber 0g, sugars 0g, protein 0g.

rich vegetable stock

This stock is excellent in meat soups and is ideal for hearty vegetarian recipes. It is stronger in flavor than the Light Vegetable Stock because mushrooms, barley, and additional herbs are added.

Preparation time **15 minutes**   Cooking time **55 minutes**   *Makes about 6 cups*

Cooking spray
1 1/2 cups mushrooms, chopped
2 small onions, chopped
1/2 cup pearl barley
3 carrots, chopped
3 celery stalks, chopped
2 tablespoons fresh parsley, chopped, or 2 teaspoons dried parsley
1 tablespoon fresh thyme, chopped, or 1 teaspoon dried thyme
1 tablespoon fresh marjoram, chopped, or 1 teaspoon dried marjoram
2 bay leaves
1/2 teaspoon salt
1/4 teaspoon black pepper

1 Heat a large saucepan coated with cooking spray over low heat. Add the mushrooms and onions, cover the pan, and cook the vegetables for 5 minutes, shaking the pan occasionally.

2 Stir in the barley, carrots, and celery. Pour in 7 cups water, increase the heat to high, and bring to a boil, skimming off any scum that rises to the surface.

3 Reduce the heat to low. Add the parsley, thyme, marjoram, bay leaves, salt, and pepper. Cover the pan and simmer for 45 minutes.

4 Strain the stock into a large, heatproof bowl and set aside to cool. Use at once or cool and then refrigerate until needed.

(**Some More Ideas**) Try making herb cubes by adding 1 teaspoon dried herbs (basil, thyme, oregano) to each cube before adding the stock. Store the cubes in the freezer and add them to tomato sauce, soups, or pasta dishes as needed.

Plus Points
• Try freezing the stock in an ice-cube tray. The cubes can be used individually as needed in place of oil when sautéing vegetables. This eliminates the need for oil and adds flavor to the vegetables as they cook.

photo, page 213

Exchanges

free food   **Each serving provides** calories 10, calories from fat 1, fat 0g, saturated fat 0g, cholesterol 0mg, sodium 130mg, carbohydrate 2g, fiber 0g, sugars 0g, protein 0g.

wild-mushroom broth with herb croutons

Mixtures of fresh wild mushrooms, widely available in supermarkets, are good for making a quick soup that tastes really exceptional. Instead of thickening or pureeing the soup, serving it as a light broth allows the individual flavors of the mushrooms, vegetables, and herbs to be fully appreciated.

Preparation time **10 minutes**   Cooking time **about 20 minutes**   *Serves 6*

Cooking spray
1 small onion, finely chopped
1 small fennel bulb, finely chopped
1 garlic clove, chopped
1 pound mixed fresh mushrooms, sliced
3 cups boiling water
1 reduced-sodium vegetable bouillon cube, crumbled, or 2 teaspoons vegetable bouillon powder
6 (1/2 inch thick) slices French bread
2 teaspoons olive oil
2 tablespoons chopped parsley or 2 teaspoons dried parsley
2 tablespoons chopped fresh mint
Salt and pepper

1 Heat a large saucepan, coated with cooking spray, over medium-high heat. Add the onion and fennel and cook, stirring frequently, until slightly softened, about 5 minutes. Stir in the garlic and mushrooms. Continue to cook, stirring frequently, for 5 minutes. Add the boiling water and stir in the bouillon cube or powder. Bring back to a boil, then reduce the heat to low and simmer the soup, uncovered, for 10 minutes.

2 Meanwhile, preheat the broiler. Brush the slices of bread lightly on one side with the oil and toast them under the broiler on each side until golden, about 1 minute. Cut the bread into cubes and place in a bowl. Add the parsley and mint and toss well.

3 Lightly season the soup with salt and pepper. Ladle the soup into bowls. Sprinkle with the parsley-and-mint croutons and serve immediately.

(Some More Ideas) Use 3 diced celery stalks in place of the fennel.

Dried wild mushrooms can be used for this soup, although it will take a bit longer to prepare. Use 1 package dried porcini mushrooms (about 1/2 ounce) and 8 ounces fresh mushrooms. Soak the porcini mushrooms in some of the boiling water for 15 minutes and add them to the soup with the water and the garlic.

Plus Points
• In Asian cultures, mushrooms are renowned for their ability to boost the immune system, and the Chinese have put them to medicinal use for over 6,000 years. Mushrooms are a useful source of vitamin B6, folate, and niacin, as well as copper.
• Lightly brushing slices of bread with olive oil and toasting under the broiler before cutting them into cubes is a good way to make low-fat, crisp croutons.

Exchanges
starch 1/2 vegetable 1
fat 1/2

Each serving provides calories 85, calories from fat 17, fat 2g, saturated fat 0g, cholesterol 0mg, sodium 130mg, carbohydrate 15g, fiber 2g, sugars 3g, protein 4g. Excellent source of riboflavin. Good source of folate, niacin, phosphorus, potassium, thiamine, vitamin C.

classic gazpacho

This traditional Spanish soup is full of wonderfully fresh flavors. It is also packed with vitamins because all of the vegetables are raw. Cool and refreshing, it is the ideal choice for a simple lunch or midsummer supper, with a crusty country-style bread or roll. Or serve it as a light appetizer on a warm evening.

Preparation time **20 minutes**   Chilling time **2 hours**   *Serves 4*

Gazpacho

1 pound fresh tomatoes,
quartered and seeded
1/2 cucumber, peeled and
coarsely chopped
1 red bell pepper, seeded and
coarsely chopped
2 garlic cloves
1 small onion, quartered
1 slice bread, torn into pieces
2 cups low-sodium
tomato juice
1 tablespoon tomato puree
2 tablespoons red wine vinegar
2 teaspoons olive oil
1/4 teaspoon salt

Garnish

1 red bell pepper
4 scallions
1/2 cucumber
2 slices bread, toasted

1 Mix all the gazpacho ingredients in a large bowl. Ladle batches of the mixture into a blender or food processor and puree until smooth. Pour the soup into a large clean bowl, cover, and refrigerate for 2 hours.

2 Prepare the vegetables to serve with the soup toward the end of the chilling time. Seed and finely dice the red bell pepper, thinly slice the scallions, and finely dice the cucumber. Cut the toasted bread into small cubes to make croutons. Place these vegetables and croutons in separate serving dishes.

3 To serve, ladle the soup into bowls and serve with the accompaniments.

(Some More Ideas) For a milder flavor, use 2 shallots instead of the small onion.

In very hot weather, add a few ice cubes to the soup just before serving, to keep it well chilled. This will also slightly dilute it.

Plus Points
• Up to 70% of the water-soluble vitamins—B and C—can be lost in cooking. In this classic soup the vegetables are eaten raw, which means they retain maximum levels of vitamins and minerals.
• Made from fermented wine, pungent red wine vinegar serves as the perfect complement for the slightly acidic tomatoes in this recipe. When vinegars are stored tightly closed in a cool area, they can last up to 6 months. They are helpful to have on hand for use in salad dressings, marinades, and in meat and vegetable dishes.

photo, page 221

Exchanges

starch 1/2 vegetable 4
fat 1/2

Each serving provides calories 159, calories from fat 33, fat 4g, saturated fat 0g, cholesterol 0mg, sodium 280mg, carbohydrate 30g, fiber 5g, sugars 13g, protein 5g. Excellent source of folate, potassium, thiamine, vitamin A, vitamin B6, vitamin C. Good source of iron, magnesium, niacin, phosphorus, riboflavin.

tomato and red pepper warmer

Sweet red bell peppers lend a unique twist to a traditional tomato soup that is sophisticated yet simple to prepare. Swirled with low-fat sour cream and accompanied by hot pesto bread, it makes an appealing special-occasion appetizer. For a more casual occasion, garnish the soup with fresh herbs instead of sour cream and serve with whole-wheat bread.

Preparation time **25 minutes**   Cooking time **25 minutes**   *Serves 6*

Soup

1 (4 ounce) baguette
3 tablespoons prepared pesto
Cooking spray
1 onion, coarsely chopped
1 garlic clove, chopped
3 red bell peppers, seeded and coarsely chopped
1 1/4 cups low-sodium vegetable broth
1 1/4 cups low-sodium tomato juice
1 teaspoon chopped fresh thyme or 1/4 teaspoon dried thyme
1/4 teaspoon ground cinnamon
1 teaspoon sugar
Salt and pepper

Garnish

4 tablespoons low-fat sour cream
6 sprigs fresh basil

1 Preheat the oven to 350°F. Slice the baguette into 1-inch-thick slices, leaving the slices attached at the base. Hold the slices apart and spread each one thinly with pesto, then press them back together. Wrap the bread in foil and set aside.

2 Heat a large saucepan coated with cooking spray over medium-high heat. Add the onion and garlic and sauté gently until softened but not browned, about 5 minutes. Stir in the peppers and cook for 5 minutes, stirring occasionally. Pour in the broth and remove from the heat.

3 Place the bread in the oven to heat for 15 minutes. Meanwhile, puree the soup in a blender until smooth. Return the soup to the pan and stir in the tomato juice, thyme, cinnamon, and sugar. Heat the soup gently without allowing it to boil. Season lightly with salt and pepper.

4 Ladle the soup into bowls and garnish each portion with 2 teaspoons low-fat sour cream and a sprig of basil. Serve with the hot pesto bread.

(Some More Ideas) Plain low-fat yogurt can be substituted for the low-fat sour cream.

Spicy version of the soup: Add 1 seeded, deveined, and finely chopped fresh red chile pepper (wear gloves when handling; they burn) with the onion, or a dash of hot sauce, such as Tabasco, with the final seasoning.

Add 2 coarsely chopped leeks and 4 sliced celery stalks with the onion instead of the red bell peppers. Cook until the leeks are softened before adding the broth, about 15 minutes. Puree the soup in a food processor or with a handheld blender and finish as in the main recipe, omitting the sugar.

Tomato and carrot soup: Use 4 diced carrots instead of the red bell peppers. After the broth is added, cover the pan and simmer the carrots until they are tender, about 10 minutes. Finish as in the main recipe, omitting the sugar.

Plus Points

• In this recipe, reduced-sodium tomato juice is used to decrease the amount of sodium by almost half.
• Pesto is made from a mixture of basil, garlic, pine nuts, and Parmesan cheese. The spread is relatively high in monounsaturated fat due to the pine nuts and olive oil. A small amount on slices of baguette serves as a special treat and complements the flavor of the red peppers and tomatoes perfectly.

photo, page 221

Exchanges

starch 1 vegetable 1 fat 1/2

Each serving provides calories 119, calories from fat 28, fat 3g, saturated fat 1g, cholesterol 4mg, sodium 239mg, carbohydrate 20g, fiber 3g, sugars 6g, protein 4g. Excellent source of vitamin A, vitamin C. Good source of folate, riboflavin, thiamine, vitamin B6.

219

garden of eden soup

An assortment of vegetables cooked in tomato juice and broth makes an utterly simple yet satisfying soup that tastes terrific. For this recipe you can take advantage of frozen vegetables, such as broccoli, beans, and peas. They cut down on preparation time, and are just as nutritious as fresh vegetables.

Preparation time **10 minutes**   Cooking time **about 20 minutes**   *Serves 4*

1 1/4 cups boiling water

1 cube reduced-sodium vegetable bouillon, crumbled, or 2 teaspoons vegetable bouillon powder

4 cups low-sodium tomato juice

2 garlic cloves, crushed

4 scallions, finely chopped

1 large potato, scrubbed and diced

1 large carrot, diced

1 cup frozen broccoli florets

1 cup cabbage, coarsely chopped

1/2 cup frozen green beans

1/2 cup frozen peas

8 large sprigs fresh basil

Salt and pepper

1 Pour the boiling water into a large saucepan. Stir in the bouillon cube or powder, tomato juice, garlic, scallions, potato, and carrot. Bring to a boil, then reduce the heat and cover the pan. Simmer the soup for about 10 minutes, stirring occasionally.

2 Use a sharp knife to cut any large frozen broccoli florets into smaller pieces, then add them to the soup with the cabbage, green beans, and peas. Bring the soup back to a boil, then reduce the heat to medium. Cook until the vegetables are just tender but still crisp, about 5 minutes.

3 Lightly season the soup with salt and pepper, then ladle it into bowls. Use scissors to snip half the basil into shreds and scatter over the soup. Add a whole sprig of basil to each portion and serve immediately.

(**Some More Ideas**) Instead of weighing out 4 types of frozen vegetables, use 8 ounces frozen mixed vegetables. Many different frozen vegetable medleys are available, and they are great for making quick soups.

For a hearty soup, add 1 can (15 ounces) cannellini beans, drained and rinsed, with the frozen vegetables. Before serving, swirl 1 teaspoon prepared basil pesto into each bowl of soup.

The soup can be varied according to the fresh or frozen vegetables you have in the house. For example, try 1 peeled sweet potato with, or instead of, the ordinary potato and add 1 peeled and diced turnip for a hearty root-vegetable soup.

Plus Points

• This is a good example of a "cold start" recipe, in which the vegetables are added straight to the liquid without being sautéed in oil or butter first. The resulting soup is virtually fat-free.

• Different fruit and vegetables contain different phytochemicals, so it is important to eat a variety. This soup includes a good mixture of vegetables.

Exchanges

starch 1   vegetable 3

Each serving provides calories 144, calories from fat 5, fat 1g, saturated fat 0g, cholesterol 0mg, sodium 100mg, carbohydrate 33g, fiber 6g, sugars 14g, protein 6g. Excellent source of folate, potassium, thiamine, vitamin A, vitamin B6, vitamin C. Good source of iron, magnesium, niacin, phosphorus, riboflavin.

garden of eden soup *p220*

tomato and red pepper warmer *p219*

carrot soup with orange *p222*

classic gazpacho *p213*

carrot soup with orange

Thickening soup with potato gives a velvety-smooth result without adding the fat used in other traditional methods. Served either hot or chilled, this beautiful soup is ideal as a dinner-party first course all through the year.

Preparation time **15 to 20 minutes**   Chilling time **4 hours** (if served cold)   Cooking time **about 25 minutes**   *Serves 4*

Soup

2 cups vegetable broth

1 pound carrots, peeled and finely diced

1 small potato, peeled and finely diced

1 medium leek, washed and bottom white part chopped

2 strips pared orange zest

4 tablespoons orange juice, or to taste

Salt and pepper

Garnish

4 tablespoons plain nonfat yogurt, stirred

2 tablespoons coarsely chopped fresh flat-leaf parsley

1 strip of pared orange zest, cut into fine shreds

1 Pour the broth into a large saucepan and add the carrots, potato, leek, and orange zest. Bring to a boil over a high heat, skimming the surface as necessary, then reduce the heat to moderate, and leave the soup to simmer until all the vegetables are very tender, about 20 minutes.

2 Remove and discard the strips of orange zest. Puree the soup in a blender or food processor until smooth.

3 If serving the soup hot, return it to the saucepan. Reheat and add the orange juice, then adjust the seasoning. Ladle the soup into bowls and add a spoonful of yogurt to each, drizzling it over the surface. Sprinkle with the parsley and shredded orange zest and serve at once.

4 To serve the soup chilled, leave to cool, then chill for at least 4 hours. When ready to serve, stir in the orange juice, then adjust the seasoning. Garnish and serve as for the hot soup.

(**Some More Ideas**) To make a filling broccoli soup, replace the carrots with 1 pound broccoli florets. Sprinkle each serving with a little grated nutmeg.

Green-bean soup: Replace the carrots in the main recipe with 1 pound green beans, trimmed and chopped. Omit the orange zest and add 1/2 cup finely chopped fennel, about 1/2 bulb. Serve sprinkled with finely chopped fresh fennel leaves (from the bulb) or dill.

Plus Points

• This low-fat soup is made with leeks instead of the usual onion. Leeks are a useful source of several water-soluble vitamins, including C and folate.

photo, page 221

Exchanges

starch 1/2 vegetable 2

Each serving provides calories 96, calories from fat 5, fat 1g, saturated fat 0g, cholesterol 0mg, sodium 539mg, carbohydrate 21g, fiber 4g, sugars 11g, protein 3g. Excellent source of vitamin A, vitamin C. Good source of folate, iron, niacin, phosphorus, potassium, riboflavin, thiamine, vitamin B6.

chunky vegetable soup

Although this is a hearty soup, laden with vegetables, it has a delicate flavor. Cooking all your vegetables in one pot makes it so easy to reach your vegetable goals! This soup is especially good on a cold wintry day.

Preparation time **15 minutes**   Cooking time **about 1 hour**   *Serves 4*

Soup

1 tablespoon olive oil
1 small onion, chopped
1 small leek, thinly sliced
1 large carrot, thinly sliced
1 bulb of fennel, sliced
1 large potato, peeled and cubed
1 bay leaf
Several sprigs of fresh thyme
Several sprigs of parsley
2 cups vegetable broth
1 can (14 ounces) chopped tomatoes
Salt and pepper to taste

Garnish

Fennel leaves (from the bulb, above) or snipped fresh chives

1 Heat the oil in a large saucepan. Add the onion and cook until softened but not browned, about 5 minutes, stirring occasionally.

2 Add the leek, carrot, fennel, and potato, and cook until slightly softened, about 5 minutes. Tie the bay leaf, thyme, and parsley sprigs together in a square of cheesecloth to make a bouquet garni. Add to the pan, together with the broth and tomatoes with their juice. Season to taste and bring to the boil, then cover the pan and reduce the heat. Simmer gently until all the vegetables are tender, about 45 minutes.

3 Remove the bouquet garni and check the seasoning. Sprinkle the soup with snipped fennel leaves or chives and serve piping hot. Whole-grain bread is delicious with this soup.

Stir 2 ounces pearl barley into the softened vegetables, just before the stock and tomatoes.

Add 1 garlic clove, finely chopped, and 2 teaspoons caraway seeds with the onion.

(Some More Ideas) For a hearty winter chowder-type soup, simply add more vegetables. Try celery root, turnips, and parsnips. Shredded white or green cabbage is also good. Add green cabbage halfway through the simmering. Cool and chill any leftovers and reheat them the next day, when the soup will taste even better.

Plus Points
• The amount of fiber in this soup is impressive. With 6 grams of fiber per serving, this soup will help you reach your daily fiber goal of 20–25 grams.
• Soup is filling. By keeping yourself satisfied, you won't need to fill up on less nutritious foods later.

Exchanges
starch 1   vegetable 3

Each serving provides calories 155, calories from fat 37, fat 4g, saturated fat 0g, cholesterol 0mg, sodium 727mg, carbohydrate 28g, fiber 6g, sugars 10g, protein 3g. Excellent source of potassium, vitamin A, vitamin B6, vitamin C. Good source of folate, iron, magnesium, niacin, phosphorus, thiamine.

artichoke soup with caraway

Jerusalem artichokes, which look like knobby new potatoes, have a distinctive and delicate flavor that goes well with other root vegetables, particularly in a smooth-textured soup. Sweetly aromatic caraway seeds complement the vegetable flavors and transform an unassuming, familiar dish into something special.

Preparation time **about 25 minutes**   Cooking time **about 40 minutes**   *Serves 6*

Soup

1 tablespoon lemon juice
1 pound Jerusalem artichokes
2 teaspoons olive oil
1 celery stalk, chopped
1 small onion, chopped
2 carrots, chopped
1 garlic clove, chopped
4 cups low-fat, low-sodium chicken broth
1 teaspoon caraway seeds
3/4 cup fat-free milk
4 tablespoons fat-free half-and-half
Salt and pepper

Garnish

1 small carrot
2 tablespoons fresh parsley, chopped

1 Add the lemon juice to a bowl of cold water. Peel and slice the artichokes, placing them into the water as soon as they are cut. (Artichokes discolor quickly once peeled and exposed to the air.)

2 Heat the oil in a large saucepan over low heat. Drain the artichokes and add them to the saucepan with the celery, onion, carrots, and garlic. Cover the pan and cook the vegetables until softened, about 10 minutes.

3 Add the broth and caraway seeds. Bring to a boil, then reduce the heat to low and cover the pan. Simmer until the vegetables are tender, about 20 minutes. Cool the soup slightly, then puree it in a blender until smooth or press it through a fine sieve.

4 Return the soup to the pan. Stir in the milk and half-and-half and season lightly with salt and pepper. Reheat the soup over medium heat without allowing it to boil. Meanwhile, cut the carrot for garnish into short matchsticks. Serve the soup hot, garnishing each portion with the carrot and chopped parsley.

(Some More Ideas) Vegetable broth (preferably homemade) can be substituted for the chicken broth.

Celery root and parsnip soup: Use 1 pound peeled and chopped celery root instead of Jerusalem artichokes, and 2 chopped parsnips instead of carrots. Omit the celery.

Bacon is delicious with artichokes and other root vegetables. Cook 3 ounces low-fat turkey bacon and use it as a garnish for the soup. Crumble the cooked bacon and sprinkle it on top of the soup instead of the carrots and parsley.

Plus Points
• Jerusalem artichokes are a useful winter vegetable. Combining them with familiar root vegetables, such as carrots, is a good way of introducing them into your diet.
• Jerusalem artichokes contain compounds called fructo-oligosaccharides—a type of dietary fiber that stimulates friendly bacteria in the intestines while inhibiting harmful bacteria.

Exchanges
vegetable 3 fat 1/2

Each serving provides calories 106, calories from fat 17, fat 2g, saturated fat 0g, cholesterol 1mg, sodium 388mg, carbohydrate 18g, fiber 3g, sugars 8g, protein 5g. Excellent source of vitamin A. Good source of iron, niacin, phosphorus, potassium, riboflavin, thiamine, vitamin C.

chilled leek and avocado soup *p227*

artichoke soup with caraway *p224*

goulash in a hurry *p229*

celery root and spinach soup *p226*

celery root and spinach soup

Celery root (celeriac) makes a rich soup with lots of flavor and a creamy texture. Young leaf spinach complements the celery root beautifully, bringing color and a light, fresh taste in the final minutes of cooking. The soup is garnished with a swirl of fat-free cream and fresh chives, creating an elegant presentation.

Preparation time **15 minutes**   Cooking time **about 20 minutes**   *Serves 4*

Soup

Cooking spray

1 large onion, thinly sliced

1 garlic clove, crushed

1 celery root (about 1 1/4 pounds), peeled and grated

4 cups boiling water

1 reduced-sodium vegetable bouillon cube, crumbled, or 2 teaspoons vegetable bouillon powder

1 pound fresh spinach, washed and trimmed

Pinch nutmeg

Salt and pepper

Garnish

2 tablespoons fat-free half-and-half

Fresh chives

1 Heat a large saucepan coated with cooking spray over medium-high heat. Add the onion and garlic, and cook until the onion is softened but not browned, about 5 minutes. Add the celery root. Pour in the boiling water and add the bouillon cube or powder. Bring to a boil, then reduce the heat to low and cover the pan. Cook the soup until the celery root is tender, about 10 minutes.

2 Add the spinach to the soup and stir well. Increase the heat and bring the soup to a boil, then remove the pan from the heat. Cool the soup slightly and then puree it, in batches, in a blender or food processor until smooth. Alternatively, you can puree the soup in the pan using a hand-held blender. The soup will be fairly thick.

3 Reheat the soup, if necessary, then stir in a dash of nutmeg, salt, and pepper. Ladle the soup into bowls. Swirl a spoonful of half-and-half into each portion and garnish with fresh chives, then serve immediately.

(**Some More Ideas**) To make a delicious potato and watercress version of this soup, use peeled and diced potatoes instead of celery root, and watercress instead of spinach. Add extra broth or a little fat-free milk if the pureed soup is too thick.

Vegetarian main-course soup: While the soup is cooking, cook 7 ounces tofu, cut into thick slices, under the broiler. Allow about 3 minutes on each side or until browned. Cut the tofu into small cubes and set aside. Toast 1 tablespoon sesame seeds in a non-stick skillet, stirring frequently, until golden. Ladle the soup into bowls, divide the tofu among the bowls, and sprinkle with the sesame seeds.

Plus Points

• Celery root, a relative of celery, complements both the flavor and texture of spinach, making the most of the modest amount of fat-free half-and-half that is used to enrich the soup. Celery root is also high in potassium.

• Onions have many health benefits. They contain sulfur compounds, which give onions their characteristic smell and make your eyes water. These compounds assist in transporting cholesterol away from the artery walls.

photo, page 225

Exchanges

vegetable 4

Each serving provides calories 95, calories from fat 8, fat 1g, saturated fat 0g, cholesterol 0mg, sodium 232mg, carbohydrate 20g, fiber 5g, sugars 7g, protein 5g. Excellent source of folate, magnesium, phosphorus, potassium, riboflavin, vitamin A, vitamin B6, vitamin C. Good source of calcium, iron, thiamine.

chilled leek and avocado soup

Cilantro and lime juice accentuate the delicate avocado flavor in this refreshing soup. It is simple yet interesting, and ideal for a summer dinner-party first course or a light lunch. Do not add the avocado too soon—not only will it discolor slightly, but its flavor will mellow and lose its vital freshness.

Preparation time **15–20 minutes**   Cooking time **25 minutes**   *Serves 4*

Soup

Cooking spray

2 leeks, halved lengthways and thinly sliced

1 garlic clove, finely chopped

4 cups reduced-sodium vegetable or low-fat, reduced-sodium chicken broth

1 ripe avocado

1/2 cup (4 ounces) plain low-fat yogurt

1 tablespoon fresh lime juice

2 tablespoons chopped fresh cilantro

Salt and pepper

Garnish

8 to 12 ice cubes (optional)

Slices of lime

Sprigs of fresh cilantro

1 Heat a large saucepan, coated with cooking spray, over medium heat, add the leeks and garlic, and cook, stirring frequently, until the leeks are slightly softened but not brown, about 10 minutes. Add the broth and bring to a boil. Cover the pan, reduce the heat to low, and simmer until the leeks are cooked, about 10 minutes.

2 Remove the soup from the heat and let it cool slightly, then puree it in a blender or food processor. Alternatively, the soup can be pureed in the saucepan with a handheld blender. Pour the soup into a bowl and allow it to cool slightly, then cool completely in the refrigerator.

3 Just before serving the soup, prepare the avocado: Halve the avocado and discard the pit. Scoop the flesh from the peel and press through a fine sieve. The avocado can also be pureed in a blender or food processor until smooth, adding a little of the chilled soup to thin the puree and ensure it is completely smooth.

4 Stir the avocado puree into the soup along with the yogurt, lime juice, and cilantro. Season lightly with salt and pepper, then ladle the soup into bowls. Float 2 or 3 ice cubes in each bowl, if you wish, then garnish with slices of lime and sprigs of cilantro. Serve immediately.

(**Some More Ideas**) This soup is also good hot. Puree the hot soup with the avocado and then stir in the yogurt.

For a slightly spicier soup, cook 1 or 2 seeded and finely chopped fresh green chile peppers with the leeks.

No-cook avocado soup: Blend 2 avocados with 2 cups low-sodium vegetable broth, then add the yogurt and lime juice and season to taste.

Vichyssoise: To make the classic chilled leek-and-potato soup, increase the broth to 5 cups and cook 2 peeled and sliced potatoes with the leeks. Omit the avocado, lime juice, and cilantro, and serve sprinkled with snipped fresh chives.

Plus Points

• Half an avocado provides a quarter of the recommended daily intake of vitamin B6 and useful amounts of vitamin E and potassium. Other substances in avocados are good for the skin.

• Leeks provide useful amounts of folate, which is important for proper blood cell formation.

photo, page 225

Exchanges

carbohydrate 1 fat 1 1/2

Each serving provides calories 121, calories from fat 75, fat 8g, saturated fat 2g, cholesterol 2mg, sodium 163mg, carbohydrate 11g, fiber 3g, sugars 4g, protein 3g. Good source of folate, potassium, vitamin B6, vitamin C.

golden lentil soup

This velvety-smooth soup owes its rich color to a combination of lentils, parsnips, and carrots. With dry sherry and a horseradish-flavored cream added for flavor, it is a perfect introductory course for an autumn dinner party. Serve it with crunchy seeded, whole-wheat crackers.

Preparation time **10 minutes**   Cooking time **about 1 hour**   *Serves 4*

1 Heat a large saucepan coated with cooking spray over low heat. Add the onion, stir well, and cover the pan. Cook the onion over low heat until softened, about 10 minutes. Stir in the parsnips, carrots, and sherry. Bring to a boil, then cover the pan again and leave to simmer gently for 10 minutes over low heat.

2 Add the lentils, broth, salt, and pepper. Bring to a boil, reduce the heat to low, and cover the pan. Simmer until the lentils are tender, about 25 minutes. Puree the soup in a blender until smooth. Return the soup to the pan if necessary, and reheat until boiling. If the soup seems thick, add a little broth or water.

3 Combine the sour cream and horseradish in a small bowl. Cut the chives into 1-inch pieces for the garnish. Ladle the soup into bowls and top each portion with 2 teaspoons of the horseradish cream. Sprinkle with chives and serve immediately.

(Some More Ideas) Celeriac can be substituted for the parsnips. Prepare and cook the soup as in the main recipe.

Dry white vermouth or white wine can be added in place of the sherry for a lighter flavor.

Plus Points
• Lentils are a good source of protein and an excellent source of fiber. High-fiber foods are bulky and make you feel full for longer, so they are very satisfying. A diet high in fiber and low in fat is good for weight control.
• Root vegetables have long been enjoyed as an excellent source of vitamins and minerals during the winter months.
• People who are reluctant to sample plain cooked vegetables will not even realize they are eating them in this tasty, colorful pureed soup.

Soup

Cooking spray
1 large onion, finely chopped
4 parsnips, diced
3 carrots, diced
1/2 cup dry sherry
1/2 cup red lentils
4 cups low-sodium vegetable broth
Salt and pepper

Garnish

3 tablespoons low-fat sour cream
2 teaspoons prepared horseradish
Fresh chives

Exchanges

starch 2   vegetable 3

Each serving provides calories 239, calories from fat 15, fat 2g, saturated fat 1g, cholesterol 4mg, sodium 180mg, carbohydrate 47g, fiber 12g, sugars 14g, protein 10g. Excellent source of folate, phosphorus, potassium, thiamine, vitamin A, vitamin C. Good source of iron, magnesium, niacin, riboflavin, vitamin B6.

goulash in a hurry

This shortcut version of classic Hungarian goulash is rich and delicious. Strips of lean pork, shredded red cabbage, and green bell pepper cook quickly and taste excellent with the traditional flavorings of paprika and caraway seeds. Serve rice or noodles and a simple green salad alongside to complete the meal.

Preparation time **10 minutes**   Cooking time **about 30 minutes**   *Serves 4*

Goulash

Cooking spray
1 large onion, finely chopped
2 garlic cloves, crushed
1 (8 ounce) pork loin, cut into thin strips
1 tablespoon flour
1 can (28 ounces) stewed tomatoes
1/2 cup dry white wine
2 tablespoons paprika
1 teaspoon caraway seeds
1/2 teaspoon sugar
1 reduced-sodium chicken bouillon cube, crumbled, or 2 teaspoons reduced-sodium chicken bouillon powder
1 green bell pepper, seeded and chopped
2 cups finely shredded red cabbage
Salt and pepper

Garnish

4 tablespoons low-fat plain yogurt
Paprika
Fresh chives

1 Heat a large nonstick skillet, coated with cooking spray, over medium-high heat. Add the onion, garlic, and pork, and cook until the meat has changed color and become firm and the onion is slightly softened, about 3 minutes. Meanwhile, blend the flour with 4 tablespoons juice from the canned tomatoes to make a smooth paste; set aside.

2 Add the wine, paprika, caraway seeds, and sugar to the skillet and stir, then add the tomatoes with the rest of their juice, breaking them up as you mix them in. Stir in the bouillon cube and the flour and tomato juice mixture. Bring to a boil, stirring, and cook until the juices thicken.

3 Add the green pepper and red cabbage and stir to coat in the cooking juices. Reduce the heat, cover the pan, and simmer the goulash until the meat is cooked and the vegetables are tender but still slightly crisp, about 15 minutes.

4 Lightly season the goulash with salt and pepper. Ladle the goulash into bowls and top each portion with a spoonful of yogurt and a sprinkle of paprika. Garnish with whole fresh chives and serve.

(Some More Ideas) *Vegetarian goulash*: Omit the pork and red cabbage. Cut 1 small eggplant into large chunks and add to the softened onion and garlic in Step 1 with 6 halved sun-dried tomatoes (not oil packed), 2 thickly sliced celery stalks, and 2 thickly sliced zucchini. Follow the main recipe, using a reduced-sodium vegetable bouillon cube or 2 teaspoons bouillon powder. Simmer until the vegetables are tender, about 25 minutes, then stir in 1 can (15 ounces) chickpeas and 1 can (15 ounces) red kidney beans, both well drained and rinsed. Cook for 5 minutes. Serve topped with plain, low-fat yogurt.

Halved small new potatoes are good in the vegetarian version, above. Add the potatoes with the other vegetables in place of the canned red kidney beans.

Plus Points

• Several studies have shown that eating garlic can reduce the risk of heart attack and stroke by making the blood less sticky and likely to clot. Garlic can also help to reduce high blood pressure.
• Onions share garlic's healthy properties, and they are also a natural decongestant. Using onions as the basis for everyday dishes contributes to good eating.

Exchanges

carbohydrate 1/2 vegetable 4
meat (lean) 1 fat 1/2

Each serving provides calories 216, calories from fat 44, fat 5g, saturated fat 1g, cholesterol 36mg, sodium 549mg, carbohydrate 29g, fiber 5g, sugars 14g, protein 17g. Excellent source of niacin, potassium, riboflavin, thiamine, vitamin A, vitamin B6, vitamin C. Good source of calcium, folate, iron, magnesium, phosphorus.

breads and snacks

black-currant tea bread

Tart black currants make an enticing tea bread that is fruity without being too sweet, while mint adds a fresh, herbal note. Orange juice is used to enhance the flavor of the bread and decrease the amount of sugar needed in the recipe. If you have extra black currants, make a few loaves of bread and freeze them for up to 2 months.

Preparation time **15 minutes**   Cooking time **about 1 hour**   *Makes 1 large loaf (14 slices)*

Cooking spray
3 cups self-rising flour
1 teaspoon baking powder
3 tablespoons reduced-calorie margarine spread
1/3 cup sugar
5 ounces fresh black currants
3 tablespoons fresh mint, chopped
3/4 cup orange juice

1 Preheat the oven to 350°F. Coat a 9 x 5-inch loaf pan with cooking spray and set aside. Sift the flour and baking powder into a large bowl, then cut in the margarine with two knives or a pastry blender until the mixture resembles coarse meal. Stir in the sugar, and make a well in the center of the dry ingredients.

2 Place the black currants and mint in the well and pour in the orange juice. Gradually stir the dry ingredients into the liquid until just combined.

3 Spoon the batter into the prepared pan and smooth the top. Bake until loaf is firm to the touch and a toothpick inserted in the center comes out clean, about 1 hour. If the loaf looks as though it is browning too much after about 45 minutes, place a piece of foil loosely over the top.

4 Allow the tea bread to cool in the pan for 5 minutes, then turn it out onto a wire rack to cool completely. The tea bread is best left overnight before serving, and can be kept in an airtight container for up to 3 days.

(Some More Ideas) Make blueberry tea bread by substituting fresh blueberries for the black currants.

Cranberry pecan tea bread: Substitute roughly chopped fresh cranberries for the black currants. Instead of mint, add 1/2 teaspoon ground cinnamon, sifting it with the flour, and stir in 1/2 cup chopped pecans with the sugar.

Plus Points
• Black currants are an excellent source of vitamin C—ounce for ounce, they contain 4 times as much vitamin C as oranges. They also provide useful amounts of potassium, and are rich in a group of phytochemicals called flavonoids, which may help to protect against heart disease.
• The oils menthol, menthone, and menthyl acetate, responsible for the characteristic flavor of mint, are believed to have powerful antiseptic properties.

photo, page 235

Exchanges
carbohydrate 2

Each serving (one slice) provides calories 135, calories from fat 13, fat 1g, saturated fat 0g, cholesterol 0mg, sodium 383mg, carbohydrate 28g, fiber 2g, sugars 7g, protein 3g. Excellent source of phosphorus, vitamin C. Good source of calcium, thiamine.

light rye bread

Rye flour is lower in gluten than wheat, so it produces a dense, moist loaf. Caraway seeds are a traditional seasoning, complementing the nutty flavor of rye to make an excellent bread for sandwiches. Try slicing the bread and using it for turkey sandwiches, paired with a bowl of steaming vegetable soup. The bread is also delicious spread with low-fat soft cheeses.

Preparation time **20 minutes, plus about 1 hour rising**   Cooking time **40–45 minutes**   *Makes 1 small loaf (24 thin slices)*

3 1/2 cups rye flour
1 cup white bread flour
1 teaspoon salt
1 teaspoon sugar
1 package instant dry yeast
2 teaspoons caraway seeds
2 tablespoons olive oil
1 cup warm water

1 Sift the rye flour, white flour, salt, and sugar into a bowl, and stir in the yeast and caraway seeds. Stir the olive oil into the tepid water, then pour this over the flour mixture. Mix the ingredients together with a wooden spoon at first, then with your hand, to make a stiff, but sticky and slightly grainy dough.

2 Turn the dough out onto a floured work surface and knead until smooth, about 10 minutes. The dough should be very firm. Shape it into an oval loaf about 7 inches long, and place it on a baking sheet coated with cooking spray. Cover loosely with plastic wrap and allow to rise in a warm place until almost doubled in size, about 1 hour.

3 Toward the end of the rising time, preheat the oven to 400°F. Uncover the loaf and bake until it is lightly browned and sounds hollow when tapped on the bottom, 40 to 45 minutes.

4 Transfer to a wire rack and leave to cool. Once cool, place the loaf in a plastic freezer bag and leave overnight (this allows the crust to soften). After this, the loaf can be kept for up to 2 days.

(Some More Ideas) To make dark rye bread, stir 2 tablespoons molasses into the water with the olive oil.

Whole-wheat flour can be substituted for the white flour.

Cumin or fennel seeds also taste good in rye bread. Toast 1 tablespoon of the seeds in a small, heavy-based skillet over medium heat until fragrant, 40 to 45 minutes. Remove from the heat immediately and allow to cool. Add to the flour in place of the caraway seeds.

Mixed-seed rye bread: Replace the caraway seeds with a mixture of 2 tablespoons poppy seeds, 2 tablespoons toasted sunflower seeds, 1 tablespoon toasted fennel seeds, and 1 tablespoon sesame seeds.

Orange and caraway rye bread: Add the grated zest of 1 large orange and 2 tablespoons light brown sugar to the flour with the seeds, and substitute canola oil for the olive oil.

Plus Points
• Choosing a variety of breads made from different types of flour helps to increase your intake of complex carbohydrates. Using whole-wheat flour increases the fiber content of the bread and provides more vitamins and minerals than plain white bread.
• Store-bought sandwich bread contains a variety of preservatives to increase the shelf life of the product. Homemade bread does not last as long as store-bought bread, but it contains only natural ingredients.

photo, page 235

Exchanges
starch 1

Each serving (one slice) provides calories 85, calories from fat 14, fat 2g, saturated fat 0g, cholesterol 0mg, sodium 98mg, carbohydrate 16g, fiber 2g, sugars 0g, protein 2g.

233

sesame cheese twists

These crisp cheese sticks are delicious served fresh and still warm from the oven. Enriched with an egg and Parmesan cheese, they are made with a combination of whole-wheat and plain flour, so that they are substantial without being too heavy.

Preparation time **10–15 minutes**   Cooking time **15 minutes**   *Makes 36 sticks*

3/4 cup whole-wheat flour
3/4 cup white flour, plus extra for rolling
1/4 teaspoon salt
2 tablespoons reduced-fat margarine spread, chilled
3 tablespoons freshly grated Parmesan cheese
1 large egg
2 tablespoons fat-free milk
1 teaspoon paprika
1 tablespoon sesame seeds
Cooking spray

1 Preheat the oven to 350°F. Sift the flours and salt into a bowl. Rub in the margarine until the mixture resembles fine bread crumbs. Stir in the Parmesan cheese.

2 Whisk the egg and milk together. Reserve 1 teaspoon of this mixture, and stir the rest into the dry ingredients to form a firm dough. Knead on a lightly floured surface for a few seconds or until smooth.

3 Sprinkle the paprika over the floured surface, then roll the dough out on it to form a 9-inch square. Brush the dough with the reserved egg mixture and sprinkle with the sesame seeds. Cut the square of dough in half, then cut into 4 1/2-inch strips that are about 1/2-inch wide.

4 Coat a baking sheet with cooking spray and then line with baking parchment. Twist the sticks and place them on the baking sheet, lightly pressing the ends of the sticks down so that they do not untwist during baking.

5 Bake for 15 minutes or until lightly browned and crisp. Cool on the baking sheet for a few minutes, then serve warm, or transfer to a wire rack to cool completely. The sticks can be kept in an airtight container for up to 5 days.

(Some More Ideas) Use finely grated low-fat cheddar cheese instead of the Parmesan.

Plus Points
• Sesame seeds are a good source of calcium as well as providing iron and zinc.
• Whole-wheat flour has a lot to offer: dietary fiber, B vitamins, and vitamin E, together with iron, selenium, and magnesium. Stone-ground whole-wheat flour has slightly more B vitamins than factory-milled whole-wheat flour, because stone grinding keeps the grain cool. Milling with metal rollers creates heat, which spoils some of the nutrients.

Exchanges
starch 1/2 fat 1/2

Each serving (two sticks) provides calories 53, calories from fat 14, fat 2g, saturated fat 0g, cholesterol 13mg, sodium 53mg, carbohydrate 8g, fiber 1g, sugars 0g, protein 2g.

sesame cheese twists *p234*

black-currant tea bread *p232*

tuscan bean crostini *p236*

light rye bread *p233*

tuscan bean crostini

Here's a delicious snack to be enjoyed hot or cold—toasted slices of baguette topped with a creamy white bean puree flavored with garlic and thyme, and finished with colorful slices of tomato and fresh herbs.

Preparation time **about 10 minutes**   Cooking time **15 minutes**   *Makes 22 crostini*

Crostini

2 teaspoons olive oil

1 small onion, finely chopped

1 garlic clove, crushed

1 can (15 ounces) cannellini beans, drained and rinsed

2 tablespoons low-fat plain yogurt

1 tablespoon chopped fresh thyme

1 thin baguette

3 plum tomatoes, thinly sliced

Salt and pepper

Garnish

Sprigs of fresh herbs

1 Heat the oil in a small skillet, add the onion and garlic, and cook gently until softened, stirring occasionally, about 10 minutes.

2 Meanwhile, place the cannellini beans in a bowl and mash with a potato masher or fork. Remove the pan of onion and garlic from the heat and stir in the mashed beans, yogurt, and thyme. Season lightly with salt and pepper and mix well. Keep warm while preparing the toasts.

3 Preheat the broiler to high. Cut the crusty ends off the baguette and discard, then cut the loaf into 22 equal slices, 1/2 inch thick. Toast the bread slices on both sides under the broiler. (The toasts can be left to cool and then kept in an airtight container; when ready to serve, top with the bean mixture, cooled to room temperature, and garnish.)

4 Thickly spread some bean mixture over each slice of toast, top with a tomato slice, and garnish with fresh herb sprigs.

(Some More Ideas) Instead of cannellini beans, use other beans such as chickpeas (garbanzo beans).

Top the bean mixture with grilled zucchini slices, lightly cooked button mushrooms, or halved cherry tomatoes.

Herbs such as fresh basil, oregano, sage, or parsley can be used in place of the thyme.

Tuna crostini: Drain and flake 1 can (7 ounces) tuna in spring water. Mix with 1 tablespoon each light mayonnaise and plain low-fat yogurt, 2 tablespoons chopped fresh chives, and pepper to taste. Spread each slice of toast with 1 teaspoon tomato relish or chutney, top with the tuna mixture, and garnish with tiny watercress sprigs.

Plus Points

• Cannellini beans, popular in Italian cooking, belong to the same family as the haricot bean and have a similar floury texture when they are cooked. Though an excellent source of dietary fiber, beans can produce side effects such as bloating. Side effects can be minimized by ensuring that canned beans are thoroughly rinsed before use.

• Here low-fat plain yogurt is used to thin the bean spread. Traditionally, oil is used, making the spread higher in fat.

photo, page 235

Exchanges

starch 1/2   **Each serving (one toast) provides** calories 45, calories from fat 5, fat 1g, saturated fat 0g, cholesterol 0mg, sodium 66mg, carbohydrate 8g, fiber 1g, sugars 1g, protein 2g.

goat-cheese toasts

Indulge your guests with these tasty morsels, made by topping toasted slices of crusty baguette with slices of plum tomato and tangy goat cheese, sprinkled with pine nuts and fresh herbs. Low-fat goat cheese is used to reduce the fat content without sacrificing the delicate flavor and soft, spreadable texture.

Preparation time **15 minutes**   Cooking time **4–5 minutes**   *Makes 16 toasts*

1 baguette (10 ounces) cut into 1-inch slices

4 tablespoons pesto

2 tablespoons sun-dried tomato paste

4 plum tomatoes

5 ounces low-fat goat cheese

1 tablespoon olive oil

1/4 cup pine nuts

Few sprigs of fresh thyme or oregano, plus extra to garnish

1 Preheat the oven broiler. Place the baguette slices on a baking sheet and place in the oven. Lightly toast both sides of the bread.

2 Mix together the pesto and tomato paste and spread a little on top of each toast, covering the surface completely.

3 Slice the tomatoes lengthways, discarding a slim slice from the curved edges, to give 4 flat slices from each tomato. Lay a slice of tomato on top of each toast.

4 Place 1 small slice of cheese on each tomato slice, and drizzle with a little olive oil. Scatter with a few pine nuts and thyme or oregano leaves.

5 Place the toasts back under the broiler and broil until the cheese is beginning to melt and the pine nuts are golden, about 4 to 5 minutes. Serve the toasts hot, garnished with sprigs of thyme or oregano.

(Some More Ideas) Use a low-fat goat cheese flavored with garlic and herbs.

Serve the toasts on a bed of mixed soft salad leaves as an appetizer or light lunch.

Plus Points

• Pine nuts, used in Middle Eastern rice dishes and stuffings and an important ingredient in Italian pesto sauce, are rich in a variety of minerals, including magnesium, potassium, iron, zinc, and copper.

• Low-fat goat cheese is a tasty source of protein and calcium, as well as B vitamins (B1, B6, B12, and niacin) and phosphorus.

Exchanges

starch 1/2   fat 1

Each serving (one toast) provides calories 93, calories from fat 37, fat 4g, saturated fat 1g, cholesterol 7mg, sodium 208mg, carbohydrate 10g, fiber 1g, sugars 1g, protein 4g.

baked potato skins with smoked salmon and fresh dill

Potato skins that are served in restaurants are often deep-fried. Brushing the skins with a little olive oil and butter and then baking them reduces the fat content of this popular appetizer. Baking gives them just as good a flavor and a nice crisp texture. Here the potato skins are filled with a creamy mixture of smoked salmon, low-fat sour cream, and fresh dill.

Preparation time **30 minutes**   Cooking time **1–1 1/2 hours**   *Serves 8*

Potato Skins

8 small (5 ounce) baking potatoes

1 tablespoon olive oil, divided

1 tablespoon butter

4 ounces smoked salmon

1 tablespoon lemon juice

1/2 cup low-fat sour cream

1 tablespoon capers, drained and chopped

2 tablespoons chopped fresh dill

Salt and pepper

Garnish

Small sprigs of fresh dill

1 Preheat the oven to 400°F. Scrub the potatoes and dry them with a paper towel. Thread them onto metal skewers (this helps them to cook more quickly). Brush the skin of the potatoes with half the oil, then sprinkle with a little salt. Arrange on a baking tray and bake until tender, about 1 to 1 1/2 hours.

2 Remove the potatoes from the skewers and cut them in half lengthways. Scoop out the flesh, leaving a layer of potato next to the skin about 1/2 inch thick. (Save the flesh for another use.) Cut each piece in half lengthways again, and place flesh side up on a large, clean baking tray.

3 Melt the butter with the remaining oil and season lightly with salt and pepper. Lightly brush this mixture over the flesh side of the potato skins. Return to the oven and bake until golden and crisp, about 12 to 15 minutes.

4 Meanwhile, cut the smoked salmon into fine strips and sprinkle with the lemon juice. Mix together the sour cream, capers, and chopped dill in a bowl, and stir in the salmon.

5 Allow the potato skins to cool for 1 to 2 minutes, then top each with a little of the salmon and sour cream mixture. Garnish each with a small sprig of dill, and serve while the potato skins are still warm.

(Some More Ideas) *Chunky guacamole topping:* Peel and dice 2 ripe avocados, and mix with 3 tablespoons lime juice, 3 tablespoons low-fat yogurt, 4 finely chopped ripe tomatoes, 1 seeded, deveined, and finely chopped fresh red chile pepper (wear gloves when handling; they burn) or a dash of hot red pepper sauce, and salt and pepper to taste.

Instead of making potato skins, bake 12 small (4 ounce) potatoes until tender, about 50 minutes. Halve the potatoes and scoop out most of the flesh, then fill with the smoked salmon and yogurt topping.

Plus Points
• Salmon is an oily fish and a rich source of essential omega-3 fatty acids. Smoking the salmon doesn't destroy the beneficial oils.
• Capers, the pickled buds of a shrub mostly grown in southern Europe, are commonly used to add a salt-sour taste, and can reduce the need for added salt in a dish.

Exchanges

starch 1 1/2 fat 1

Each serving provides calories 167, calories from fat 46, fat 5g, saturated fat 2g, cholesterol 12mg, sodium 178mg, carbohydrate 26g, fiber 4g, sugars 2g, protein 6g. Good source of copper, iron, niacin, potassium, vitamin B6, vitamin C.

caramelized onion tartlets

The shells for these tartlets are made by pressing pieces of bread into muffin tins. The shells are brushed lightly with melted butter and baked until crisp. They are then filled with a mixture of onions and sun-dried tomatoes. Both the shells and the filling can be prepared ahead, then warmed and assembled for serving.

Preparation time **20 minutes**   Cooking time **35 minutes**   *Serves 12*

Cooking spray
1 tablespoon melted butter
12 thin slices white bread
2 teaspoons olive oil
2 large onions, thinly sliced
12 sun-dried tomatoes packed in oil, drained and roughly chopped
2 teaspoons finely chopped fresh thyme
1/2 cup toasted walnut pieces
Salt and pepper

1 Preheat the oven to 450°F. Lightly spray a 12-cup muffin tin with cooking spray. Using a 3-inch pastry cutter, cut a disc from each slice of bread. Flatten each bread disc with a rolling pin, then press into the muffin cups to line them evenly, curving the edge of the bread slightly to make large scallop shapes.

2 Brush the bread cases with the melted butter and bake until crisp and golden, about 8 to 10 minutes. Set aside in a warm place until ready to fill. (If made ahead, keep the bread cases in an airtight container.)

3 Heat the oil in a large, heavy skillet. Add the onions and stir well. Cover with the lid and cook over a low heat for 20 minutes or until the onions are very soft.

4 Remove the lid, turn up the heat, and cook rapidly, stirring, until the onions turn a dark golden brown. Remove from the heat and stir in the sun-dried tomatoes and thyme. Season lightly with salt and pepper. (If made ahead, cool the filling and keep in the fridge, then reheat just before filling the bread cases.)

5 Divide the onion filling among the bread cases, then sprinkle the chopped walnuts over the top. Serve hot.

(Some More Ideas) *Ratatouille tartlets*: Soften 1 finely chopped onion in 2 teaspoons olive oil, then stir in 2 chopped garlic cloves and 1 small red bell pepper, seeded and finely diced. Cook, stirring frequently, for 2 minutes. Add 1 small eggplant and 1 zucchini, both cut into small dice. Cook for 1 minute, then add 12 finely chopped sun-dried tomatoes and 1 teaspoon chopped fresh thyme. Stir, then cover tightly and cook gently until the vegetables are tender, about 15 to 20 minutes. Season lightly with salt and pepper, then divide among the warm bread shells. Sprinkle with 1/4 cup toasted pine nuts and serve.

Plus Points
• Eating walnuts in moderation but on a regular basis may help to reduce blood cholesterol levels and guard against heart disease and cancer. This is because of the antioxidant nutrients found in walnuts: selenium, zinc, copper, and vitamin E.
• Traditionally, the shells for mini tartlets are made from pie dough prepared with a high percentage of shortening or butter. In this recipe, the bread "shells" are brushed with just a small amount of butter and baked for much of the same result with a lot less fat.

photo, page 243

Exchanges
carbohydrate 1/2 fat 1

Each serving provides calories 83, calories from fat 48, fat 5g, saturated fat 1g, cholesterol 3mg, sodium 52mg, carbohydrate 8g, fiber 1g, sugars 3g, protein 2g.

tortilla chips with fresh mango and tomato salsa

Here is a fresh-tasting, colorful salsa that is rich in vitamins and valuable antioxidants.
It is a perfect dip for crunchy, homemade tortilla chips, quickly baked rather than deep-fried for a healthy,
low-fat result. Either corn tortillas or flour tortillas can be used to make the chips.

Preparation time **10 minutes**   Cooking time **15 minutes**   *Serves 12*

2 ripe mangoes
1 large ripe tomato
Grated zest and juice of 1 lime
1 medium-hot fresh green chile pepper, seeded and finely chopped
1 garlic clove, crushed
2 tablespoons chopped fresh cilantro
1 tablespoon snipped fresh chives
Salt and pepper
8 (10 inch) corn tortillas

1 Peel the mangoes and cut the flesh away from the pit. Chop the flesh into small pieces and place in a large bowl. Chop the tomato into small pieces and add to the mango.

2 Add the lime zest and juice, chile pepper, garlic, cilantro, and chives. Stir well, then season lightly with salt and pepper. Spoon into a serving bowl, cover, and refrigerate while preparing the tortilla chips.

3 Preheat the oven to 325°F. Cut each tortilla into 6 wedges using kitchen scissors. Spread out the wedges on a large baking sheet and bake until crisp and firm, about 15 minutes. Transfer to a wire rack and leave to cool.

4 To serve, place the bowl of salsa on one side of a large serving platter and scatter the tortilla chips next to it.

(**Some More Ideas**) *Fresh peach salsa*:
Use 4 ripe peaches instead of the mangoes.
There is no need to peel the peaches.
Just cut them in half, remove the pit, and chop them.

Nachos: Prepare the tortilla chips and allow to cool. Finely chop 3 scallions, 2 green bell peppers, and 1 medium-hot fresh green chile pepper, seeded, and place in a bowl. Sprinkle with 1/4 teaspoon cumin. Spread the tortilla chips out on a baking sheet lined with aluminum foil and sprinkle with the vegetables. Top with 1 1/2 cups reduced-fat shredded cheddar cheese. Bake in a preheated 375°F oven until the cheese has melted, about 10 to 15 minutes.

Plus Points
• Fresh mangoes contain the antioxidant vitamin C.
• Chile peppers are another source of vitamin C, containing more, ounce for ounce, than citrus fruit such as oranges and lemons.

Exchanges
starch 1 fruit 1/2

Each serving provides calories 109, calories from fat 9, fat 1g, saturated fat 0g, cholesterol 0mg, sodium 59mg, carbohydrate 24g, fiber 3g, sugars 7g, protein 2g. Excellent source of vitamin A, vitamin C. Good source of folate, phosphorus.

241

crab dip with crudités

This creamy dip is based on ingredients that can be kept in the pantry and rustled up quickly if guests drop by unexpectedly. It is served with celery and cucumber sticks as well as juicy pineapple wedges, all of which add important nutrients to this snack. Crisp breadsticks are another good dipper.

Preparation time **15–20 minutes**   *Serves 4*

Dip

1 can (7 ounces) white crabmeat, drained

2 tablespoons low-fat mayonnaise

2 tablespoons plain low-fat yogurt

1 teaspoon tomato puree

Grated zest of 1 lime

6 sun-dried tomatoes packed in oil, drained and finely chopped

1 small pickle, finely chopped (optional)

Few drops of hot red pepper sauce, or to taste

Crudités

2 celery stalks

1 medium cucumber

1 small pineapple

1 To make the dip, place the crabmeat, mayonnaise, yogurt, tomato puree, lime zest, sun-dried tomatoes, and pickle in a bowl and stir together thoroughly. Season with hot sauce to taste. Place the dip in a small serving bowl, cover, and refrigerate while preparing the crudités.

2 Cut the celery and cucumber into chunky sticks. Remove the crown of leaves from the pineapple (wash and keep the leaves for garnish, if desired). Cut the flesh into wedges, leaving the skin on, then cut away the core.

3 Arrange the celery, cucumber, and pineapple on a platter with the bowl of dip. Garnish with the pineapple leaves, if desired, and serve.

(Some More Ideas) Use the crab dip to fill the hollows in 2 halved and pitted avocados, piling up the dip over the surface. Scatter a little diced cucumber and red bell pepper over the top, and serve with salad leaves and bread as a light lunch.

For a fancier presentation, serve the crab dip on rounds of cucumber, cut about 1/2 inch thick. Garnish with thin strips of radish or little watercress leaves.

Plus Points

• Crab is a good source of phosphorus, a mineral needed for the development and maintenance of healthy bones. Phosphorus also plays an important role in releasing energy from food.

• Celery, first grown as a medicinal herb, only became a popular vegetable in the late 17th century. It provides potassium, and green celery stalks and leaves contain the antioxidant beta-carotene.

Exchanges

fruit 1 vegetable 1 meat (very lean) 1

Each serving provides calories 131, calories from fat 20, fat 2g, saturated fat 0g, cholesterol 30mg, sodium 228mg, carbohydrate 21g, fiber 3g, sugars 17g, protein 9g. Excellent source of vitamin C. Good source of folate, magnesium, phosphorus, potassium, thiamine, vitamin B6.

caramelized onion tartlets *p240*

crab dip with crudités *p242*

greek meatballs with lemon dip *p245*

pissaladière *p244*

gingered crab phyllo dumplings

These Asian-style, triangular dumplings of crisp, light phyllo pastry envelop a ginger-flavored filling of crab, water chestnuts, and corn. They look and taste wonderful, and are surprisingly simple to make. Prepare them ahead for a party, then bake just before serving with a sweet chili dipping sauce.

Preparation time **45–50 minutes**　　Cooking time **12–13 minutes**　　*Makes 18 dumplings*

Dumplings

1 can (7 ounces) white crabmeat

1 can (4 ounces) water chestnuts, drained and coarsely chopped

1 1/2 cups frozen corn, thawed

4 scallions, chopped

1 tablespoon finely chopped fresh ginger

1 fresh red chile pepper, seeded, deveined, and finely chopped

2 tablespoons Chinese cooking wine or dry sherry

2 tablespoons canola oil

1 tablespoon toasted sesame oil

6 sheets phyllo pastry (20 x 12 inches)

1 tablespoon sesame seeds

Salt and pepper

Garnish

Thai sweet chili dipping sauce

Scallions

1 Preheat the oven to 400°F. Combine the crabmeat, water chestnuts, corn, scallions, ginger, red chile pepper (wear gloves; they burn), and wine in a bowl, and season lightly with salt and pepper. Mix the canola and sesame oils in a cup.

2 Roll up the 6 sheets of phyllo pastry loosely, rolling from a short side. Using a sharp knife, cut the roll across evenly into 3 pieces. Cover 2 of these shorter rolls with plastic wrap to prevent them from drying out. Unravel the third roll, remove one of the strips, and set the rest aside, covered.

3 Lay the strip of phyllo flat on the work surface, with a short end nearest to you, and brush with a little of the oil mixture. Place a heaping teaspoon of the crab mixture near the bottom, toward the right-hand corner of the short end, and fold the pastry diagonally over it. Continue folding diagonally, over and over, until you reach the end of the strip, making a neat triangular parcel. Place on a baking sheet, seam side down.

4 Repeat with remaining strips of phyllo, uncovering them only when needed, until all of the crab mixture is used. (The dumplings can be prepared in advance; cover the baking sheets with plastic wrap

and keep in the refrigerator. The baking time may need to be increased to 15 minutes if the dumplings are very cold.)

5 Lightly brush the tops of the dumplings with any remaining oil mixture and sprinkle with the sesame seeds. Bake until crisp and golden, about 12 to 13 minutes.

6 Transfer the dumplings to a wire rack and cool slightly. Meanwhile, shred the tops of the scallions for garnishing, to form "brushes." Serve the dumplings warm, on a tray garnished with the scallion brushes and a little dish of Thai sweet chili dipping sauce to accompany.

(Some More Ideas) *Shrimp phyllo dumplings*: Use 6 ounces chopped, cooked, peeled shrimp in place of the crabmeat.

Mini spring rolls with a vegetable filling: Mix together 1 cup bean sprouts, 1 grated carrot, 1 can sliced bamboo shoots, drained and chopped, 4 chopped scallions, and 1/2 cup chopped mushrooms. Heat 2 teaspoons canola oil in a large pan, add 1 tablespoon finely chopped fresh ginger, and 2 crushed garlic cloves, and stir-fry for 30 seconds. Add the vegetable mixture and stir-fry for 1 minute.

Exchanges

starch 1/2 fat 1/2

Each serving (one dumpling) provides calories 63, calories from fat 16, fat 2g, saturated fat 0g, cholesterol 7mg, sodium 67mg, carbohydrate 9g, fiber 1g, sugars 1g, protein 3g. Good source of vitamin C.

Sprinkle over 1 tablespoon light soy sauce and 1 tablespoon Chinese cooking wine or dry sherry, and stir-fry for 1 minute, then cool. Cut the phyllo pastry into strips as in the main recipe. Mix together 2 tablespoons canola oil and 1 tablespoon toasted sesame oil. Lightly brush a strip of phyllo with a little of the oil mixture, then place a heaped teaspoon of filling on the center base. Fold in the sides and roll up to make a little cigar shape. Repeat with the remaining phyllo and filling. Finish and bake as in the main recipe.

Plus Points

• Using phyllo for these parcels keeps the fat content low. This is because only a light brushing of oil is needed to stick the pastry edges together and to give a golden-brown sheen and crisp texture.

smoked turkey and apricot bites

Dried apricots soaked in orange juice, then wrapped in lean turkey bacon, make a tasty snack to pass around at a party. Take care when grilling the turkey bacon because it will dry out if overcooked. A tangy mustard mixture helps to add moisture during cooking.

Preparation time **10-15 minutes**   Cooking time **2 minutes**   *Makes 24 bites*

Bites

24 dried apricots

Juice of 1 orange

2 teaspoons no-sugar-added orange marmalade

2 teaspoons Dijon mustard

6 slices lean turkey bacon

1 teaspoon olive oil

Garnish

Chopped fresh parsley

1 Place the apricots in a small bowl, pour over the orange juice, and toss so that the apricots are moistened all over (this will prevent them from burning under the grill).

2 Mix the marmalade with the mustard. Spread each slice of turkey bacon with a little of the mustard mixture; then, using scissors, cut it in half lengthways. Cut each piece in half again, this time across the middle, to make a total of 24 strips of turkey bacon.

3 Preheat a ridged grill pan or oven broiler to medium. Drain the apricots. Wrap a strip of turkey bacon around each apricot and secure it with a toothpick.

4 Arrange the turkey bites on the grill pan, then brush each with a little oil. Grill on each side until the turkey is just cooked, about 1 minute.

5 Pile the bites in a small, shallow bowl and sprinkle with chopped parsley, if using. Serve hot.

(Some More Ideas) Instead of the mustard and marmalade mixture, spread the turkey bacon with a little commercially prepared pesto sauce.

Cherry tomatoes can be used instead of dried apricots. They do not need to be moistened with orange juice.

Turkey and banana chutney bites: Cut 3 medium bananas into chunky pieces (8 pieces each) and toss in a little lemon or lime juice to prevent them from discoloring. Wrap each piece in a strip of turkey bacon that has been spread with a little mango chutney, then grill for 1 minute on each side. Serve hot.

Plus Points
• Because the apricot bites are made with turkey bacon and grilled, they make a fairly healthy snack that seems succulent and indulgent. The combination of the sweet dried apricots and salty turkey bacon will impress any crowd.

photo, page 251

Exchanges

fruit 1/2

Each serving (one turkey bite) provides calories 29, calories from fat 8, fat 1g, saturated fat 0g, cholesterol 3mg, sodium 54mg, carbohydrate 5g, fiber 1g, sugars 3g, protein 1g.

smoked turkey and apricot bites *p248*

chewy date and walnut bars *p250*

stuffed mushrooms *p253*

spicy date, apple,
and cheese dip *p249*

rosemary marinated olives

The flavor of olives is greatly enhanced by marinating them in fruity olive oil with fresh herbs and citrus juices. When served with colorful chunks of red and yellow bell peppers and little cherry tomatoes, they look and taste fabulous. For the best flavor, allow about 2 days of marinating.

Preparation time **10 minutes**   Marinating time **2 days**   *Serves 8*

1 Place the olives in a large bowl and add the olive oil, lemon juice, chunks of orange, rosemary sprigs, and chile pepper. Stir together, then cover. Place in the refrigerator.

2 For the next 2 days, every 12 hours or so, take the olive mixture from the fridge, uncover, and stir. Cover again and return to the fridge to continue marinating.

3 When ready to eat, combine the marinated olives with the red and yellow bell peppers and tomatoes, and stir well.

7 ounces olives, preferably a mixture of black and green

2 tablespoons olive oil (preferably extra virgin)

1 tablespoon lemon juice

1 thin-skinned orange, scrubbed but not peeled, cut into small chunks

2 sprigs of fresh rosemary

1 fresh green chile pepper, seeded and thinly sliced

1 red bell pepper, seeded and cut into small chunks

1 yellow bell pepper, seeded and cut into small chunks

1/2 cup halved cherry tomatoes

(Some More Ideas) Add the marinated olives to salads, such as spinach leaves with chickpeas, or tuna and cucumber.

Garlicky marinated olives with feta: Instead of orange, rosemary, and the chile pepper, add 2 roughly chopped garlic cloves, 4 or 5 chopped sun-dried tomatoes, and a small handful of roughly torn fresh basil leaves to the olive oil and lemon juice. Before serving the olives, toss them with 1 ounce cubed feta cheese, the red and yellow bell peppers, 4 halved baby plum tomatoes, and some fresh basil leaves.

Plus Points

• Olives are highly valued for their oil content, which is mostly the healthier monounsaturated type. Green olives provide more vitamin A than black olives.

• Extra-virgin olive oil is the premium of all the olive oils. It has a low level of acidity and a wonderful aroma and flavor. As it is produced with minimal heat and refining processes, it retains more of its essential fatty acids and phytochemicals.

• The name rosemary comes from the Latin and means "sea dew." This strong, pungent herb was often found growing on the coast. In Roman times it was used mainly as a medicinal herb, to soothe the digestive system.

Exchanges

vegetable 1 fat 1

Each serving provides calories 81, calories from fat 53, fat 6g, saturated fat 1g, cholesterol 0mg, sodium 299mg, carbohydrate 7g, fiber 2g, sugars 3g, protein 1g. Excellent source of vitamin C. Good source of vitamin A.

stuffed mushrooms

Filled with a delicious mixture of finely chopped zucchini, spinach, and hazelnuts, then topped with grated Parmesan cheese and baked, these mushrooms make delicious, hard-to-resist party bites. They look their best if the mushrooms are all about the same size.

Preparation time **25–30 minutes**   Cooking time **15 minutes**   *Makes 16 mushrooms*

Mushrooms

16 large mushrooms

1 tablespoon butter

2 shallots, finely chopped

1 garlic clove, crushed

1 small zucchini, finely chopped

1 cup finely chopped baby spinach leaves, plus a few leaves to serve

Garnish

1/2 cup fresh whole-wheat bread crumbs

1/2 cup finely chopped hazelnuts

2 tablespoons finely chopped parsley

1/3 cup grated Parmesan cheese

Salt and pepper

1 Preheat the oven to 350°F. Remove the stems from the mushrooms and chop them finely. Melt the butter in a large skillet over medium heat. Add the chopped mushroom stems, shallots, garlic, and zucchini, and cook for 5 minutes, stirring occasionally.

2 Remove the pan from the heat and stir in the chopped spinach, bread crumbs, hazelnuts, parsley, and salt and pepper to taste.

3 Place the mushroom caps, hollow side up, in a single layer in a lightly sprayed shallow ovenproof dish or on a lightly sprayed baking tray. Heap some of the shallot and zucchini mixture into each mushroom cap and sprinkle the Parmesan cheese over the top. (The mushrooms can be prepared 2 to 3 hours ahead and kept, covered with plastic wrap, in the refrigerator.)

4 Bake until the mushrooms are tender and the cheese has melted, about 15 minutes. Serve warm, on a bed of spinach leaves, if desired.

(Some More Ideas) *Mushrooms with red bell pepper and pine nut filling*: Sauté the mushroom stems in 2 teaspoons olive oil with 4 finely chopped scallions, 1 small seeded and finely chopped red bell pepper, and 1 crushed garlic clove for 5 minutes. Stir in 1/2 cup chopped pine nuts, 1 cup chopped watercress, 1/2 cup fresh bread crumbs, 2 tablespoons finely chopped parsley, and salt and pepper to taste. Fill the mushroom caps with this mixture and sprinkle with 1/3 cup finely grated mozzarella cheese. Bake as in the main recipe.

Plus Points

• Mushrooms provide useful amounts of some of the B vitamins and are a good source of the trace mineral copper. This mineral has several functions—it is found in many enzymes, and is needed for bone growth as well as for the formation of connective tissue.

• Stuffed mushrooms are a classic party appetizer. Traditionally the mushrooms are made with plenty of melted butter to hold the filling together. In this recipe, only 1 tablespoon of butter is used and the zucchini provides extra needed moisture and serves as a binder.

• Hazelnuts were known in China 5,000 years ago and were also eaten by the Romans. They are a particularly good source of vitamin E and most of the B vitamins (with the exception of vitamin B12).

photo, page 251

Exchanges

vegetable 1 fat 1/2

Each serving (one mushroom) provides calories 53, calories from fat 34, fat 4g, saturated fat 1g, cholesterol 4mg, sodium 34mg, carbohydrate 4g, fiber 1g, sugars 1g, protein 2g. Good source of vitamin A.

desserts and drinks

mango smoothie

Smoothies are speedy and satisfying fruit drinks, loaded with vitamins and antioxidants, that can be made with milk and yogurt or with pure fruit juices and pieces of fruit. Almost any fresh fruit can be used, on its own or in combination. To serve more than 2, simply make a second batch of smoothies.

Preparation time **5 minutes**   *Serves 2*

1 ripe mango
1/2 cup plain low-fat yogurt, chilled
1 cup fat-free milk, chilled
1 teaspoon honey, or to taste
Seeds from 6 cardamom pods (optional)

1 Peel the skin off the mango and cut the flesh away from the pit. Chop the flesh roughly and place it in a blender or food processor. Process until smooth.

2 Pour in the yogurt and milk, and continue to process until well mixed and frothy. Sweeten with honey to taste.

3 Pour into 2 tall glasses and sprinkle the cardamom seeds over the top. Serve immediately.

(**Some More Ideas**) *Tropical banana smoothie*: Replace the mango with 1 large sliced banana.

Kiwi and raspberry smoothie: Use 1 peeled and chopped kiwifruit and 1/2 cup raspberries in place of the mango.

Plus Points

• Smoothies are made very quickly, using raw fruit, so they retain the maximum nutritional value of their ingredients. They are a great refresher in the morning or after a workout.
• When made with low-fat milk and yogurt, a smoothie will also contain protein, calcium, and many B vitamins.

Exchanges
fruit 1 1/2 milk (fat-free) 1

Each serving provides calories 168, calories from fat 14, fat 2g, saturated fat 1g, cholesterol 7mg, sodium 109mg, carbohydrate 33g, fiber 2g, sugars 30g, protein 8g. Excellent source of calcium, phosphorus, riboflavin, vitamin A, vitamin C. Good source of potassium, thiamine, vitamin B6, vitamin B12.

citrus wake-up

Instead of plain orange juice in the morning, whisk up this frosty blend of citrus fruits. Begin with sweet, juicy oranges; be sure to pick ones that feel heavy for their size, as this usually means they are filled with juice. Add a pink grapefruit, lime, and lemon, plus some shredded fresh mint. It's a great way to start the day!

Preparation time **15 minutes**   *Serves 6*

Juice

1 large lime

4 large oranges

1 medium pink grapefruit (about 12 ounces)

1 large lemon

1/2 cup cold water

2 tablespoons sugar

2 tablespoons finely shredded fresh mint leaves

Garnish

4 thin round slices unpeeled lemon

4 thin round slices unpeeled lime

1 Using a citrus zester or peeler, remove the zest from the lime; set aside 1/2 teaspoon.

2 Cut the lime, oranges, grapefruit, and lemon in half crosswise. Juice the fruits by using either an electric juicer or a citrus squeezer, preferably one that strains out seeds while allowing a generous quantity of pulp. If you don't have a juicer, poke a fork into the flesh several times, then squeeze the juice from the fruit by hand.

3 In a large pitcher, stir the citrus juices with the reserved lime zest, the water, sugar, and shreds of mint. Pour the drink over ice into 6 glasses. Garnish the drinks with slices of lemon and lime.

(Some More Ideas) *Mexican fruit gazpacho*: Omit the lime and grapefruit; increase the lemons to 2. Juice only 2 of the oranges; peel and section the remaining 2. Cut up 1 small pineapple (3 cups fruit); peel and thinly slice 1 kiwifruit (1/2 cup). Mix and serve as a chunky fruit gazpacho or whirl it all up in a blender or food processor until it is frothy. Decorate with fresh mint leaves, if you wish.

Summery sparkler: For a nonalcoholic summery drink, add 3/4 cup chilled lime- or lemon-flavored seltzer to the juicy mixture in the pitcher, just before pouring into the glasses (Step 3).

Plus Points

• Naturally, citrus fruits are one of the best sources of vitamin C. Being an antioxidant, vitamin C protects against cell damage by free radicals, which are produced in the body when oxygen is burned.

• Oranges and their juice contain a B vitamin called folate that is important for women of child-bearing age because it helps prevent birth defects.

• Fruit juices can be combined with seltzer water to make a bubbly nonalcoholic cocktail that contains half the amount of calories of a full glass of juice.

photo, page 259

Exchanges	
fruit 1 1/2	

Each serving provides calories 99, calories from fat 3, fat 0g, saturated fat 0g, cholesterol 0mg, sodium 3mg, carbohydrate 26g, fiber 4g, sugars 18g, protein 2g. Excellent source of vitamin C. Good source of folate.

frozen pineapple and berry slush

It looks like a frozen drink, it eats like a sorbet, and it tastes like a fresh-fruit treat. This frozen fruit slush is quick to whip up in the morning. Try it as an afternoon snack or spoon it into sherbet glasses and serve as dessert. Keep a selection of chopped fresh fruit in your freezer so you can make slushes anytime.

Preparation time **20 minutes**   Freezing time **at least 1 1/2 hours for freezing fruit**   *Serves 6*

Slush

1 pint (2 cups) ripe
strawberries, hulled
2 cups fresh pineapple chunks
1 cup ice cubes (about 8 large)
1/2 cup pineapple juice
2 tablespoons sugar,
or to taste

Garnish

Sprigs of fresh mint

1 Freeze the fresh fruit ahead of time so the slush is extra thick. To prepare the fruit for freezing: Peel, core, and cut the pineapple into chunks and place in a plastic freezer bag or covered container. Slice the strawberries and place them in a separate plastic bag or container. Place the fruit in the freezer or until very firm, at least 1 1/2 hours.

2 Place the ice cubes in a food processor or heavy-duty blender and pulse until they are finely crushed. Or, drop the ice cubes into a plastic bag and close; crush them with a rolling pin, then finish crushing them in a food processor or blender.

3 Add the frozen strawberries and pineapple chunks, the pineapple juice, and sugar. Pulse on high just until blended, but not liquefied. Small pieces of fruit and ice should still remain.

4 Taste and add a little more sugar if you wish. Process a few more seconds just until blended.

5 Spoon the slush into 4 tall glasses and garnish each with a sprig of mint, if desired. Serve with long spoons.

(Some More Ideas) *Three-berry slush*: Substitute 1/2 pint (1 cup) fresh blueberries and 1/2 pint (1 cup) fresh raspberries for the pineapple. Use 1/2 cup cranberry juice instead of the pineapple juice.

Rosy peach slush: Instead of the fresh fruits, use 3 cups frozen peach slices and 1 cup frozen raspberries (both are available in your supermarket's frozen-food section). Omit the pineapple juice and use only 1/2 cup cranberry juice instead.

Tropical slush: Substitute 2 cups frozen chopped, peeled mangoes and 2 cups frozen cantaloupe chunks for the strawberries and pineapple. Instead of pineapple juice, use orange juice.

Slush-in-an-instant: When you have slush left over, freeze it in ice-cube trays. Later, to quickly make a slush, just crush the cubes in a food processor or blender. If the mixture is too thick, add a little extra fruit juice.

Plus Points

• A wide variety of fruit is now available packaged and frozen. This is convenient to have on hand and may be a better source of vitamins than some "fresh" fruit that may have been poorly stored, badly handled, or kept too long on the shelf. It is particularly useful for slushes and smoothies, where the texture of the fruit is not important. Slushes are a great, refreshing drink on a hot summer day. They are also an easy way to incorporate several servings of fresh fruit into your diet.

Exchanges

fruit 1

Each serving provides calories 68, calories from fat 4, fat 0g, saturated fat 0g, cholesterol 0mg, sodium 1mg, carbohydrate 17g, fiber 2g, sugars 15g, protein 1g. Excellent source of vitamin C.

iced melon and berry soup *p260*

frozen pineapple and berry slush *p258*

citrus wake-up *p257*

flambéed asian pears with oranges *p261*

iced melon and berry soup

Honeydew melon is perfect for this dazzling display, but it is essential that the melon be very ripe and sweet. Serve the soup as a refreshing first course when the weather is hot, dressing up each bowlful with a swirl of berry puree and some whole berries as a garnish.

Preparation time **20 minutes**   Chilling time **30 minutes**   *Serves 4*

1 ripe honeydew melon (about 2 pounds)

1 tablespoon fresh lime juice

1-inch piece fresh ginger, peeled and grated

3/4 cup blueberries

1/2 cup orange juice

2 tablespoons low-fat plain yogurt

3/4 cup raspberries or strawberries

1 Halve the melon, discard the seeds, and use a spoon to scoop the flesh out of the peel into a blender or food processor. Add the lime juice and ginger. Puree until smooth, pausing occasionally to push the pieces of melon to the bottom of the goblet or bowl. Pour the puree into a bowl, cover, and refrigerate until completely cool, about 30 minutes.

2 Put the blueberries into the blender or food processor. Add the orange juice and yogurt and puree until smooth. Transfer to a second bowl, cover, and refrigerate until completely cool, about 30 minutes.

3 Divide the melon soup among 4 chilled glass bowls. Swirl a quarter of the blueberry puree in the center of each bowl. Scatter the raspberries or strawberries on top. Serve immediately.

(**Some More Ideas**) Try making the soup with cantaloupe instead of honeydew, and top the soup with sliced kiwifruit instead of the red berries.

Watermelon can also be used instead of the honeydew. Chop about 3 pounds of the flesh, discarding the seeds, then puree with the lime juice and 1 seeded and chopped fresh green chile pepper instead of the ginger. Coarsely crush the blueberries with the raspberries and/or strawberries, adding 1 to 2 tablespoons orange juice for the berry puree. Omit the yogurt.

Plus Points
• All melons provide vitamins B and C and are very low in calories. Their high water content makes them a delicious and refreshing thirst quencher.
• Ginger is thought to be an anti-inflammatory agent that can help ease some of the symptoms of arthritis.

photo, page 259

Exchanges

fruit **1 1/2**

Each serving provides calories 84, calories from fat 5, fat 1g, saturated fat 0g, cholesterol 1mg, sodium 19mg, carbohydrate 20g, fiber 3g, sugars 16g, protein 2g. Excellent source of vitamin C. Good source of potassium.

flambéed asian pears with oranges

An impressive dessert! Asian pears are large, round, and yellowish-green. Look for these crunchy, juicy fruits from late summer through early fall. Simmer them up with oranges and a touch of brown sugar, then flambé them elegantly with brandy.

Preparation time **20 minutes**   Cooking time **10 minutes**   *Serves 6 (recipe can be doubled)*

Pears

2 large Asian pears

2 to 3 tablespoons fresh lemon juice

3 large navel oranges

2 tablespoons unsalted butter

3 tablespoons light brown sugar

3 tablespoons brandy

Garnish

3 tablespoons coarsely chopped pistachios

Sprigs of fresh lemon balm

1 Peel, quarter, and core the Asian pears. Cut them lengthwise into slices. To prevent the pears from turning brown, immediately sprinkle them with the lemon juice and toss until coated.

2 Peel the oranges, removing the white pith. Cut the oranges crosswise into slices, 1/2 inch thick.

3 In a large skillet, melt the butter over medium heat. Add the sugar, stirring constantly, so it doesn't burn. Quickly add the pear slices and cook gently on each side or just until tender yet firm to the touch, about 3 minutes. Add the orange slices and cook just until warmed and well coated with the juices in the skillet, about 1 minute more.

4 Using a slotted spoon, transfer the pears and oranges to a shallow serving dish and keep warm. Increase the heat to high and boil the juices in the uncovered skillet until reduced to about half, then pour over the fruit. Pour the brandy into the skillet, heat it, stand back, and ignite. Pour over the fruit.

5 Serve the flambéed fruits on 6 warmed plates. Sprinkle with the pistachios and decorate with the sprigs of lemon balm.

(Some More Ideas) *Flambéed pineapple with orange*: Substitute 3 cups fresh pineapple spears for the Asian pears. Flambé with 3 tablespoons dark rum in place of the brandy and sprinkle with 3 tablespoons chopped toasted pecans instead of the pistachios.

Flambéed apples with Calvados: Substitute 2 large, peeled, cored, and sliced Granny Smith apples for the pears. Flambé with the brandy and sprinkle with chopped toasted hazelnuts.

Plus Points

• Oranges are famous for their vitamin C, a water-soluble vitamin that the body doesn't store. Consequently, it is essential that we eat fruits and vegetables containing vitamin C every day.

• Sautéed fruit makes an elegant low-fat dessert. The fruit can be served alone, topped with a dollop of low-fat vanilla yogurt, or served as a topping for low-fat vanilla frozen yogurt.

photo, page 259

Exchanges

fruit 2 fat 1

Each serving provides calories 175, calories from fat 57, fat 6g, saturated fat 3g, cholesterol 10mg, sodium 5mg, carbohydrate 28g, fiber 6g, sugars 21g, protein 2g. Excellent source of vitamin C.

saffron and vanilla grilled fruit

Pick a collection of luscious fruits, spice them elegantly with saffron and vanilla, then grill them until they release some of their juices and are warm and fragrant. Top with frozen yogurt.

Preparation time **15 minutes**   Marinating time (optional) **1 hour**   Grilling time **5 minutes**   *Serves 6*

Marinade

1 small pinch saffron threads or 1/2 teaspoon ground saffron
1/4 cup hot water
1/4 cup fresh orange juice
1 tablespoon Marsala wine or sweet sherry
1 teaspoon vanilla extract
1 teaspoon honey

Salad

1/2 large papaya
1 large navel orange
1 large kiwifruit
1 large banana
1/2 cup seedless black or purple grapes

To serve (optional)

6 (1/2 cup) scoops fat-free, sugar-free frozen vanilla yogurt

1 First, make the marinade. Heat a small, dry saucepan over high heat until hot, about 1 minute. Add the saffron and toast, stirring, until fragrant, about 30 seconds. Chop the saffron finely or place in a mortar and crush it with a pestle. Place the saffron in a medium bowl and add the hot water. Stir in the orange juice, Marsala wine, vanilla, and honey.

2 Prepare the fruits, adding them to the marinade as you go. Peel the papaya, remove the seeds, and cut into bite-size chunks. Using a serrated knife, peel the orange, removing all the white pith; cut between the membranes and lift out the sections.

3 Peel the kiwi, then cut it lengthwise into 6 wedges. Peel the banana, halve it lengthwise, then cut into bite-size chunks. Add the grapes. You will have about 4 cups of fruit. Stir gently to coat the fruit with the marinade. If time permits, let the fruit marinate for 1 hour before cooking.

4 Preheat the broiler or heat a grill pan on the stovetop. Pour the fruit and marinade into a shallow ovenproof dish if using the broiler. Spread out the fruit in an even layer. Broil until all the fruit is heated through, about 5 minutes. If using the grill pan, place the fruit in an even layer in the pan and cook until heated through, 5 minutes (or sauté fruit in a large skillet over medium-high heat for 5 minutes). Ladle the fruit into 6 dessert dishes. Serve warm with a scoop of frozen yogurt.

(Some More Ideas) *Tropical marinade*: Use 3/4 cup fresh lime juice, 2 tablespoons white rum, 1 tablespoon golden honey, 2 teaspoons vanilla extract, and 1 teaspoon ground cinnamon. Sprinkle with seeds from 1 large pomegranate.

Tropical grilled fruit: Omit the papaya and grapes. Substitute 2 cups fresh pineapple chunks and 2 cups unpeeled plum slices.

Summer grilled fruit: Substitute 2 cups peeled fresh peach or nectarine slices for the kiwi and 1 cup pitted Bing cherries, cut in half, for the grapes.

Plus Points

• Kiwifruits are cultivated in California and New Zealand. Because these two places have opposite seasons, kiwifruits are available year-round. They can be kept in the refrigerator for up to 3 weeks and serve as a healthy snack. Try simply cutting the fruit in half and scooping the flesh out with a spoon.
• The banana, kiwi, and citrus fruit provide potassium, which keeps body fluids and blood pressure in balance.

Exchanges

fruit 1

Each serving (without frozen yogurt) provides calories 78, calories from fat 3, fat 0g, saturated fat 0g, cholesterol 0mg, sodium 3mg, carbohydrate 19g, fiber 2g, sugars 14g, protein 1g. Excellent source of vitamin C.

saffron and vanilla grilled fruit *p262*

citrus soufflés *p264*

grilled fruit en brochette *p266*

plums en papillote with honey *p265*

citrus soufflés

These deliciously light, individual citrus soufflés will be a tempting and refreshing end to any meal. Here low-fat sour cream provides valuable nutrients such as calcium without adding too many calories. The accompanying strawberry coulis looks pretty and complements the soufflés perfectly, as well as contributing vitamin C.

Preparation time **30 minutes**   Cooking time **15–20 minutes**   *Serves 6*

Soufflés

Cooking spray

6 tablespoons sugar, divided

5 egg whites

2 egg yolks

2 tablespoons flour

1 (8 ounce) container low-fat sour cream

Zest of 1 lime

Zest of 1 small orange

Strawberry Coulis

1/2 pound ripe strawberries, halved

2 teaspoons sugar

2 teaspoons liqueur such as kirsch (optional)

Confectioners' sugar for dusting

1 Preheat the oven to 375°F. Coat 6 individual 7-ounce soufflé dishes with cooking spray, then coat lightly with sugar, shaking off the excess. Set the dishes aside.

2 Place the egg yolks, 2 tablespoons sugar, and the flour in a bowl and whisk together until light and creamy. Add the sour cream and the lime and orange zests, and whisk until thoroughly combined.

3 In a clean mixing bowl, whisk the egg whites until stiff peaks form. Add the remaining 4 tablespoons of sugar to the egg whites in a slow, steady stream while whisking. Carefully fold the whisked egg whites into the sour cream mixture.

4 Spoon the mixture into the prepared soufflé dishes and set them on a baking sheet. Bake until the soufflés have risen and are golden brown, about 15 to 20 minutes.

5 Meanwhile, make the Strawberry Coulis: Puree the strawberries in a blender or food processor until smooth. Sweeten the sauce with 2 teaspoons sugar, then stir in the liqueur (if using).

6 Serve the hot soufflés straight from the oven, dusted lightly with confectioners' sugar. Serve the coulis on the side.

(**Some More Ideas**) Instead of flavoring the soufflés with lime and orange zests, try lemon and orange, or pink grapefruit and orange.

After spraying the dishes with cooking spray, coat them lightly with finely crushed macaroons or ground hazelnuts instead of sugar.

Mixed berry soufflé: Coat a 1 1/2-quart soufflé dish with cooking spray and dust with sugar. Make the soufflé mixture as in the main recipe, flavoring with the finely grated zest of 1 lemon and 1 lime. Place 1 1/2 pints mixed berries, such as raspberries, strawberries, and blackberries, into the prepared soufflé dish. Spoon the soufflé mixture over the fruit, covering it completely, and bake until well risen and golden brown, about 30 minutes. Dust with sifted confectioners' sugar and serve immediately.

Plus Points

• When recipes call for heavy cream, use low-fat sour cream, fat-free half-and-half, or evaporated milk instead, to decrease the fat content.

• Eggs are a good source of zinc, a mineral that is vital for growth, reproduction, and efficient working of the immune system.

photo, page 263

Exchanges

carbohydrate 1 1/2 fat 1

Each serving (one soufflé) provides calories 150, calories from fat 45, fat 5g, saturated fat 3g, cholesterol 84mg, sodium 74mg, carbohydrate 21g, fiber 1g, sugars 17g, protein 7g. Excellent source of vitamin C. Good source of riboflavin, vitamin A.

plums en papillote with honey

The French term *en papillote* refers to baking foods in packets of parchment. Look for parchment paper at a gourmet or specialty cookware store. The packets puff in the oven, and when opened, release a wonderful spicy aroma is released. The fruit is served in the packet and crowned with a scoop of frozen yogurt for a crowd-pleasing presentation.

Preparation time **20 minutes**   Cooking time **20 minutes**   *Makes 8 individual papillotes*

Papillotes

1 large juice orange,
such as Valencia

8 squares parchment paper
(14 x 14 inches)

8 large ripe plums,
pitted and sliced 1 inch thick

2 tablespoons unsalted butter,
cut into bits

4 cinnamon sticks, halved

16 whole cloves

1/4 cup honey

Garnish

8 (1/2 cup) scoops frozen
fat-free, sugar-free frozen
vanilla yogurt

4 tablespoons coarsely
chopped toasted pecans

1 Preheat the oven to 400°F and set out a large, shallow pan with sides. Using a citrus zester or vegetable peeler, remove the zest from the orange; cut into thin shreds. Juice the orange (you need 1/2 cup juice). Set aside.

2 For each of the 8 papillote packets, lay out a square of parchment. Spoon 1/8 of the plum slices in the center of each parchment. Add a bit of butter, a piece of cinnamon stick, and 2 whole cloves. Drizzle with 1 1/2 teaspoons honey. Top the plums with 3 or 4 strips of orange zest and drizzle with some of the orange juice.

3 For each papillote, bring two opposite sides of the parchment paper together over the fruit filling and fold two or three times. Fold over the other opposite ends twice, tucking them under, to make a neatly sealed packet.

4 Place the packets in the baking pan, folded ends up. Bake until the packets are puffed up and light brown, about 20 minutes. The fruit inside will be bubbling hot.

5 Place the packets on 8 individual dessert plates. Carefully open up each one (stand back to let the steam escape). Discard the whole cloves. Top each with a scoop of frozen yogurt and sprinkling of pecans. Serve immediately.

(Some More Ideas) *Fresh pineapple and banana en papillote*: For the plums, substitute 1 small ripe pineapple, peeled, cored, and cut into bite-size wedges, and 2 bananas, sliced 1/2 inch thick. Proceed as directed in Step 2.

Maple papillotes: Substitute 1/4 cup pure maple syrup for the honey.

Plums and clementines en papillote: Substitute 5 fresh medium clementines (sweet, bright orange, thin-skinned, seedless oranges) for 4 of the plums. Peel, section, and mix with the plums.

Plus Points

• Plums contain a fair amount of vitamin E, an important antioxidant that recent studies indicate may protect against some conditions associated with aging.

• Many foods can be baked *en papillote*. The same technique can be used to steam fish and vegetables or a combination of the two.

photo, page 263

Exchanges

carbohydrate 2 1/2 fat 1

Each serving (one papillote) provides calories 221, calories from fat 51, fat 6g, saturated fat 2g, cholesterol 8mg, sodium 66mg, carbohydrate 39g, fiber 2g, sugars 20g, protein 5g. Excellent source of vitamin C. Good source of calcium, phosphorus, riboflavin, vitamin A.

grilled fruit en brochette

The French term *en brochette* refers to food cooked on skewers. Fresh fruit is grilled on skewers long enough to heat the fruit and caramelize the sugars. Be careful not to leave the brochettes on the grill too long, as fruit can brown quickly. A coulis, an uncooked fruit or vegetable puree, is simple to prepare and creates a beautiful presentation on the plate.

Preparation time **30 minutes**   Cooking time **7 minutes**   *Serves 8*

Brochettes

4 fresh figs, or 4 dried figs, soaked and drained

1/2 large fresh pineapple (1 pound)

2 large pears, ripe but firm (1 pound)

2 large peaches, ripe but firm (1 pound)

2 large bananas, ripe but firm

1/3 cup fresh lemon juice

1 tablespoon sugar

Fresh raspberries

8 bamboo skewers, 10 to 12 inches long

Coulis

2 cups fresh raspberries (1 pint)

1 1/2 teaspoons grated orange zest

1/2 cup orange juice

1 tablespoon sugar

1 Soak the bamboo skewers in cold water for 20 minutes.

2 Meanwhile, make the coulis: In a blender or food processor, puree the raspberries, orange zest and juice, and sugar. Strain the mixture to remove the seeds, if you wish, but it's not necessary. Set aside.

3 Preheat the grill or broiler. Cut the figs lengthwise into four equal pieces (about 2 cups). Peel, core, and cut the pineapple into bite-size chunks (3 cups). Core (do not peel) the pears and cut into 1 1/2-inch cubes. Pit (do not peel) the peaches and cut into 1 1/2-inch cubes. Peel the bananas and cut crosswise into 1 1/2-inch pieces. Thread the fruit onto the soaked skewers, alternating them to make a colorful arrangement. Mix the lemon juice and sugar in a measuring cup. Baste the brochettes with half of the mixture; set aside the rest.

4 Grill or broil the brochettes about 4 minutes. Turn the brochettes, baste with the remaining lemon juice mixture, and grill or broil until light golden brown, another 3 or 4 minutes.

5 For each serving, spread about 1/4 cup coulis on a plate and arrange a fruit brochette on top. Garnish with whole raspberries, if you wish. Serve hot.

(Some More Ideas) *Fall fruit brochettes*: Substitute 1 pound red-skinned apples, such as Cortland, Rome, or York Imperial (do not peel), for the peaches. Use 1 pound plums (do not peel) for the figs and omit the bananas.

For appetizers, serve uncooked brochettes.

Other substitutes: For peaches, substitute the same amount of ripe nectarines. Fresh figs are available only from June through October in most markets. To use dried figs instead, soak and drain according to package directions.

Plus Points

• This delicious recipe provides an excellent amount of the antioxidant nutrient vitamin C, which comes from the pineapple, the raspberries, and the orange and lemon juices. The peaches provide a little beta-carotene, which the body converts to vitamin A. Additionally, bananas are an excellent source of potassium.

• Plenty of dietary fiber, essential for keeping the digestive tract healthy, is present in this array of fruit. Pectin, a soluble dietary fiber, regulates intestinal functions and can help to reduce blood cholesterol levels. Cellulose, an insoluble fiber, provides bulk and prevents constipation by promoting normal functioning of the intestines.

photo, page 263

Exchanges

fruit 3

Each serving (one brochette) provides calories 184, calories from fat 8, fat 1g, saturated fat 0g, cholesterol 0mg, sodium 6mg, carbohydrate 47g, fiber 8g, sugars 34g, protein 2g. Excellent source of vitamin C. Good source of potassium, riboflavin, vitamin B6.

peach and blackberry phyllo pizzas

For this impressive dessert, layers of light and flaky phyllo make crisp, elegant pizza "shells." The phyllo bases are sprinkled with almonds and then topped with an arrangement of sliced peaches and blackberries. A light sprinkling of sugar caramelizes slightly in the oven, bringing out the natural sweetness of the fruit.

Preparation time **30 minutes**   Baking time **15 minutes**   *Makes 6 individual pizzas*

5 sheets phyllo pastry
(14 x 18 inches)
Butter-flavored cooking spray
2 tablespoons ground almonds
3 large ripe peaches
1 cup fresh blackberries
2 tablespoons sugar

To serve (optional)
1 cup reduced-fat sour cream
1 tablespoon light brown sugar

1 Preheat the oven to 400°F and coat a baking sheet with cooking spray. Lay out the 5 sheets of phyllo and immediately cover with plastic wrap, then a damp towel (phyllo dries out in a couple of minutes if left uncovered). Work fast!

2 Place a sheet of phyllo on the work surface and spray with cooking spray. Layer 4 more phyllo sheets, spraying with cooking spray each time, and finally spray the top sheet with cooking spray. Using a 5-inch saucer as a guide, cut out 6 circles from the layered phyllo. Transfer each layered circle to the baking sheet and sprinkle with the ground almonds.

3 To decorate, cut the peaches in half (do not peel), twist apart, and remove the pits. Slice the peaches very thin. Place the peach slices on the phyllo pastry circles in a pinwheel design. Divide the blackberries among the pizzas. Sprinkle 1 teaspoon sugar on top of each pizza.

4 Bake pizzas until the pastry is golden brown and the peaches are very tender and light brown, about 15 minutes. These pizzas are best served within 15 minutes, as the pastry can lose its crispness quickly if the fruit is juicy. If desired, serve with sour cream sweetened with the brown sugar.

(Some More Ideas) *Pear and raspberry phyllo pizzas*: Substitute 1 pound ripe pears (preferably Bartlett) for the peaches; core the pears (do not peel) and cut into slices 1/8 inch thick. Use 1/2 pint (1 cup) fresh raspberries instead of the blackberries. If you wish, drizzle the pizzas with a little brandy after decorating and before sprinkling them with the sugar.

Nectarine and raspberry phyllo pizzas: Substitute 1 pound ripe nectarines for the peaches (do not peel) and 1/2 pint (1 cup) fresh blueberries for the blackberries. Toss the sugar with 1/4 teaspoon ground cinnamon before sprinkling over the pizzas.

Quick brandied peach pizzas: Substitute well-drained sliced peaches (canned in juice) in brandy for the fresh peaches.

Plum and raspberry phyllo pizzas: Use 1 pound ripe, pitted, unpeeled plums for the peaches. Slice 1/8-inch thick. Substitute 1/2 pint fresh raspberries for the blackberries.

Plus Points

• Spraying the sheets of phyllo with cooking spray assures a nice crispness and browning effect during baking without using butter.

• The reduced-fat sour cream mixed with brown sugar creates a mock whipped cream and dresses the plate up a bit when serving the fruit pizzas to a crowd.

Exchanges
carbohydrate 1 1/2

Each serving (one pizza) provides calories 107, calories from fat 15, fat 2g, saturated fat 0g, cholesterol 0mg, sodium 50mg, carbohydrate 22g, fiber 3g, sugars 13g, protein 2g. Good source of vitamin C.

pear and red currant phyllo lattice

This lovely tart uses sweet and tangy red currants with juicy pears for a winning combination. The bright red juice of the currants tints the pears and looks attractive under the pastry lattice. Although red currants only have a short season, they freeze well, so put some in the freezer to make a tart later in the year.

Preparation time **25 minutes**   Cooking time **15–20 minutes**   *Serves 6*

Tart

3 sheets phyllo pastry,
(12 x 20 inches each)
Butter-flavored cooking spray

Filling

2 tablespoons red-currant jelly
(or raspberry jam)
1 teaspoon lemon juice
3 medium ripe, firm pears
4 ounces red currants
(or gooseberries)
1/2 cup ground almonds

1 Preheat the oven to 400°F and put a baking sheet in to heat. For the filling, place the red-currant jelly and lemon juice in a small saucepan and heat gently over medium heat until melted. Remove from the heat.

2 Peel the pears and slice thinly. Add to the jelly glaze and toss gently to coat. Stir in the red currants.

3 Lay out 2 sheets of phyllo on top of each other. (Keep the third sheet covered to prevent it from drying out.) Cut into quarters. Separate the 8 pieces and coat with cooking spray. Use them to line a 9-inch loose-bottomed tart pan, overlapping them slightly, scrunching and tucking in the edges.

4 Sprinkle the ground almonds over the bottom of the lined tart pan. Top with the pear and red-currant mixture, spreading the fruit out evenly.

5 Cut the remaining sheet of phyllo cross-ways in half and spray with cooking spray. Place one half on top of the other, then cut into 10 strips about 3/4 inch wide, trimming off excess pastry. Twist the doubled strips gently and arrange them in a lattice pattern over the filling, tucking in the ends neatly.

6 Place the pan on the hot baking sheet and bake until the pastry is crisp and golden brown, about 15 to 20 minutes. Serve warm.

(Some More Ideas) Make a pear and raspberry phyllo lattice by using raspberries instead of red currants, and seedless raspberry jam for the glaze rather than red-currant jelly.

Mango and gooseberry phyllo tart: Sprinkle the bottom of the lined tart pan with 3 tablespoons shredded coconut. Peel and dice 2 ripe mangoes and mix with 4 ounces halved gooseberries. Toss the fruit gently with 2 tablespoons each of lime juice and light brown sugar, then spoon into the pastry and spread out evenly. Top with the pastry lattice and bake as in the main recipe.

Plus Points
• Unlike most fruits, pears contain only a small amount of vitamin C. However, in this recipe they are combined with red currants, which are a useful source of vitamin C. Pears do offer good amounts of potassium as well as soluble fiber.
• Red currants contain more beta-carotene than white currants and less than black currants.

Exchanges
carbohydrate 2 fat 1

Each serving provides calories 170, calories from fat 55, fat 6g, saturated fat 0g, cholesterol 0mg, sodium 64mg, carbohydrate 28g, fiber 4g, sugars 15g, protein 3g. Excellent source of vitamin C. Good source of magnesium, riboflavin.

vanilla angel food cake

Virtually fat-free, this light sponge cake really could be the food of angels. It is made using egg whites only, no yolks, and during baking develops a delicious golden crust that hides the tender, pure white interior. Here it is served with creamy low-fat yogurt and summer berries, but it is just as tempting with juicy peaches, mangoes, or apricots.

Preparation time **15 minutes**   Cooking time **35 minutes**   *Serves 12*

Cake

1 cup sifted cake flour

1/3 cup sugar

8 large egg whites, at room temperature

1 teaspoon cream of tartar

1/2 cup sugar

1/4 teaspoon salt

1 teaspoon pure vanilla extract

Garnish

8 ounces strawberries, cut into quarters

8 ounces (1/2 pint) raspberries

8 ounces (1/2 pint) blueberries

1 container (8 ounces) light vanilla yogurt

1 Preheat the oven to 350°F. Sift the flour and 1/3 cup sugar onto a large plate and set aside.

2 Place the egg whites and cream of tartar in a large bowl and whisk until frothy. Combine 1/2 cup sugar and salt and add to the whipping egg whites in a slow, steady stream. Add the vanilla extract, and continue whisking until the mixture forms stiff peaks.

3 Sift the flour mixture over the egg whites and fold in very gently with a large metal spoon until well blended.

4 Spoon the mixture into an ungreased 10-inch tube pan, gently smoothing the top. Bake until golden brown and cake springs back when lightly touched in the center, about 35 minutes.

5 Invert the cake, still in the pan, onto a wire rack and leave to cool completely, upside down. When it is cool, slide a long knife around the side of the pan to loosen the cake, then invert it onto a serving plate. (The cake can be kept, wrapped in plastic or stored in an airtight container, for 1 to 2 days.)

6 Just before serving, mix together the strawberries, raspberries, and blueberries. Spoon the fruit into the hollow in the center of the cake. Serve each slice with a dollop of vanilla yogurt.

(Some More Ideas) *Lemon and lime angel food cake*: Add the finely grated zest of 1 lemon and 1 lime to the beaten egg whites with the sifted flour and sugar. While the cake is cooling, peel a cantaloupe and remove the seeds. Cut the melon into small chunks and place in a bowl. Squeeze the juice from the lemon and lime, sprinkle it over the melon, and toss to coat well. Serve the cake with the melon pieces piled up in the center.

Chocolate angel food cake: Sift 2 tablespoons cocoa powder with the flour and sugar. Decorate the cake by dusting it with a mixture of 1 tablespoon cocoa powder and 1 tablespoon confectioners' sugar, sifted together.

Coffee angel food cake: Sift 1 tablespoon instant coffee powder (not granules) with the flour and sugar. Garnish with sifted confectioners' sugar.

Plus Points

• Low-fat yogurt is a useful source of calcium, which is an essential component of bones and teeth—the adult skeleton contains nearly 3 pounds of calcium, and 99% of this is present in the bones.

• Angel food cake is relatively high in sugar, so when cooking for a person with diabetes, it should be eaten in moderation. Because it is fat-free, a slice can easily be worked into a healthy diet, especially when topped with fresh berries.

photo, page 273

Exchanges

carbohydrate 2

Each serving provides calories 133, calories from fat 2, fat 0g, saturated fat 0g, cholesterol 0mg, sodium 96mg, carbohydrate 29g, fiber 2g, sugars 17g, protein 4g. Excellent source of vitamin C. Good source of riboflavin.

baked almond-stuffed peaches

Turn fresh peaches into a fabulous warm dessert by stuffing them with dried apricots, toasted almonds, and crushed amaretti cookie crumbs, then baking them in the oven until they are brown and bubbly. Try a variation featuring apples and stuffing them with a cinnamon macaroon filling. The fruit can be served with low-fat sour cream or vanilla ice cream.

Preparation time **30 minutes** Cooking time **about 35 minutes** *Serves 8 (half a peach each)*

Peaches

5 large peaches, ripe but firm

Stuffing

10 dried apricot halves, finely chopped

6 packaged amaretti cookies, crumbled

2 teaspoons almond extract

1 tablespoon brandy

1 large egg white

1/3 cup chopped, blanched almonds

1/4 cup packed light brown sugar

To serve (optional)

Low-fat sour cream or vanilla ice cream

1 Preheat the oven to 350°F. Half-fill a large saucepan with water and bring to a boil over high heat. Cut 4 of the peaches in half (do not peel) and remove the pits. Slide the peaches into the boiling water and cook just until they begin to soften, about 2 minutes. Using a slotted spoon, transfer to paper towels to drain. Place the peaches cut side up in a shallow baking dish.

2 To make the filling, peel, pit, and finely chop the remaining peach and place in a medium bowl. Add the dried apricots, amaretti crumbs, almond extract, brandy, and egg white. Stir until thoroughly mixed.

3 Heat a small skillet over high heat for 1 minute, add the almonds, then turn and toss them until golden and lightly toasted. Add the almonds to the fruit mixture and toss.

4 Spoon the filling into the cavities of each peach half, heaping up the filling and pressing it together gently. Sprinkle with the brown sugar. Cover the baking dish with foil.

5 Bake the peaches until tender, about 25 minutes. Remove the foil, increase the oven temperature to 400°F, and bake until the topping is golden brown, 5 minutes more. Serve warm with a scoop of low-fat sour cream or ice cream, if desired.

(Some More Ideas) *Baked raisin-stuffed apples*: Instead of the peaches, substitute 5 large red-skinned baking apples (about 2 1/2 pounds), such as Cortland, Jonathan, or Rome Beauty. Cut 4 of the apples in half (do not peel) and core. Instead of the amaretti filling, use the remaining peeled, cored, chopped apple, 1 cup coconut macaroon crumbs, 1/2 cup golden raisins, 1 teaspoon vanilla extract, 1 tablespoon light rum, 1 teaspoon ground cinnamon, and 1 large egg white.

Baked cherry-stuffed pears: Substitute 5 large ripe pears for the peaches and 3/4 cup dried cherries for the apricots.

Baked cranberry-stuffed nectarines: Use 5 large ripe nectarines for the peaches and 3/4 cup dried cranberries for the apricots. Use 1/3 cup chopped pistachios in place of the almonds.

Plus Points

• Dried apricots are a good source of potassium, which is needed to maintain normal blood pressure.

• Amaretti cookies are a type of macaroon made with whipped egg whites and almond paste. Because they are made with a meringue, they are lower in fat than many other cookies.

photo, page 273

Exchanges

carbohydrate 2 fat 1/2

Each serving provides calories 174, calories from fat 48, fat 5g, saturated fat 1g, cholesterol 4mg, sodium 56mg, carbohydrate 30g, fiber 3g, sugars 21g, protein 3g. Good source of riboflavin, vitamin A, vitamin C.

black forest mousse cake

Here's one of those heavenly warm, dense chocolate cakes that is very light, surprisingly low in fat, and much easier to make than you might think. Cocoa delivers a rich, chocolaty flavor with less fat than plain chocolate. A dollop of mock whipped cream spiked with cherry brandy adds a delightful touch to each slice of cake.

Preparation time **20 minutes**   Baking time **25 minutes**   *Serves 6*

Cake

1 cup all-purpose flour
1/2 cup granulated sugar
1/3 cup unsweetened cocoa
1/4 teaspoon salt
5 large egg whites
1 teaspoon vanilla extract
1 pound fresh Bing cherries, pitted and cut in half (1 1/2 cups)
1 tablespoon confectioners' sugar

Cream

4 ounces reduced-fat cream cheese, at room temperature
3 tablespoons low-fat sour cream
2 tablespoons cherry preserves
1 tablespoon Kirsch (cherry brandy) or rum (optional)

1 Preheat the oven to 350°F and line a 9-inch round cake pan (2 inches deep) with parchment paper. Sift the flour, 1/4 cup of the granulated sugar, the cocoa, and salt on a piece of wax paper.

2 Using an electric mixer on high, beat the egg whites in a clean, grease-free large bowl until soft peaks form. With the mixer running, beat in the remaining 1/4 cup of the granulated sugar, 1 tablespoon at a time, and the vanilla extract. Continue beating until the egg whites are glossy and smooth, and stand up in stiff peaks.

3 Sift the flour-cocoa mixture over the egg whites and fold in gently with a wire whisk, just until the flour disappears. Do not overmix. Using a rubber spatula, lift the batter into the pan. Smooth out the surface, mounding it slightly in the center, then sprinkle the cherries evenly over the top of the cake.

4 Bake the cake until the cake has risen and is just firm to the touch yet still moist on top, about 25 minutes (a toothpick inserted into the center should come out with moist crumbs). Transfer the cake to a wire rack to cool slightly.

5 Sprinkle the cake with the confectioners' sugar before serving. If you wish to serve with the mock whipped cream, blend together all of the ingredients and serve each slice of the warm cake with a generous spoonful.

(Some More Ideas) *Warm strawberry-chocolate mousse cake*: In place of the cherries, use 1 1/2 cups sliced ripe strawberries (about 1 pint whole berries).

Raspberry-chocolate mousse cake: In place of the cherries, buy 1 pint fresh raspberries. Use 1 1/2 cups whole fresh raspberries in place of the cherries in the cake and garnish the warm cake with the rest of the berries.

Winter Black Forest mousse cake: When fresh Bing cherries are not in season, substitute 1 1/2 cups of canned, pitted sweet dark cherries. Drain the cherries well before sprinkling them over the top of the cake batter.

Plus Points

• Like egg yolks, egg whites also provide protein but do not contribute any of the fat or cholesterol found in the yolks.

• Ounce for ounce, cocoa contains 79% less fat than baking chocolate and five times as much iron. Your body does not absorb this iron as well as the iron in meat, but the vitamin C in the cherries helps.

Exchanges
carbohydrate 3

Each serving provides calories 195, calories from fat 11, fat 1g, saturated fat 0g, cholesterol 0mg, sodium 143mg, carbohydrate 42g, fiber 3g, sugars 23g, protein 6g. Good source of folate, riboflavin, thiamine.

black forest mousse cake *p272*

baked almond-stuffed peaches *p271*

vanilla angel food cake *p270*

fig bars *p275*

cranberry and almond biscotti

Biscotti means "twice baked," a reference to the technique that gives these Italian cookies their characteristically hard texture. They are best dipped in coffee or tea as an afternoon or evening treat.

Preparation time **30 minutes**   Cooking time **30–35 minutes**   *Makes 24 biscotti*

1/2 cup blanched almonds

1 egg

1 egg white

1/2 cup sugar

1 teaspoon vanilla extract

1 1/2 cups flour

3/4 teaspoon baking powder

1 teaspoon ground cinnamon

1/4 teaspoon baking soda

1/2 cup dried cranberries

1 Preheat the oven to 350°F. Spread the almonds on a baking sheet and toast them in the oven until lightly browned, about 10 minutes. Set aside to cool.

2 Place the egg, egg white, sugar, and vanilla in a bowl and whisk with an electric mixer until very thick and pale; the mixture should be thick enough to leave a trail on the surface when you lift the beaters.

3 Sift the flour, baking powder, cinnamon, and baking soda onto a sheet of parchment paper, then sift the mixture again onto the whisked egg mixture. Using a spatula, carefully fold the sifted mixture into the egg mixture, then stir in the toasted almonds and cranberries to make a stiff dough.

4 Spoon the dough onto a baking sheet coated with cooking spray. With floured hands, form the dough into a neat log shape about 10 inches long and 2 inches wide and flatten slightly. Bake until golden brown, about 20 to 25 minutes. Leave to cool on the baking tray for 5 minutes, then transfer to a cutting board.

5 Using a serrated knife, cut the log across, slightly on the diagonal, into 24 slices. Arrange the slices on the baking sheet and return to the oven. Bake until golden brown, about 10 minutes. Cool on the baking sheet for 5 minutes, then transfer to a wire rack and cool completely. The biscotti can be kept in an airtight container for up to 2 weeks.

(Some More Ideas) Substitute dried cherries or golden raisins for the cranberries.

For a stronger almond flavor, use 1/2 teaspoon pure almond extract instead of cinnamon.

To make chocolate biscotti, replace the cranberries with 1/3 cup coarsely chopped good dark chocolate. Add 1 teaspoon pure vanilla extract when you whisk the egg and sugar.

Plus Points

• Absolutely no fat is needed to prepare the biscotti. They are purposely hard and crisp so they can be dipped without crumbling.

• Both fresh and dried cranberries are a good source of vitamin C.

Exchanges

carbohydrate 1

Each serving (one cookie) provide calories 71, calories from fat 14, fat 2g, saturated fat 0g, cholesterol 9mg, sodium 30mg, carbohydrate 13g, fiber 1g, sugars 6g, protein 2g.

fig bars

Here's a classic—a crisp shortbread cookie wrapped around a rich fig filling. The natural sweetness and full flavor of dried figs need little embellishment other than lemon juice to add a zesty tang. Figs are also high in fiber, making these bars a healthful snack.

Preparation time **35 minutes, plus 30 minutes chilling**   Cooking time **12–15 minutes**   *Makes 20 bars*

1 cup white flour
1 cup whole-wheat flour
5 tablespoons reduced-calorie margarine spread
5 tablespoons unsweetened applesauce
1/3 cup light brown sugar
1 teaspoon vanilla extract
1 egg
1 package (8 ounces) dried figs, finely chopped
2 tablespoons lemon juice

1 Sift the flours into a mixing bowl. Using two knives or a pastry blender, cut in the margarine until the mixture resembles coarse meal.

2 Add the applesauce, sugar, vanilla extract, and egg, and mix to form a firm dough, adding 1 to 2 teaspoons water if necessary to bind. (Alternatively, blend the flours and margarine in a food processor, then add the applesauce, sugar, vanilla, and egg, and blend briefly to make a dough.) Wrap the dough in plastic and refrigerate for 30 minutes.

3 Place the figs in a small saucepan with 6 tablespoons water. Bring to a boil, then reduce the heat to low, cover, and simmer until the figs have plumped up slightly and absorbed the water, about 3 to 5 minutes. Transfer to a bowl and mash lightly with a fork to break up the pieces. Add the lemon juice and stir, then allow to cool.

4 Preheat the oven to 375°F. Roll out the dough on a lightly floured surface to a 20 x 6-inch rectangle. Cut the dough rectangle in half lengthways to make 2 strips.

5 Spoon half the fig puree evenly over half of each strip, along one of the long sides. Bring the opposite long side up and over the filling, to form a log shape, and press the edges of the dough together to seal.

6 Flatten each of the logs slightly. Using a sharp knife, cut each log across into 10 bars and transfer to a baking sheet coated with cooking spray. Prick each bar with a fork or score with a sharp knife. Bake until slightly darkened in color, about 12 to 15 minutes.

7 Transfer the bars to a wire rack to cool. The bars can be kept in an airtight container for 2 to 3 days.

(Some More Ideas) To make cherry and apple rolls, gently simmer 1/2 cup dried cherries in a saucepan with 5 tablespoons water and 1 cored and finely chopped apple until the water is absorbed. Use instead of the fig filling.

Plus Points

• Dried figs are a good source of fiber and also contain compounds known to have mild laxative effects. Drying the fruit concentrates their nutrients, making them a useful source of calcium and iron.

• Unsweetened applesauce can often be used in recipes for baked goods to replace half the fat. It ensures a moist product and drastically reduces the amount of total fat in each serving.

• Unsweetened applesauce works especially well in recipes for quick breads and muffins and adds a pleasant fruit flavoring to the product.

photo, page 273

Exchanges
carbohydrate 1 1/2

Each serving (one bar) provides calories 104, calories from fat 17, fat 2g, saturated fat 0g, cholesterol 11mg, sodium 25mg, carbohydrate 21g, fiber 2g, sugars 11g, protein 2g.

creamy baked custards

These creamy baked custards, delicately flavored with vanilla and accompanied by a fresh cherry compote, are easy to make and sure to be popular with all ages. Take care not to overcook the custards—they should be just set when you take them out of the oven. This dessert is perfect for dinner parties because the custards can be prepared ahead of time and refrigerated until serving.

Preparation time **about 40 minutes**   Cooking time **30–35 minutes**   *Serves 6*

Custards

2 cups 1% milk
1 vanilla bean, split
2 eggs
2 egg yolks
3 tablespoons sugar
1/2 teaspoon flour

Compote

1 tablespoon sugar
1 pound fresh cherries, pitted
2 teaspoons cornstarch

1 Place the milk and vanilla bean in a medium saucepan and heat over medium-high heat until almost boiling. Remove from the heat, cover, and set aside to infuse for 15 minutes.

2 Preheat the oven to 325°F. Place the whole eggs, egg yolks, 3 tablespoons of sugar, and flour in a bowl and lightly whisk together.

3 Bring the milk back to a boil, then remove the vanilla bean, and slowly pour the hot milk over the egg mixture, whisking constantly. Strain the mixture into a pitcher, then divide among six 4-ounce ramekin dishes that have been coated with cooking spray.

4 Set the ramekins in a shallow roasting pan and pour enough hot water into the pan to come halfway up the sides of the ramekins. Bake until the custards are lightly set, about 30 to 35 minutes. The custards should be slightly wobbly in the center as they will continue to cook for a few minutes after being removed from the oven. Lift the custards out of the pan of hot water and place on a wire rack to cool. After cooling, refrigerate until ready to serve.

5 For the compote: Place 1 tablespoon sugar and 6 tablespoons water in a medium saucepan and heat over medium-high heat until the sugar has dissolved. Bring to a

boil, then reduce the heat to low, and add the cherries. Cover the pan and simmer gently, stirring occasionally, until the cherries are tender, 4 to 5 minutes. Use a slotted spoon to remove the cherries and place them in a small serving bowl; set aside.

6 Mix the cornstarch with 1 tablespoon cold water and then stir mixture into the cherry juices in the saucepan. Bring the mixture to a boil, then reduce the heat to low and simmer, stirring, until thickened and clear, about 1 minute. Allow to cool for a few minutes, then pour the sauce over the cherries. (The compote can be served warm or at room temperature.) Spoon a little of the cherry compote over the top of each custard, and serve the rest of the compote on the side.

(**Some More Ideas**) If you want to turn the custards out for serving, line the bottom of each ramekin with a circle of baking parchment, and add 1 extra egg yolk to the mixture. After baking, chill for at least 4 hours or preferably overnight. To turn out, lightly press the edge of each custard with your fingertips to pull it away from the dish, then run a knife around the edge. Place an inverted serving plate on top of the ramekin, then turn them

Exchanges

carbohydrate 1 1/2   fat 1

Each serving provides calories 165, calories from fat 44, fat 5g, saturated fat 2g, cholesterol 145mg, sodium 65mg, carbohydrate 25g, fiber 2g, sugars 21g, protein 7g. Excellent source of riboflavin. Good source of calcium, phosphorus, vitamin A, vitamin B12.

both over, holding them firmly together, and lift off the ramekin.

Chocolate custard pots with poached pears: Flavor the milk with a thin strip of pared orange zest instead of the vanilla bean. In Step 2, use light brown sugar, and add 1 tablespoon sifted cocoa powder. Continue making the custards as in the main recipe. For the pears, heat 1 cup water with 1/4 cup sugar and a split vanilla bean until the sugar dissolves, then bring to a boil, and simmer for 2 to 3 minutes. Add 4 small, firm dessert pears, peeled, cored, and thickly sliced. Cover and simmer gently until just tender, about 12 to 15 minutes, turning the pear slices in the syrup occasionally. Lift out the pears with a slotted spoon and transfer to a serving dish. Simmer the syrup for 5 minutes to reduce slightly, then cool for 5 minutes. Remove the vanilla bean and pour over the pears.

Plus Points

• When cooking for people with diabetes, it is important to limit high-cholesterol foods whenever possible. Only two egg yolks are needed in this recipe to stabilize the custards. This limits the amount of total cholesterol in the dessert.

• Cherries are rich in potassium and provide useful amounts of vitamin C.

five-star cookies

These nutty, moist cookies will cheer up midmorning coffee or an after-school snack. They are satisfying and packed full of healthy ingredients to restore lagging energy levels, without being too sweet. The addition of dried fruit instead of chocolate, nuts, and seeds make these cookies a much healthier option than store-bought packaged cookies.

Preparation time **10–15 minutes**   Cooking time **10 minutes**   *Makes 16 cookies*

2 tablespoons hazelnuts, finely chopped

2 tablespoons sunflower seeds, finely chopped

1/4 cup dried apricots, finely chopped

1/4 cup pitted dried dates, finely chopped

1/2 cup whole-wheat flour

1/2 cup quick oats

1 tablespoon light brown sugar

1/2 teaspoon baking soda

2 tablespoons canola oil

4 tablespoons reduced-calorie apple juice

1 Preheat the oven to 350°F. Mix the chopped hazelnuts, sunflower seeds, apricots, and dates together in a large bowl. Add the flour, oats, sugar, and baking soda, and stir until all the ingredients are thoroughly combined.

2 Combine the oil and apple juice, and pour over the dry mixture. Stir until the dry ingredients are just moistened.

3 Drop by rounded teaspoonfuls onto a baking sheet coated with cooking spray. Using the back of a fork dipped in flour, gently flatten each ball, and neaten the edges with your fingers.

4 Bake the cookies until golden brown, about 10 minutes. Transfer to a wire rack and cool. The cookies can be kept in an airtight container for up to 4 days.

(Some More Ideas) Try substituting unsalted cashew nuts for the hazelnuts.

Use dried peaches and figs instead of the apricots and dates.

Plus Points

• Sunflower seeds are a good source of the antioxidant vitamin E, which helps to protect cell membranes from damage by free radicals. Sunflower seeds are rich in polyunsaturated fats and also provide good amounts of vitamin B1 and the minerals zinc, iron, phosphorus, selenium, magnesium, and copper.

• Store-bought cookies are usually prepared with hydrogenated shortening that is high in saturated fat and contributes to the buildup of plaque in the arteries over time. In this recipe, canola oil is used as an unsaturated, healthier fat and the apple juice helps to contribute moistness.

Exchanges
carbohydrate 1/2 fat 1/2

Each serving (one cookie) provides calories 67, calories from fat 27, fat 3g, saturated fat 0g, cholesterol 0mg, sodium 40mg, carbohydrate 9g, fiber 1g, sugars 4g, protein 1g.

orange and pecan cookies

These are slice-and-bake cookies—the roll of dough can be prepared in advance and kept in the refrigerator. Then, whenever you want cookies, you simply slice the roll into rounds, top with pecans, and bake. They are perfect not-too-sweet little treats served with a cup of tea or coffee.

Preparation time **15 minutes, plus 2 hours chilling**   Cooking time **8–10 minutes**   *Makes 24 cookies*

3/4 cup whole-wheat flour, plus extra for kneading
1/2 cup self-rising white flour
1/3 cup light brown sugar
2 tablespoons pecans, chopped
Zest of 1 orange
4 tablespoons canola oil
2 egg whites
12 pecan halves, sliced in half

1 Place the flours, sugar, chopped pecans, and orange zest in a bowl, and stir until well combined.

2 In a small bowl, beat the oil and egg whites together with a fork. Add this mixture to the dry ingredients and mix with a fork until a soft dough forms.

3 Knead the dough very lightly on a floured surface until smooth, then roll into a log shape about 12 inches long. Wrap the roll in plastic and refrigerate for 2 hours. (The dough can be kept in the fridge for 2 to 3 days before slicing and baking.)

4 Preheat the oven to 350°F. Unwrap the roll of dough and slice across into 24 slices, using a sharp knife. Arrange the slices, 2 inches apart, on 2 large baking sheets coated with cooking spray. Top each slice with a piece of pecan, pressing it in slightly.

5 Bake until firm to the touch and lightly golden, about 8 to 10 minutes. Transfer the cookies to a wire rack to cool completely. The cookies can be stored in an airtight container for up to 5 days.

(Some More Ideas) Chopped hazelnuts can be used in place of the pecans, with whole hazelnuts to decorate.

Almond-polenta cookies: Mix 2 ounces instant polenta with 3 ounces confectioners' sugar and 4 ounces self-rising flour. Rub in 2 ounces butter until the mixture resembles bread crumbs. Beat 1 large egg with 1/2 teaspoon pure almond extract, add to the crumb mixture, and mix to form a soft dough. Roll, wrap, and chill as in the main recipe. Before baking, scatter 2 tablespoons slivered almonds over the slices.

Plus Points
• Like other nuts, pecans are rich in fat—but little of this is saturated fat, the majority being present as polyunsaturated fat. Pecans also provide generous amounts of vitamin E.
• Canola oil is extracted from grape seeds and is believed to be lower in saturated fat than any other oil (6%). It works well in cookies and other baked goods in place of saturated fats such as butter.

Exchanges
starch 1/2 fat 1/2

Each serving (one cookie) provides calories 66, calories from fat 31, fat 3g, saturated fat 0g, cholesterol 0mg, sodium 39mg, carbohydrate 8g, fiber 1g, sugars 3g, protein 1g.

279

mocha ricotta tiramisu

This delectable version of the popular Italian dessert includes the traditional sponge cakes soaked in coffee and liqueur for the base. Instead of layering the ladyfingers with whipped high-fat mascarpone cheese, a light and creamy mixture of sweetened ricotta cheese and yogurt is used. A sprinkling of grated dark chocolate is the finishing touch.

Preparation time **20 minutes, plus at least 30 minutes chilling**   *Serves 4*

8 ladyfingers, halved

1 teaspoon instant espresso powder

1/2 cup boiling water

2 tablespoons coffee liqueur or brandy

1 teaspoon sugar

1 cup low-fat ricotta cheese

1 cup plain low-fat yogurt

1/4 cup sifted confectioners' sugar

1 teaspoon vanilla extract

1 square (1 ounce) semi-sweet dark chocolate, grated

1 Break each of the ladyfingers into 3 pieces, then divide evenly among four 8-ounce glass tumblers or dessert glasses.

2 Place the coffee in a glass measuring cup and add the boiling water. Add the liqueur or brandy and 1 teaspoon sugar, and stir to dissolve. Pour evenly over the ladyfingers. Leave to soak while you prepare the topping.

3 Beat the ricotta with the yogurt, confectioners' sugar, and vanilla extract until smooth and creamy. Pile on top of the soaked ladyfingers.

4 Sprinkle the top of each dessert with grated chocolate. Cover and chill for at least 30 minutes (but no more than 3 to 4 hours) before serving.

(**Some More Ideas**) Low-fat vanilla yogurt can be substituted for the plain yogurt to add a bit more flavor.

Instead of grated chocolate, decorate the tops of the desserts by dusting each with 1/2 teaspoon cocoa powder.

Plus Points

• Ricotta cheese is much lower in fat and calories than the creamy mascarpone that is traditionally used for tiramisu. Adding yogurt to the ricotta provides creaminess and helps to decrease the fat content even further.

• Dark chocolate is a good source of copper, a mineral that helps the body to absorb iron. As dark chocolate is also a source of iron, there is a double nutritional benefit to including it in this dessert.

Exchanges
carbohydrate 2 1/2 fat 1

Each serving provides calories 242, calories from fat 41, fat 5g, saturated fat 4g, cholesterol 42mg, sodium 162mg, carbohydrate 36g, fiber 1g, sugars 29g, protein 13g. Excellent source of calcium, phosphorus. Good source of riboflavin, vitamin A.

rich fruit ring cake

Most fruitcakes are high in fat and sugar, but this one is relatively low in fat and depends on dried fruits soaked in apple juice for natural sweetness. The cake is baked in a tube pan and garnished with nuts and cherries, making it an elegant treat. The taste deepens over time, and the cake can be stored in the refrigerator for 2 weeks prior to serving.

Preparation time **about 30 minutes, plus soaking**   Cooking time **about 1 hour and 15 minutes**   *Serves 18*

Cake

1/4 cup dried cranberries
1/4 cup raisins
1/4 cup dried pears, chopped
1/4 cup pitted dried dates, chopped
1 cup apple juice
1/4 cup pecans, chopped
1 tablespoon candied ginger, chopped
Zest and juice of 1 lemon
Cooking spray
5 tablespoons canola oil
1 egg
1/4 cup light brown sugar
1 cup self-rising white flour
1 cup self-rising whole-wheat flour
1 teaspoon baking powder
1 teaspoon ground cinnamon
Pinch ground nutmeg
3–4 tablespoons fat-free milk, as needed

Decoration

2 tablespoons apricot jam
15 maraschino cherries
6 whole hazelnuts
12 pecan halves
6 walnut halves
Confectioners' sugar to dust

Exchanges

carbohydrate 2 fat 1

1 Place all the dried fruit in a medium saucepan. Add the apple juice, place over medium heat, and bring to a boil. Cover and simmer gently until the fruit begins to absorb the liquid, about 3 to 4 minutes.

2 Remove the pan from the heat and let stand, covered, until completely cold. Stir in the pecans, ginger, and lemon zest and juice.

3 Preheat the oven to 300°F. Coat a 9-inch tube pan with cooking spray. In a bowl, beat the oil, egg, and sugar until smooth.

4 Sift the flours, baking powder, cinnamon, and nutmeg into a large bowl. Add the soaked fruit and the egg mixture, and stir well to combine. Add in enough milk to make a fairly soft mixture.

5 Spoon the mixture into the prepared pan and smooth the top with a spatula. Bake until the cake is firm and a toothpick inserted in the center comes out clean, about 1 hour and 15 minutes.

6 Allow the cake to cool in the pan for at least 1 hour before running a knife around the edge and turning it out. Wrap in aluminum foil, and store in the refrigerator for 1 to 2 weeks before serving to allow the flavors to mature.

7 To decorate the cake, gently heat the jam with 1 teaspoon water, then press through a fine sieve. Brush the top of the cake with the jam. Arrange the cherries and nuts on top, pressing them gently into the jam. Finally, dust the cake lightly with sifted confectioners' sugar.

(Some More Ideas) For easier slicing, bake the cake in a long loaf pan, about 5 cups in capacity.

Soak the fruit in a mixture of 1/2 cup cherry brandy and 1/2 cup apple juice.

Plus Points
• Only 5 tablespoons of oil is needed for the entire cake, which serves 18 people, making it very low in fat compared to many iced layer cakes.

Each serving provides calories 170, calories from fat 58, fat 6g, saturated fat 1g, cholesterol 12mg, sodium 206mg, carbohydrate 26g, fiber 2g, sugars 13g, protein 2g. Good source of phosphorus.

eat to beat diabetes

It wasn't too long ago that a diagnosis of diabetes was followed by "the talk", a particularly frustrating conversation with the doctor about your future. You'll have to watch your diet far more closely now, the doctor would say. Cut out the sugar. Cut way back on carbohydrates. Watch the fat. Lots of steamed green vegetables. No indulgent restaurant meals. Lose the dessert habit. There's no other choice.

It was depressing, disheartening, annoying. What a difference a few years can make. Thanks to ever-improving research, a whole new mind-set has emerged in the health community for how to eat to beat diabetes. And what a wonderful mind-set it is! Blandness is out; flavor is in. Overly tight restrictions are out; intelligent moderation is in. The new thinking about eating for diabetes is to eat delicious, healthy, creative food, with a sensible eye toward the right mix of nutrients and the right portion sizes. It's a more open-ended food prescription, but with proven results.

This new thinking is part of a bigger, more intuitive approach that is emerging for treating diabetes. As you probably know, diabetes is a condition in which your cells become less adept at absorbing glucose—better known as blood sugar and the key ingredient cells use for fuel. There are two main causes for this: Either you are no longer creating enough insulin (the hormone secreted by your pancreas that transports glucose from the bloodstream into the cells), or the cells are no longer receptive to the insulin you are creating. In either case, the result is that there is too much sugar in your bloodstream, and not enough in your cells. A myriad of complications can follow.

Today we know that the art of managing diabetes is in good part about controlling blood sugar. There are three key ways to do that:

- First, make sure your body has enough insulin so that your cells can get the fuel they need to function.

- Second, develop lifestyle habits to make your body less susceptible to blood sugar swings and your cells less resistant to insulin. At the top of the list is losing weight. Also included are exercise, relaxation, better sleep habits, and even a vitamin and supplements program.

- Third, adjust your diet to make sure that you are getting the right nutrients throughout the day, without big surges in blood sugar.

The last item is what this cookbook is all about: developing a way of eating that is healthy, delicious, well balanced, and defensive against blood sugar surges. In the pages ahead, you will learn about the science and practice of healthy eating for diabetes. We will explain why the recipes in this book are so appropriate for your condition. And best of all, we'll make clear how easy and delicious it is to eat to beat diabetes.

Understanding nutrients

Another aspect of diabetes management that has changed is the demise of a "one size fits all" nutritional program. Not only are the scope, impact, and cause of the condition different for each person, but each person's lifestyle and priorities differ as well. So in this new world of diabetes, it's far more common for the newly diagnosed to be sent to a nutritionist to help craft a unique plan of attack. The eating plan that will emerge will factor in the need for weight loss, the intensity of the condition, personal food tastes, as well as lifestyle issues (exercisers have different nutritional needs than sedentary people, for example).

Yet ultimately there are core truths about nutrition and diabetes that transcend individual needs and preferences. Among those is that you must be sensible about your mix of nutrients. Here, then, is an overview of the key nutrients that a person with diabetes must be smart about. Understand these, and you'll have a

> # > Diabetes at a glance

All cells use glucose, or blood sugar, as their main source of fuel. Diabetes is a medical condition in which the process that transfers glucose into your cells breaks down. The result is that glucose builds up in your bloodstream, while your cells starve without it. There are two main forms of diabetes:

Type 1 Diabetes

Type 1 diabetes occurs when the body's immune system destroys the insulin-producing cells in the pancreas. This can cause a total halt in insulin production. People with type 1 diabetes must take insulin shots daily or use an insulin pump. Without such treatment, glucose levels build up to dangerous levels in the blood, which if left untreated, could lead to coma and even death. Type 1 diabetes usually occurs in children or young adults, and often appears suddenly. It is a lifelong condition. Its symptoms include:

- High levels of sugar in the blood
- High levels of sugar in the urine
- Frequent urination
- Extreme thirst
- Extreme weight loss
- Weakness and fatigue
- Moodiness

Type 2 Diabetes

With type 2 diabetes, the pancreas does produce insulin, but the body's cells begin to "resist" insulin's message to let blood sugar inside the cells—a condition called insulin resistance. This form of diabetes is often linked to being overweight, and tends to develop slowly. It is more easily treated than type 1 diabetes, but its spread is becoming epidemic in the United States. Its symptoms include:

- Increased thirst
- More frequent urination
- Edginess, fatigue, and nausea
- Increased appetite
- Weight loss
- Blurred vision
- Hard-to-heal infections
- Tingling or numbness in the hands and feet

much better grasp on what makes for safe and healthy eating for diabetes.

Carbohydrates

Carbohydrates are your main source of energy. They come in two forms. **Simple carbohydrates** are foods that are easily digested into glucose. Examples include table sugar, bleached flour, and white rice.

Complex carbohydrates are exactly that—starches made up of more complex sugars, fiber, and a rich assortment of other nutrients. These carbohydrates take longer to digest and have more beneficial ingredients in them. They make up the bulk of whole grains and vegetables.

Since carbohydrates are easily broken down into sugars, they have the most

> All about sugar substitutes

Until 1994 sugar was considered the most evil of foods for people with diabetes. But then, new research showed that eating table sugar doesn't raise your blood sugar levels much more than eating other starches. The conclusion: Sugar can be had in moderation, particularly if your diet is otherwise well rounded.

So what's the deal with all those little blue, pink, and yellow packets of sugar substitutes? The answer: Table sugar (or sucrose) is not very sweet when compared to sugar substitutes. When recipes call for sugar, it is usually in large amounts to get to the desired sweetness. This can cause the total number of calories and carbohydrates per serving to be too high. Sugar substitutes can give the sweetness desired for none of the calories or carbohydrates.

But even with improvements in taste, many people dislike the flavor of sugar substitutes. And not everyone is convinced of their healthiness. Here is a look at what's on the market today:

Sucralose Sold under the name Splenda. Sucralose is the only sugar substitute made from sugar. It has no calories, is not recognized as a sugar or a carbohydrate in the body, yet is 600 times sweeter than sugar. Sucralose has no unpleasant or bitter aftertaste, and it is very heat stable, making it ideal for baking and cooking. Approved by the FDA in 1998, it is also sold as packets and in granular form for baking.

Acesulfame Potassium or Ace-K Sold under the name Sunett, Ace-K is 200 times sweeter than sugar and is not metabolized by the body (meaning no calories). Like Sucralose, it remains stable at high temperatures, making it ideal for cooking and baking. It tastes sweet with no lingering aftertaste. It also works well when combined with other sugar substitutes. The FDA approved Ace-K for use in soft drinks in 1998 and continues to approve its use in many products.

Aspartame Sold under the name NutraSweet. Aspartame is made from amino acids and is 200 times sweeter than sugar. Aspartame was the first sugar substitute to be approved by the FDA for tabletop use and in various foods in 1981 after a 25-year absence of new substitutes. The taste is sweet and similar to that of sugar. It has the ability to intensify fruit flavors in foods and beverages. Some people report that the sweet flavor does not hold up as well under heating as Sucralose or Ace-K, but aspartame can be used for baking and cooking.

Saccharin Sold under the name Sweet'N Low, saccharin has been used to sweeten foods for over a century. Saccharin was popular until the 1970s, when it was taken off the market for safety reasons. Those fears were proven unfounded, and it has returned to the marketplace. Since the creation of newer sugar substitutes, saccharin has been combined successfully with them in a variety of commercial products to increase the flavor, improve stability, and lower production costs. Saccharin is not metabolized by the body and provides little or no calories.

impact on your blood sugar levels. In particular, simple carbohydrates are so easy to digest that they almost instantly flood your body with blood sugar. It's no wonder, then, that carbohydrates have long been seen as the enemy of people with diabetes.

The American Diabetes Association still says that some people need to lower their carbohydrate intake to better manage their diabetes. But it is now widely recognized by the medical community that following a strict low-carbohydrate food program may do more harm than good. Why? Because, ultimately, carbohydrates are the best source of fuel for your body. And since carbohydrates are about half the amount of calories of fat per gram, a food program that includes carbohydrates also gives you wider food choices with less risk of gaining weight.

The trick is not to reduce "carbohydrates" to a single category of food. A bagel is mostly carbohydrates. Broccoli is mostly carbohydrates. Pretty different foods, no? And yet many of the popular low-carbohydrate diets do not differentiate adequately between the two. Many of these plans limit all carbohydrates regardless of the source.

The problem with simple carbohydrates—foods like bagels, candy, cake—isn't just that they are high in sugar. Most people with diabetes can handle such treats every now and then—eaten in small portions. Rather, it's that such foods are often full of fat and short of vitamins, minerals, and other healthy nutrients. They're all the bad stuff with almost none of the good.

Complex carbohydrates, on the other hand, not only have more complex, slower-to-digest sugars in them, but also far more beneficial nutrients. In particular, they have lots of fiber.

Fiber, simply put, is the stuff in plants that your body can't digest. It's the husks on the grains, the stringy threads in celery. How wonderful is fiber? Let us count the ways. Fiber is bulky and absorbs water, so it fills you up faster. Fiber slows down digestion, so it prolongs feelings of satiation. Both of those are critical for maintaining healthy weight. Fiber binds together waste, keeping you regular. Fiber sweeps out your digestive tract, keeping your insides clean. Fiber helps reduce fat and cholesterol in your blood system, protecting your heart. Fiber helps keep blood sugar levels steady. And since fluctuating blood sugar levels influence feelings of hunger and irritability (as well as your energy levels), high-fiber foods such as vegetables, whole grains, and beans also help to keep you on a more even keel. (See the next page for ways to add fiber to your diet.)

Fiber is not the only desirable constituent of complex carbs. Compelling new research suggests that eating the right vegetables, whole grains, and beans every day may help you to reap even more health benefits. Potent ingredients called phytochemicals that are found in these foods may play a role in helping prevent disease. For instance, the phyto-chemicals in broccoli may play a role in the prevention of certain cancers; onions' allium compounds may help reduce cholesterol, an important factor for people with diabetes; oats and some soy products may also reduce cholesterol.

So there is no need to follow a faddish low-carbohydrate plan to control your diabetes. Carbohydrates, particularly complex ones, help you manage one of the most important factors in diabetes: your ability to control your blood sugar, while maintaining high energy levels and reaping the benefits of the many vitamins and minerals they provide.

Fats

What's creamy, crunchy, flavorful, and pleasurable? Fat has a way of fitting all these descriptions.

Fat: You know it when you see it (some-one, please hide that butter!). And you certainly know it when you taste it. But describing it in words is a little complicated. Fats are a class of organic chemicals that scientists refer to as fatty acids or lipids. When digested, they create nearly double the energy of the same amount of carbohydrates or protein. In your body, fats are crucial to the health of all cell membranes, are used to create hormones, and have other key functions. Indeed, you need a layer of body fat to protect organs and have a reserve of fuel. Even lean athletes have body fat.

Fat is only a problem when you eat too much of it. Fat molecules that you eat are easily stored in your body as . . . fat. And that means weight gain, which is rarely a good thing for your health. That also means lots of fat-related molecules in your bloodstream, which is bad for your heart and circulatory system.

But don't go to extremes. There is a solid case for eating some fat. First, it is an amazingly rich source of energy. And fat slows the digestion, causing sugar to enter the bloodstream more gradually—a goal of blood sugar control.

And as with carbohydrates, it is wrong to speak poorly of all forms of fat. There are three categories of fats, and two of those categories offer health benefits so impor-tant that you might wish to add them to your diet.

We won't go into the science of fat deeply here. But here's what it boils down to. The type of fat that is least healthy for you is the type that maintains a solid shape at room temperature. Primarily, this means butter, cheese, and the fat on meat. While this kind of fat (known as saturated) offers incredible amounts of fuel, it has few other health benefits and has the most detriments. Fats that are in liquid form at room temperature (primarily, plant oils, such as corn, olive, or canola oil) are split into two categories: polyunsaturated and monounsaturated. Both have benefits, but "mono" oils are best for you. There is evidence that monounsat-urated fat raises your HDL cholesterol (the good one), important for people with dia-betes because they run an increased risk for heart disease. Monounsaturated fat also has been shown to reduce insulin resistance.

So while fat isn't evil, it's not a perfect angel either. You will still need to watch how much and what kind of fat you eat. Monounsaturated fat, the fat you should be concentrating on, is still rich in calories. Try to stick with small amounts of olive oil, canola oil, or foods like avocados and almonds to get the best sources of monounsaturated fat.

Protein

Protein, the third main category of nutrient, also plays a role in blood sugar control; it is digested more slowly compared to carbohydrates and causes a more gradual rise in blood sugar levels. So should you pack on the steaks and hamburgers? Appealing as that may sound to some, the answer is a resounding no!

A "protein" is part of a large class of chemicals called amino acids. They are digestible into energy, but also serve many other functions in the body. In particular, your body uses the proteins you eat to build and repair muscles and tissues.

In developed countries, it is rare for people to suffer from a deficiency of protein. That's because protein is in so many of the foods we eat, even those generally considered carbohydrates. Proteins are in plant foods—vegetables, grains, beans, nuts, soy products—and are the main ingredient in animal foods like beef, poultry, seafood, and dairy products.

So yes, your body needs proteins for everyday function and health, and as an energy source. In fact, proteins are particularly good for steady energy and stable blood sugar. Just remember that protein is in lots of food; you probably already get more than you need for health and growth. So don't seek out big

portions of meat in the name of health. In fact, meat is usually both surrounded and infused with fat. So keep it lean.

The role of weight

One part of that doctor conversation that hasn't changed much over the years is

the need to keep your weight down if you have diabetes. The reason is simple and direct: The more fat you carry, the more insulin resistant your cells become. Even losing a small amount of weight can improve insulin resistance. For many people with diabetes, a 10-pound change is enough to have measurable results in your blood sugar.

> ## > The fiber fill-up

You can do it! You can reach the recommended daily fiber level of 20 to 30 grams. Here's how:

Don't skimp on breakfast. A modest morning meal of whole grains and fruit provides a golden opportunity to get as much as a third of your daily fiber. Look for a cereal with 5 grams of fiber or more (make sure you still look at total carbs and it fits your program). Enjoy whole-grain bread instead of bagels and rolls made with white flour. Change the flour in your pancake and waffle mixes to whole wheat. Add fruit to the batters.

Eat the skins (and some seeds). Scrub the skins on edible fruits and vegetables, but don't peel! A potato goes from 3.6 grams of fiber to 2.3 when it is skinned. The seeds in berries, kiwifruit, and figs also supply fiber, so be sure to try these and add variety to your diet.

Be a booster. Add wheat germ or bran flakes to meat loaf and casseroles. Or sprinkle some in yogurt. Add bran or wheat germ into bread crumbs. Each tablespoon of bran adds 1 gram of fiber.

Think beans. Beans are a great source of fiber. A half-cup serving supplies anywhere from 4 to 10 grams of fiber. Try split-pea or lentil soup for a fiber-rich lunch. Add beans to a salad, or fill a soft tortilla with heated beans.

Add produce too. Vegetables like carrots and celery are good sources of fiber. Add extra into casseroles, soups, salads, sandwiches, and pasta. Fresh, frozen, or even canned—it doesn't matter.

Switch from white to brown. Think whole-wheat pasta, brown rice, and whole-wheat flour versus the white versions. Be aware, however, that even if a food looks brown, it does not necessarily mean it is high in fiber. Check the label. In order to be considered a good source of fiber, a product has to have 3 grams of fiber per serving; a high source, 5 grams. Don't be fooled by brown bread that actually has little whole-grain flour; it's getting its brown look from coloring or molasses.

Weight loss can be extremely complicated, or it can be extremely simple. If you are the type to follow fads and research announcements, then you know that an overflow of weight-loss theories have risen and fallen in the past 15 years. For much of the '80s and '90s, the message was low-fat eating: By reducing the most calorie-dense foods from your diet, you'd naturally lose weight. Most of us tried. Most of us failed. As it turned out, fat helps us feel satiated; many people on low-fat diets ended up consuming far more calories than when they allowed themselves some steak.

Today high-protein, low-carb diets are all the rage. The idea is this: When you cut out all or most of the carbs from your diet, your body no longer has glucose to burn as energy. So instead, it burns body fat. However, this is an inefficient way to generate fuel, leading to weight loss.

Trouble is, protein foods are often rich with saturated fats. The debate continues over whether high-protein diets are safe either in the short or long term.

A thousand theories, a thousand diets. You can easily get lost in all the conflicting science (and pseudo-science). And millions of people have. Which is why obesity remains such a problem.

Then there's the simple theory of weight loss: Just burn more calories in a day than you consume, and you'll lose weight! To do that, you exercise a little more, and eat a little less. You find ways other than eating to relieve stress or cure boredom or show love, and instead eat

> Eating for junior

For pregnant women with the temporary condition of gestational diabetes, a nutritionally balanced diet is essential to maintaining a healthy mother and a successful pregnancy. While all pregnant women should choose nutritious foods to ensure a healthy fetus, a sound diet during pregnancy can also help avoid complications such as high blood pressure for women diagnosed with gestational diabetes.

A mother-to-be only needs 300 extra calories a day during the second and third trimesters of pregnancy. While many women really believe they are "eating for two," excess food leads to weight gain, which makes the diabetes worse. Here are a few tips for eating for two with gestational diabetes:

Be diligent about sugar. In pregnant women, sugar is rapidly absorbed into the blood and requires a larger release of insulin to maintain normal blood sugar levels. Since insulin is temporarily impaired in gestational diabetes, it is so important that sugary foods be kept to a minimum.

The same for fat. Remember, the weight you gain makes you even more insulin resistant, and eating fat puts

you on the fast track to weight gain. While you need small amounts in your diet for your own health, as well as fetal growth, you probably already get what you need.

Eat high-fiber foods. Constipation is often a problem in pregnancy, and by increasing your fiber content, you can ward it off. Make sure you get at least two servings of fruit and three servings of vegetables every day. Eat the whole fruit, skin and all.

Have a bedtime snack. Women with gestational diabetes tend toward lower-than-normal blood sugar levels during the night. This can be prevented by having a bedtime snack that provides both protein and complex carbohydrates.

Eat steadily. Women with gestational diabetes need at least three meals plus a bedtime snack. Another snack may also be added to the day. Blood sugars will be easier to keep in the normal range if meal times and amounts are evenly spaced. Do not skip meals—it can cause hypoglycemia, which may be harmful to the fetus and make you feel irritable or shaky.

only when you're hungry. In this simpler approach, you eat a well-balanced, diverse array of food. Lots of complex carbs, healthy oils, lean meats, and fish. Cooked with pizzazz, served in sensible portions. Interestingly, not only does it work for a lifetime of healthy weight, it also matches almost perfectly the new

thinking about healthy eating for diabetes. Go figure!

In fact, you do need to do a little figuring. If healthy eating really is about calories, just how many should you eat in a day? Calorie requirements vary from person to person, depending on body size, physical activity, and basal metabolic rate. One thing is for sure, any food program that is set below 1,200 calories a day will make it extra hard to get all the vitamins and minerals you need. Eating too little can lead to fatigue and deprivation, which in turn only lead to more overeating.

To maintain your current weight, multiply your weight by ten. This is the number of calories your body needs per day to function while at complete rest. To adjust your daily calorie needs for physical activity, do the following:

- If you're totally **sedentary**, add 300 calories.
- If you're **moderately active,** add 500 calories.
- If you're **very active,** add 700 calories.

And there you have a very rough estimate of your daily calorie needs. If you want to keep your weight stable, that's how many calories you should eat. Want to lose weight? Essentially, one pound equals 3,500 calories. So to lose a pound per week, burn an extra 500 calories a day through exercise, or cut 500 calories from your diet, or come up with some combination. To lose two pounds a week, you need a caloric imbalance of 1,000 per day, achieved by exercise, diet, or both. It's a pretty simple formula.

We're not making light of all diets and weight-loss programs. Many are outstanding at addressing not only harmful eating patterns, but lifestyle issues as well. By all means, develop a walking habit, find a few food tricks that work for you, and do what it takes to lose weight! It is probably the single most important thing you can do to help your diabetes.

Keeping portions under control

Back in the 1980s nouvelle cuisine— or as some called it, the art of small portions—was the rage among upscale restaurants. The trend didn't last long. People laughed at how ridiculous a small portion of food looked on a large plate. They felt they should get more for their money than an artful presentation and a sample-size portion.

Today, value rules—and value, unfortunately, means lots of food. More and more restaurants serve massive, hard-to-finish portion sizes.

Where we should have ended up is somewhere in between the two. The perfect meal is one in which you are served a reasonable-sized portion of wonderful, surprising, delicious food. You shouldn't feel stuffed at the end of the meal, but you shouldn't be hungry either. You should feel satiated and happy.

It's a nice food philosophy, isn't it? Eating smaller portions of your favorite foods works in many ways. First and foremost, you get to eat the foods you love. It's fine for people with diabetes to have sweets, for example; they just need to be portion-controlled. Better to eat a small portion of something you really love than set yourself up for deprivation. You'll begin to have a healthier view of food too. Food does not have to be divided into only two camps, bad or good.

Although the food guidelines today allow people with diabetes to choose from a wide array of foods, portion size still matters. It may seem impossible that just one more chicken wing or another teaspoon of oil makes a difference, but they do. Those extra 100 calories make it that much more difficult to lose weight or manage blood sugar.

Until you can really eyeball serving sizes correctly, it may be helpful to rely on a few useful tools. Purchase measuring spoons and cups and a food scale. This way you can accurately see what 1 ounce of cereal is. Make a mental note about what 1 ounce looks like so eventually you will only need to rely on your eyes to judge portion sizes. Other visual tools include:

- 3 ounces of meat = your palm, a deck of cards, a cassette tape
- 6-ounce fish fillet = a checkbook
- 1 cup cereal/pasta = a tight fist, a baseball
- 1 ounce cheese = a thumb
- 3 ounces lunch meat = 2 CDs
- 1 cup milk, yogurt, soup = diner coffee cup

Putting it all together

It's one thing to have a philosophy about healthy eating. But putting it into practice and making it an everyday reality takes more than discipline—it takes clever thinking and specific actions. With that in mind, here is a collection of hints and tips to help you on your road to eating to beat diabetes.

Eat from the earth and the vine.

If we had to be graded on our consumption of fruits and vegetables, most of us would fail! Fresh produce rarely plays a dominant role in our meal planning. Yet it is such an important part of a balanced food program.

Vegetables don't raise blood sugar very much and add so few calories. In fact, they are the most nutrient-dense, low-calorie foods you can eat. And if you load up on them, you won't have as much room for less healthy, calorie-dense foods.

The exception, of course, would be the starchier vegetables like potatoes, corn, peas, and winter squash, but they should not be counted out. In fact, it is probably wiser to consume your starches in the form of starchy vegetables more often than bread or pasta. Starchy vegetables provide more vitamins, minerals, and fiber than the more processed and refined breads, pastas and some grains.

As for non-starchy vegetables, eat them with gusto! Try to aim for three to five servings a day.

Fruit, while healthy, has to be more carefully managed than vegetables. Fresh fruit is brimming with natural sugars, and so can raise blood sugar levels faster and higher than vegetables. The trick is to determine how fruit raises your own sugar levels. One way to do this is to eat a standard-size portion of fruit (see the exchange lists on page 302), and then test your sugar level one to two hours later. Some fruits may raise your blood sugar more than others. Monitoring is the only way to know.

Fruits are excellent sources of vitamins A and C and minerals such as potassium and magnesium. Your goal should be two servings a day, but work with a registered dietitian to determine how you can work fruit into your diet.

Using this cookbook will help; the recipes include a wide variety of fruits and vegetables prepared in tasty ways. But go the next step by "fortifying" your everyday meals with extra produce. Some ideas:

- Add vegetables into the cooking water when preparing pasta.
- Add tomato and cucumber slices to sandwiches.
- Use canned salsa as a salad dressing.
- Top a baked potato with stir-fried vegetables.
- Add vegetables to eggs and omelets.
- Drink low-sodium vegetable juices.
- Add orange slices or tangerines to green salads or chopped apples to coleslaw.
- Add fruit to breakfast cereal, yogurt, and pancake and waffle mixes.

Pour on some fat, but keep the spout small. As mentioned earlier, you need fat in your diet for healthy cells. Another reason that fat is so important in managing diabetes is that it keeps you feeling satisfied. That's because fat takes longer to leave your stomach than either carbohydrate or protein does. The more

(see the exchange lists on page 302)

> ## The right amounts

Amazing how big portions have gotten. Here's what you save in calories by reining in portions:

muffin

Standard, size of a small apple, 125–150 calories

Mega, size of a medium grapefruit, 850–1000 calories

> calories saved: 725–850

bagel

Small, 1-inch-high, 160 calories

Large, 2-inch-high, 850 calories

> calories saved: 690

pasta

1/2 cup cooked, size of a tennis ball, 80 calories

3 cups cooked, half a soccer ball, 565 calories

> calories saved: 485

cookie

Small, size of half a yo-yo, 50 calories

Mega, size of a coffee saucer, 550 calories

> calories saved: 500

fast-food fries

small order, 210 calories

supersize order, 540 calories

> calories saved: 330

pizza

Slice of thin-crust cheese pizza, 340 calories

Slice of deep-dish pizza with sausage, pepperoni, and double cheese, 640 calories

> calories saved: 300

satisfied you are, the less likely it will be that you will start rummaging through the fridge for more to eat!

Eat more than you need, though, and those fat calories wind up stored on your hips (and arms and belly and so on). So be choosy about the amount and type of fat you use. Some ideas:

- Add a tablespoon of nuts, particularly almonds or walnuts to a salad, soup, or main-dish entrée.
- Instead of using low-fat salad dressings (which are often loaded with more sugar than you need and have questionable taste), drizzle on 1 or 2 tablespoons of olive oil paired with flavorful vinegars.
- Add a slice or two of avocado to a sandwich or omelet.
- Occasionally indulge the child in you and have a peanut butter sandwich.

Get the natural kind and combine 2 tablespoons of it with some low-sugar jam or slices of banana spread on whole-grain bread. Or spread some peanut butter on crisp apple slices!
- Boil up a bag of edamame, or soy-beans. A little salt and pepper, and you have a truly wonderful snack.

The bottom line: Choose fats that actually do something! Olive oil, nuts, nut butters, and foods like avocados actually add interest and flavor that satisfies.

Eat for healing. As we mentioned, many natural foods are filled with micronutrients—organic chemicals with extraordinary healing powers and important benefits to your body. Since having diabetes may increase the risk for high cholesterol, heart disease, kidney problems, and high blood pressure, you'll want to be sure to eat foods that play a role in the prevention of these problems. Examples:

- Garlic can lower cholesterol levels and blood pressure. The phytochemical it contains is called allicin. In fact, members of the allium family—onions, garlic, leeks, and shallots—can all contribute to lower cholesterol and lower blood pressure.
- You've heard that red wine may also play a role in preventing heart disease. But drinking alcohol regularly may not be the best idea for a person with diabetes. The good news: Scientists now suspect the benefits of red wine are actually from the nonalcoholic flavonoids, particularly in the grape skins. The phytochemical in the

skins is called resveratrol. So there seems to be some benefit to eating a small portion of red grapes or a small glass of grape juice.
- The evidence for eating oatmeal to lower cholesterol is so conclusive it's approved by the Food and Drug Administration as a claim.
- The phytochemical called lutein found in spinach and other dark green leaves may help fight macular degeneration, a major cause of vision problems.

Drink water constantly. One way to calculate your water needs is to divide your weight in half. This is the number of ounces of fluid you should get daily. Why? Every system of your body needs water—in fact, your lean muscle, blood, and brain are each more than 70% water. Water is the most important ingredient your body needs every day. And yet, most people do not consume enough.

Never underestimate the value of water. Water regulates body temperature, transports nutrients and oxygen, carries away waste, helps detoxify the kidneys and liver, dissolves vitamins and minerals, and cushions the body from injury. Even mild dehydration can lead to health problems such as fatigue and constipation. There is also some evidence that drinking adequate water may help prevent some diseases such as kidney stones and may be associated with a lower incidence of colon cancer.

Water is best, but milk, juices, and decaffeinated tea can also count. But be aware you also add calories. Caffeinated beverages and alcohol do not count. They act as diuretics and increase fluid loss. In fact, add an extra glass of water for each cup of these liquids you drink.

Don't leave your water intake to chance. Develop a regular program by keeping water bottles and pitchers near you as a reminder. And don't wait until you are thirsty. You may be already dehydrated. When in doubt, fill your glass again. You'll need to drink extra amounts of water in dehydrating conditions such as hot, humid, or cold weather or high altitudes.

Eat more frequently. In other words, migrate away from three big meals a day and shift to pleasant but smaller meals, plus lots of healthy snacks. Studies indicate that staggering your food throughout the day not only helps to stabilize blood sugar but also may lower cholesterol levels. Of course, your body is unique, and the nature of your diabetes will affect the frequency with which you should eat. Work with a dietitian to come up with a good plan for dividing your meals up throughout the day.

Dine with people you like. That's because you are going to do a lot of food sharing! Particularly at restaurants, get in the habit of splitting entrées, sharing appetizers, ordering a sampling menu. The reason: Portions are often out of control at restaurants. By making the food communal, you can enjoy lots of unique flavors without overdoing it. Not only is this good for your weight, but when you are consistent with food portions day in and day out,

> ## > A bit of the bubbly

Is there room for alcohol in your diet if you have diabetes? Perhaps, if you are particularly vigilant about its use. The first problem with alcohol is that it lowers blood sugar levels due to its effect on the liver. The second is that it is high in calories—almost as high as fat—but with few nutrients. If you get the green light from your health-care team that it is okay to drink on occasion, here are some useful tips:

Pair alcohol with food. Food acts like a sponge, helping to absorb some of the alcohol and in turn minimizing its effect on blood sugar. Likewise, sip your drink slowly to further slow absorption.

Don't drink when your blood sugar is low. By taking consistent daily blood sugar readings, you will be in a much better position to make an intelligent decision whether to drink or not. If your blood sugar is already low, there is no need to cause more problems by drinking.

Make the exchange wisely. If you drink, you will have to exchange it for another food in your diet if you are using the exchange system (detailed in the next chapter). Although it is not advisable to consistently exchange alcohol for food with equivalent values, know that a serving of alcohol counts as two fat exchanges. A beer counts as 1 1/2 fat exchanges and one starch exchange.

One drink is best. There are fewer risks to your diabetes, and possible benefits, by keeping to only one drink a day. But be sure your diabetes is well controlled. If weight loss is a goal, drinking may hinder progress, so discuss this with your health-care team.

Keep the mixers calorie-free. If you choose hard liquor, watch out for added calories due to the mixers. Stick with club soda, mineral water, diet soda, tonic waters, Bloody Mary mix, or coffee for hot drinks.

your blood sugar has a greater chance of staying stable.

As you can see, there is not just "one" diabetes diet. Every food fits. And there are many meal-planning approaches to manage your diabetes, as you'll discover in the next chapter. You don't have to eat all sugar-free foods or restrict fat to a bare minimum. You can eat out, be a vegetarian, enjoy the holiday foods. But the bottom line is keeping the blood sugar stable by eating a healthy mix of nutrients.

You'll increase your chances of success by taking a two-pronged approach: Pay attention to what you eat and how much you eat. Build your diet on the foundation of good food in modest amounts. Eat about the same amount of food each day at about the same time each day, and don't skip meals. Within those few guidelines, you can build a delicious diet that will provide lifelong health.

buying and stocking food

Supermarkets are treacherous places. Cookie displays here. Piles of salami there. Ice cream, potato chips, sugary cereals everywhere! Grocery-store owners are in the business of getting you to buy on impulse. And they're good at it.

But you are better. And after you read this, you'll be better still. Your goal, of course, is to buy healthy, tasty foods, in the right quantities, at good prices, without succumbing to the temptations around you. Here is your guide.

General shopping principles

Shop from a list. Once you have designed your meals for the week, then outline a list. Numerous studies have shown shopping from a list saves time and helps to avoid impulse buying. Although it is fun to explore new stores, try to find a grocery store you are comfortable with. This way you can get to know the store well, and you can organize your shopping list according to the layout of the store.

Focus on the store's perimeter. This is where the food is most healthy. Begin your trip with the produce aisle and then work your way around—usually, it's the meats, the seafood, the dairy, the juices, the breads. The less time in the inner aisles, the better.

Don't be tempted by the end displays. Every business uses psychology to get you to buy, and supermarkets are no exception! The end displays on the aisles are usually highly processed, not-so-nutritious foods that are packaged brilliantly. Despite their allure, if they aren't on your list and aren't everyday staples of your home, walk on by.

Start with a full stomach. You've heard it before, but it bears repetition. Never shop when you are hungry. The temptation is too great to rip open a bag of something you'll later regret, and to fill your cart with foods you don't need but look awfully tempting at the moment.

Ponder the P foods. That is: prepared, presliced, precooked. You pay a lot for that extra service, and often prepared foods are oversalted, oversugared, and over-chemicaled for flavor. That said, convenience is important in these crazy times.

You are safest in the produce section. Prewashed and sorted mixed greens might very well be worth the extra dollar if it's the difference between a healthy vegetable side dish and no side dish at all.

Create a shopping system. For example, once a month, buy the staples: the canned goods, oils, frozen vegetables, dried herbs that you use regularly for cooking. In the in-between weeks, only buy perishables that you'll need that week—meats, seafood, fruits, vegetables, milk. This approach keeps you out of the central aisles of the grocery store three out of four weeks, and saves you lots of time and temptation.

Shop for value. So many of us are buying more of our foods in bulk at warehouse clubs. But buying in bulk doesn't always mean buying more frugally. With a coupon or in-store sale, we've found that a grocery-store price may be far cheaper than the warehouse-club price. Likewise, the grocery store's house brand may be the cheapest route, even in small quantities. How do you measure? We recommend you get acquainted with the price of food per pound. It's the only way to comparison-shop effectively.

Don't be too good. Ever buy lots of produce, and 10 days later, end up throwing out half of it because it's no longer good for eating? Don't feel alone—it happens all the time. Again, use your weekly planner as a guide.

If you are finding you are throwing out more produce than you are eating, consider purchasing frozen and canned versions of fruits and vegetables. Nutritionally, there's very little difference between fresh, frozen, and canned. Just check the label for added sugars and sodium.

Near is better than far. When it comes to produce, locally grown food is typically tastier and healthier than produce shipped in from thousands of miles away. So while many vegetables and fruits are now available year-round thanks to more open trade agreements, you should emphasize buying foods in season—that is, your seasons.

Shopping for produce

Perhaps no other department in the market will give you more variety and abundance of nutrition than the produce department. The dizzying array of selections can confuse anyone. Here is what you need to be a savvy consumer.

Take your time. Many shoppers go to the same old bins, buy the same old things, and head off to the next section of the store. If time permits, and your food plans are somewhat flexible for the week, slow down and give the entire section a once-over. What looks fresh? What looks interesting? What's on sale? The produce section is the one area of a

grocery store that you should be willing to shift from the shopping list and buy based on what's available.

Fear no fruit. Break out of your rut! Add a new fruit or vegetable to your cart once every other week. The key to a well-balanced food program is variety. Ask the produce manager for tips on how to use the fruit or vegetable.

Look for quality. Avoid any fruit or vegetable that is bruised or looks old. There is often a separate shelf in the market labeled "Reduced for Quick Sale." Although it may be appealing to purchase really inexpensive produce, the nutritional value of these foods is less than that of their fresher, crisper equivalents.

Look for nutrition. Most vegetables

will not come with nutritional labeling, but this information is often available. Many markets now offer nutritional information in the form of posters and pamphlets displayed in the produce department. So if you want to determine if broccoli has more fiber than green beans, the answer is probably available right there.

Vegetables

Asparagus Choose tender, straight green stalks. Avoid spreading or woody stems. Can be stored in plastic bags in the refrigerator crisper for one to three days. Best season: April to June.

Bell peppers Peppers should be firm and well shaped with shiny flesh. Avoid limp, soft, or wrinkled peppers. Can be stored in the crisper for four to five days.

Broccoli Look for dark green heads with tightly closed buds. Stalks should be tender yet firm, and the leaves should be fresh and unwilted. Avoid yellow buds or rubbery stems. Can be stored in plastic bags in the refrigerator crisper for two to four days.

Cabbage Choose heads that are solid and heavy for their size. Avoid heads with splits or yellowed leaves. Can be stored in the crisper for three to seven days.

Carrots Choose well-shaped, firm, bright-orange carrots. Avoid those with splits or blemishes. Can be stored in the crisper for one to four weeks.

Cauliflower Select firm, compact heads with white florets and bright green leaves. Avoid any heads with brown spots or yellowing leaves. Store in the crisper for two to four days.

Celery Choose celery that has crisp stalks. Leaves should be light or medium green. Avoid limp or yellowed leaves. Can be stored in the crisper for one week.

Green beans Search for smooth, crisp pods. Avoid limp, wrinkled or fat, over-mature pods. Can be stored in plastic bags in the refrigerator crisper for one to three days.

Greens Greens for cooking include spinach, kale, collards, and Chinese cabbage (napa and bok choy are the best known). They should be crisp and fresh-looking, with good color and no brown spots or yellowing leaves. Keep greens in a plastic bag in the refrigerator. They keep two to four days, but try to use as soon after purchase as possible.

Mushrooms Should be firm and white and relatively clean. Avoid dark, bruised ones. Can be stored unwashed, loosely covered, on a refrigerator shelf for four days. Avoid placing mushrooms in the crisper drawer, as they have a tendency to become soft.

Onions Select onions that do not appear to be ready to sprout. They should be heavy for their size. Store in a cool, dry place but not in the refrigerator.

Parsnips Choose young, straight, firm roots without blemish. Avoid large roots; they tend to be woody. Can be stored unwashed in a perforated bag in the refrigerator for one week.

Potatoes Look for firm, well-shaped potatoes. Avoid any that are blemished, sprouted, or cracked. They should be stored in a cool, dry place away from the sunlight. Most potatoes will keep for two weeks at room temperature.

Scallions Scallions should have firm white bulbs with crisp green tops. Avoid those with withered or yellow tops. Can be stored in plastic bags in the refrigerator for two to three days.

Shallots Choose firm, well-shaped bulbs that are heavy for their size. The papery skins should be dry and shiny. Store in a cool, dry place. They will keep for several months.

Summer squash (zucchini, yellow, or crookneck) The youngest zucchini and yellow squash taste the best. Look for summer squash that is about 5–7 inches long. They should be firm, heavy for their size with bright vivid color and free of brown spots or cuts. Keep in a loose bag in the refrigerator. Use in two to three days.

Tomatoes Should be vine-ripened and fully colored. Tomatoes should feel heavy for their size. Flavor is best in tomatoes that are stored at room temperature. Avoid tomatoes from refrigerated sections of the market. Best season: late spring through early fall.

Turnips Choose small, firm, slightly rounded turnips. Avoid large ones, as they tend to be strong-flavored and woody. Can be stored unwashed in the refrigerator for one week.

Fruit

Apples Fruit should be firm and of good color for the variety. Keep cold and humid. Buy apples with a fresh fragrance; they should not smell musty. All varieties of apples except for Red Delicious can be used for baking as well as eating out of hand. Available all year.

Avocados Color ranges from purple to black to green according to variety. Irregular brown marks on surface are superficial and don't affect the quality. Hold at room temperature until fruit yields gently to pressure, then refrigerate. Available all year.

Bananas Fruit should be plump. Color varies from green to dark yellow with brownish flecks, according to degree of ripeness. Avoid grayish yellow fruit, which indicates chilling injury. Ripen at room temperature. When at the stage of preferred ripeness, eat or refrigerate. Skin color turns brown, but flesh keeps well for several days. Available all year.

Berries Choose plump, firm, full-colored berries. All varieties, with the exception of strawberries, should be free of their hull.

Avoid any baskets showing signs of bruised or leaking fruit. Cover and refrigerate. Use within a few days. Available mainly June to August.

Cantaloupes They should be free of any stem and should "give" when pressed gently. Hold at room temperature for a few days, then refrigerate and use as soon as possible. Available May to September.

Cherries Sweet cherries are bright and glossy, ranging from deep red to black in color. They should be attached to fresh green stems. Avoid cherries that are hard, sticky, or light in color. Refrigerate and use within a few days. Available May to August.

Clementines Clementines are a type of mandarin orange grown primarily in Spain and have surged in popularity in recent years. They are small with a thin skin and a sweet orange flesh. Store in refrigerator like oranges. Mostly available in the winter months. Late-season clementines are often more sweet than the first of the season (this is generally true for oranges as well).

Cranberries Select plump, firm, lustrous red to reddish black berries. Refrigerate and use within two weeks. Can be frozen in original package. Available September to December.

Dates Fruit should be soft and a lustrous brown. After package is opened, refrigerate. Keep them well wrapped to avoid drying and hardening. Available all year.

Grapefruit Should be firm, not puffy or loose-skinned. Look for fruits that are heavy for their size, indicating juiciness. Green tinge does not affect eating quality. Refrigerate or keep at room temperature. Available all year.

Grapes Choose plump, well-colored grapes that are firmly attached to green, pliable stems. Green grapes are sweetest when yellow-green in color. Red varieties are best when rich, red color predominates. Grapes won't increase in sweetness, so there's no need to hold them for further ripening. Refrigerate and use within one week. Available June through February.

Honeydew melons Look for a creamy or yellowish white rind with a velvety feel. Avoid stark-white or greenish tinged rinds. Hold at room temperature for a few days, then refrigerate. Peak: June to October.

Lemons/Limes Look for a fine-textured skin, indicating juiciness. Select those that are heavy for their size. Keep at room temperature or refrigerate. Available all year.

Mangoes Skin color generally green with yellowish to red areas. Red and yellow color increases with ripening. Avoid any having grayish skin discoloration, pitting, or black spots. Keep at room temperature until soft. When fully soft, refrigerate. Peak: May to August.

Oranges Should be firm and heavy with a fine-textured skin. A green skin color does not affect eating quality. Store at room temperature or refrigerate. Available all year.

Papayas Select medium-sized, well-colored fruit—that is, at least half yellow. Ripen at room temperature until skin color is primarily golden, then refrigerate. Peak: October to December.

Peaches and nectarines Background color of peaches should be yellowish or cream-colored; nectarines are yellow-orange when ripe. Fruit should be firm with a slight softening along the "seam" line. Avoid green or greenish tinged fruits and any that are hard, dull, or bruised. Peak: June to September.

Pears Color varies according to variety. Pears generally require additional ripening at home. Hold at room temperature until stem end yields to gentle pressure, then refrigerate. Year-round availability due to different varieties.

Persimmons Look for plump, smooth, highly colored fruit with a green cap. Keep at room temperature until soft. When ripe, refrigerate. Peak: October to December.

Pineapple Select large fruit with fresh green leaves. Shell color is not an indicator of maturity. Pineapples don't "ripen" after harvest, so may be eaten immediately. Keep at room temperature or refrigerate. Available year-round. Peak: March to June.

Plums Appearance and flavor differ widely by variety. Hold at room temperature until they yield gently to pressure. Peak: June to September.

Pomegranates Rind should be pink or bright red with a crimson seeded flesh. Avoid any that appear dry. Keep cold and humid. Available September to November.

Strawberries Choose berries that are fresh, clean, bright, and red. The green caps should be intact, and the fruit should be free of bruises. Strawberries are best eaten immediately, but if they must be stored, refrigerate them with their caps intact. Available year-round with peak supply April through June.

Tangelos Look for firm, thin-skinned fruits that are heavy for their size. Keep at room temperature or refrigerate. Available October to January.

Tangerines Choose fruit heavy for its size. A puffy appearance and feel is normal. Refrigerate and use as soon as possible. Peak: November to January.

Watermelons Difficult to determine ripeness of uncut melons. Choose firm, smooth melons with a waxy bloom or dullness on the rind. Underside should be yellowish or creamy white. Avoid stark white or greenish colored underside. With cut melons, select red, juicy flesh with black seeds. Keep at room temperature or refrigerate. Peak: May to August.

Shopping for frozen foods

Since you may not have the opportunity to grocery shop each week, stocking up on frozen foods can be a good idea. There are many healthy foods to choose from today's freezer case.

Vegetables Although many people believe that fresh vegetables are the only way to go, frozen vegetables can be equally tasty and sometimes have more nutrition than fresh. Since so many of us today do not grow our own vegetables, we have to rely on our supermarket's produce selection. Often vegetables will be out of the ground as many as seven days before we consume them. Vitamins and minerals will be lost during this delay to our table. Frozen vegetables have been flash-frozen, thus preserving the nutrients.

- Always choose vegetables that are plain, not dressed with cream or cheese sauces.
- If possible, buy vegetables in bags versus boxes. It is much easier to seal up whatever you do not use.
- Try to use up frozen vegetables within four months. Rotate the vegetables every time you purchase more. Place older vegetables up front and new ones in the back.

Fruits When berries or other fruits are out of season, consider purchasing the frozen. Buy these fruits with no sugar added. Berries are a great source of vitamin C and fiber that you should be able to enjoy all year long.

Entrées It would be great to have a home-cooked meal every night, but for many of us, this may never be a reality. Frozen entrées today can give you a complete meal, with less fat and calories than the old days of TV dinners. Check the nutritional labeling for the total carbohydrates, fats, and sodium. Be sure to check the portion size too. Supplement frozen entrées with a fresh salad or other vegetables.

Desserts Ice cream and frozen yogurt are always a treat. Today there is a myriad of options, and fortunately for people with diabetes, there are low- and no-sugar brands as well as fat-free brands. Make sure to read the label and look at total carbohydrate and fat grams to figure into your daily allotment.

Shopping for the pantry

The shelves are bursting with so many foods and ethnic foods formerly only available in specialty shops. Reading the label will be your key to whether or not you should purchase the product. Let's go aisle by aisle and explore what's on the shelves.

Canned fruits and vegetables For many people, purchasing canned fruits and vegetables is a time-saver. Try to use canned fruits and vegetables within a year of purchase. Canned fruits are packed many ways. You will need to look for fruit that is unsweetened and packed only in its own juice. Fruits in syrup—heavy or light—will probably add too many extra carbohydrates to your food plan.

For vegetables, just be sure the label states "No Salt Added." Often salt is added to canned vegetables during the processing.

Canned beans These are a wonderful addition to your food plan. They are more convenient than dried beans, which must be soaked and cooked. Read the label and look for no added fats. And buy as low-sodium a version as you can get.

Tomatoes To many cooks, canned tomatoes are indispensable. They add flavor to cooked rice, pasta, and numerous other dishes. Another bonus: Research indicates that eating cooked tomato products gives you a cancer-fighting phytochemical called lycopene.

Look for no-salt-added tomatoes. Any of the common forms will do: whole tomatoes, crushed tomatoes, tomato paste, tomato puree, tomato sauce, and diced tomatoes.

Condiments Bottled condiments add lots of flavor yet contain little if any fat. Here are some to keep on hand:

- Chili sauce
- Low-sodium ketchup
- Fat-free mayonnaise
- Dijon mustard
- Salsa
- Low-sodium soy sauce
- Worcestershire sauce

Oils and vinegars

All oils are 100% fat and thus contain about 13 grams of fat per tablespoon. But as mentioned, certain fats are healthier for you than others. Seek out monounsaturated fats like olive and canola oils. The less saturated fat you can eat, the better; this means cutting down on butter and other animal fats.

Keep oils stored in a cool, dry place or in the refrigerator for best freshness. Remove oil from the refrigerator 15 minutes prior to preparing your recipe to allow it to decloud.

Vinegars can add great flavor to your foods. Many vinegars are wine vinegars, but some—like apple cider vinegar—are made from fruits other than grapes. Once opened, vinegars should be used within a year. Keep vinegars in a cool, dry place.

Here are more specifics on both oils and vinegars:

No-stick sprays Whether you purchase the aerosol cans of vegetable sprays or place your own oil in a pump spray, the advantage of using the sprays is that you will use far less oil than if pouring from a bottle. Spray oils can be used for sautéing, stir-frying, roasting, and grilling.

Canola oil Use canola oil for salad dressing, sautéing, and baking. Canola oil has a less heavy taste than olive oil does, so it can be an alternative choice to get your monounsaturated fats.

Olive oil Renowned for its taste, olive oil is probably the best loved of the oils. You can select olive oil according to its grade; most cooks prefer an extra-virgin oil, from the first pressing of the olives. This is the best-tasting of the olive oils and has the lowest acidity and richest flavor.

Flavored oils Oils can be flavored with lemon, garlic, herbs, and spices. Just a dab on foods can give it great flavor.

Balsamic vinegar Balsamic vinegar is made from dark grapes that produce a dark, sweet, mellow, and highly aromatic vinegar. Balsamic vinegar is aged in wooden casks for years. Add it to salad dressings or use as part of a marinade for poultry.

Wine vinegar Wine vinegar can be made from red or white wine. Its flavor can vary from mild to strong. Sherry vinegar is especially tasty and can be used as a substitute for balsamic vinegar.

Rice vinegar Rice vinegar is Asian and is clear and mild. It has a nice sweet-and-sour taste. Splash rice vinegar on salads.

Herb vinegars Often herbs, spices, or fruits are added to vinegar. Products like these are great because you do not need oil to accompany them, since the vinegar is so tasty to begin with.

Prepared soups

Buying canned soup is certainly convenient when you don't have the time to make a homemade pot. There are so many to choose from, so here is what you should look for. In any and all cases, consider tossing in extra vegetables (frozen work fine) to add fiber and extra nutrition.

Dehydrated soups These are great, because they store well in your desk drawer and also pack well for traveling. Just add water, stir—and in less than 7 minutes you have soup. Be aware that some brands are very high in sodium, so check the label.

Ready-to-eat soups Look for more vegetable, bean, and non-cream-based soups. For a main meal, look for a heartier soup without too much salt added.

Canned broth Broth is a healthy staple to keep on hand. Look for canned low-fat, lower-sodium chicken and beef broths. Avoid bouillon cubes; although convenient, they are packed with too much sodium.

Pasta, rice, and other grains

Everyone loves a bowl of pasta or nutty rice, and there are so many varieties to choose from. But all are carbohydrates, so you need to be selective and particularly careful about portion sizes. In general, use grains as a side dish, not the main entrée. Here's a smart way to approach it: Mentally split your dinner plate into fourths. One-fourth should be a protein like lean meat or fish; one-fourth should be a healthy, fiber-rich grain; the remaining two-fourths should be non-starchy vegetables.

Here's what you need to know to make smart choices:

Pasta Consider buying whole-wheat versions. Whole-wheat pasta has about three times the fiber of regular pasta made with white flour. Colored pastas such as carrot, beet, or spinach are certainly pretty and add variety, but they don't count as a vegetable serving (sorry!). Make sure you just add a vegetable to the pasta dish to get its nutrient content higher. Keep your pastas in a cool, dry pantry. Use them within a year.

As for fresh pasta: It cooks in as little as 1–3 minutes, a time-saver indeed. The disadvantage is that you have to use it up within 24 hours of purchase. Fresh pasta may also contain more eggs, which may be restrictive for some people. If you can find fresh whole-wheat pasta, so much the better!

Rice Try brown rice instead of white rice. Brown rice has more nutrients than white and more fiber. Wild rice is actually a long-grain marsh rice and has more protein, riboflavin, and zinc than brown rice. If you purchase the rice mixes, use half the seasoning packet or omit it entirely, because it is usually heavy in salt. To get rid of excess starch, rinse rice several times. When rinse water no longer turns cloudy white, it's ready for cooking. Of all the grains, rice freezes the best.

Other grains From amaranth and barley to quinoa and wheatberries, grains are making a comeback in kitchens and restaurants everywhere. Consider them for healthy, fiber-rich side dishes. While each has its own personality and cooking needs, there are some commonalities. Most come in a dry form that needs cooking in a liquid to plump and soften it. Use water or low-sodium, low-fat chicken broth. Be sure to fit the lid on tightly—the grain needs all the steam it can get to swell properly. Do not stir while grain cooks. That will loosen the starch and the grain will be gummy. Most grains can be found in natural food stores and some major supermarkets. Buy in bulk to save money. Store in glass containers either in the refrigerator or in a cool, dry place.

how to plan meals

Did you know that at 4 p.m. today, the majority of us still won't know what we are going to have for dinner? It sounds surprising at first—but that's because we make the false assumption that everyone else is better organized than we are.

Truth is, for most of us, life is busy, life is unpredictable, and many of us leave such mundane issues of "what's for dinner?" to the last moment.

There are lots of benefits to planning your week's meals: less time wasted shopping, one less daily hassle to worry about, saving money by buying just what you need. Then there are the health reasons. For those with diabetes, getting the right mix of nutrients is crucial. And not just some days—all days.

But don't think that meal planning means spending your Saturday mornings picking seven dinner recipes, a full week of lunch menus, and a daily breakfast. Unless your diabetes is severe, your meal plans need not be so restrictive. Merely by keeping lots of fresh, healthy foods on hand and planning the main ingredient for your dinner entrées—shrimp on Monday, chicken breasts on Tuesday, a bean soup on Wednesday—you will have gone a long way toward getting your nutrition under control.

Of course, doctors and nutritionists recommend a little more rigor than that. They would prefer that you use a meal-planning system that more formally guides you to the optimal mix of nutrients. For many years, doctors have advocated that people with diabetes use the exchange system created by the American Diabetes Association and the American Dietetic Association to get the right blend of foods in their diet. It's an effective and well-established system, but it takes lots of monitoring and scoring (more on that in a moment). Luckily, for those with more mild cases of diabetes, there are other, easier ways to effectively monitor your nutrient mix and plan your meals, ranging from carbohydrate or calorie counting to merely pursuing a wide diversity of foods through the day.

The beauty of all these methods is that they rarely tell you what specific food to eat. Rather, they tell you what food *categories* to eat. They say "vegetable," but only you decide whether that means broccoli, green beans, or artichoke. This type of freedom is essential, since we all have unique food preferences.

Another thing these food-monitoring approaches have in common is a pencil. Not only does writing down your meal ideas give you the discipline to eat more consistently and shop more effectively, it becomes a food diary that helps you see how your diet is affecting your weight, your mood, your health, and of course, your blood sugar levels. By planning, you will come to know whether you actually need a snack at 4 p.m. or if it's better to have one at 10 a.m. By planning, you will know how much insulin you will need to cover you and whether you should delay eating—or eat sooner.

As we mentioned in the last chapter, people newly diagnosed with diabetes are strongly encouraged to meet with a registered dietitian to discuss their nutritional needs and preferences. A dietitian will not only tell you what types of food to eat but also give you a time schedule for when to eat. By using a meal-planning system, you can work through challenges like having an irregular work schedule, meeting the food needs of people you live with, food budgets, and food allergies. You can use a written planning sheet (see page 308) each week to plan your meals. Or perhaps you'll want to use your computer. Whatever avenue you choose, writing down your plan, rather than planning it in your head and leaving it there, is a much more organized approach. You'll meet your diabetes-management goals much better by writing your plan down.

In this chapter we'll explore the various meal-planning methods, and then give you a sample of a week's worth of food incorporating some of the delicious recipes from this book. Let's get started!

Understanding the exchange system

"I'll trade you one slice of bread for three crackers." Sounds like a conversation in the school lunchroom. But in fact, trades like this one are the method behind one of the most popular tools available for helping people with diabetes eat sensibly. Called "the exchange system," this meal-planning process was designed specifically to help people with diabetes choose the right mix of foods to eat each day.

The idea behind the exchange system was to group together foods that have about the same amount of carbohydrate, fat, protein, and calories. That is why any food on a list can be "exchanged" or traded for any other food on the same list. There are 3 main exchange lists, and those are broken down into 12 subcategories. Once you know how many portions you can eat in a day from the lists, you get to choose the foods you want (each recipe in this book provides the exchanges per serving).

The exchange system was created in 1950, and has been used by many thousands of people with diabetes. To stay current, the ADA updates the exchange lists regularly; its most recent update was in February 2003. The program's strengths are many. In particular, the exchange system concentrates not only on the right foods but also on the right portion sizes. You'll never need to guess what is the right amount of a food to eat. However, the system does have drawbacks. For one, it requires a lot of math,

a lot of food measuring, a lot of journaling and food tracking. If your life is busy, this type of vigilance can be difficult.

A key principle of the exchange system is that each person should have a customized eating plan. In fact, the ADA goes to great lengths not to put out sample programs. Rather, a person with diabetes needs to work with a nutritionist to set up a unique program based on weight, intensity of the diabetes, food preferences, and everyday life issues (work, kids, exercise, travel, and so on).

The lists are organized by three main groups: the carbohydrate group, the meat and meat substitutes group, and the fat group. The lists then are further broken down. Starch, fruit, milk, other carbohydrates, and vegetables are food lists within the carbohydrate group. The meat and meat substitutes group is divided into very lean, lean, medium-fat and high-fat foods. Foods in the fat group consist of monounsaturated, polyunsaturated, and saturated lists.

Serving sizes for each exchange are measured by weight. Realize, though, that the weight doesn't refer to the whole food or dish, but rather the amount of the dish that is that particular nutrient. Generally the foods in the carbohydrate group have 15 grams per serving, except for vegetables, which have 5 grams. The meat group contains 7 grams of protein per serving, and the fat group contains about 5 grams of fat per serving.

Is the ADA's exchange system right for you? Here are questions to ask yourself:

- Do I lack the knowledge or willpower to get the right mix of food each day?
- Do I mind keeping count of the foods I eat?
- Do I need help in resisting snacks or eating too much at a meal?
- Am I willing to work with a nutritionist?

To help you better understand the exchange system, we've provided details of the food lists—the portion sizes, what nutrients each exchange contains, and sample foods within each, courtesy of the American Diabetes Association.

The carbohydrate group

Starches

One starch exchange equals 15 grams of carbohydrate, 3 grams of protein, 0–1 grams of fat, and generally about 80 calories. In terms of food portions, one starch exchange is:

> 1 ounce of a bread product (such as 1 slice)
>
> 1/2 cup cooked cereal, grain, pasta, or starchy vegetable (such as corn)
>
> 3/4 to 1 ounce of most snack foods

One serving of beans, peas, and lentils is counted as one starch and one very lean meat, since they are rich in protein.

There are some starchy foods that are prepared with fat. For instance, a 2 1/2-inch biscuit should be counted not only as one starch but also as one fat.

Fruit

One fruit exchange equals 15 grams of carbohydrate and about 60 calories. In general, one fruit exchange is:

> 1 small to medium piece of fresh fruit
>
> 1/2 cup canned or fresh fruit or fruit juice
>
> 1/4 cup dried fruit

Exchanges for canned fruit are based on "no sugar added" or fruits packed in their own juice. Try to eat whole fruits rather than juices, since the fiber content is higher and you will feel much more satisfied.

Count cranberries or rhubarb as a free food if sweetened with low-calorie sweeteners.

Milk

One milk exchange equals 12 grams carbohydrate and about 8 grams protein. Notice that no fat is included, the assumption being that you will use nonfat choices. One milk exchange is:

> 1 cup milk
>
> 3/4 cup plain yogurt
>
> 1 cup yogurt sweetened with low-calorie sweetener

Cheeses and cream cheese are found on the fat list, rice milk is on the starch list, and soy milk is on the medium-fat meat list. Ice cream, fruit-flavored yogurt, chocolate milk, and frozen yogurt are on the other carbohydrates list.

Other carbohydrates

This is where you can have your cake and eat it too! While the portions are small, you can still savor a piece of cake or some ice cream. These foods can be substituted in your meal plan from the starch, milk, or fruit choices. Bear in mind they do not contain as many vitamins and minerals, but with careful planning they can be included in a balanced program.

One exchange in this category equals 15 grams of carbohydrate or one starch, one fruit, or one milk. Examples include:

> Brownie, 2 inches square (1 carbohydrate, 1 fat)
>
> Cookies, 2 small (1 carbohydrate, 1 fat)
>
> Energy/breakfast bar, 2 ounces (2 carbohydrates, 1 fat)
>
> Fruit juice bar (1 carbohydrate)

Vegetables

Vegetables that contain small amounts of carbohydrates, fat, and calories are on this list. One vegetable exchange equals 5 grams of carbohydrate, 2 grams of protein, 0 grams of fat, and about 25 calories. One vegetable exchange is:

> 1/2 cup cooked vegetables or vegetable juice
>
> 1 cup raw vegetables (non-starchy versions, such as spinach or broccoli florets)

If you consume more than 4 cups of raw vegetables or 2 cups cooked vegetables at one meal, count them as 1 carbohydrate.

The meat and meat substitutes group

This list is broken down into the amount of fat the food contains:

Very lean meat and substitutes group
One exchange equals 0 grams carbohydrate, 7 grams protein, 0–1 grams fat, and 35 calories.

Lean meat and substitutes group One exchange equals 0 grams carbohydrates, 7 grams protein, 3 grams fat, and 55 calories.

Medium-fat meat and substitutes group
One exchange equals 0 grams carbohydrate, 7 grams protein, 5 grams fat, and 75 calories.

High-fat meat and substitutes group
One exchange equals 0 grams carbohydrate, 7 grams protein, 8 grams fat, and 100 calories.

In general, you should strive for very lean meat choices, and should limit your medium- and high-fat choices to three times a week or less. In general, one meat exchange is:

> **1 ounce cooked (weighed after cooking) meat, poultry, fish**
>
> **1 ounce cheese**
>
> **1/2 cup beans, peas, or lentils**
>
> **1 egg**
>
> **3 bacon slices (1 high-fat meat and 3 fat)**
>
> **1 tablespoon peanut butter (1 high-fat meat and 2 fat)**

The fat group

Fat is divided into three groups, based on the main type of fat they contain—monounsaturated, polyunsaturated, and saturated. One fat exchange equals 5 grams of fat and 45 calories regardless of the type of fat. But it is important to choose monounsaturated more often than polyunsaturated or saturated fats.
One fat exchange is:

> **1 teaspoon of margarine, vegetable oil, butter, or mayonnaise**
>
> **1 tablespoon regular salad dressing**
>
> **6 almonds or cashews**
>
> **Avocados, olives, and coconut are on the fat list**

The free-foods group

Like not having to pay the price for something? The free-foods group is any food or drink that contains less than 5 grams of carbohydrates and 20 calories per serving. This list includes:

> **Fat-free or reduced-fat spreads**
>
> **Sugar-free soft drinks**
>
> **Coffee**
>
> **Carbonated water**
>
> **Tea**
>
> **Salsa**
>
> **Nonfat broth**

Other approaches

In addition to the exchange system, there are other ways to monitor your daily food intake. Here are the two most common:

Carbohydrate counting

Many people like the ease of tracking their intake of just one nutrient: carbohydrate. Since carbohydrate has the most dramatic effect on blood sugar, it is a pretty reliable nutrient to use in matching up insulin needs and food intake. Once you and a dietitian take a good look at lifestyle, medications, and activity level, you can come up with the number of carbohydrate grams you need each day.

Using this method means you can eat foods that contain sugar—as long as you count them as part of your total carbohydrate allotment for the day. But do keep in mind that foods high in sugar are often high in fat and calories too. The recipes in this book list the carbohydrate grams per serving, as well as the carbohydrate exchange numbers.

Calorie counting

For people with diabetes who are overweight but do not take insulin, calorie counting is another option. This method would involve keeping a diary of foods you eat every day. You and a dietitian come up with the amount of calories you should have each day based on your goals. You decide how a food might fit into your plan. Say you desire to eat something that is 600 calories and your allotment for the day is 1,500. You would then decide how to "spend" the remaining 900 calories. By using calorie counting, you can also decide on your portion size. Perhaps you'll have "room" for a double portion of rice or maybe you only have enough calories left to have just a half portion.

The drawback of calorie counting is that it is tedious and time consuming. Plus, you need a very accurate calorie counter. But most of all, it leaves nutritional choices completely up to you. If you are diligent and wise, you'll be sure to eat healthy vegetables, whole grains, and lean meat. But not everyone can resist the temptations of eating ice cream and cheeseburgers to get to their daily levels.

A week of great eating

And then there's common sense. No matter how you are monitoring your diet, no matter what formal system you are using to protect against blood sugar fluctuations, having good intuition about healthy eating makes everything a little easier, a little safer.

Good, healthy food: You should know it when you see it. Usually, it's colorful. Usually, the portions are modest. Usually, there are lots of vegetables. If the meat takes up more than a quarter of the plate, it's probably a problem. If noodles, rice, or potato take up most of the plate, it's probably a problem.

When it comes to eating right, nothing serves you better than visual training. If you can see a good plate of food, then you are more likely to eat a good plate of food. And if you see a bad plate of food, with the right knowledge, you are more likely to eat the right stuff that's on it, and politely pass on the remainder.

There's a second intuition you need to develop to be truly on top of your diet. And that is what a healthy *day* of food looks like. To eat

> ## > Exchanges sample plan
>
> Here are the general exchange counts we used to create the week's menu, as well as how the exchanges might change for different calorie targets:
>
> | exchange category | daily exchanges for these calorie levels | | |
> |---|---|---|---|
> | | 1,500 | 1,200 | 1,800 |
> | Meat/Meat substitutes | 6 | 4 | 6 |
> | Starches | 7 | 6 | 9 |
> | Fruits | 3 | 2 | 3 |
> | Vegetables | 3 | 3 | 4 |
> | Fats | 3 or less | 2 or less | 4 or less |
> | Milk | 2 | 2 | 2 |

to beat diabetes, you need to eat smart throughout the day to keep blood sugar stable and your nutrient mix optimal.

To help you there, we've prepared a sample one-week eating plan, using several of the recipes in this book but also throwing in a few grab-bag meals. Each day in this sample plan provides about 1,500 calories—a level appropriate for an average woman seeking to slowly lose weight. As we've said, each person is unique, and your own caloric needs could range anywhere from 1,200 calories per day to 2,400.

If you actually want to try to eat according to this plan, terrific! We're sure you will be delighted by the mix of flavors. And if you want to try just one day, that's great too. But even if you have no interest in following such a meal plan, read it anyhow. As we've said, having good intuition about how much food

is appropriate in a day will serve you well in managing diabetes.

Our one-week eating plan is on page 306 and 307. But first, on the facing page, you'll find another useful tool: a form for tracking your day's eating. We strongly recommend you make seven copies and fill one out at the end each day this week. Doing this will give you invaluable insight into your eating habits. If it serves you well, make lots more copies and create a notebook!

Then, on page 308 and 309, you'll find one more tool: a weekly food planner. Make four copies for the coming month and fill one out each weekend to sketch out your eating plans for the week. Put in fully developed menus, or just entrée ideas. But use it to get in the habit of planning your meals.

daily food and
health tracker

monday ●

tuesday ●

wednesday ●

thursday ●

friday ●

saturday ●

sunday ●

exchange lists

Meat/Meat substitutes
1 2 3 4 5 6 7 8 9 10

Starches
1 2 3 4 5 6 7 8 9 10

Fruits
1 2 3 4 5 6 7 8 9 10

Vegetables
1 2 3 4 5 6 7 8 9 10

Fats
1 2 3 4 5 6 7 8 9 10

Milk
1 2 3 4 5 6 7 8 9 10

monitoring your day

Snacks
1 2 3 4 5 6 7 8 9 10

Glasses of water
1 2 3 4 5 6 7 8 9 10

**Times ate out of
boredom, stress, habit**
1 2 3 4 5 6 7 8 9 10

Rate your energy today:
1 2 3 4 5

Rate your attitude today:
1 2 3 4 5

Rate your health today:
1 2 3 4 5

**Rate the quality of your
eating today:**
1 2 3 4 5

How was breakfast?
☐ Skipped it
☐ Balanced
☐ Not so balanced
☐ Correct portions
☐ Too much

How was lunch?
☐ Skipped it
☐ Balanced
☐ Not so balanced
☐ Correct portions
☐ Too much

How was dinner?
☐ Skipped it
☐ Balanced
☐ Not so balanced
☐ Correct portions
☐ Too much

daily comments

_____
_____
_____
_____
_____
_____
_____
_____
_____
_____
_____
_____
_____
_____
_____
_____
_____
_____
_____
_____
_____

a week
of great eating

day 1

breakfast

1 cup **shredded-wheat cereal** (2 starch)

1 cup **skim milk** (1 milk)

3/4 cup **blueberries** (1 fruit)

lunch

Stir-Fried Chicken and Avocado Salad with Hot Balsamic Dressing, *page 94* (1/2 carbohydrate, 1 vegetable, 2 meat, 1 fat)

1 slice *1 ounce* **whole-grain bread** (1 starch)

1 *4 ounce* **apple** (1 fruit)

dinner

Grilled Halibut Steaks with Tomato and Red Pepper Salsa, *page 147* (1/2 fruit, 2 vegetable, 3 meat, 1 fat)

1 cup cooked **brown rice** (2 starch)

1/2 cup cooked **broccoli** (1 vegetable)

snack

1 cup **skim milk** blended with 1/2 cup **strawberries**, to make a **milkshake** (1 milk, 1 fruit)

day 2

breakfast

1 **Blueberry Popover,** *page 10* (1 starch, 1/2 fruit, 1/2 fat)

1/4 cup **plain yogurt,** (1 milk)

lunch

Seafood with Watercress Dressing, *page 157* (1 vegetable, 3 meat)

2 **breadsticks** *2/3 ounce each* (1 starch)

1 medium fresh **peach** (1 fruit)

1 cup fat-free **milk** (1 milk)

dinner

3-ounce broiled lean **pork tenderloin** (3 lean meat)

Roasted-Pepper Salad, *page 181* (2 vegetable, 1 fat)

1 cup **whole-wheat penne noodles** (2 starch)

1/2 cup cooked **green beans** (1 vegetable)

1 small **orange** (1 fruit)

snack

3 cups air-popped **popcorn** with 1 tablespoon lower-fat **margarine,** melted (1 starch, 1 fat)

day 3

breakfast

1 cup cooked **oatmeal** (2 starch)

1/2 cup **fat-free milk** (1/2 milk)

1/4 cup **raisins** (1 fruit)

1 tablespoon chopped **walnuts** (1 fat)

lunch

Chickpea and Pita Salad, *page 165* (2 1/2 starch, 1 vegetable, 1 fat)

1 ounce **cheese** *3 grams or less per ounce* (1 lean meat)

1/2 cup chopped **mango** (1 fruit)

1 cup **fat-free milk** (1 milk)

dinner

Shrimp Provençal, *page 156* (2 1/2 starch, 3 vegetable, 2 very lean meat, 1/2 fat)

Garlicky Tomato Salad, *page 180* (2 vegetable, 1 fat)

snack

1/4 cup nonfat **ricotta cheese** (1 lean meat)

15 **red grapes** (1 fruit)

day 4

breakfast

Breakfast Muffin, *page 13*
(1 1/2 carbohydrate, 1 fat)

1 cup **fat-free milk** (1 milk)

1 cup **cantaloupe** cubes
(1 fruit)

lunch

3 ounces sliced **turkey**
(3 meat)

1 *6-inch* **pita bread**
(2 starch)

1-ounce **avocado** (1 fat)

1 cup raw **carrots**
(1 vegetable)

3 **dates** (1 fruit)

dinner

Spiced Stir-Fried Duck,
page 128 (1 fruit, 2 vegetable,
2 meat, 1/2 fat)

1/3 cup cooked **couscous**
(1 starch)

1 cup raw **green salad**
with nonfat dressing
(1 vegetable, 1 free food)

snack

1 cup **fat-free milk** (1 milk)

day 5

breakfast

3/4 cup cold **cereal,**
unsweetened (1 starch)

1/2 cup **fat-free milk** (1/2 milk)

1/2 cup **mixed fruit** (1 fruit)

lunch

(on the road at fast-food joints)

1 plain **hamburger**
(2 carbohydrate,
1 medium-fat meat, 1 fat)

1 small order **French fries**
(2 carbohydrate, 2 fat)

1 cup **garden salad** with
fat-free dressing
(1 vegetable, 1 free food)

2 **tangerines** *you pack*
(1 fruit)

dinner

Golden Lentil Soup, *page 228*
(2 starch, 3 vegetable)

2 tablespoons grated
Parmesan cheese
(1 lean meat)

1 cup **red and green pepper**
strips (1 vegetable)

1 **baked apple** (1 fruit)

snack

1 cup nonfat fruit-flavored
yogurt with nonnutritive
sweetener (1 milk)

day 6

breakfast

1 **waffle,** 4 1/2 inch squares
(1 starch, 1 fat)

1/4 cup low-fat **cottage cheese**
(1 very lean meat)

1 tablespoon light **syrup**
(1/2 carbohydrate)

1 cup fresh **raspberries**
(1 fruit)

lunch

**Chicken and Potato
Chowder,** *page 204*
(1 1/2 starch, 1 vegetable,
1 lean meat, 1/2 fat)

1 cup **mixed green salad**
with 1 teaspoon **olive oil** and
balsamic vinegar
(1 vegetable, 1 fat, 1 free food)

5 whole-wheat, fat-free
crackers (1 starch)

1 cup **fat-free milk** (1 milk)

dinner

Spinach-Stuffed Meat Loaf,
page 72 (3 vegetable, 3 very
lean meat)

1/2 cup **mashed potatoes**
made with 1 teaspoon **olive oil**
(1 starch, 1 fat)

1/2 cup cooked **broccoli**
(1 vegetable)

Vanilla Angel Food Cake,
page 270 (2 carbohydrate)

snack

3/4 cup canned **mandarin
oranges** in their own juice
(1 fruit)

day 7

breakfast

Huevos Rancheros, *page 19*
(2 1/2 starch, 3 vegetable,
1 medium fat meat, 2 1/2 fat)

1 cup **fat-free milk** (1 milk)

1/2 cup **pineapple** chunks
(1 fruit)

lunch

Grilled Salmon Salad,
page 131 (2 fruit, 4 lean meat)

1 cup **red and green pepper**
strips (1 vegetable)

1 small *1 ounce* **whole-
wheat roll** (1 starch)

dinner

Minted Barley and Beans,
page 173 (1 1/2 starch,
1 vegetable 1/2 fat)

1/2 cup sliced **asparagus**
(1 vegetable)

1 *6-inch* **pita bread** (1 starch)

snack

Five-Star Cookies, *page 278*
(1/2 carbohydrate, 1/2 fat)

1 cup **fat-free milk** (1 milk)

weekly planner

shopping

trip 1

*when*_____

list

_____

_____

_____

_____

_____

_____

_____

_____

trip 2

*when*_____

list

_____

_____

_____

_____

_____

_____

_____

_____

_____

meals

monday	tuesday	wednesday
breakfast	breakfast	breakfast
lunch	lunch	lunch
dinner	dinner	dinner
snacks	snacks	snacks
social activities involving food	social activities involving food	social activities involving food

thursday	friday	saturday	sunday
breakfast	breakfast	breakfast	breakfast
lunch	lunch	lunch	lunch
dinner	dinner	dinner	dinner
snacks	snacks	snacks	snacks
social activities involving food	social activities involving food	social activities involving food	social activities involving food

Glossary

Acesulfame Potassium, or Ace-K A sugar substitute, 200 times sweeter than sugar, that contains no calories.

Allergen A substance foreign to the body that causes an allergic reaction.

Allicin The chemical responsible for garlic's odor and health effects.

Amino Acids Organic (carbon-containing) acids that the body links to make proteins. Nine amino acids are termed essential, because they must be provided in the diet; the body produces the remaining 11 as they are needed.

Anemia A condition in which there is a shortage of red cells in the blood or a deficiency of hemoglobin (the oxygen-carrying pigment) in these cells.

Anthocyanins Antioxidant flavonoids found in many plant pigments.

Anticarcinogens Compounds that are thought to counteract certain cancer-causing substances.

Antioxidant A substance that protects cells from the damaging effects of free radicals. Some antioxidants are made by the body; others, such as vitamins C and E, are obtained through diet or supplements.

Asparagine An amino acid found in certain plants, especially legumes.

Aspartame An artificial sweetener that is 200 times sweeter than sugar.

Bacteria Single-celled microorganisms that are found in air, food, water, soil, and other living creatures, including humans. "Friendly" bacteria prevent infections and synthesize certain vitamins; others cause disease.

Basal Metabolic Rate The energy required to maintain vital processes in the human body.

Beta-Carotene One of a group of nutrients known as carotenoids. An immune-system booster and powerful antioxidant, beta-carotene neutralizes the free radicals that can damage cells and promote disease.

Beta-Glucans The soluble dietary fiber component of barley and oat bran.

B-Group Vitamins Although not chemically related to one another, many of the B vitamins occur in the same foods, and most perform closely linked tasks within the body. B vitamins are known either by numbers or names, or both: B1, thiamine; B2, riboflavin; B3, niacin; B5, pantothenic acid; B6, pyridoxine; B12, cobalamin; biotin; and folate.

Biotin One of the B vitamins.

Calcium The most plentiful mineral in the body; a major component of bones, teeth, and soft tissues. Calcium is needed for nerve and muscle function, blood clotting, and metabolism.

Calorie The basic unit of measurement for the energy value of food and the energy needs of the body. Because 1 calorie is minuscule, values are usually expressed as units of 1,000 calories, properly written as kilocalories (kcal), or simply calories.

Capsanthin A carotenoid. Capsanthin contributes to the red color in paprika.

Carbohydrates *Simple carbohydrates* are foods that are easily digested into glucose, such as table sugar, bleached flour, and white rice. *Complex carbohydrates*, which make up the bulk of whole grains and vegetables, are starches composed of complex sugars, fiber, and other nutrients. They take longer to digest and have more beneficial ingredients in them.

Carcinogen A substance that can cause cancer.

Carotenes Yellow and red pigments that color yellow-orange fruits and vegetables and most dark green vegetables. They are among the antioxidants that protect against the effects of aging and disease. The human body converts one such pigment—beta-carotene—into vitamin A.

Carotenoids A group of red and yellow pigments similar to carotenes.

Chromium A trace mineral that ensures proper glucose metabolism.

Cobalamin (see B-Group Vitamins; Vitamin B12).

Complex Carbohydrates (see Carbohydrates).

Copper A trace mineral necessary for the production of red blood cells, connective tissue, and nerve fibers. It is a component of several enzymes.

Cruciferous Vegetables Members of the mustard family of plants, which includes broccoli, cabbage, cauliflower, cress, mustard, radish, and turnips.

Daily Value (DV) The percent numbers on food labels that refer to the recommended daily amounts of vitamins, minerals, and major nutrients.

Diabetes Also called diabetes mellitus. A disorder of carbohydrate metabolism, characterized by inadequate production or utilization of insulin and resulting in excessive amounts of glucose in the blood and urine. There are two main forms: *Type 1 diabetes* occurs when the body's immune system destroys the insulin-producing cells in the pancreas, which can cause a total halt in insulin production. In *type 2 diabetes*, the pancreas does produce insulin, but the body's cells begin to "resist" insulin's message to let blood sugar inside the cells—a condition called insulin resistance.

Diuretic A substance that causes the body to excrete excess urine.

E. coli (Escherichia coli) Bacteria that occur naturally in the intestines of humans and other animals; one of the common causes of diarrhea and urinary tract infections.

Electrolytes Substances that separate into ions that conduct electricity when fused or dissolved in fluids. In the human body, sodium, potassium, and chloride are electrolytes essential for nerve and muscle function and for maintaining the fluid balance as well as the acid-alkali balance of cells and tissues.

Essential Fatty Acids The building blocks that the body uses to make fats.

Estrogen A female sex hormone produced in both sexes, but in much greater quantities in females.

Fats A class of organic chemicals, also called fatty acids or lipids. When digested, they create nearly double the energy of the same amount of carbohydrates or protein.

Fiber Indigestible material in food that stimulates peristalsis in the intestine.

Flavonoids Plant pigments that are potent antioxidants.

Folate One of the B vitamins, also known as folic acid.

Free Radicals Waste products of oxygen metabolism that can damage cell components.

Fructose A naturally occurring, simple (monosaccharide) fruit sugar.

Glucose A simple sugar (monosaccharide) that the body converts directly into energy; blood levels of glucose are regulated by several hormones, including insulin.

Glucosinolates A group of phytochemicals found in cruciferous vegetables.

Gluten The tough nitrogenous substance remaining when wheat or other grain is washed to remove the starch.

Glycemic Index A scale of numbers for foods with carbohydrates that have the lowest to highest effects on blood sugar. There are currently two indexes. One uses a scale of 1–100, with 100 representing a glucose tablet, which has the most rapid effect on blood sugar. The other common index uses a scale with 100 representing white bread (so some foods will be above 100).

Glycogen A form of glucose stored in the liver and muscles, which is converted back into glucose when needed.

Gram (g) A metric unit of weight; one gram is equal to 1,000mg. There are 28.4g to an ounce.

High-Density Lipoproteins (HDLs) The smallest and "heaviest" lipoproteins, they retrieve cholesterol from the tissues and transport it to the liver, which uses it to make bile; called "good cholesterol," because high blood levels of HDLs do not increase the risk of a heart attack.

Hormones Chemicals that are secreted by the endocrine glands or tissue; they control the functions of all the body's organs and processes, including growth, development, and reproduction.

Hydrogenation The process for transforming an oil (unsaturated liquid fat) into a hard fat by incorporating hydrogen. Hydrogenated fat is similar to saturated fat and linked to an increased risk of heart disease.

Hypertension Elevation of the blood pressure.

Hypoglycemia An abnormally low level of glucose in the blood.

Indoles Nitrogen compounds found in vegetables and believed to protect against certain cancers by accelerating the elimination of estrogen.

Insulin A hormone that regulates carbohydrate metabolism.

Insulin Resistance (see Diabetes).

Iodine A mineral that is essential for the formation of thyroid hormones.

Iron A mineral that is essential for the manufacture of hemoglobin and the transport of oxygen.

Lactose The natural sugar in milk.

Lipid A fatty compound made of hydrogen, carbon, and oxygen. Lipids are insoluble in water. The chemical family includes fats, fatty acids, carotenoid pigments, cholesterol, oils, and waxes.

Lipoprotein A combination of a lipid and a protein that can transport cholesterol in the bloodstream. The main types are high density (HDL), low density (LDL), and very low density (VLDL).

Low-Density Lipoproteins (LDLs) These abundant, so-called "bad" lipoproteins carry most of the circulating cholesterol; high levels are associated with atherosclerosis and heart disease.

Lutein A phytochemical found in spinach and other dark green leaves.

Lycopene The main pigment in certain fruits, such as tomato and paprika.

Lysine A basic amino acid essential in human nutrition.

Macronutrients Nutrients the body requires in large amounts for energy—specifically, carbohydrates, proteins, and fats.

Magnesium A trace mineral that is needed for healthy bones, the transmission of nerve signals, protein and DNA synthesis, and the conversion of glycogen stores into energy.

Metabolism The body's physical and chemical processes, including conversion of food into energy, that are needed to maintain life.

Microgram (mcg) A unit of weight equivalent to 1/1000 milligram.

Micronutrients Essential nutrients that the body needs in only trace or very small amounts.

Milligram (mg) 1/1000 gram.

Monosaccharide (see Fructose; Glucose).

Monounsaturated Fats Fats that are liquid at room temperature and semisolid or solid under refrigeration. They are believed to help protect against heart disease.

Niacin (see B-Group Vitamins; Vitamin B3).

Omega-3 Fatty Acid (see also Essential Fatty Acids). A polyunsaturated fatty acid, essential for normal retinal function, that influences various metabolic pathways, resulting in lowered cholesterol and triglyceride levels, inhibited platelet clotting, and reduced inflammatory and immune reactions.

Oxalic Acid A potentially toxic chemical found in certain plants that inhibits the absorption of calcium, iron, zinc, and other minerals. Can promote the development of oxalate kidney stones.

Oxidation A chemical process in which food is burned with oxygen to release energy.

Pancreas A large gland, situated near the stomach, that secretes a digestive fluid into the intestine and also secretes the hormone insulin.

Pantothenic Acid (see B-Group Vitamins).

Pectin Soluble dietary fiber that regulates intestinal function and can help to lower blood cholesterol levels.

Peristalsis Wavelike muscle contractions that help propel food and fluids through the digestive tract.

Phosphorus A mineral needed for healthy bones and teeth, nerves, muscles, and for many bodily functions.

Phthalides A group of secondary phytochemical compounds. A component of celery, 3-n-butyl phthalide, gives this plant its characteristic smell and taste.

Phytochemicals Chemicals derived from plants; some have powerful effects, including both the prevention and the promotion of certain cancers, heart disease, and degenerative conditions linked to aging.

Polyphenols Organic compounds, including tannins, that combine with iron and can hinder its absorption; found in a number of foods, tea, and red wines.

Polyunsaturated Fat A fat containing a high percentage of fatty acids that lack hydrogen atoms and have extra carbon bonds. It is liquid at room temperature.

Potassium A trace mineral that is needed to regulate fluid balance and many other functions (see Electrolytes).

Protein Part of a large class of chemicals called amino acids. The body uses proteins to build and repair muscles and tissues. Proteins are in plant foods—vegetables, grains, beans, nuts, soy products—and are the main ingredient in animal foods like beef, poultry, seafood, and dairy products.

Pyridoxine (see B-Group Vitamins; Vitamin B6).

Recommended Dietary Allowance (RDA) Defined as "the level of intake of essential nutrients considered, on the basis of available scientific knowledge, to be adequate to meet the nutritional needs of healthy persons." Standards, which are revised periodically, are set between a minimum below which deficiency occurs, and a ceiling, above which harm occurs, to provide a margin of safety.

Recommended Dietary Intake (RDI) Standards established by the World Health Organization (WHO). RDIs are lower than RDAs, because the WHO experts do not believe stores need to be as high as those recommended in the United States.

Resveratrol A phytochemical derived from grape skin.

Riboflavin (see B-Group Vitamins; Vitamin B2).

Saccharin A sugar substitute. Saccharin is not metabolized by the body and provides little or no calories.

Saturated Fat A lipid with a high hydrogen content; the predominant fat in animal products and other fats that remain solid at room temperature. A high intake of saturated fat is linked to an increased risk of heart disease, certain cancers, and other diseases.

Selenium An essential trace mineral with antioxidant properties.

Serotonin A neurotransmitter that helps promote sleep and regulates many body processes, including pain perception and the secretion of pituitary hormones.

Simple Carbohydrates (see Carbohydrates).

Sodium A trace mineral essential for maintenance of fluid balance; it combines with chloride to form table salt.

Soluble Fiber A dietary fiber that becomes sticky when wet and dissolves in water.

Starch A complex carbohydrate that is the principal storage molecule of plants and the major source of carbohydrate and energy in our diet.

Sucralose The only sugar substitute made from sugar. It has no calories and is 600 times sweeter than sugar.

Sucrose A sugar composed of glucose and fructose. The sugar obtained from cane and beets; it's also present in honey, fruits, and vegetables.

Sugar Substitutes (see Acesulfame Potassium, Aspartame, Saccharin, Sucralose).

Sulforaphane An antioxidant phytochemical compound.

Tannin An astringent substance derived from plants that can contract blood vessels and body tissues.

Thiamine (see B-Group Vitamins; Vitamin B1).

Triglycerides The most common form of dietary and body fat; high blood levels have been linked to heart disease.

Tryptophan An essential amino acid found in many animal foods; a precursor of serotonin. Its use as a dietary supplement has been linked with serious illness, most likely due to contamination during the manufacturing process.

Very Low Density Lipoproteins (VLDLs) Fat-carrying proteins that transport mostly triglycerides in the blood.

Vitamin A A fat-soluble nutrient occurring in foods such as green and yellow vegetables and egg yolk, essential to growth and the prevention of night blindness.

Vitamin B1 (thiamine) A water-soluble compound of the vitamin-B complex essential for the normal functioning of the nervous system. Found in natural sources such as green peas, liver, and the seed coats of cereal grains.

Vitamin B2 (riboflavin) A vitamin-B complex factor, essential for growth, found in milk, fresh meat, eggs, leafy vegetables, and enriched flour.

Vitamin B3 (niacin) Also called nicotinic acid, it controls blood sugar, keeps skin healthy, and maintains the proper functioning of the nervous and digestive systems.

Vitamin B6 (pyridoxine) Found in foods such as whole-grain cereals, meats and fish. Among other functions, this vitamin forms red blood cells, helps cells make protein, and manufactures brain chemicals (neurotransmitters) such as serotonin.

Vitamin B12 (cobalamin) Obtained from liver, milk, eggs, fish, oysters, and clams. Important for red blood cell production, maintains the protective sheath around nerves, helps convert food to energy, and plays a critical role in the production of DNA and RNA, the genetic material in cells.

Vitamin C (ascorbic acid) A water-soluble vitamin occurring in citrus fruits and green vegetables.

Vitamin D A fat-soluble vitamin found in milk and fish-liver oils.

Vitamin E An important antioxidant found in vegetable oils, whole-grain cereals, butter, and eggs.

Water-Soluble Vitamins Vitamins that dissolve in water, specifically vitamin C and the B-group vitamins.

Zeaxanthin A carotenoid found in collards, kale, mustard greens, and spinach.

Zinc A trace mineral that is essential for many processes, including metabolism, the healing of wounds, and normal growth.

Index

metric conversion charts

Temperature

Fahrenheit   Celsius

  0°F = -18°C (freezer temperature)

  32°F = 0°C   (water freezes)

180°F = 82°C   (water simmers)

212°F = 100°C (water boils)

250°F = 120°C (low oven)

350°F = 175°C (moderate oven)

425°F = 220°C (hot oven)

500°F = 260°C (very hot oven)

Length

U.S.   U.K./Australia

1/2 inch = 1.3 centimeters

1 inch = 2.5 centimeters

12 inches = 1 foot = 30 centimeters

39 inches = 1 meter

Abbreviations

mm = millimeter

cm = centimeter

m = meter

in = inch

ft = foot

ml = milliliter

l = liter

tsp = teaspoon

tbsp = tablespoon

oz = ounce

fl oz = fluid ounce

qt = quart

gal = gallon

g = gram

kg = kilogram

lb = pound

C = Celsius

F = Fahrenheit

Baking Pan Sizes

U.S.	Metric
8 x 1 1/2-inch round baking pan	20 x 4 cm-cake tin
9 x 1 1/2-inch round baking pan	23 x 3.5-cm cake tin
11 x 7 x 1 1/2-inch baking pan	28 x 18 x 4-cm baking tin
13 x 9 x 2-inch baking pan	30 x 20 x 3-cm baking tin
2-quart rectangular baking dish	30 x 20 x 3-cm baking tin
15 x 10 x 1-inch baking pan	30 x 25 x 2-cm baking tin (Swiss roll tin)
9-inch pie plate	22 x 4- or 23 x 4-cm pie plate
7- or 8-inch springform pan	18- or 20-cm springform or loose-bottom tin
9 x 5 x 3-inch loaf pan	23 x13-7-cm or 2-pound narrow loaf tin
1 1/2-quart casserole	1.5-liter casserole
2-quart casserole	2-liter casserole

Cooking Equivalents U.S., U.K./Australia   *All numbers have been rounded.*

Volume

U.S.   U.K./Australia

1/8 teaspoon = 0.5 ml

1/4 teaspoon = 1 ml

1/2 teaspoon = 2 ml

1 teaspoon = 5 ml

1 tablespoon = 15 ml

1/4 cup = 2 tablespoons = 2 fluid ounces = 60 ml

1/3 cup = 1/4 cup = 3 fluid ounces = 90 ml

1/2 cup = 1/3 cup = 4 fluid ounces = 120 ml

1 cup = 3/4 cup = 8 fluid ounces = 240 ml

1 1/4 cups = 1 cup

2 cups = 1 pint

1 quart = 1 liter – 3 tablespoons

1 gallon = 4 liters – 1 1/2 cups

Weight

U.S.   U.K./Australia

1/4 ounce = 7 grams

1/2 ounce = 14 grams

3/4 ounce = 21 grams

1 ounce = 28 grams

8 ounces = 1/2 pound = 225 grams

12 ounces = 3/4 pound = 341 grams

16 ounces = 1 pound = 454 grams

35 ounces = 2.2 pounds = 1 kilogram

Phrases

Most of the recipe ingredients in this book are available throughout the world. However, some are known by different names in other English-speaking countries. Here are some common American ingredients and their possible counterparts:

All-purpose flour = plain household flour or white flour

Baking soda = bicarbonate of soda

Beet = beetroot

Cilantro = fresh coriander

Cornstarch = cornflour

Eggplant = aubergine

Golden raisins = sultanas

Green, red, or yellow sweet peppers = capsicums

Ground beef = minced beef

Jumbo shrimp = king prawns

Light-colored corn syrup = golden syrup

Low-fat milk = semi-skim milk

Powdered sugar = icing sugar

Sugar = granulated or caster sugar

Vanilla = vanilla essence

Zucchini = courgette